LITTLE RESILIENCE

MCGILL-QUEEN'S UNIVERSITY PRESS
MONTREAL & KINGSTON ♦ LONDON ♦ CHICAGO

© McGill-Queen's University Press 2020

ISBN 978-0-2280-0348-9 (cloth)
ISBN 978-0-2280-0349-6 (paper)
ISBN 978-0-2280-0481-3 (ePDF)
ISBN 978-0-2280-0482-0 (ePUB)

Legal deposit third quarter 2020
Bibliothèque nationale du Québec

Printed in Canada on acid-free paper that is 100% ancient forest free (100% post-consumer recycled), processed chlorine free.

This book has been published with the help of a grant from the Canadian Federation for the Humanities and Social Sciences, through the Awards to Scholarly Publications Program, using funds provided by the Social Sciences and Humanities Research Council of Canada.

We acknowledge the support of the Canada Council for the Arts.
Nous remercions le Conseil des arts du Canada de son soutien.

Library and Archives Canada Cataloguing in Publication

Title: Little resilience : the Ryerson poetry chap-books / Eli MacLaren.
Names: MacLaren, Eli, author.
Description: Includes bibliographical references and index.
Identifiers: Canadiana (print) 20200269321 | Canadiana (ebook) 20200270621 | ISBN 9780228003489
 (cloth) | ISBN 9780228003496 (paper) | ISBN 9780228004813 (ePDF) | ISBN 9780228004820 (ePUB)
Subjects: LCSH: Ryerson poetry chap books. | CSH: Canadian poetry (English)—20th century—History and criticism. | CSH: Canadian poetry (English)—20th century—Publishing. | CSH: Poets, Canadian (English)—20th century. | LCSH: Poetry—Authorship.
Classification: LCC PS8153 .M33 2020 | DDC C811/.509—dc23

Set in 11/13.5 Bembo Std with Blacker Pro and Golden Cockerel ITC
Book design and typesetting by Lara Minja, Lime Design

For Jody, Xavier, Simon, and Charles

CONTENTS

FIGURES AND TABLES ix

ACKNOWLEDGMENTS xiii

INTRODUCTION 1

ONE

"The Quickening Spirit of the Times"
Publishing in 1920s Canada

12

TWO

"Significant Little Offerings"
Launching the Ryerson Poetry Chap-Books

41

THREE

Modern Romantic
Nathaniel A. Benson

73

FOUR

Broadcasting Authority
Anne Marriott

105

FIVE

Chap-Book, Deafness, Sacrifice
M. Eugenie Perry
148

SIX

A Responsible Home
Dorothy Livesay
175

SEVEN

Romantic Modern
Al Purdy
204

CONCLUSION 241

APPENDIX
List of the Ryerson Poetry Chap-Books, 1925–62
245

NOTES 253

BIBLIOGRAPHY 281

INDEX 295

FIGURES AND TABLES

FIGURES

1.1 / Front cover and spine of Jack Miner, *Jack Miner and the Birds: Some Things I Know about Nature* (Toronto: Ryerson Press, 1923). Private copy.
24

1.2 / Laura Goodman Salverson, "Chant of the Deep," in *Wayside Gleams* (Toronto: McClelland & Stewart; printed by Warwick Brothers and Rutter, 1925), 69.
28

1.3 / Title page from A.M. Stephen, *The Rosary of Pan* (Toronto: McClelland & Stewart; printed by Warwick Brothers and Rutter, 1923).
28

1.4 / H.B. Wollen, *The Canadians at Ypres*, frontispiece to Jesse Edgar Middleton, *Sea Dogs and Men at Arms: A Canadian Book of Songs* (New York: G.P. Putnam's Sons, 1918; issued in Canada by McClelland & Stewart).
29

2.1 / Charles G.D. Roberts, *The Sweet o' the Year and Other Poems*, Ryerson Poetry Chap-Book no. [1] (Toronto: Ryerson Press, 1925), front cover.
52

2.2 / Page 1 of Roberts, *Sweet o' the Year*
53

2.3 / Inside back cover of Roberts, *Sweet o' the Year*
54

3.1 / Nathaniel A. Benson, circa 1907. Courtesy of Julian Benson.
76

3.2 / Poets at the Muskoka Assembly, undated photograph (circa 1930). Courtesy of Julian Benson.
76

3.3 / Nathaniel A. Benson, *Twenty and After*, Ryerson Poetry Chap-Books [no. 17] (Toronto: Ryerson Press, 1927), 1.
77

3.4 / The publishing agreement for Nathaniel A. Benson, *Twenty and After*. Courtesy of Ryerson University Library.
78

3.5 / Charles G.D. Roberts, E.J. Pratt, Pelham Edgar, and Nathaniel A. Benson judging the Toronto *Daily Star*'s Royal Family Poetry Contest, March 1939. Courtesy of Julian Benson.
84

3.6 / Nathaniel A. Benson, *Dollard: A Tale in Verse*, illustrated by Walter J. Phillips (Toronto: Thomas Nelson & Sons, 1933), 14.
87

3.7 / Keith Bissell, *The Ballad of the Rawalpindi*, for unison or two-part voice and piano, text by Nathaniel A. Benson (Toronto: Gordon V. Thompson, 1959), 2–3.
90

4.1 / Front of the production card for *The Wind Our Enemy*, Ryerson Press Collection, Ryerson University Library.
129

4.2 / Back of the production card for *The Wind Our Enemy*, Ryerson Press Collection, Ryerson University Library.
129

4.3 / Anne Marriott, *Salt Marsh*, Ryerson Poetry Chap-Books no. 100 (Toronto: Ryerson Press, 1942).
132

6.1 / Dorothy Livesay, *Call My People Home*, Ryerson Poetry Chap-Books no. 143 (Toronto: Ryerson Press, 1950).
186

6.2 / A 1940s musical arrangement of the spiritual "Go down Moses." *Fireside Book of Folk Songs*, selected and edited by Margaret Bradford Boni, arranged by Norman Lloyd, illustrated by Alice and Martin Provensen (New York: Simon and Schuster, 1947), 316.
188

TABLES

4.1 / Terms of publication for the Ryerson Poetry Chap-Books
117

4.2 / Works by Anne Marriott broadcast on CBC Radio
140

5.1 / Chronological list of books by M. Eugenie Perry
162

6.1 / Textual variants in editions of Dorothy Livesay, "Call My People Home"
186

7.1 / Textual variants in Al Purdy, "At Roblin Lake"
232

ACKNOWLEDGMENTS

FUNDING FOR THIS BOOK was provided by a SSHRC-Banting Postdoctoral Fellowship, the Groupe de recherches et d'études sur le livre au Québec, the Aid to Scholarly Publishing Program, and McGill University. The Department of English at McGill shaped the writing of it by allowing me to teach Canadian poetry and book history. Key conversations with colleagues at McGill, as well as with librarians, invited guests, research assistants, students, and others connected to the English department, refined the study. I would not have completed it without the freedom granted by a junior-faculty research leave and, later, a sabbatical. The resources of McGill Library were indispensable – not only the complete collection of the Ryerson Poetry Chap-Books, but also the many original print books from the 1920s and '30s available for regular loan, the excellent digital collections, and the interlibrary loan services. I am grateful to the librarians and staff of Rare Books and Special Collections at the McLennan Library for their patient assistance over the past nine years. Equal thanks are due to the librarians and archivists at Queen's University Archives, Ryerson Archives and Special Collections, University of British Columbia Rare Books and Special Collections, British Columbia Archives, and the Concordia Centre for Broadcasting and Journalism Studies. The Word in Montreal, Julian Benson, and Karen Smith also provided crucial access to primary material. Stages of the research were presented at conferences and talks organized by the Bibliographical Society of Canada; the Society for the History of Authorship, Reading and Publishing; the Friends of the Fisher Library; the Early Modern Conversions project at McGill; the Montreal Book History Group; Groupe de recherches et d'études sur le livre au Québec graduate students at the Université de Sherbrooke; and the McGill English Graduate Student Association. I appreciate the discussions that occurred with members of these associations. Several research assistants helped advance the work with enthusiasm: Sarah Mycio, Valerie Silva, Jeff Weingarten, Laura Cameron, Gavin Currie, and Alex Barnes. I offer special thanks to McGill-Queen's University Press: to Mark Abley, acquisitions editor; to the two anonymous peer reviewers; to the copyeditor, Carolyn Yates; and to the marketing and publicity staff. Friends and family have shaped this book in more ways than I can list, and I hope that the finished product reflects their wisdom and trust.

LITTLE RESILIENCE

INTRODUCTION

THE RYERSON POETRY CHAP-BOOKS comprise two hundred short books of poetry by English Canadian writers published over the course of thirty-five years, 1925 to 1960, with a final outlier in 1962. In their day, they were by far the longest-running poetry series that the country had ever seen. Indeed, if we foreground the single-handed perseverance of the editor, Lorne Pierce (1890–1961), and if we pay due attention to the fact that he carried out the bulk of his work without aid or incentive from the Canada Council, the achievement appears even more remarkable. Subsequent publishers now loom larger in Canadian poetry in English – Fiddlehead Poetry Books (established in 1954, reborn as Goose Lane Editions in 1981), Brick Books (established in 1975), Signal Editions of Véhicule Press (established in 1981), or McClelland & Stewart (established in 1906) in its heyday around the Canadian centennial – but their familiar achievements all belong to a later time. They have distributed their work across the devoted energies of several editors during the era of state sponsorship of the arts, whereas Pierce persisted with less assistance through a prior period in Canadian history, challenged by the Great Depression and the Second World War. No mention of the Ryerson Poetry Chap-Books as a series is made in the *Literary History of Canada*. This omission should be redressed. The Ryerson achievement is well worth examining.

The motivations for this book are bibliographical and literary. What were the material conditions for the publishing of Canadian poetry in roughly the middle decades of the twentieth century? What practices of authorship developed from such publishing? What sorts of poetry were created? The conjunction of these questions is at the core of the present study, which is both a publishing history full of literary interpretation and a literary history preoccupied with the ins and outs of publishing.

Raymond Williams writes that culture is ordinary; Robert Darnton, that enlightenment is a business; Michel Foucault, that authorship has a history; Pierre Bourdieu, that the consecration of art is a function of its social coordinates; Janice Radway, that middlebrow reading generates its own value scales; and D.F. McKenzie, that sweeping forces of history are manifest in a piece of letterpress type. To hold, as this study does, that the meaning of literature intersects not tangentially but fundamentally with the materials and circumstances of books is to follow these influential thinkers in exploring the effect of social and economic structures on literary form and content. The writing and publishing of the Ryerson Poetry Chap-Books have much to teach us, especially if we consider these two facets of their production together.

What, then, do they teach us? In short, they show how little poetry weighs and how much it matters. The present study revolves around this thesis – that the Chap-Books were insufficient as income and negligible as commodities but replete with the supreme value that poetry possessed for the scores of people who took part in their production. They are fascinating for the ways in which they make tangible the fluctuation of poetry between failure and success.

The following chapters will develop this theme through four interrelated arguments. First, the Chap-Books are a major example of the difficult conditions that average Canadian writers faced in the middle of the twentieth century as they laboured hopefully to make poetry reflect something of themselves and their homes. These booklets are elegant in design but slight, even paltry, in mass. They are striking when their covers are viewed squarely, but turn them sideways and they almost vanish. This contradictory form is the first sign of the weakness or marginality of their commercial character and also, conversely, of the strength and stubbornness of their ideological character. There was not much money to be made in the Chap-Books, but the cost of joining the honourable ranks of poetry was also not too high. How else could such a series have survived the 1930s? During the Great Depression, the Chap-Books plummeted from a high of thirteen new titles a year (1927) to only one (1933). Nevertheless, the series continued.

Correspondence preserved in the Lorne and Edith Pierce Collection at Queen's University and contracts archived at Ryerson University Library confirm this portrait of austerity. Publishing a Chap-Book demanded a sacrifice on the part of the writers, even as orchestrating the series demanded the same of the editor. As demonstrated in the case studies below, many of the contributing poets were more or less self-publishing, in so far as Ryerson required of them a financial guarantee to make up any shortfall that might occur if after a period (often set at one year) the edition had not sold well enough to cover its printing costs. These were the terms of contract under which promising poets entered the series in the 1920s, and they were a factor in the mixed careers that most of the writers ultimately pursued. The austerity persisted in one form or another for decades, varying from author to author. In 1939, Anne Marriott was offered a 10 per cent royalty on *The Wind Our Enemy* (no. 80)[1] but still had to take charge of distribution and sales, unpaid responsibilities that encouraged her to find other opportunities for her talent as a writer. As late as 1947, M. Eugenie Perry secured her second Chap-Book through a pledge to help finance it. Finally, the average terms of publication relaxed to a level that represented no direct negative impact on the writer, with contributors in the late years of the series such as Al Purdy being offered a number of author copies in lieu of royalties. The fibre and the grain of the publishing conditions of Canadian poetry at the time grow visible through these details.

Moreover, in the context of Ryerson's wider activities as an educational publisher and a distributor for foreign publishers, the Chap-Books are a shadow of the agency system that dominated twentieth-century Canadian book publishing. That system, in which Canadian firms acted as the agents for foreign publishers that sold books in Canada, accorded little space and few resources to original writing by new domestic authors. Approximately 90 per cent of Ryerson's business consisted of agency publishing, while only 10 per cent was specialist publishing (the first publication of original works by Canadian authors).[2] The slightness of the Chap-Books, in this light, indicates the vulnerability of Canadian literature. They were not an experimental student magazine fuelled for a year or two on coffee, but the premiere poetry series of one of the country's three mainstream book publishers, printed at the heart of the Canadian book trade – and still they were tiny. "In 1930," writes Sandra Campbell, describing the onset of the Depression, "some three-quarters of the Ryerson publication list – sixty-two titles out of the eighty-four published that year – were textbooks or chapbooks. Lean times indeed."[3] In order to put the publishing of the Chap-Books in perspective, chapter 1 describes the contexts of publishing and of poetry in 1920s Canada that affected Pierce's creation of the series. To a surprising extent, Pierce was obliged to invent the role to which he aspired, that of the publisher. The irregular process and the burden placed on authors will show what an accomplishment the launching of a national poetry series was in this period, when literary publishing in Canada generally possessed such little resilience.

Second, in their dogged loyalty to poetry despite a protracted failure to incentivize it monetarily, the Chap-Books constituted a model for the small press in Canada. The small press and its close cousin, the little magazine, are often logically associated with literary modernism on the grounds that their uncommercial marginality accorded perfectly with modernist revolt. They seemed to break from the conventions of print culture – the mass-market novel, the schoolbook of nineteenth-century poetry, the advertisement-laden newspaper – precisely as intelligent experimenters were breaking from the stock imagery, sweet sentiments, and predictable rhythms of mass-produced verse. Harriet Monroe's publication of T.S. Eliot's "Love Song of J. Alfred Prufrock" in the pages of *Poetry* (Chicago) in 1915 is one of the classic examples of this association, which received eloquent application to Canada in an article that Louis Dudek wrote for the *Canadian Forum* in 1958: "The little magazine is a recognizable and peculiar phenomenon associated with the growth of the modern poetry movement in this century." Thus Dudek opened a survey that highlighted the *McGill Fortnightly* (Montreal, 1925–27), *Contemporary Verse* (Vancouver, 1941–52), *Preview* and *First Statement* (Montreal, 1942–45), *Northern Review* (Montreal, 1945–56), and *Contact* (Toronto, 1952–54), among others, as narrow but important channels in the development of Canadian modernist poetry, branching out from the stream of mass culture represented by a magazine such as the ubiquitous *Time*. As Dudek writes, "The veritable 'little magazine' of literature is a vociferous reaction to this latter form of readership; also to the radio, movies, and TV, that supplement and now replace the printed page; and to any deaf traditionalism that hopes to carry on without immersing in the destructive element of reality."[4] A vociferous medium for a vociferous poetry, the little magazine thus becomes to the modernist poem what the pipe organ was to the fugues of J.S. Bach. This association of form and content is frequently repeated. Tony Tremblay and Ellen Rose, for example, evaluate online literary magazines today against a standard defined by the "rapidity" with which the little magazines of the twentieth century "served to institutionalize cultural engagement in Canada in mid century, thereby moving avant-garde modernism from the margins closer to the centre of literary concern."[5]

If there was a powerful connection between the little magazine and the literary modernist, however, it was not necessary or exclusive. It was not "peculiar." This is not to deny the association sketched above, only to contextualize it in an enlarged view of the small press. When printing technology grew more affordable in the late nineteenth century, little magazines and small presses of all stripes sprang up with diverse individual agendas. Many of them had special claims to cultural defiance or artistic experiment, but the claims flew pell-mell in all directions, from the elaborate aestheticism of *The Knight Errant* (Cambridge, MA, 1892–93) to the social protest of *The Philistine* (East Aurora, NY, 1895–1915). No one movement embraced them all, and all preceded literary modernism per se. Starting from a bibliographical rather than a literary angle, Kirsten Macleod describes over three hundred little magazines published in the United States in the 1890s and the first few years of the twentieth century. She argues that "the apparent lack of avant-gardist radicalism in American little magazines of the 1890s has been largely responsible for their critical neglect. In broad terms, little magazines of this period featured content quite similar to both their genteel and mass-market mainstream counterparts and, at the same time, followed the trends towards brevity and a lively journalistic style. Many engaged with timely literary and artistic culture, featuring popular genres of fiction and poetry, such as local colour writing and historical romance."[6] A generation before Ezra Pound and Eliot, then, little magazines abounded.

Another bibliographer, David McKnight, has expanded the census of the little magazine and the small press in twentieth-century Canada. McKnight defines the small press as "the non-commercial production of books and periodicals with a literary orientation, issued in limited runs for specialized readerships, and often dedicated to experimental writing or identity-based perspectives." Between 1918 and 1980, he counts approximately 465 little magazines and 325 small presses in English, and fifty little magazines and fifty small presses in French, calculating their average lifespan in either language at two years. The vast majority of them appeared after 1960, and one of the first initiatives that McKnight lists is the Ryerson Poetry Chap-Books.[7] Indeed, if the accent is placed on book production rather than poetic school, it is clear that Pierce blazed a trail that many small-press publishers in Canada would follow. His activity conforms to McKnight's definition exactly. The succeeding case studies will document his printing of poetry in small editions of 150 to 500 copies, with an Arts and Crafts design reminiscent of that patron saint of the small press, William Morris. The author was not only obliged but usually eager to help cover the costs of printing, and where this did not happen, as with Susan Frances Harrison's Chap-Book, publication nevertheless proceeded at a loss – subsidized, in effect, by Ryerson's other business.[8] Although imagined for a national audience, the Chap-Books were in practice often distributed to readers in the author's personal orbit. The venture as a whole proceeded out of Pierce's commitment to Canadian national identity rather than any opportunity for profit. Two decades before *Preview* and *First Statement*, and continuing well after their demise, the Chap-Books operated as an anti-commercial cultural institution for the production of Canadian poetry. When at last the Canadian government decided to invest in the creation and publication of literature, which caused the post-1960 boom that McKnight records, it was simply a matter of funding a practice that had already existed for decades. The resilient little Chap-Books provided the model.

Third, because of Pierce's nationalist commitment, and because of an Irish heritage that set him at a critical distance from imperialism,[9] the Ryerson Poetry Chap-Books were politically responsible. They reflect a broad, far-flung, middlebrow culture of poetry in twentieth-century Canada as it was really practised. Edited more on a principle of representative inclusion than discriminating exclusion, more as a rambling anthology than a concentrated manifesto, the Chap-Books assemble in the manner of a parliament many different poetic voices, subject positions, and aims. Of the 144 contributors, over half (seventy-six) were women, a remarkable count in a period known for the masculinist gendering of serious authorship.[10] One of them was Elsie Fry Laurence, the future mother-in-law of the novelist Margaret Laurence. Fry Laurence's example as a published author encouraged Laurence to pursue her vocation as a writer at a crucial moment in the latter's life.[11] Pierce's editorial inclusivity was thus diametrically opposed to the notorious dismissal of the average Canadian woman writer manifest in F.R. Scott's "The Canadian Authors Meet" (1927; 1936).

The inclusivity was geographical, too. The Chap-Books drew in writers such as Lenore Pratt from Newfoundland, Alexander Louis Fraser and John Hanlon Mitchell from the Maritimes, Leo Cox from Quebec, Kathryn Munro and Raymond Souster from Ontario, Elaine M. Catley and Sara Carsley from Alberta, and Ernest Fewster and Mary Matheson from British Columbia. Writers from every region of Canada except the

Far North were included. Immigrants were included, such as Geoffrey Drayton, whose 1950 Chap-Book, *Three Meridians* (no. 141), describes scenes from his native Barbados. Before airlines or highways, Pierce crossed the continent by train to meet authors, sell books, secure educational contracts, and take in the diverse geography of Confederation. The land was vast, and Pierce worked to bring writers all across it into contact with each other through his series.

Age was not a barrier, either. Old poets and young were accepted. Dorothy (Gostwick) Roberts was twenty-one years old when her first Chap-Book was published (in 1927). Arthur Stringer was seventy-four (in 1948). Some of the poetry is even expressly written for the ear of the preliterate child. The title poem of May P. Judge's *Way to Fairyland and Other Rhymes* (no. [52], 1931), for example, is a galloping ballad that holds a three-year-old's attention with its rhyme, animal imagery, and fantastical notions of what fairies eat:

> They took me to the market, nothing very nice for sale,
> The only thing I wanted was sweet honey in a pail;
> I did not fancy bird's eggs, nor fat, home-cured butterflies,
> And toadstools for a pie-crust hardly seemed quite overwise.
> So had to say, "No, thank you," and I had no wish to dine, –
> And no, I really *could* not taste their sweet blackbeetle wine.
> I shuddered at their scalloped snail, and caterpillar steak,
> And chose instead a water ice, and sorrel-seeded cake.[12]

Like Dennis Lee decades later, Judge made good her belief that poetry is for everyone by including the youngest listeners.

Discrimination based on disability or class was also less than one might expect. Disabled people have a presence at a few levels. Pierce's own life with disseminated lupus and his near-total hearing loss by the early 1920s[13] disposed him favourably both to deaf poets themselves, such as Annie Charlotte Dalton, author of *The Ear Trumpet* (no. [5], 1926), and to allies of the deaf community, such as M. Eugenie Perry (see chapter 5). There are also working-class writers who take their place alongside wealthy ones. Al Purdy was working in a Vancouver mattress factory when he wrote the poems that became *Pressed on Sand* (no. 157, 1955). By contrast, W.V. Newson, when his *Vale of Luxor* (no. [6], 1926) appeared, was the deputy treasurer of Alberta.

Even with respect to race and ethnicity, which one might well expect to be homogeneous in a poetry series that concluded decades before the passage of the Multiculturalism Act in 1988, there is a diversity of representation that calls for a closer look. Hyman Edelstein, a Montreal Jew, published two collections in the series in the 1940s. Another contributor was the Ukrainian Canadian writer Maara Haas (Myra Lazechko-Haas). R.D. Cumming, a native of Glasgow, grew up near Lillooet, British Columbia, where he learned the St'at'imc and Chinook languages. He represents the struggle of the First Nations against colonization sympathetically in his long poem, *Paul Pero* (no. [29], 1928), giving the eponymous protagonist speeches such as the following:

> Who is this unwelcome white man
> With his fables of repentance,
> With his tales of sins unnumbered,
> With his laws, and jails, and justice,
> With his police, and prisons and handcuffs,
> Who has come unasked among us?
> Why must we bow down before him, –
> He who stole our fish and mowitch,
> Feeds us with his own religion?[14]

In its focus on land and policing, the poem frankly acknowledges core issues of First Nations politics in Canada. The series does not appear to have included any Indigenous, Asian, or Black writers, but this lack was not the result of any deliberate exclusion on Pierce's part, as far as his archives indicate.[15] On the contrary, representation, or the responsibility of the series to the people and places that constituted Canada, is a substantial dimension of the Chap-Books. This dimension contributed to the formation of the very standards by which we now judge as regrettable the lack noted above. This third argument – of the series' parliamentary responsibility – is expanded in chapters 5 and 6.

Fourth, the collective literary character of the Ryerson Poetry Chap-Books is a mixture of romantic and modernist. As Campbell shows, Pierce, a child of the 1890s, was raised in powerful currents of nineteenth-century thought, and it is no surprise that they flow through the books that he published over the course of his lifetime. His mother instilled in him the core values of Methodism: radical faith in God, literacy through the Bible, temperance, and sacrificial service. At the age of six, he attended a revival with his mother and signed a pledge never to touch alcohol. His religion adjusted and deepened during his undergraduate studies in the humanities at Queen's University from 1908 to 1912, where the Social Gospel and philosophical idealism were in the air. Pierce was profoundly inspired by idealists such as John Watson and W.D. Jordan, who taught that individual fulfillment is found in self-dedication to the good of society and that the Christian church, at its best, is an instrument through which society can realize the goal of "beauty betrothed to truth." Pierce was ordained a Methodist minister, fulfilling his mother's hopes, and he ultimately conceived of his work as a publisher as a form of extended ministry at the national level: "Somehow I feel," he wrote in his diary on 1 June 1924, "that my life is ordained to more than ordinary burdens and possibly to equally great achievements." Moreover, between 1917 and 1920, he cultivated an interest in Russian literature – Dostoevsky, Tolstoy, Pushkin, and Gogol. He was fascinated by their epic revelation of religious values at work in national evolution.[16] The romantic quest for transcendence, therefore, wove itself profoundly into Pierce's upbringing, worldview, and professional vocation. Naturally he looked around for the Canadian equivalent of Dostoevsky and was fiercely loyal to the idealistic nationalism he found in the work of the Confederation Poets. Chapter 2 documents Charles G.D. Roberts's influence in Pierce's inauguration of the Chap-Books, and chapter 3 tells the story of Nathaniel A. Benson, who carried the torch of romantic poetry into the mid-twentieth century as Roberts's heir.

Pierce's parliamentary inclusivity, however, ultimately compelled him to open the Chap-Books to modernist poetry. The University of Toronto professor E.K. Brown was a key intermediary in persuading Pierce of the merit of the new poetry, despite its explicit hostility to romance. Brown's collaboration with Duncan Campbell Scott to bring out previously unpublished poems by Archibald Lampman, in the form of *At the Long Sault and Other New Poems* (Toronto: Ryerson Press, 1943), won Pierce's trust, and he published works by younger poets whom Brown recommended – Earle Birney's *David and Other Poems* (1942), A.J.M. Smith's *News of the Phoenix* (1943), Dudek and P.K. Page's *Unit of Five* (1944), and F.R. Scott's *Overture* (1945), to name a few.[17] It is worth returning to Dudek's 1958 essay for a glowing tribute to Pierce's contribution to Canadian modernism. Although Dudek restricts his definition of the little magazine to heighten its modernism, and excludes prior small-scale initiatives such as the Chap-Books, he acknowledges that Pierce worked exceptionally against the reactionary "profit-motive literature of mass-readership": "The conservatism of Toronto publishers has also been remarked, though in fact the Ryerson Press alone has done more to advance our literature than any other single force."[18] Dudek, after all, had a Chap-Book of his own by this point. *Romantic* and *modernist* are blunt terms, but they describe the basic polarity that Pierce experienced in the 1940s and '50s. In nonhierarchical combination, they remain useful in discerning the competition and blending of poetic traditions and innovations as the series wound its way to its conclusion in 1960. Moreover, as chapter 7 will argue, they help to explain the phenomenal success of Purdy, who seized the mixed romantic-modernist character of the series and forged it into his own distinct voice.

All in all, the Ryerson Poetry Chap-Books are a major example of the possibilities and constraints under which Canadian literature took shape in the mid-twentieth century as a sociopolitical and artistic cultural product. The process that produced them and the literary vision that they project are in the end inseparable, and in reading them with an open mind and interpreting their content and form with regard to their authors' and their editor's lives, we can learn much about the texture of Canadian poetry stretching from one celebrated Canadian poet, Charles G.D. Roberts, to another, Al Purdy.

Ultimately this book contends that the Chap-Books should be lifted out of the neglect into which many of them have fallen. Taken individually, cer-tain numbers have garnered extensive critical attention, such as Anne Marriott's *The Wind Our Enemy*. Most, however, have not received any critical commentary, let alone detailed analysis. The reasons for this neglect may be several. Justifiably, the person at the centre of most literary studies is the author. In the past few decades, the history of the book has sought to counteract this gravity and has mounted compelling arguments for the cultural importance of publishers, readers, and other agents in the life of the book. Nevertheless, the natural inclination to know who wrote a text and why remains irresistible, and so the attempt to study a publisher's creation – the series – falls back to studying the author's – the poetry.[19] To examine the 144 contributors to this series exhaustively would be a formidable and encyclopedic task. I have not succeeded in completing it. Instead I offer what I hope will be an interesting defeat, presenting well-considered avenues into the rich essence of the series, avenues for others to multiply and extend.

The Chap-Books are physically slight. They are slim, bound in paper until 1953, and blank on their spines until 1960, and therefore all but invisible on a shelf. Printed in modest runs, they were collectors' items from the outset, and if a number of them can still be had relatively easily through the dealer's network, the original editions really belong in the rare book departments of university libraries in which they tend to reside. Digitization, such as through the Internet Archive project, will help to counteract this inaccessibility, as will republication along the lines of the new editions put out by Ronald P. Frye & Company between 2009 and 2011, but scholarship and criticism must play their essential part in discovering the value of the poetry if it is not to lapse into oblivion.

Cultural nationalism is also in play, and the desire for an ideal Canada appears over and over again through these booklets. Some readers today will wish to ignore it. To do so, however, would be to discount the grave and awful patriotism that ensued from the First World War, the institutionalized centrality of the Ryerson Press to the English Canadian book trade as it was then constituted, the life of an editor whom his biographer styles "inescapably a 'Maker of Canada,' the creator and promoter of a potent construct of the nation,"[20] and the real structures of government and culture that constitute the evolving phenomenon of Canada. The ideal of Canadian literary nationalism unfolded dramatically and extensively in the thirty-five years of the Ryerson Poetry Chap-Books. The ephemerality and endurance of these two hundred little books tell a valuable story of that unfolding.

ONE

"The Quickening Spirit of the Times"
Publishing in 1920s Canada

AT THEIR ORIGIN, the Ryerson Poetry Chap-Books were a product of the 1920s, a period of excitement, renewal, and struggle in Canadian publishing. Writers, publishers, and readers all eagerly responded to the sense of nationalism awakened by the First World War, but the war had not altered the fundamental challenges of making books in Canada. The 1917 conscription crisis had emphasized the country's linguistic division. It was difficult to publish original trade books in English when so many were available from American publishers. American copyright formalities continued to prevent Canadian publishers from marketing their books in the United States. The war had raised the possibility of Canada defining itself in literature apart from Europe's cultural authority, but to develop a Canadian culture of literary authorship was a complex undertaking. To publish original trade books in Canada was to walk onto thin ice, and the corollary was often a burden of self-reliance for aspiring authors. This chapter will describe three contexts for Lorne Pierce's creation of the Chap-Books: the operations of the Ryerson Press as a book publisher; the examples set by two other leading Canadian book publishers; and the culture of poetry in Canadian magazines. Together these contexts show the vision, experimentation, and disarray that characterized publishing in

Canada in the 1920s. Like so many other periods in Canadian literature, the decade was a time of real and perceived beginnings, and the Ryerson Poetry Chap-Books reflected them.

※✝※

ENVELOPING THE ACTIVITIES of the Ryerson Press was the church. The publisher traced its origin to the Methodist Revival in eighteenth-century England, "to the hymns that Charles Wesley wrote, to the preaching of John and Charles Wesley and [George] Whitefield, and to the multitude of books and pamphlets issued by John Wesley."[1] In Canada, Methodist publishing took firm root in 1829, when Egerton Ryerson founded the *Christian Guardian*, at York (Toronto), Upper Canada.[2] The *Christian Guardian* attracted a wide readership and actively expanded public discourse with its commentary on local and international politics, especially under its charismatic founding editor, while remaining above all a religious weekly magazine.[3] It had a ready sales force in the ministers of the Methodist church in Canada, who were explicitly made its agents, "and every agent who may procure fifteen subscribers, and use his best endeavours to make collections and obtain subscribers annually, shall be entitled to paper gratis."[4] Profits from publication went into a pension fund for retired ministers. The relation between preaching and publishing was thus a symbiotic one and successful. By 1920, the *Christian Guardian* may have had as many as 40,000 subscribers, more than any other Canadian weekly magazine.[5]

From the outset, the printing office set up to produce the magazine took all sorts of other jobs, too, and printed newssheets, reports, pamphlets, and books of various description for the growing colony. The first book that Egerton Ryerson published was *The Doctrines and Discipline of the Methodist Episcopal Church in Canada* (1829), but another early imprint was the *Report of the Select Committee of the House of Assembly, on the Petition of George Rolph* (1830).[6] Religious and secular publication were thus intermixed and bookselling was also included. In 1833, Ryerson and other Methodist leaders created a Book Room, which "initially ... served as a depository from which the ministers and congregation could obtain decent publications. Over time it transmuted into a large-scale retail and wholesale operation that came to be stocked not only with the merchandise of foreign publishers but with its own publications as well as those of other Canadian publishers."[7] From these beginnings in printing and bookselling, the Methodist Book and Publishing House grew under successive book stewards, especially William Briggs from 1879 to 1919, into one of Canada's most important publishers. The superlative can be let stand as long as it is recognized that the house also twisted every way to avoid risking its own money on new works by local writers. From 1913 to 1915, the house built the Wesley Building for itself, a grand, five-storey office and factory at the corner of Queen Street West and John Street in Toronto with an ornate, cathedral-like entrance. It remains part of the downtown landscape today.[8]

Briggs had printed, published, and sold trade titles under his own name. When Samuel Wesley Fallis succeeded him as book steward in 1919, he adopted the imprint "the Ryerson Press" instead. The name was retained through 1925, when the union of the Methodist, Congregational, and most of the Presbyterian churches created the United Church of Canada.[9] The Ryerson Press (the general trade division) reported to the church's Board of Publication and operated alongside the United Church Publishing House (the ecclesiastical division). On 1 December 1970, church ownership ceased with the sale of the Ryerson Press to the American publisher McGraw-Hill. The event shocked the public and made an impact on Canadian cultural policy for years to come.[10]

It was Fallis who hired Lorne Pierce. Pierce was raised a strict Methodist in the small town of Delta, Ontario (northeast of Kingston).[11] He studied at Queen's University and Victoria College (University of Toronto), served as a missionary among immigrant settlers on the Prairies, and received a bachelor of divinity degree from the Union Theological Seminary in New York. He was ordained in 1916. That year, he married Edith Chown, a classmate at Queen's with whom he would have two children, and he began work as a parish minister in Ottawa. The growing crisis of the war prompted him to enlist, and he served with the medical corps at a military hospital in Kingston. However, his own lifelong health problems had manifested by this time and cut short his military career. What was initially diagnosed as tuberculosis eventually proved to be disseminated lupus, and it caused Pierce to experience profound hearing loss. He was all but deaf by age thirty. He was discharged from active service but the Great War left its devastating mark on him nonetheless when he received belated word that his beloved cousin, Clifford Pierce, had been killed at Vimy Ridge.

After the war, Pierce took a position as the minister of a rural church in Brinston, between Cornwall and Brockville, but the annual meeting of the Montreal Methodist Conference in nearby Kemptville on 2 June 1920 altered his vocation again. He dazzled the audience with a lecture on moral idealism in Russian literature, the topic of the doctorate that he was pursuing by correspondence from the United Theological College in Montreal. Samuel Fallis was among the assembled. Eager for someone to help him regenerate the book publishing program of the Methodist Book and Publishing House, he promptly offered Pierce the position of literary critic and advisor. It was a vague, hopeful role that Pierce eventually shaped by dint of will and Edith's support into that of editor-in-chief.

The job of editor at the Ryerson Press was an inheritance in the double sense of being both honour and burden. Pierce felt himself to be carrying on in the illustrious tradition of Egerton Ryerson and William Briggs, spreading literacy and literary culture, educational and spiritual edification, national purpose, and self-fulfillment. At the same time, he saw that none of these would move an inch unless he carried the weight. His own description of the situation that he inherited along with his desk in the Wesley Building offers a valuable account of Canadian publishing in 1920, an account well worth dissecting. Because of Briggs's success as a distributor of international books, it was necessary for the ninety-year-old house to reinvent itself almost from scratch as an original publisher:

> During the last decade of the régime of Dr Briggs the book publishing programme of the House gradually slowed down to almost zero. The House had taken on a large number of important foreign agencies, which provided each year roaring sales of best-sellers from New York and London. It was a time when the trade departments dominated the policy of the House. If agency titles could be had, with little or no risk, why waste time and money on Canadian ventures? Moreover, some of our most experienced and enterprising sales executives moved out to found publishing houses of their own: S.B. Gundy, John McClelland, George Stewart, Thomas Allen, Fred Goodchild and G.J. McLeod. In a very short time these new Houses became the publishing centres of Canadian books, and under the imprint of McClelland and Stewart they were the most distinguished looking books yet to appear in Canada. The publisher had become artist as well as architect, with an assist from J.E.H. MacDonald, R.C.A., and his son, Thoreau MacDonald.

When the House of Ryerson once again began to take its place as a Canadian publishing concern, it was necessary to recover lost ground. Since much of the territory had been pre-empted, the House was forced to begin where it could, and with some lines that other Houses had ignored as unprofitable or uninteresting. If one must somehow make a beginning, one must begin somewhere. This was a slow business, and a costly one, but gradually the House came once again into its own, and today [i.e., in 1954] covers nearly all the important categories, history, biography, travel, fiction, poetry, *belles lettres*, religion, theology, economics and so on, as well as text books for the primary grades, through high school and vocational school to college and professional schools. In the founding of our educational list we were fortunate in having the advice of Professor Peter Sandiford, Dean Harold Innis, Dean O.D. Skelton and others, whose names are now permanently identified with Canadian scholarship and public affairs. We were also fortunate in having the loyalty of many members of the learned societies and educational associations as well as other leaders of opinion.

We place this in the record, for it is true that no man stands alone. Strong forces were in our favour, the quickening spirit of the times, the loyal co-operation of leaders in many areas of Canadian life, the supporting tradition of the House itself.[12]

Since its founding in the nineteenth century, the house had produced hundreds of books for an expanding Canada. Yet, as this commentary indicates, Pierce was obliged to build up its activities as an original publisher from "almost zero," competing with others who had left the firm to take the lead elsewhere.

"Why waste time and money on Canadian ventures?" was the problem that Pierce faced. What his question acknowledges is that dealing in American books was more profitable. Between 1880 and 1940, American book publishers generally shifted from family concerns to modern corporations. A new class of professional managers reorganized the trade to attack the challenge of national and international mass distribution more rationally, including distribution to Canada. The big American trade houses such as D. Appleton & Company and Houghton Mifflin Company produced books in every genre, offered writers large advances, ran advertisement-based monthly magazines to lure in readers, hired travellers to advise and control retailers more effectively, and increasingly concentrated themselves in New York City. At the same time, elite publishers such as Copeland & Day of Boston, Stone & Kimball of Chicago, and Alfred A. Knopf of New York flourished and invested private capital into books of remarkable artistic quality.[13] American publishers set the standard in producing the "roaring ... best-sellers" that the canny William Briggs sold so successfully to Canadian readers. In distributing these books and making rules around their distribution, such as the Copyright Amendment of 1900, the Canadian book suppliers and politicians of his generation had cemented the agency system of publishing.[14]

Cutting against this grain, Pierce adopted a number of strategies to reincorporate original publishing into Ryerson's operations. Perhaps his greatest career achievement was in educational publishing, a field that shared the nationalist goals and some of the content of his literary publishing but far surpassed it in readers and profits. Canadians born in the middle decades of the twentieth century grew up with the schoolbooks that Pierce published jointly with the Macmillan Company of Canada, namely the Treasury Readers and the Canada Books of Prose and Verse. They were adopted across English Canada and went through approximately forty printings between 1930 and 1965: "By 1961, the textbooks for grades 7 to 12, still in use, had a combined national sale of 200,000 copies per year." The profit margins, not extraordinary, were nevertheless "solid," and Pierce, as an author, made royalties that surpassed his Ryerson salary – $5,855.55 in 1948, for example, when his salary was $5,599.92.[15] The *Picture Gallery of Canadian History*, illustrated by the artist C.W. Jefferys, became the basis for a generation's understanding of Canada's past. Statistically speaking, it was in educational publishing that Pierce came closest to his dream of a national literature. Moreover, he was exemplary in supporting Jeffrys materially through the last three decades of the artist's career.[16]

In trade publishing, Pierce's accomplishments were smaller, but he did perceptibly widen the channel for Canadian writing and a number of his authors achieved books of lasting value. Enthusiasm and difficulty, prestige and shortcomings characterize Pierce's efforts "to recover lost ground" for the Ryerson Press in original literature in the 1920s. His bringing out E.J. Pratt's first major collection of poetry, *Newfoundland Verse* (1923), was a major accomplishment that Canadian literary history continues to honour. However, there were printing errors in the book as a result of the aftermath of the printers' strike of 1921, and Ryerson soon lost Pratt as an author.[17] Wilson MacDonald's *Miracle Songs of Jesus* (1923) sold a thousand copies in two weeks, but then Pierce rashly offered MacDonald a $250 advance (about $3,710 today) for a novel that was never published, and their relations soured.[18] When Pierce courageously published Frederick Philip Grove's *Settlers of the Marsh* (1925), a landmark of Canadian realist fiction, it raised a storm of controversy outside and inside the Ryerson Press that Pierce only escaped thanks to a letter of praise from the Canadian prime minister, Arthur Meighen. Pierce's later dealings with Grove were "mutually disappointing."[19] In general, Pierce's work as a specialist literary publisher careened through peril, frequently risking the wrath of the book steward. He continually skirted financial disaster on the one hand and authors' displeasure on the other. The fact that a volatile, ad hoc, and unique process seems to lie behind every book is a measure of the amplitude of the obstacles that were ranged against him.

Pierce's quest to find the way to publish Canadian literature impelled him to consider unusual manuscripts and unorthodox arrangements. He was "forced to begin where [he] could, with some lines that other Houses had ignored as unprofitable or uninteresting." In order to better understand the challenge of becoming and remaining an original publisher, it is worthwhile to look more deeply into some of these "ignored" books from the 1920s, with which Pierce was willing to engage in order to extend Ryerson into the various genres of the general publisher. Amateurism on the part of both author and publisher characterizes the three books described below. The authors were novices willing to cover a significant portion of the costs. The publisher was conducting a nascent practice in which his role had to be renegotiated case by case. The publishing terms were unpredictable and idiosyncratic, no matter the genre. Both author and publisher ran up hard against their limits, and yet their persistence in the ventures evinces the devotion of the amateur to a cause. The publishing of poetry chapbooks emerged from this context of experiment and fluidity.

In April 1925, Senator Andrew Haydon, friend and ally of William Lyon Mackenzie King, approached Pierce with his pioneer history of the Ontario counties of Lanark and Renfrew. The fifty-eight-year-old Haydon had been gathering material on the settlement of the Ottawa Valley, his native locale, for over twenty years, but when it came to book publication the seasoned politician was a beginner. "I would be greatly interested in knowing whether you think the manuscript is worthy of publication," he wrote. "If so, I would like to know upon what terms you might be willing to take it, and in that case I have a number of illustrations, photographs, &c."[20] Pierce's reply caused Haydon to adjust his expectations about their relative responsibilities. His next letter frankly asked how much a good edition would cost him, "and I mean the cost according to the way you think you would like to produce it." If Haydon was surprised by the terms that Pierce offered, he did not balk: six weeks later he returned the galley proofs to Ryerson with his compliments on the care taken in typesetting, adding, "I now enclose my cheque for $500., which is the payment due at the end of May, as promised." (This payment would equal about $7,420 today.) He also asked, however, for the insertion of a proper scholarly apparatus to note his sources, a request that threw Ryerson for a loop. Contrary to his hopes, the book was not ready for a summer reunion of old-timers in Perth, and Haydon corrected two more sets of proofs in July and October. When at last publication drew near, the author broached the matter of author copies, and indicated a further willingness to pay: "I want fifty copies for myself whether you are to be paid for them or not must be, of course, according to your arrangements whatever they are."[21]

Pioneer Sketches in the District of Bathurst, volume 1, appeared in December. It is a substantial book that runs to slightly over three hundred pages. The title-page verso states that Haydon retained the copyright. If the design efforts were minimal, care was nevertheless taken over the half-tone illustrations, which are not lumped together but inserted intelligently where their subject comes up in the text. As for the letterpress printing, it inevitably reflects the last-minute addition of the notes.[22] Haydon expressed pleasure upon receiving his two boxes of copies. "I will make no difficulty for you from a business point of view in any kind of way," he promised, thanking Ryerson for its willingness to look after the commercial distribution, which he acknowledged might well be "very limited." Still, he had suggestions for the list of newspapers to which review copies should be sent.[23] Overall, the publication of *Pioneer Sketches* cut its own path, thanks to a wealthy and determined author. Elements standard to modern publishing agreements — whether notes and illustrations would be included, how many complimentary copies the author should receive, who would sell the edition — appear to have been handled informally as they arose. As the next example shows, the complete cost of printing *Pioneer Sketches* almost certainly exceeded $500, and it is therefore fair to conclude that a particular division of expenses between author and printer enabled its publication. History was one of the categories that Pierce wished to promote.

In August 1925, Walter McRaye of Winnipeg floated an opportunity to print a biographical encyclopedia on terms that demanded some entrepreneurial vim. A bolder and more settled publisher might have either immediately rebuffed McRaye's inquiry or turned to advantage his request for credit, but Pierce did neither: he considered the project while being careful not to overcommit, skirting the risk of real investment. McRaye was an actor and reciter of poetry. He had been the friend and stage partner of Pauline Johnson, with whom he had toured across North America and as far as England, and he had performed the *habitant* poems of William Henry Drummond for fellow soldiers during the First World War.[24] These qualifications interested Pierce. According to McRaye's pitch, his proposed *Pioneers and Prominent People of Manitoba* would be a better book than the similar volume on Saskatchewan that Ryerson had printed the year before. The publication department estimated the price to print the edition at $2,200 (about $32,700 today) and Pierce or a colleague pencilled an immediate reaction in the margin of McRaye's letter: "500 down." This would be the sticking point, for McRaye needed financial assistance: "I have assets of over $5000 in contracts from the cream of Manitobas citizenry. Now here is the point, will the Ryerson Press print this for me, holding contracts as security until the money starts to come in ... My subscribers are all well to do people, two thirds of them the leading people of Winnipeg. Manitoba has a wonderful crop this season to back it up."[25] Pierce was not averse to the book. Its Canadian-historical focus was in line with his larger objectives, and Ryerson would print two other books by McRaye some years later. In September McRaye travelled by train from Winnipeg to Toronto to discuss the venture, but crop or no crop Ryerson refused to be pushed into moving capital around to accommodate him:

> Frankly, we want very much to do your book, particularly when the four or five others to come, including the Ontario volume, are in view ... However, just as frankly, we cannot see very favourably the proposition of assuming the responsibility of a bank in regard to those contracts. Perhaps if we had not had the experience with the two or three other cases I spoke of this morning the situation might be different, but as you will thoroughly appreciate, by reason of the

difficulties resulting from these other cases, we are a bit careful. Under all circumstances it seems that the request of a deposit of $500. as suggested in our wire, is fair and reasonable. You are the logical man to handle these contracts. They should not go out of your hands. To avoid any negotiation with them we should be very glad to accept your Note at ninety days with an endorsement by Mr Bagshaw covering the remainder of the amount, approximately $1,700.[26]

McRaye could not meet these cash-payment deadlines. He went on alone with the publication of *Pioneers and Prominent People of Manitoba*, which appeared later that year under the otherwise unknown imprint of the Canadian Publicity Co (where he was manager); Bulman Brothers of Winnipeg printed it. At 376 pages, it is slightly longer than *Pioneer Sketches*, but its illustrations are less and comprise only one inserted plate (the frontispiece) and eight small images incorporated into the letterpress formes. The total production costs of the two books therefore compare. As for the subsequent encyclopedias that McRaye envisioned, they never materialized; after showing genuine interest in the project, Ryerson eventually shied away from financing it.

Of the novice, self-publishing Canadian author there is perhaps no more colourful case than the naturalist Jack Miner. This third example of Ryerson's tentative involvement in original publishing reveals not only an author's experimental initiative but also the limitation of the press to Canada despite the allure of the larger North American market. Miner owned a brick and tile factory on a rural homestead three kilometres north of Kingsville, Ontario, where his family had moved from Ohio in 1878. He was a born woodsman. The fifth child and second son among ten children, he had no formal schooling and would not learn to read until age thirty-five.[27] Rather, by his own account, he "took to the woods as naturally as a park hare" and studied birds and mammals as a hunter. After his older brother died in a moose hunting accident in 1898, Miner began to transform his land into a bird sanctuary. It continues to thrive today under the auspices of a charitable foundation that bears his name. From the first wild ducks he hatched in 1902, Miner attracted ever greater numbers of wildfowl, including Canada geese and swans, to return to him annually for protection and food. He invented a practice of tagging to trace their migration, each tag bearing his address and a verse of Scripture meant to inspire respect for the creature on whose leg it was found.[28]

The flocks of birds and the tags distinguished him as an early leader in the conservation movement. In 1910, in order to raise money for feed, he began to give public lectures about his work. His help was enlisted in the campaign to make nearby Point Pelee a national park, which succeeded in 1918.[29] He became a celebrated speaker and ultimately travelled across North America delivering addresses to clubs, schools, universities, and associations, one high point being a ninety-minute speech to the Izaak Walton League of America at a banquet in Chicago in 1927 where the other speaker was future US president Herbert Hoover. His lectures, many given at Massey Hall in Toronto, included a filmstrip about birds produced with the assistance of another eminent friend, Henry Ford, who sent a technician from his own motion picture studio to Kingsville. Miner died in 1944, and three years later, by unanimous votes in both the House of Commons and the Senate, the Canadian Parliament passed a special act to declare the week of 10 April to be National Wild Life Week in honour of the day in 1865 when this illustrious Canadian had been born.[30]

Miner's first book, *Jack Miner and the Birds and Some Things I Know about Nature* "by Jack Miner Himself," is a jocular and heartfelt account of his becoming a conservationist. In its introduction it pretends to have been penned in solitude, in a tent pitched in the woods, as its author drank in the purity of nature: "And while I am very thankful to my many friends who have offered to write it for me if I would only dictate it, yet I firmly believe the majority of readers will enjoy these facts right from the awkward hand of Jack Miner better than if they were polished too much. While it may read very unreasonable, yet please don't forget that outside of a little joke I may attempt to crack, the rest is all facts gathered from personal experience and observation, and I assure you these views are not second-hand, as I am a very poor reader and have never read a book through in my life." Mingling humility and pride, Miner justifies his climb into the world of letters despite his relative illiteracy. Direct experience is one kind of authority he claims; the other is a spiritual attitude of transcendence toward language: "when I entered the tent and sat down to write, I first whispered a few words of silent prayer of thankfulness, and asked God to guide my untrained hand so that you will understand my meaning." The text seems to originate from this divine inspiration. In fact the writing process was more complex. In moments of spare time over six years, from 1916 to 1922, Miner recounted his stories about the birds to his son, Manly Forest Miner, who transcribed and organized them.[31] The text runs to thirty-six chapters and is a well-designed whole, initially drawing the reader in with humour and then coherently building through various episodes to Miner's crowning achievement, his unprecedented success in trapping and banding Canada geese by the thousands. Halftone illustrations from photographs accompany the text throughout and are integral to it, evidencing a diligent gathering of materials and a careful coordination of word and image. The "awkward hand of Jack Miner" is thus a rhetorical construction, the invention of an enterprising father-son team forcing their way into print with knowing innocence.

The composition complete, Manly began to look about for a publisher. He approached the Ryerson Press but ran into a complication that was typical of the agency system. Rather than decide on its own, Ryerson forwarded the manuscript to the New York publisher George H. Doran (an expatriate Canadian who published many Canadian authors). Doran rejected it, and Ryerson therefore followed suit.[32] Undaunted, Manly proceeded to self-publish the book through Ryerson, taking the title of sales manager for himself while reserving that of author for his father. Ryerson typeset the manuscript, cast monotype plates, incorporated the four dozen half-tone illustrations, and in the fall of 1923 printed a book that consisted of thirteen gatherings.[33] It was no small enterprise, and the print run reached five thousand copies.[34]

The edition is not without its qualities. The leaves of paper are large (25.7 × 17.4 cm), smooth, and heavy; the typographical errors few, a letter of type slipping here, a word misspelled there; and the dust jacket handsome and printed from an engraving. In other respects, serious flaws marred it. Ryerson bound the first batch using a cheap glue that soon failed. With charming country manners on full display, Manly wrote to Ryerson's publication department, voicing his worry: "I am not sending this book back in way of complaint only to show you its cover is not sticking as it should. I have received eight or ten back like this and was not going to say anything about it to you only when I got a thinking perhaps its in the fault of the glue or something which you people should know about."[35] Some readers had returned books to him because of binding failure, "the green cloth rising from the paste board cover"; other copies showed defective printing: "one had a big black spot of ink size of your hand other two had holes clear through centre of page size of American half dollars"[36] (see figure 1.1).

A lengthy copyright statement proudly confirms the original Canadian manufacture, naming both the Miners and the Ryerson Press and reflecting

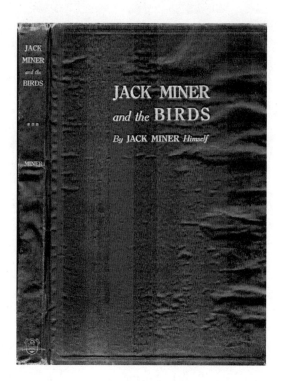

1.1 / Front cover and spine of Jack Miner, *Jack Miner and the Birds: Some Things I Know about Nature* (Toronto: Ryerson Press, 1923). Private copy. The poor binding is visible in the rippling of the cloth where the glue has failed. At the foot of the spine is the ornament of the Ryerson Press, which symbolized the heritage Lorne Pierce was shouldering – a crest with the bust of Egerton Ryerson and the phrase "Ryerson Press Founded 1829."

the idiosyncratic publication process.³⁷ Equally peculiar were the modes Manly invented to sell the book. Generally, the retail price was $2.50, but in the mecca of Kingsville Manly struck a deal with a store owner named Pickard, giving the latter a local monopoly that allowed him to raise the price to $3.00. Manly, not Ryerson, controlled the wholesale distribution of the edition, and when a copy of the book showed up in the store of a different Kingsville retailer he wrote to Ryerson in concern.³⁸ The Miners not only financed the Canadian edition but also devised their own ways to sell it. Manly would later estimate that he sold four thousand copies in the first nine months "by direct mail, the profit being channeled into advertising of the book."³⁹

Unlike Haydon or McRaye, Miner did not write for a distinctly Canadian audience; on the contrary, the experiment of having hunters from Texas to Hudson Bay report the birds' tags wherever they were taken was essentially transnational in character. At first the Miners ignored the border, and filled orders for example from customers in Albany, New York.⁴⁰ It was not long, however, before they realized the massive dimensions of the

US market. The baseball star Ty Cobb had visited the bird sanctuary and told them that he had been offered ten thousand dollars for his life story by a New York syndicate. Writing to Pierce's senior colleague, E.J. Moore, a manager in Ryerson's publishing department, Manly wondered, "Say Mr Moore do you know father could make a fine lot of money writing stories. Why I never knew there was so much money in it. Syndicates like 'King,' 'Allman,' 'International,' 'Associated News Bureau' have all written re articles."[41] Despite the earlier rejection by Doran, he now pushed ahead with an American edition, engaging Reilly and Lee of Chicago. On the afternoon of 19 February, Manly went to Pere Marquette station in Walkerville (Windsor), met the freight train from Toronto, and oversaw the unloading of the monotype plates that Ryerson had made to print his father's book. The next day he personally imported them into the United States, paying a duty of 2 1/8 cents per pound on the lead in the metal. In the Detroit railyard he gave one of the workers a tip, saw his plates put in a freight car going directly to Chicago, lingered to make sure the train departed as planned, and then sent a telegram to Reilly asking him to meet it with his own truck so that the plates would be handled gently.[42]

Reilly and Lee modified the monotype plates slightly before they printed the first American issue of *Jack Miner and the Birds*.[43] By rearranging some of the illustrations, Reilly reduced the book to twelve gatherings. This change saved money, as did a reduction in paper: the leaves of the US issue are much smaller (22.8 × 15.7 cm). The list of illustrations is different; the title page, of course, is different, too. The typography is identical except for some corrections. The most important difference is the addition of a second preface by the author, which candidly describes the book's journey from individual experiment toward industry norms: "After privately publishing this book in Canada, I am pleased to say the sales so far exceeded my expectations that I am hustling out a second edition." If the original printing was private and Canadian, the implication is that a more standard and American publishing agreement now governed the book. Having safely delivered his book into the hands of a US firm, Manly reflected to E.J. Moore on his own adventure as a publisher over the preceding fourteen months: "However a year has past and don't you think I have got along fine for a green ham at the book business. By me handling it as I have too been the means of getting Reilly-Lee in the States to handle it. As you people tried U.S. houses when it was in MSS. form didn't you and by owning plates and buying type am getting practically

20% and book to sell at $2.50 So thats not too bad Eh.'"[44] The American issue appeared in April and sold well: one travelling salesman from Detroit ordered five hundred copies at once, and it went through several print runs.[45] In the fall of 1925, Manly wrapped up the Ryerson edition, asking Moore to bind, cover, and ship him the final batch of one thousand copies, which arrived in Kingsville in three crates mid-December.[46]

Congratulating themselves on their earnings in money and in fame, the Miners appear to have remained blissfully unaware of their one error as publishers: that by originally printing outside of the United States they had technically contravened US copyright formalities. Was the book pirated? An online catalogue search does not turn up a host of unauthorized editions, at least not under the author's original name and title. Nevertheless, their publishing experiment ran this risk.[47] If a pair of brick manufacturers in Kingsville knew nothing about manufacturing clauses or deposit requirements, the same was not true of Fallis, Pierce, E.J. Moore, and others at the Ryerson Press who were the heirs of William Briggs's knowledge of asymmetrical North American copyright. A book had to be printed from type set in the United States to qualify for US copyright. Because of this technicality, Ryerson held itself to the role of printer and binder of *Jack Miner and the Birds* even though it proved to be a bestseller and the author became a celebrity. Even after learning that the edition would be large – five thousand copies – Ryerson refused to manage it, instead looking on as the old pattern of Canadian author finding American publisher repeated itself.[48]

Andrew Haydon's, Walter McRaye's, and Jack and Manly Miner's books show Pierce beginning where he could. They are evidence of the unsettled book publishing practices at the Ryerson Press in the 1920s, one important context of the Ryerson Poetry Chap-Books at their origin. A cautious openness to the Canadian writer, divided financing, cancelled sheets and last-minute additions, casting monotype plates, deferral to an American industry counterpart, faulty glue, unique copyright statements that name several parties, peculiar retail arrangements, and inability to publish for the American market: all of these facts reveal how much Pierce had to overcome in striving to catch up with the industry specialization that had occurred in the United States and Britain, whose publishers still supplied most of the books read in Canada. It is important to appreciate all that had to go into a book for it to be published. Before any poem can rise off the page, it must first be properly set down onto it.

Pierce's description of the conditions he faced at the start of his career as an editor is also useful for the view it provides of other publishers. In his words, quoted above, "No man stands alone." Beyond the sphere of the Ryerson Press, Canadian poetry was being written and published by many who shared the sense of service and opportunity that flooded the country because of the Great War. Their contributions to the culture of poetry in Canada constitute another key context for Pierce's initiative.

Pierce wished to emulate McClelland & Stewart, who had leapt ahead of Ryerson in the publishing of poetry circa 1920. John McClelland and Frederick D. Goodchild had been employed under Briggs but they left the Methodist Book and Publishing House in 1906 to found their own bookselling company. (George Stewart joined them in 1913, and Goodchild departed in 1918.) Within a few years of setting up shop, the firm was acting as the Canadian agents for several foreign publishers and issuing titles under its own imprint. During the war, they moved to the fore in the publication of work by Canadian writers. As Carl Spadoni and Judy Donnelly write, "Many of these authors, such as Ralph Connor, Marian Keith, Duncan Campbell Scott, and Hiram Cody, came to M&S as a result of agency contracts. In other instances, however ... the company assumed a primary role in publication, and oversaw both the manufacture and marketing of indigenous books. Most notably, the firm became the literary agent of L.M. Montgomery in 1916 and published her book of verse *Watchman and Other Poems*, when relations with her American publisher, L.C. Page and Co, became intolerable."[49] McClelland & Stewart published a dozen books of Canadian poetry in 1917 and 1918, and then settled into a pattern of a few each year until the 1930s. Some of them, such as Duncan Campbell Scott's *Lundy's Lane and Other Poems* (1916) and Robert Norwood's *The Piper and the Reed* (1917), were issued from the edition of an American publisher, usually Doran or Putnam of New York. Others, like Tom MacInnes's *The Fool of Joy* (1918), were printed independently by Warwick Brothers and Rutter in Toronto, with whom McClelland & Stewart developed a good working relationship. Although they did not form an explicit series, these editions nevertheless announced a commitment to Canadian poetry through a degree of homogeneity. They are elegant in design and tend toward a uniform size (approximately 19.5 × 14 cm). Some employ a distinctive typeface; some are graced by woodcuts by J.E.H. MacDonald, as Pierce remembered. (See figures 1.2 and 1.3.)

The war caused the upswell in McClelland & Stewart's publishing of poetry; several books are clearly direct responses to it. Thomas Harkness

1.2 / (*left*) Laura Goodman Salverson, "Chant of the Deep," in *Wayside Gleams* (Toronto: McClelland & Stewart; printed by Warwick Brothers and Rutter, 1925), 69. The typeface gestures toward a medieval hand with a bulging *h*, an *e* with a slanted crossbar, ligatures for *fi* and *fl*, slanted serifs, and the contrast between thicks and thins.

1.3 / (*right*) Title page from A.M. Stephen, *The Rosary of Pan* (Toronto: McClelland & Stewart; printed by Warwick Brothers and Rutter, 1923). The woodcut and the endpapers are the work of J.E.H. MacDonald, a member of the Group of Seven.

Litster dedicated his *Songs in Your Heart and Mine* (1917) "To my Stepson Lieut. George Murray Fraser, 1st Battalion, Canadians, France" (5). The frontispiece to Jesse Edgar Middleton's *Sea Dogs and Men at Arms: A Canadian Book of Songs* (1918) is a colour plate of H.B. Wollen's painting *The Canadians at Ypres*, which commemorates the landmark victory of the Canadian army in the Second Battle of Ypres in the spring of 1915 (see figure 1.4). Bernard Freeman Trotter, a literature student at McMaster University, imagined the plight of his Belgian peers in "To the Students of Liège (August 1914)" and recorded his own determination to enlist:

1.4 / H.B. Wollen, *The Canadians at Ypres*, frontispiece to Jesse Edgar Middleton, *Sea Dogs and Men at Arms: A Canadian Book of Songs* (New York: G.P. Putnam's Sons, 1918; issued in Canada by McClelland & Stewart).

In old Liège, when those dark tidings came
Of German honor callously forsworn,
And the red menace that should bring the scorn
Of ages on the Kaiser's name and shame,
And crown their city with a deathless fame,
The students wrote, they say, that summer morn
For their degrees, then joined the hope forlorn
Of Liberty, and passed in blood and flame.
O valiant souls! who loved not Duty less
Than Honor, whom no fears could move to shirk
The common task, no tyrant's threat subdue
When Right and Freedom called in their distress, –
Not vain your sacrifice nor lost your work:
The World's free heart beats high because of you!

Trotter was killed by a high-explosive missile in France on 7 May 1917. His parents, Ellen and Thomas Trotter, collaborated with W.S.W. McLay, professor of English and dean of arts at McMaster, to publish their son's collection, *A Canadian Twilight and Other Poems of War and of Peace* (1917), posthumously.[50] The same sublimity attaches to *Songs of an Airman and Other Poems* (1918) by Hartley Munro Thomas, a Queen's University student who likewise died in the war.[51] The title poem of Lilian Leveridge's *Over the Hills of Home* (1918) was "written as a tribute to Corporal Frank E. Leveridge, who died in France, after being wounded in action." It achieves pathos through a childlike rhythm, repetition, and rhyme that belie the adult speaker's grief:

> Brother, soldier brother, the Spring has come back again,
> But her voice from the windy hilltops is calling your name in vain;
> For never shall we together 'mid the birds and the blossoms roam
> Over the hills of home, brother, over the hills of home.[52]

McClelland & Stewart began to publish poetry with books like these, which helped readers come to terms with the ineffable feelings stirred up by the war.

After 1918, the momentum carried on into other Canadian poetry collections. Charles E. Royal wrote a book of Klondike poems, *The Trail of a Sourdough: Rhymes and Ballads* (1919), in the style of Robert Service. Frank Oliver Call, who would publish a Chap-Book with Pierce in 1944, experimented with free verse in *Acanthus and Wild Grape* (1920), as did James Lewis Milligan in *The Beckoning Skyline and Other Poems* (1920), a collection on the theme of emigration from England to Canada.[53] In 1922 Isabel Ecclestone MacKay not only published her own book, *Fires of Driftwood*, but also saw Marjorie Pickthall's *The Wood Carver's Wife* to press after the latter's death. MacKay wrote in her foreword that she had listened to Pickthall read aloud from the manuscript on a day in June while the two of them sat on a rock near the ocean: "Below lay the Pacific and above and far back the mountains rose. Forest sounds, secret and musical, accompanied the rise and fall of the poet's voice as she turned the pages, reading here and there."[54] Both her book and Pickthall's were designed by J.E.H. MacDonald and his son, Thoreau.[55] Recondite diction and a riddling mysticism set apart A.M. Stephens's *The Rosary of Pan* (1923). The McClelland & Stewart list also accumulated more work by the Confederation Poets in Duncan Campbell Scott's *Beauty and Life* (1921) and Bliss Carman's *Later Poems* (1921), *Ballads and Lyrics* (1923), and *Far Horizons* (1925).

In addition to original poetry, McClelland & Stewart published a handbook that introduced readers to the art of verse. It is valuable in retrospect for the light that it sheds on the culture of poetry from which the Ryerson Poetry Chap-Books emerged. *The Appeal of Poetry* by Donald G. French (1923) is an introduction to the poetics that prevailed in Pierce's generation, before T.S. Eliot and Ezra Pound introduced new standards. Rereading it helps to recover the meaning and purpose of the poetry that thrived in Canada circa 1920, which critics such as Munro Beattie, voicing the next generation's judgment in the *Literary History of Canada*, tended to reject.[56] French was the literary editor at McClelland & Stewart for more than twenty years, beginning in 1920.[57] His handbook, addressed to the general reader and appropriate for high school, opens with the principle that poetry is essentially moral, idealist, and aesthetic: "'He that hath eyes to see, let him see.' That is, in a great measure, the message of the poet to us. The poet is the great observer, and not only does he see things as they are objectively – he sees them in their relation to the soul of man; he sees their spiritual significance. And so it happens that the poet very often reaches our souls through the eye of imagination by appealing to our sense of the beautiful."[58] Poetry, by this definition, is the perception of virtue. It demonstrates compassion, grace, and loveliness in both form and ethical import, with the express purpose of counteracting cruelty, despair, and materialism. In other words, the realism that Beattie and others later used to appraise this decade's poetry was not one of the goals of many of the writers.

True poetry, French continued, was also general: "The poet does not concern himself with the analytical detail of the scientist, nor even with the idealistic detail of the painter ... we must supply the details for ourselves" (13). This assertion, too, contrasts later expectations, schooled by imagism to prefer concrete specificity. Beattie wrote (of Raymond Knister), "Sometimes a poem does no more than round off a succession of details with the intimation of a mood or the hint of an impression."[59] From his pen, this was praise, but French preferred the upsweep of a poem (by Carman) designed to make the reader "feel the inspiring power of spring, the call to adventure forth upon new voyages, whether upon the ocean azure, or upon the vast ocean of the unexplored regions of the soul ... Just observe how much is suggested and how little really told (a characteristic of fine artistry in poetry)" (14–15). The two critics agree on the power of suggestion but differ on the value of detail, oppositely assessing its place in the constitution of a good poem.

In French's poetics, sound was "the essential quality of poetic form – the singing quality, the music of it" (38). The printed line placed in a certain way on the page was only necessary in so far as it furthered the poem's aural quality. Mere typographic layout was not in itself poetic. French emphasized quantitative and accentual effects of metre: "long vowels and short measures are in keeping with verse of dignity and deep thought; longer measures with shorter vowel sounds produce a form of metre suitable to lighter themes" (39). Without resorting to the technical terms, he thus contrasted the iambic foot ("short measures") with the anapestic or dactylic ("longer measures"), combining them with an appreciation of vowel length based on classical Greek and Roman prosody. Metre and rhyme, even in their most traditional guises, were not to him worn out conventions. In *The Appeal of Poetry*, the literary editor at McClelland & Stewart bore witness to a culture that defined poetry as idealistic, moral, musical, and, as the title makes clear, appealing to everyone, and he did so entirely with examples from Canadian poets. This was the approach to poetry that Pierce espoused.

The other leading Canadian publisher of poetry books in the 1920s was the Macmillan Company of Canada. Like McClelland & Stewart but a step or two behind, Macmillan was in the process of becoming a specialist publisher of original trade books. Its Canadian office had been founded two decades earlier, in 1905, as a branch of the venerable British firm, Macmillan and Company (established in London in 1843), and its American offshoot, the Macmillan Company of New York (established 1869). Its main purpose was to sell the books published in London and New York to the Canadian market. Its other initial purpose was to develop authorized textbooks for use in Canadian schools.[60] From the outset, it also distributed other foreign publishers' books through agency agreements.

Gradually the presidents of the Canadian branch – Frank Wise, from 1905 to 1921, and Hugh Eayrs, from 1921 to 1940 – expanded into original literary publishing. "By the late 1930s, Macmillan had become a significant publisher of award-winning, internationally successful Canadian trade titles,"[61] thanks largely to the charisma of Eayrs, who acquired new works by Canadian writers such as Mazo de la Roche, Stephen Leacock, Morley Callaghan, Frederick Philip Grove, Raymond Knister (his novel *White Narcissus*, 1932), Irene Baird, and Louis Hémon (in translation) for the Macmillan list. From the early 1920s, the Macmillan Company of Canada was on the path toward original publishing.

Fiction constituted the bulk of its achievement, but Macmillan's Toronto office did publish verse, selectively. Its first poetry title was Thaddeus A. Browne's *The Belgian Mother, and Ballads of Battle Time* (1917).[62] As with McClelland & Stewart's first books of verse, the urgency of the war explains the exception. The title poem is a dramatic monologue in heroic couplets that compares to Pauline Johnson's "A Cry from an Indian Wife" in tone, topic, and form. The mother, who has suffered injury and the murder of her children during the German invasion of Belgium, apostrophizes God and asks whether justice exists. Her "torn bosom, 'neath the Prussian heel, / Crimson and breastless challenges Thy sky."[63] Her refrain, "shall Prussia pay," hardens from a question into an exclamation over the course of the five stanzas. The reader, implicitly, is tasked with fulfilling it. The collection contains much else besides war ballads – there is a variety of occasional verse – but the war again seems to have been decisive in overcoming the obstacles to publication. Propaganda opened a channel for poetry, and the volume went into a second edition within a year.[64]

Five years passed before another poetry collection appeared under the Macmillan Canada imprint. In 1922, a steady trickle began with Louise Morey Bowman's *Moonlight and Common Day*.[65] Bowman described the firm as encouraging but limited in its reach: "I seem to be tied up with 'Macmillans In Canada,' who seem to be rather a power unto themselves. They did well for me here, but almost nothing in either England or the States. The President (Mr Eayrs) of the Canadian house is a good sort; far the best publisher in Canada I think. He seems much the most modern of any of the Macmillan people anywhere. He handles the Borzoi books here too and is keenly alive, in many ways."[66] The comment is a snapshot of Canadian book publishing, which was striving to be "here," "modern," and "alive" while also inevitably rooted in the agency system. The association with Macmillan sufficed for Bowman, who saw her second collection, *Dream Tapestries*, published by the company in 1924. It included her Montreal poem "The Mountain that Watched," a dramatic lyric that explicitly sifts through images, wanders in and out of iambic pentameter, and acknowledges the English Romantics – with a difference:

Docks! There's a magical word! Not unpoetical
let me tell you, if you'll only close your eyes
and use that "inward eye" your Wordsworth used
for daffodils. My God! you'd think he had secured that "eye"

to be hereafter used for "daffodils," and "solitude" and "thrills,"
exclusively!
Come now! Just try it on for once to-day
with river docks filled with the motley throng ...
old world and new.
Deep searching eyes that seek the "golden West" –
wild eyes that hold the primal hunger lure,
young eyes that hold the secrets of the dawn,
sad eyes that hold the fury of the night –
We'll have to stand the dirty docks I think,
and the crowded station –
holding a daffodil to your nose to smell
you'll soon forget the nose and the daffodil![67]

In 1923 Macmillan published Florence Randal Livesay's *Shepherd's Purse*, Albert E.S. Smythe's *Garden of the Sun*, Marian Osborne's *The Song of Israfel and Other Poems*, and an anthology, *A Book of Canadian Prose and Verse*, edited by Edmund Kemper Broadus and Eleanor Hammond Broadus.[68] Osborne's book was designed and published in London by Erskine Macdonald and printed by the Stanhope Press of Strood, England, but the title page includes the Toronto imprint. The author, a second cousin of Sir William Osler, was a native of Montreal, had lived in Wales, had worked in England during the First World War, and resided in Ottawa when *The Song of Israfel* was published.[69] Dedications inside it – to Osler, Sir Andrew Macphail, Bliss Carman, and the landscape painter Elizabeth Knowles – make explicit the author's Canadian milieu, as does the imagery in "Forest of Mine," a nature poem with a stately rhythm in Alexandrines:

Thrice blessed forest, keep my heart and hold my dreams,
Where birches raise their queenly heads, tender and pure,
Where pines like sentinels stand straight and proud – it seems
Their soul is old as truth and ever must endure –
Where joyous maples kissed by frost, the artisan,
Bear jewelled leaves of splendour exquisitely wrought,
Where oaks give peace, the peace that cometh unto man
Where men dwell not, and where no walls confine his thought.[70]

The catalogue of trees is typical of the mixed forest of the St Lawrence and the Ottawa watersheds; it is as descriptive of Canada as Bowman's imagery of the Port of Montreal. In this case, however, the presentation of it in a book depended in some measure on a publishing arrangement that spanned between Canada and England. In 1924 the Macmillan Company of Canada brought out Annie Charlotte Dalton's *Flame and Adventure* and Gertrude MacGregor Moffat's *Book of Verses*, with Lyon Sharman's *The Sea-Wall and Other Verse* the following year. Macmillan's school edition of Sir Walter Scott's *Lay of the Last Minstrel* (1925) probably outsold them all.

These enumerations begin to characterize McClelland & Stewart's and Macmillan's roles as publishers of Canadian poetry in the 1920s. To take the evaluation further, it would be necessary to determine how much and how frequently Canadian authors were left to pay for the production of their books and how well they sold. What culture of literary authorship did these publishers enable? This is the analysis that will be pursued with respect to the Ryerson Poetry Chap-Books in the chapters that follow. E.J. Pratt became Macmillan's prize poet with *The Witches' Brew* (1925) and enjoyed special treatment from then on. On the other hand, when Dorothy Livesay published her first collection, *Green Pitcher*, with Macmillan in 1928, her parents covered the bill. All in all, it is clear that McClelland & Stewart and the Macmillan Company of Canada were building reputations as Canadian publishers – reputations that included a small but notable amount of poetry. Pierce's undertaking to publish Canadian poetry coincided with and emulated theirs.

TO PUBLISH WORK in the enduring, collectible, and cataloguable form of the book may have been the poet's ultimate goal, but it would be misleading to suggest that the book was the only context for poetry. Canadian poetry also flourished in magazines, which were cheaper, printed in greater numbers, fresher in their appearance from month to month, better paying, and more social in the sense of mingling many contributors together in each issue. Yet American production here, too, outstripped Canadian. Like books, most of the magazines read in Canada after the First World War were published in the United States. By 1918, "millions of copies of American magazines were being sold annually in Canada, and American consumer magazines outsold their Canadian counterparts by a four to one ratio."[71] The Canadian government had long sought to counteract this preponderance of American print by subsidizing domestic periodicals through a second-class postal rate, which allowed Canadian newspapers and magazines to reach subscribers for a fraction of the normal mailing costs. Nevertheless, "by 1918 the Canadian periodical market was [still] swamped with American publications, and throughout the 1920s and 1930s Canadian periodical publishers lobbied the government for more protection than the established postal subsidy."[72] The publishing of poetry in Canadian magazines thus proceeded against the odds, with lower circulation and smaller author payments in an asymmetrical continental market largely saturated with American products that benefited from greater economies of scale.

"We have no Poetry journals at all and our magazines are in a horrible mess," Louise Morey Bowman wrote to Amy Lowell in December 1923.[73] Her lament points out that Canada had no equivalent to *Poetry* (Chicago), which was exclusively devoted to verse. This lack was partly what moved Pierce to launch the Ryerson Poetry Chap-Books. It should be noted, however, that several Canadian magazines did publish poetry. The *Canadian Magazine* (1893–1937) was the oldest of them and the broadest in appeal. Published monthly in Toronto by the Ontario Publishing Company, it offered a breezy variety of political articles, literary essays, travel writing, paintings, photographs, short fiction, and book reviews. A touristy article by Frank Yeigh, for example, enticed readers north from Toronto by train and steamboat to the cottage country of Haliburton, while in "The Pearl of Baghdad," Lyman B. Jackes spun an exotic tale from the Great War, in which British officers and archeologists outwit the German-Ottoman enemy and local Arab traders in a scramble for buried treasure after Baghdad's fall to the British in 1917.[74] Poetry had a secure place in this variety. In the early 1920s, the *Canadian Magazine* published poems by Martha Ostenso, Wilson MacDonald, Wilfrid Eggleston, and many others, including Bowman and several future Chap-Book authors, such as Agnes Joynes, John Hanlon, and Frederick B. Watt. Watt's poem, "Edmonton, the Gateway," explains the epithet that continues to attach to his home city, describing the passage of "Trader, trapper and engineer" through it on their way north (Jan. 1924, 214).

Although the May 1922 issue of the *Canadian Magazine* printed only a single poem – Christina Willey's "Return, O Shulamite!" (54) – poetry pervaded the magazine. It was frequently the object of discussion in the articles. In his essay, "Percy Bysshe Shelley," Charles Morse defended Shelley as the fourth-greatest English poet of all time (Aug. 1922, 340–1). In June 1922, J.D. Logan explained the "genius" of Marjorie Pickthall (154–61), and in January 1924 he turned to the expatriate Gilbert Parker, whose poems he judged "noble in conception, beautiful in diction" and suffused "with spiritual elevation and poetic or religious significance" (179–82 [180]). "The Library Table," Florence Deacon Black's book review column, was full of news about Canadian poetry. Her blurb on Beatrice Redpath, a Montreal-born poet, includes the telling detail that both of Redpath's collections, *Drawn Shutters* (1916) and *White Lilac* (1922), were published in London by John Lane, with agency distribution to Canada (Dec. 1923, 154–8). Black's description of Vancouver's burgeoning poetry scene is rightly checked by an accurate observation of what that city lacked: "The Pacific Coast is rapidly becoming a centre for writers. And no wonder! With the mountains, the sea, the soft air, the lovely gardens, there is everything to attract. If the publishing houses were there too, it would be ideal for authors" (78–84 [79]). The *Canadian Magazine* of the 1920s treated poetry as an object of general interest and common patriotism, one associated with refined taste and emotional sensitivity while being in no way at odds with popular consumption. Whether or not this added up to a "horrible mess" depends on one's perspective.

The *University Magazine* (1907–20), a prestigious quarterly edited in Montreal by Andrew Macphail, had a more demanding and elite character. It proposed poetry to be among the highest matters of national importance, to be considered, like the economy, by those striving to define the direction Canada should take. Macphail, a medical doctor, professor of the history of medicine at McGill University, driving member of the Pen and Pencil Club, and essayist, aimed "to express an educated opinion upon questions immediately concerning Canada, and to treat freely in a literary way all matters which have to do with politics, industry, philosophy, science, and art."[75] Faculty from McGill, the University of Toronto, and Dalhousie University constituted the editorial board of a venture squarely led and financed by Macphail himself. The conservatism that Macphail promulgated, like that of Sara Jeannette Duncan, was attractive, and he reached a considerable audience. Subscriptions cost $1.00 per year ($0.25 per issue) and circulation peaked at nearly six thousand in 1912. From the outset, he made it a point to pay contributors. Marjorie Pickthall and John

McCrae thrived in the pages of the *University Magazine*. Duncan Campbell Scott, Frank Oliver Call, Edward Sapir, Alexander Louis Fraser, and a host of others also appeared, rubbing shoulders with the political, historical, economic, scientific, and literary essayists whom the magazine published. The First World War eroded the magazine, not least because Macphail was away at the front serving as a medical officer; upon his return it briefly rallied before ceasing publication with the February 1920 issue.[76] Nevertheless, it set an example for the discriminating and serious publication of original Canadian poetry, publishing it more selectively than did the *Canadian Magazine*, and it was an example of which Pierce, through his editorial work on Pickthall, became aware.

The long-lived and critically robust *Canadian Forum* (1920–2000) appeared on the scene as Pierce began his work at the Ryerson Press. Perched near the University of Toronto and the professoriate who sustained it, the monthly surveyed a range of poetic activity both conventional and experimental in its inaugural years. Light and witty verse of an undergraduate flavour was the product of its frequent literary competitions: a five-dollar prize went to "A Soliloquy of Hamlet on Seeing Himself in the Movies" in November 1920 (48), and to an "Epitaph on the Board of Commerce" in January 1921 (110). Some years would go by before the *Forum* established its signature alliance with modernism. The first issues clearly reflect the continuing stature of the Confederation Poets in Canadian poetry. Bliss Carman's three-page "Open Letter" (Dec. 1920, 80–2) narrates, in ballad rhythm, an ill speaker's journey north into the winter forest, where a vision of deceased friends' spirits during a snowstorm restores him to health. C.W. Jefferys, with whom Pierce would develop an enduring partnership as noted above, paid tribute to Archibald Lampman with an illustrated excerpt from "In November," visualizing the metaphor that recasts a stand of dead mulleins as a company of hermits; the layout, in which elaborate drawings flourish around a dense column of text, evokes an illuminated manuscript (Nov. 1921, 431). Modernism appeared nascently in short poems by A.J.M. Smith ("The Smile," Feb. 1925, 149) and Robert Finch ("Were I to Take Away My Mask," June 1925). The poet featured most prominently was E.J. Pratt, who was a frequent contributor from the second issue (Nov. 1920) on, and who dominated the November 1925 issue with his long poem "The Cachalot" (46–51), accompanied with a full-page illustration.

A book review published in the *Canadian Forum* in August 1921 signalled the opportunity to produce a national chapbook series. In Halifax,

Archibald MacMechan was writing and publishing the Nova Scotia Chap-Books pamphlet series. Some contained verse, some prose. MacMechan's goal was to preserve, in book form, poems and essays that he had written pertaining to the history and character of his home province. Four of these chapbooks came across the editorial desk at the *Forum*: *Three Sea Songs* (no. 1, [1919]), *The Orchards of Ultima Thule* (no. 5, [1919]), *The Log of a Halifax Privateer* (no. 6, 1920), and *Twelve Profitable Sonnets* (no. 14, 1920). Approving of them, the reviewer suggested that their concept be expanded and applied to Canada as a whole: "The example might well be followed and chap-books be published to give semi-permanent form to the distinctive legends, narratives and verses of the various provinces. Many anecdotes are too slight in bulk to achieve magazine or book form and it is of great importance that they should be preserved."[77] The idea of publishing a chapbook series to represent Canada's many regions thus circulated in Pierce's Toronto before he seized hold of it.

There were many other periodicals that acted as channels for Canadian poetry. The *Canadian Bookman* (1919–39), established by B.K. Sandwell, collected the excitement around the formation of the Canadian Authors Association when it briefly became the association's official magazine in 1921. It passed under new management later that year but continued to publish texts by and about poets from across the country who joined the movement to organize Canadian authors.[78] In Montreal, A.J.M. Smith and F.R. Scott rebelled against this organization through their editing of three short-lived magazines: a literary supplement to the *McGill Daily* (1924–25), the *McGill Fortnightly Review* (1925–27), and the *Canadian Mercury: A Monthly Journal of Literature and Opinion* (1928–29). Smith's manifesto, "Contemporary Poetry," denounced Victorian conventions and called for a revolution in form and subject matter following the examples of T.S. Eliot and Wallace Stevens. The circulation of these magazines was tiny, but they stood out to later poets, critics, and anthologists interested in pinpointing the inauguration of modernism in Canadian poetry.[79] This sample of magazines suggests the wide extent of the poem in Canadian publishing in the 1920s. Moreover, in addition to magazines, countless newspapers across the country also regularly printed poetry. Several of the poets discussed in the following chapters first published their writing in a newspaper. Together these forms of print media added to the general culture of the poem upon which the more specialized activity of publishing books of poetry depended.

IN TAKING UP HIS WORK as poetry editor at the Ryerson Press, Pierce joined an active field that was thick with others' achievements and infused with the energy of the First World War. He brought his Methodist upbringing, his Queen's University education, his admiration for the nineteenth-century Russian novel, and an acute sense of his own mortality to the inchoate position of literary editor at the country's oldest publishing house, with which the illustrious John and Charles Wesley, Egerton Ryerson, and William Briggs were associated. Against the dominant pattern of agency publishing, he had to reinvent what it was to be an original Canadian book publisher. In his authors, who often helped to finance their books, he found willing allies in his struggle to release original books against the norm of agency publishing. Pierce was determined to catch up with Donald French, the literary editor at McClelland & Stewart, who by 1925 presided over an impressive list of books that had responded to the terrible reality of the war and affirmed the existence of Canadian poetry in popular titles by Bliss Carman and Marjorie Pickthall. Competing alongside Pierce was Hugh Eayrs at the Macmillan Company of Canada, who had drawn the talented E.J. Pratt and Louise Morey Bowman into his stable. Canadians' interest in poetry – their high regard for the genre and their regular participation in it through writing and reading poems – was more than clear in the contents of the magazines that crossed the thresholds of homes across the country every month. Collectively the texts were a complex mingling of topics: religion and patriotism, grief and experiment, world politics and idealism, music and nature. What this busy field did not yet have was a single publisher's series of books explicitly devoted to Canadian poetry. In response to the quickening spirit of the times, Pierce would be the one to make this unprecedented contribution.

TWO

"Significant Little Offerings"

Launching the Ryerson Poetry Chap-Books

FROM THE OUTSET, the Ryerson Poetry Chap-Books were a defiant attempt to publish Canadian literature independently, in Canada alone, in book form, over the long term. Both the editor and the poets faced relatively discouraging profits, but this discouragement makes their contributions all the more noteworthy. This chapter will reconstruct Lorne Pierce's creation of the series over its first two years, looking at its financial limits and situating some of the poetry within them. Part luxuries, part sacrifices, the Chap-Books originated as little, self-published collections that served the Canadian poetic tradition defined by Charles G.D. Roberts and that accumulated because their idealistic authors were willing to bear the expense of production.

AS EXPLAINED IN CHAPTER I, Samuel Fallis, book steward at the Ryerson Press, was impressed with Pierce when he hired him in 1920 to advise in the selection of book manuscripts, but by 1925 a rift had opened between them.[1] Pierce had assumed the responsibilities of a businessman but held a doctorate in theology, had trained as a minister, and was inclined toward the pleasures of reading and writing. He collected books and manuscripts, liked to command a good view of a subject, strived to set the record straight, and dreamed of gathering a community of admirers around a great monument. Looking up from the pages of a good book, blinded with insight, almost certainly meant more to him than reporting a short-term departmental profit; nevertheless, as book editor of the Ryerson Press, he had to get used to the latter task.

Friction between literary ideals and money characterized the immediate circumstances from which the Chap-Books sprang. Since the autumn of 1922, Pierce had been hard at work on a more ambitious canonical undertaking: the Makers of Canadian Literature, a series of anthologies that aimed to introduce the general reader to the country's best authors. Each volume included a biography, selections of the author's work, a critical appraisal, a bibliography, and an index. Pierce commissioned various experts to write the commentary, at a rate of four hundred dollars upon completion plus one hundred more upon publication, irrespective of the number of copies that actually sold and regardless of the fact that Pierce worked on each project a great deal himself, especially when it came to the bibliography. The series was, in the end, an abortive attempt to reinvent the way in which literature was published in Canada. Pierce tried single-handedly to heave the country toward the better remuneration of authors, but the Makers series soon collapsed under its own weight. Of the forty volumes planned, only thirteen were published, all but one in the initial surge from 1923 to 1925.[2]

Duncan Campbell Scott's manuscript on Archibald Lampman encapsulates the mismanagement of the series. In February 1925, having completed his assignment, Scott wrote to Ryerson peremptorily to request payment: "You may inform the management that my contract calls for $500.00 on the acceptance of the manuscript, and I should like them to send me the balance as soon as possible. My agreement with Dr Pierce also calls for $300.00 for the copyright of Lampman's poems and my own. This should also be sent."[3] The matter was soon resolved to his satisfaction, for in April he wrote to thank Miss D. Dingle, editorial department secretary, for a cheque for one hundred dollars, the last of the money owed him.[4] "Archibald Lampman," however, was never published: the book got as far as typesetting but stopped there. In other words, Pierce paid an author $800 for a manuscript that never returned a cent. Given that it sits in the Queen's University archives with ten other Makers manuscripts, likewise finished but unpublished, this loss was only part of a larger financial debacle.[5]

What brought the series to its fatal crisis was a dispute between Fallis and Pierce – a dispute that sprang from different concepts of authorship and publishing. Recent copyright legislation had provoked a furor over compulsory licensing and international authors' rights, and in February 1925 the government of William Lyon Mackenzie King appointed a special committee to investigate the matter. Like William Briggs before him, Fallis understood the copyright disadvantages under which the Canadian book trade had long laboured. In his testimony to the committee, he, like most printers, supported the new licensing clause that aimed to increase the manufacture of books and magazines in Canada by allowing printers to reprint foreign works without the permission of the copyright owner if the latter had not arranged for a Canadian edition.

Canadian authors, on the other hand, denounced the clause as a retrogressive measure that would deprive them of their livelihood. Thomas Guthrie Marquis, whom Pierce had hired in 1924 to promote the Makers series, hotly contradicted Fallis and declared in an 11 April 1925 letter to the committee that the Ryerson Press in fact endorsed the authors' cause. As proof, he enclosed a note from Pierce. Fallis angrily repudiated Marquis's representation and demanded his resignation. When Pierce protested, Fallis ordered him to reduce his department's expenses, and in the next annual report to the book committee on 9 April 1926, Fallis recorded the indefinite suspension of the series: "After investing a considerable sum in producing and promoting it, we have called a halt until times become more propitious." The same report had the following to say about Pierce's department in general: "The Educational Department, which was undertaken to get more seriously into the field of the best literature, and to enhance the name of the Ryerson Press as something more than a jobber of popular reading, is still in the experimental stage, and has made its blunders, with consequent problems."[6]

This stiff rebuke for the largesse of the Makers series, which included at least one huge copyright fee to a dead author, chastened Pierce. In future, he would not pay his authors so liberally; indeed, he would have to curtail his activity as specialist publisher per se, shifting most of the risk of publication onto the authors while retaining for Ryerson the lesser role of printer and continuing as editor in a more modest fashion. The extreme leanness of the next series that he launched would reflect the lesson.

A CHAPBOOK is the leanest of books. When Pierce turned to it as the solution for publishing Canadian poetry, the unassuming form was in the midst of a historic change. This evolution is apparent today in the two distinct senses of *chapbook*. In its modern sense, it is an appurtenance of the aspiring author – a small book written and designed to artistic standards, printed by the author at personal expense, bound cheaply, and all in all produced outside the mainstream commercial book trade. In the nineteenth century, by contrast, it denoted cheap, popular literature of a prior age – that is, what the labouring classes read before the advent of mass-produced penny papers. In this sense, a chapbook was an old broadside or pamphlet containing a ballad, tale, or tract, often illustrated by a stock woodcut, and sold across the countryside by a peddler or chapman.[7] According to the *Oxford English Dictionary*, the root of the word derives from the Old English *céapian*, meaning "to bargain, trade, chaffer, buy." One apparent connection between its two senses, then, is low expense. Another is the antiquarian element: the chief value that a self-published booklet of original poems can be said to have is that which it acquires at a later date, when in light of the writer's subsequent fame it takes on the lustre of a rare artifact from their apprentice phase. Like an antique copy of "Jack the Giant Killer," the modern poetry booklet is essentially a collectible, for the time before an author's renown is, as the eighteenth century was to the nineteenth, a bygone era.

The self-published poetry book existed before this label was applied to its slimmer manifestations. For example, Shelley had *Queen Mab* (1813) printed privately in a run of 250 copies, which he gave away to prominent poets of the day.[8] George Meredith paid the publisher John W. Parker to print his first book of poems (1851), and even his late *Poems and Lyrics of the Joy of Earth* (1883), although it appeared under the imprint of Macmillan and Company, was his own investment.[9] In Canada, Thomas Cary's *Abram's Plains: A Poem* (1789) was printed "for the author," as its title page states, after Cary raised the necessary money through subscriptions.[10] Charles Sangster printed his first book, *The St Lawrence and the Saguenay, and Other Poems* (1856), at his own expense and strove to recoup the cost latterly through sales.[11] Many a subsequent writing career in this country unfolded in similar fashion. The interesting historical development in which to contextualize the Ryerson Poetry Chap-Books is therefore not the mere practice of poets' self-publishing, which was common enough, but rather the shift to recognizing it under a term, *chapbook*, newly appropriated to designate it.

Use of the word in this sense appears to date from the fin-de-siècle American boom in the printing of little magazines. In the 1890s, a new culture of independent printing swept through the United States and spawned hundreds of periodicals that defined themselves against the book trade's ever-increasing mass production. According to Kirsten MacLeod, between 1894 and 1903 at least 334 of these "ephemeral bibelots," "freak magazines," "decadents," or "chap-books," as they were variously called, appeared[12] – so many, in fact, that as a phenomenon they evade precise count or definition. Elbert Hubbard, the publisher of one of the most successful ones, the *Philistine* (1895–1915), estimated that there were 1,100 such little magazines in 1895–96 alone.[13] Slim, cheap, short-lived, irregular in format and size, striking in layout, bizarre in typography, low in circulation, aesthetically or politically radical, and financially precarious: these are the elements that generally characterize the cluster, but any one specimen may fail to exhibit most of them, especially since exceptionality was a guiding principle.

The fin-de-siècle little magazines were a complex middle-class phenomenon. They served as platforms for revolt against middle-class norms but flourished on increasing bourgeois access to printing technology, whether in the form of a newspaper press after hours, a school press, or a novelty press at home.[14] They reflected a middle-class desire for self-improvement that drew strength from the Arts and Crafts movement, especially the revival in fine printing spearheaded by William Morris, which contemporaries called "the book beautiful": "Through its link with the revolution in fine printing and its remediation of the fine press book, the little magazine became a 'magazine beautiful,' accruing the status of a collectible print object at an affordable price for a class seeking to assert its distinction."[15]

One of the most prominent little magazines was the *Chap-Book* (1894–98), founded by Harvard undergraduates Herbert S. Stone and Hannibal Ingalls Kimball, Jr, to promote the book-publishing firm that they had established the year before.[16] MacLeod explains their choice of title as an evocation of pre-machine-age folk culture:

> *The Chap-Book* educated its readership about the form, including, for example, a feature on [early-modern] chap-books by historian

John Ashton, and by printing examples of chap-book woodcuts. Though the chap-book represented an historically cheap format, its appearance was in keeping with private press ideals that looked to the preindustrial hand press era, favouring old style fonts, woodcut or woodblock illustrations, handmade paper, uncut pages, wide margins, and rubrication. Instead, however, of recreating the laborious and time-consuming methods that had been employed in the expensive, low-circulation *Knight Errant*, Stone and Kimball found ways to economise in order to enable production in numbers of 10,000 or more to sell at a cost of five and, later, ten cents, while still maintaining an attractive publication.[17]

Stone and Kimball, the well-connected sons of businessmen, combined their admiration of antiquarian book-collecting, the book beautiful, and decadent aesthetics with serious commercial ambition. The *Chap-Book* strove to surprise and educate its readers, asserting the value of art to a society perceived to be drifting into soulless materialism. Its success lay in its clever "commodification of the critique of commodification."[18] With its stylized woodcuts, trenchant literary criticism, and accomplished contributors (among them Henry James, W.B. Yeats, Paul Verlaine, and Thomas Hardy), it rapidly found a niche. The proprietors were soon obliged to engage a mainstream printer and chose the Lakeside Press of Chicago. By 1896, the little magazine had reached a circulation of 16,500 and attracted dozens of imitators and even a parody, the *Chop-Book*.[19] The residue of this flurry of activity was an altered word: chapbook, absorbing the peculiar hue of the *Chap-Book*, came to designate the fin-de-siècle little magazine generically, and became synonymous with *bibelot* and other contemporary terms.

This meaning further refined itself into the modern sense of the word over the next two decades. In London, Claud Lovat Fraser, Harold Monro, and A.T. Stevens involved themselves with small-press chapbooks around the time of the First World War.[20] Archibald MacMechan self-published his series of Nova Scotia Chap-Books beginning in 1919 (see chapter 1). Arthur Leonard Phelps published a booklet of poetry entitled *A Bobcaygeon Chapbook* in 1922. Annie M. Anderson and other students at the University of British Columbia collaborated on *A Chapbook*, which was printed in a limited edition of 500 copies in Vancouver in 1922. Three years later, the Vancouver Poetry Society engaged Charles Bradbury to print *Three Poems* by Ernest Philip Fewster, Bromley Coleman, and A.M. Stephen, and styled the book "VPS Chapbook no. 1" although no further numbers followed. Two decades later, society members claimed that theirs was the one that had inspired Pierce's series: "A tradition of the Society, later recorded in print by A.M. Stephen, is that 'Dr Lorne Pierce caught the idea of printing chapbooks while on a visit to Vancouver; he saw the possibilities embodied in this first Canadian chapbook,' and The Ryerson Press chapbook series, now numbering well over a hundred, was the result."[21] Given Pierce's connections with the society, it is plausible that their book attracted his attention, but *Three Poems* was not the first Canadian chapbook. It was also not the only model at Pierce's disposal, for by the 1920s the new chapbook had broadly established itself as a feature of English-language print culture.

There is also the detail of spelling. From the outset, Pierce's books were always "Chap-Books" – with a hyphen – which recalls the most famous of the little magazines of the 1890s. Stone and Kimball's *Chap-Book* is especially pertinent because it was briefly an outlet for the Confederation Poets. The editor for the first few months was Bliss Carman. The first issues contain contributions by both him and Charles G.D. Roberts. Number 1 (15 May 1894), for example, contains Roberts's poem "The Unsleeping," in which a Shelleyesque speaker declares that he, the voice of poetry, will survive all the wrecks of space and time and sail through the ages as the witness of God's mind. Given that Pierce was studying Roberts's life and collecting his work for the Makers series, and given that a copy of this number of the *Chap-Book* is preserved in the Pierce Collection in the W.D. Jordan Library at Queen's University, it seems likely that it, too, substantially influenced his choice of form and title. His undertaking must thus be situated in the international culture of the modern chapbook.

※✝※

MANY OF THE EARLY Ryerson Poetry Chap-Books enshrine Roberts's poetics. Roberts was not only the author of the inaugural number, *The Sweet o' the Year and Other Poems* (1925), but also the prime influence over several that followed. As the series unfolded, successive numbers showed that its firm purpose was to build national character through an affirmation of the Canadian-romantic idealism that Roberts and his fellow

Confederation Poets had modelled in their prime over three decades earlier. Its principles included classically inspired metre and rhyme, belief in spiritual immanence, reverence for rural life and nature, and interest in stories attached to Canadian landscapes. In this aesthetic program Pierce deferred to Roberts, and with the repatriated father of Canadian poetry lending ready assistance he strove to recuperate, assert, and anchor an identity in Canadian poetry by looking backward. The difficulty of the undertaking was surely part of the attraction.

Having been drafted to assist his old English professor at Queen's University, James Cappon, in writing the Makers book on Roberts, Pierce was gathering primary materials from Roberts's son, Lloyd, in 1924 when he learned that the latter had drawn his father back to Canada. "This is to announce the good news," Lloyd wrote in November, "that we have induced Charles G.D. to come to Canada on a lecture tour ... You might give some thought to the subject, as from what you said to me last year I know the Ryerson Press will be closely interested."[22] The success of Carman's "triumphal" reading tour of Western Canada in 1921–22 had tempted Roberts to follow suit.[23] During his New York years Roberts had visited Canada intermittently, but since 1907, while he travelled through Europe, settled in London, and served in the First World War, his absence had been unbroken.[24] His return after nearly eighteen years caused a sensation.

It also presented an obvious opportunity. It was not a straightforward process, however, for Ryerson to sell the Canadian author's books, no matter how the national demand might swell in response to his presence. An entirely new book seems to have been out of the question, primarily because, although Roberts's output in fiction had been prodigious, his creative energies were flagging; as for his poetry, it slowed to a trickle after *The Book of the Rose* (1903). Worse, most of his best-known works were jealously guarded by the Boston publisher L.C. Page and Company, with whom Roberts had fallen out over *The House in the Water* (1908). L.C. Page, who had published the book in the United States, was angry that the author had permitted an English edition and had retaliated by withholding all royalties due Roberts on that book or any other.[25] Pierce ran into this obstacle while planning the anthology section of Cappon's book. "Why not select as much as you like from any Dent or Ward Lock volume in the public library?" Lloyd advised, referring to English reprints such as *Some Animal Stories* (1921), which defied the American publisher's claim to any international copyright. When Pierce came back with selections from *Earth's Enigmas* (1895) and *The Kindred of the Wild* (1902), however, Lloyd warned that Page owned both.[26] Pierce evidently took the circumspect but expensive path of negotiating with the American publisher, whom he did not feel confident enough to resist. When Cappon's *Charles G.D. Roberts* appeared sometime in 1925, it included only a handful of poems, all of them deferentially acknowledged to be owned by L.C. Page and Company.

Page, too, realized that Roberts's reading tour would buoy his book sales. On 27 June 1925 he fired off a threatening letter to declare that Roberts had assigned to his company "all his right, title, and interest, of every nature, in all countries, in each and every book of his, published by us."[27] Given that Page had taken legal action against the English publishers, Ryerson could expect similar treatment if it attempted to republish any of the works on the exhaustive list attached. At the end of August, Pierce turned to the Canadian Patent and Copyright Office in an attempt to gauge the strength of Page's claims. The response was turbid: *By the Marshes of Minas* (1899) had indeed been assigned to Page, but no Canadian registration of *Songs of the Common Day* (1893) had ever occurred, and "Ave! An Ode for the Shelley Centenary" (1892) remained under the author's name.[28] Unsure quite where to draw the line around Page's expansive proprietary claims, Pierce proceeded with caution and ultimately chose to reprint a text that lay well beyond the Boston publisher's grasp. Republishing Roberts's writing in conjunction with his homecoming proved to be a thorny affair, at a time when Pierce was suffering Fallis's sharp criticism.

The first Ryerson Poetry Chap-Book was an accessory to Roberts's reading tour, a trinket for his audiences to take home and keep, a bit of national treasure. Pierce was involved in the tour's organization from the beginning. Lloyd Roberts and his wife, Leila, had booked the auditorium of the Jarvis Collegiate Institute in Toronto for the first event on 5 February 1925.[29] Pierce helped to place advertisements and sell tickets, although he admitted to being "a poor impresario" when W.A. Deacon of *Saturday Night* asked why no complimentary passes had been issued to the press.[30] There were also doubts about whether the event would draw a good crowd, because it was a reading rather than a more dramatic recital.[31] Nevertheless, the Toronto arts community came out in force and Roberts conducted himself with aplomb, reading from *The Book of the Rose* (Boston: L.C. Page, 1903) and *New Poems* (London: Constable, 1919) and filling the intervals with amiable talk about himself and his work. A series of similar engagements rapidly followed and took Roberts across Ontario.[32]

Meanwhile Pierce set off for the West to prepare an itinerary for the poet. Roberts followed at the end of March, giving readings accordingly.[33] In Edmonton, Emily Murphy looked forward to his visit but regretted that it would coincide with Easter: "We are expecting Dr Roberts this week and although he will be here in the poorest week in all the year for a recital – Christmas only excepted – we are going to give him a capacity house. I am eagerly anticipating the pleasure of meeting him personally and of – yes, yes, having him autograph those books of his which I reviewed in the long ago when I was young and miserable."[34] While the dispute between Fallis and Pierce was exploding in Toronto, Roberts was en route to Vancouver, where Fewster, Stephen, Annie Charlotte Dalton, and other members of the Vancouver Poetry Society fêted him royally and held a dinner in his honour on 22 April.[35] Dalton would follow Roberts into the Chap-Book series with *The Ear Trumpet* the next year (no. [5], 1926). Fewster, too, would contribute, although some years later, with his *Litany before the Dawn of Fire* (no. 96, 1942).

Upon his return to Toronto, the perennially hard-up Roberts took up residence in a third-floor suite at the Ernescliffe, "an ultra-modern apartment house" with attractive Ionic columns at the corner of Sherbourne and Wellesley.[36] There he began to plan the next leg of his national tour. A joyful reunion with Carman took place in the first week of August at the Muskoka Assembly, a summer literary, musical, and theosophical retreat run by the Canadian Chautauqua Institution two hundred kilometres north of Toronto. The two cousins, the guests of honour for Canadian Authors' Week, brought their participation in it to a resounding finish by giving a joint, open-air reading on the veranda of the Chautauqua president's cottage.[37] In attendance were two lesser poets, W.H.F. Tenny and Wilson MacDonald. The jocular Tenny, a retired chemical and pharmaceutical supplier from Buffalo, New York, had ingratiated himself with Pierce by writing poems about the pure and virile North. He would be the second Chap-Book author. MacDonald, also a resident of the Ernescliffe, is by contrast conspicuously absent from the series. He introduced Roberts to a twenty-six-year-old admirer, Constance Isabel Davies Woodrow, a native of Liverpool who had recently moved to Toronto and taken up writing, contributing poems to several magazines and literary news to the *Canadian Bookman*, where she became assistant editor. Davies Woodrow had married John Merritt Woodrow, an artist and illustrator, the previous year, and they too lived at the Ernescliffe. Roberts was long since estranged from his wife, May. MacDonald looked on in outraged disbelief as Roberts and Davies Woodrow flirted and fell in love.[38]

Plans for a book were struck in the midst of this scandalous romance. Pierce was aware of the circumstances, and worried in his diary that Roberts "lives in a state of sexual excess. He can never write anything great again, I fear. There is no sustained core to his thinking and living."[39] If the author was preoccupied, the editor was morally disappointed, financially constrained, and worried about copyright. Out of this confusion in August came the plan to print a small volume of poems selected from what little Roberts had published in London after the break with Page, some of which he was reading on tour. "In launching my Poetry Chapbook idea," wrote Pierce in his diary on 20 August 1925, "I have been looking about for someone to commence with, who will give the whole thing standing and distinction. Roberts has consented to give me a few poems for this initial number."[40] Pierce read and liked Roberts's *New Poems*. Eight of them were chosen for *The Sweet o' the Year and Other Poems*, the first Ryerson Poetry Chap-Book. To reprint poems first published elsewhere some years earlier marked an inauspicious beginning for a series of original poetry; it also shows Pierce's relative comfort in the skin of the Canadian publisher-agent, whose work was more literary dissemination than innovation. The ninth and final poem, that taken for the book's title, was not new either, having been published in a London magazine five years before.[41] In Roberts's next book, *The Vagrant of Time* (Ryerson, 1927), some of these poems would appear yet again.[42]

The continuation of Roberts's national tour whisked him off to Montreal and the Maritimes in September. Pierce, meanwhile, shared his plans with Carman, who sent his blessing in October – "The Chapbook idea is fine."[43] The series launch was now imminent, for when Pierce printed a program for Roberts's tour he included the following advertisement:

THE SWEET O' THE YEAR and OTHER POEMS – – – .50
by Charles G.D. Roberts
This is the first offering in the Ryerson Poetry Chap-books. It contains several of Dr Roberts' favorites among his later work, together with new material. Limited to 500 copies. Boxed.[44]

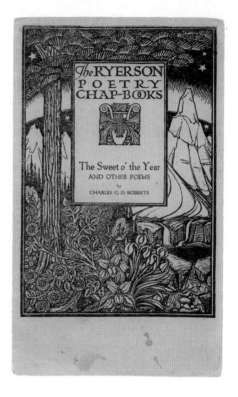

2.1 / Charles G.D. Roberts, *The Sweet o' the Year and Other Poems*, Ryerson Poetry Chap-Book no. [1] (Toronto: Ryerson Press, 1925), front cover. The initials of the designer, J.E.H. Macdonald, appear on the stone in the bottom right corner. The flowers in the foreground symbolize Nova Scotia (trailing arbutus), Quebec (lily), Ontario (trillium), Alberta (wild rose), and British Columbia (Pacific dogwood). Behind the glacier and the mountains is an arch that represents the aurora borealis.

The description of the reprinted contents is euphemistic, but the limited print run and the slipcase, together with the very name "Chap-book," reveal the heart of Pierce's plan to market the little books as collector's items. "Ever so many thanks for the programmes, – which are *fine*," Roberts wrote at the beginning of November from Fredericton, where he was in the throes of "recitals, receptions & functions of all kinds." In the same letter he asked, "When will *my* Chap Book appear? If this month, will you please send me several copies to c/o Professor Henry Munro, 246 Jubilee Road, Halifax, which will be my address for the next few weeks while I 'do up' the rest of the Nova Scotia Towns."[45] Roberts looked forward to receiving the promised reinforcements in his self-promotional campaign.

The Sweet o' the Year and Other Poems was published later that month, in November 1925. It consisted of a single unsigned letterpress sheet folded into four leaves (eight pages) and fastened with two staples into a paper cover.[46] According to the inside front cover, the print run was the advertised 500. (After the third Chap-Book, the normal print run would be 250.)

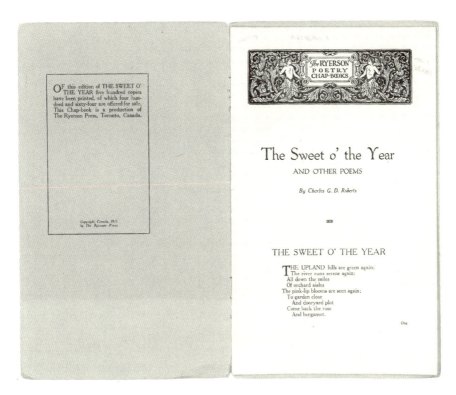

2.2 / Page 1 of Roberts, *Sweet o' the Year*. The influence of the "book beautiful" movement is seen in the series ornament by J.E.H. Macdonald, the typography (curves and thick-thin contrasts), the spacious layout, and the large initial for the first line of verse. In addition, from 1926 on, many of the Chap-Books were printed on paper with a watermark consisting of a circle around a capital S and a beaver with the indication "Bard of Avon MADE IN CANADA."

Pierce had J.E.H. Macdonald of the Group of Seven design the book, and his front-cover woodcut, signed "J.M 25" on a stone at the bottom right, matched the former's literary-nationalist vision. Canada appears as a land of pure and rugged beauty in which wild roses, trilliums, lilies, mayflowers, and Pacific dogwoods – provincial symbols, all – intertwine at the foot of lordly pines; a rocky river, a lake, cataracts, a glacier, and mountains lead the eye up to the aurora borealis and to the stars beyond; finally, the central icon features pine cones that emanate from a lyre, symbolizing the power of poetry to create a nation. Macdonald's woodcut, which left space at the centre for title and author, would adorn most of the Chap-Books

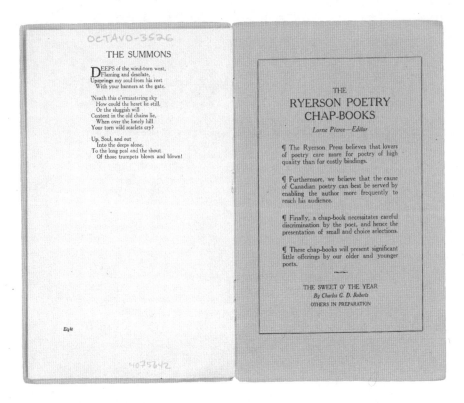

2.3 / Inside back cover of Roberts, *Sweet o' the Year*, declaring Lorne Pierce's mission for the Ryerson Poetry Chap-Books.

until 1942, when an updated design by his son, Thoreau, replaced it. (In 1950, this updated woodcut was abandoned for a simpler design, although it was resurrected for ten books between 1953 and 1955.)[47] The series advertisement on the inside back cover is equally noteworthy, for it is here that Pierce proclaimed his editorial principles, making a virtue out of the cords that bound him:

> The Ryerson Press believes that lovers of poetry care more for poetry of high quality than for costly bindings.
>
> Furthermore, we believe that the cause of Canadian poetry can best be served by enabling the author more frequently to reach his audience.

Finally, a chap-book necessitates careful discrimination by the poet, and hence the presentation of small and choice selections.

These chap-books will present significant little offerings by our older and younger poets.

Besides its binding, the book's defects are its lack of a proper title page and a glaring typographical error on the second page: the "The Unk[n]own City."

This poem is a good example of the idealism that generally suffuses the series in its initial phase.

The Unknown City

There lies a city inaccessible,
Where the dead dreamers dwell.

Abrupt and blue, with many a high ravine
And soaring bridge half seen,
With many an iris cloud that comes and goes
Over the ancient snows,
The imminent hills environ it, and hold
Its portals from of old,
That grief invade not, weariness, nor war,
Nor anguish evermore.

White-walled and jettied on the peacock tide,
With domes and towers enskied,
Its battlements and balconies one sheen
Of ever-living green,
It hears the happy dreamers turning home
Slow-oared across the foam.

Cool are its streets with waters musical
And fountains' shadowy fall.
With orange and anemone and rose,
And every flower that blows
Of magic scent or unimagined dye,
Its gardens shine and sigh.

Its chambers, memoried with old romance
And faëry circumstance, –
From any window love may lean some time
For love that dares to climb.

This is that city babe and seer divined
With pure, believing mind.
This is the home of unachieved emprise.
Here, here the visioned eyes
Of them that dream past any power to do,
Wake to the dream come true.
Here the high failure, not the level fame,
Attests the spirit's aim.
Here is fulfilled each hope that soared and sought
Beyond the bournes of thought.
The obdurate marble yields; the canvas glows;
Perfect the column grows;
The chorded cadence art could ne'er attain
Crowns the imperfect strain;
And the great song that seemed to die unsung
Triumphs upon the tongue.[48]

The opening alliteration encapsulates the idealistic theme: art, the place where the dead live, is the paradox of attempting to articulate ineffable beauty. The first verb of the poem, "lies," has a double meaning that plays with the simultaneity of art's substance and shadow: the unknown city (1) exists and (2) deceives. The poem moves deliberately through images of landscape, architecture, flora, sculpture, and instrumental music before it self-reflexively climaxes with poetry itself in the final lines, which reprise the concept of immaterial substance in their juxtaposition of death and triumph. The image of dreamers rowing a boat recalls Duncan Campbell Scott's "The Piper of Arll" ("The sailors launched a sombre boat, / And bent with music at the oars");[49] that of the city itself echoes the description of Camelot in Tennyson's *Idylls of the King*, both in the veil of fleeting clouds ("Far off they saw the silver-misty morn / Rolling her smoke about the Royal mount") and in the contradictory state of being-in-art ("'the city is built / To music, therefore never built at all, / And therefore built for ever'").[50] Like these and other romantic works, "The Unknown City" draws on the concept of poetry as a "high failure" – as a spiritual quest for more than can possibly be attained. Roberts's poem is an uplifting expression of an ideal, metrically crafted to speak clearly to a listener's imagination.

The second Ryerson Poetry Chap-Book, Tenny's *Companionship and the Crowd*, veered away from the aesthetics of the Confederation Poets. Roberts soon put a decisive stop to experiments of its sort. Ryerson had printed Tenny's *Songs of the North* in 1923 and Tenny continued to share his writing with Pierce, whom he held in high esteem. "I am sending a sort of revision of the sonnet I dedicated to you," Tenny wrote affectionately to Pierce in October. "Now you know, I am not competent to write as beautiful a tribute as you deserve. You are giving the very best that is in you to the development and assistance of a lot of writers, not one of them able to do nearly as good work as you can, and it seems to me almost sacrilege for me to attempt what I have."[51] Nine poems were chosen for his Chap-Book, which was also dedicated to Pierce. The title poem anxiously contemplates love and religion in light of the prospect of global mass education – "Bold, fearless, mighty host of the newly enlightened, / What, when they think?" – in 130 lines of free verse. Upon receiving copies of the first two Chap-Books, however, Roberts chided Pierce for the blunder of including Tenny. In subsequent numbers, Pierce hastened to include the poets whom Roberts next recommended, who were not only connected to the latter personally but also similar to him in style:

> So glad you like my brother Theodore's poems. I think that, in authentic, *essentially poetic* quality, he ranks with our best. It is the fact that he has not published in book form that has so delayed his due recognition. But the *best* American magazines have long accepted him, — & American anthologies. I am writing him to send you more stuff. A Chap book of his verse would be one of the choicest of the series. By the way, how is the series going? And when does the book of our incomparable Lady Connie appear? And *Tenny's*, — I *can't* find that his verse, however popular, will add to the prestige of such a series!! Do *you* think it will? ... P.S. I am enclosing some poems by my gifted 19-year-old niece, Gostwick Roberts. If you like any of them, perhaps you would pass them on to the Editor of the *New Outlook*. I think she has amazing promise; & I am sending some of her stuff to the London Mercury.[52]

It was a decisive editorial moment. Roberts's influence over the early series is palpable in that successive numbers would eschew the free-form musings on social upheaval of the sort Tenny offered. The inclusion of Theodore Goodridge Roberts (*The Lost Shipmate,* no. [7], 1926) and Dorothy (Gostwick) Roberts (*Songs for Swift Feet,* no. [22], 1927) within the next two years confirms Roberts's effectiveness in drawing the Chap-Books toward his aesthetic nucleus. He knew what it was to direct and promote a poetic movement[53] and he exerted his seasoned strength. At the same time, Pierce's inclusion of Tenny is a sign of his own tendency as an editor toward parliamentary inclusion, which only grew as Roberts's strength ebbed.

As the letter above implies, before he left Toronto Roberts saw to it that Davies Woodrow would get a Chap-Book. Their affair burned through the fall, generating several impassioned letters, and he carried copies of her poems with him on tour and read them aloud to his audiences. Her Chap-Book, *The Gypsy Heart* (no. [4], 1926), appeared the following spring, prefaced by an appreciative introductory note by Roberts, which he sweated over in Fredericton and submitted to Pierce at the beginning of November:

> It is a pleasure to associate myself with this modest collection of poems by Constance Davies-Woodrow. Among the qualities to be looked for in all poetry those of sincerity, simplicity and candour always make a particular appeal to me. Equally essential, according to my own artistic faith, are music in phrase and cadence, the quest of beauty in both thought and form, and conscientious workmanship. These qualities seem to me to characterize, in no small measure, the poems here gathered; and they make the little book a refreshing protest against the defiance of sound technique, the mistaking of violence for strength and of ugliness for originality, which mark so much of our contemporary verse.
>
> Authentic emotions, expressed with such brave directness, yet with a grace so persuasive, should carry these brief lyrics into the hearts of many readers.

This concise manifesto applies to dozens of early Chap-Books. *The Gypsy Heart* is an especially strong example of Roberts's sway, both because of this introduction and because his affair with Davies Woodrow is the key to several poems in the collection, such as "Grey Seas Are Sobbing," which obliquely voices the emotional turmoil of illicit love. Apart from his own book, Roberts's involvement in shaping the Ryerson Chap-Books was nowhere more intimate and is nowhere more evident than in *The Gypsy Heart*.

※✝※

ANALYZED ECONOMICALLY, the Chap-Books largely fall into the category of authorial self-publication and thus cement the modern sense of *chapbook*. Pierce offered editorial advice, but they were mainly self-published in that the authors assumed the ultimate responsibility for the cost of printing and engaged themselves to promote and sell their work. The terms were relatively lenient. In most cases in the early years, Pierce had the authors promise to pay the press a set amount in the event that their books did not sell (see table 4.1). This guarantee against loss on Ryerson's part, formalized by contract, was accommodating in that the author was not obliged to front the capital: production could begin in the hope of adequate sales. Even so, publication depended on the author's willingness to bear the risk.

A business plan did not coalesce until the third Chap-Book, *Forfeit and Other Poems* (1926) by Kathryn Munro. Like many of her successors in the series, Munro, a minister's wife in Sutton, Ontario, was looking for a way to collect the various pieces that she had placed in newspapers and magazines: "Chimney Tops," for example, was first published in the *Canadian Magazine* in April 1925. Upon learning of the publication of *The Sweet o' the Year* in November 1925, Munro posed Pierce several practical questions: "Will you please let me know about how many poems of magazine length would be required to make a Chapbook? That is, what would be the smallest number of pages considered, or have you a set size? Also, if in the case of a very few poems, whether a number of short essays could be added. I would be glad to know, too, if the work of unknown poets is likely to appear in Chapbook form, or only that of our established poets."[54]

Pierce had answers for these questions but vacillated on the basic question of retail price. Upon seeing the proofs in February 1926, Munro noticed that the price had dropped from $0.60 to $0.50 and asked whether this was correct.[55] It was – $0.50 would be the price of an eight-page Chap-Book until 1950, with others at $0.60, $0.75, and $1.00, depending on the length – but it is noteworthy that this policy was still taking shape three months in. The first surviving formal publishing agreement for a Ryerson Poetry Chap-Book appears to be the one that Munro signed for *Forfeit and Other Poems*. It specified the following terms:

> The Author agrees to assign his copyright in the said work to the Publisher, subject to the following:
> (1) A royalty of ten (10) per cent shall be paid on the retail price of all copies sold.
> (2) The royalty shall not apply to author's copies, however which may be secured at manufacturing cost.
> (3) The publisher agrees to promote the sale of the book.
> (4) The author guarantees to protect the publisher against loss on the unsold copies remaining one year from the date of publication, the amount of this subvention not to exceed eighty-five dollars.[56]

Thus began the policy of demanding a guarantee against loss: the author was saddled with the liability for the edition, reckoned here at a maximum of eighty-five dollars, to be paid twelve months after publication. These terms are gentler than those imposed on Andrew Haydon, Walter McRaye, and Jack Miner (see chapter 1); still, like them, Munro became the financial backer of her book. Although the contract states that Ryerson would promote the book, Munro effectively took charge. She "wasn't hoping for 'Author's copies,' as I think the agreement said they were not to be given out, in the Chap Book series," but purchased several for herself at the manufacturing price when her book appeared in April. She suggested people and bookstores to whom copies might be sold. Finally, Pierce arranged for the book to be sold in the United States through a Philadelphia publisher, Macrae Smith Company. The American distribution plan faltered at the outset – in answer to a letter from Munro's sister, Macrae Smith claimed to have no knowledge of *Forfeit* – and it was abandoned partway through the following year.[57] Alexander Louis Fraser's *By Cobequid Bay* (no. [18], 1927) was the last to mention the US publisher on the inside front cover.

The eleventh Ryerson Poetry Chap-Book, *The Prophet's Man* (1926) by Geoffrey B. Riddehough, provides more information about financing. Born in England in 1900 and raised in Penticton, British Columbia, Riddehough had studied English and Latin at the University of British

Columbia and gone on to a master of arts at the University of California at Berkeley.[58] He was teaching at the University of Alberta in April 1926 when he wrote to Pierce about publishing his poems as a Chap-Book: "I am sending under separate cover some verse and verse-translations, with a view to possible publication in chapbook form. Some of the shorter poems have been published in the *Vancouver Daily Province*, but I could get permission to republish them. If you feel that any of them could be used to make a volume, please let me know."[59] An academic career and a newspaper had enabled his literary creativity to date; now, he investigated what book publication might offer. Pierce liked the poems but ruled out the translations and responded with the proposal that the author underwrite the venture. Riddehough accepted: "you suggest that you publish a chapbook of twelve pages, containing some original verse of mine and entitled 'The Prophet's Man'. I notice that you would like me to give a guarantee of $70 to protect you against loss from unsold copies. Your proposal is quite agreeable to me, and I should like you to make out a contract to the above effect. There is, by the way, one point on which I should like to be clear. In the event that the edition does not sell, shall I, on reimbursing you, receive the unsold copies?"[60] Riddehough thus discovered that having a book of poetry published in Canada was tantamount to buying it for oneself.

Pierce did, however, control the physical form of the book and therefore contributed to the selection of poems that would fill its twelve pages. Riddehough, not knowing the size of type or paper to be used, listed ten poems that he most hoped might be included. Pierce took eight of these and added nine others from the author's April package, the result being a seventeen-poem Chap-Book.[61] If a distinction is made between *publish* and *edit*, what comes into view is an author-financed process that was lightly shaped by an intermediary's judgment.

To what extent did Pierce act as a critical gatekeeper to the series, on aesthetic grounds refusing a poet who was willing to pay? Archibald Otto Lampman, the son of the Confederation Poet, was denied a Chap-Book. Duncan Campbell Scott urged Pierce to ignore his "derivative" poetic efforts in hopes of preserving the literary reputation of the Lampman name.[62] Campbell writes that, "from the moment he launched the chapbooks, Pierce was inundated by mediocre manuscripts on hackneyed themes, leading him to ban 'all religious and patriotic poetry' from the series," and cites a letter Pierce received from George Whalley in

1945.⁶³ Euphoria over the end of the Second World War may well have obliged Pierce to implement a simple policy against jingoism in that year. Otherwise, if there were indeed such a ban, it must only have touched crude effusions, for religion and patriotism are everywhere in the early Chap-Books, albeit in restrained and dignified form.

The Prophet's Man, for example, is a profoundly religious book that wrestles throughout with the problem of unbelief. Beginning with the title poem, which Riddehough considered his best, the collection skeptically explores faith and probes the disparity between the individual's dream and his need for public recognition and material reward. Several poems juxtapose the ardour of the visionary with the suffering that he causes himself and others, foregrounding the friction between belief and doubt, subject and society, personal desire and cosmic order. For example, the sonnet, "Peculium" (Latin for "savings") figures the religious life as a doubtful practice of self-deprivation, a questionable abstaining from pleasures now in the hope of storing them up in the afterlife:

> The Roman bondsman, so the old writers tell,
> Would leave a portion of his daily food
> Untasted in his hunger; he would sell
> Strength of his life for every coin that could
> Be added to the tiny hidden store
> Which after many years the weary slave
> Finally drew from underground, and gave
> Unto his lord, to be a slave no more.
>
> Masters, O masters whom I may not see!
> Lo, in this earthen vessel here I bring
> The price of freedom – all that was denied
> To me when through the days of scarcity
> The treasures of my heart lay tarnishing
> In the earth, sourly ... Are you satisfied?⁶⁴

Faith is peculiar: it is a strange purchase in which the object bought is hard to distinguish from the price paid for it, and the enjoyment of it is entirely subjective. In another sonnet, "Conceit," Riddehough presents character as an outward show of strength despite crumbling self-confidence:

A Spanish captain, many years ago,
Thus in his crumbling castle held at bay
The Moorish cannonaders: lest the foe
Should see his broken walls, at close of day
He hung a painted cloth, whereon were seen
Lines of unbroken rampart, while his men
Rebuilt their weak defence; the canvas screen
Beguiled his foes till succour came again.

O best of friends! if I should seem to you
Vain and self-centred, if my lips have spoken
Too flippant boasts and foolish mockeries,
Know that in these same vanities I too
Behind a screen am building ramparts broken
By many a rush of fierce anxieties.[65]

Riddehough's style is philological: he revels in the unfolding of a single word into the splendid meanings hidden in its etymology. Here, the title refers not only to pride but also to an extended metaphor: the likening of the speaker to a Spanish castle is a metaphysical conceit indebted to Donne's "Holy Sonnet XIV" ("Batter my heart, three-personed God / ... / I, like an usurped town, to another due, / Labor to admit You, but Oh, to no end!").[66] The topic is conversation, friendship, and isolation. Layered under this is a self-reflexive dimension in which the speaker ("I") is the poet, the "best of friends" ("you") is the reader, and the "painted cloth" and "lines" of self-aggrandizement are the poem itself. Communication in general and poetry in particular are thus presented as a process of ambitious construction besieged by a sense of failure. Like Lionel Stevenson, who also published a Ryerson Poetry Chap-Book in 1926, Riddehough went on to a mainly academic career, but his creative work evinces a fine ability to explore complexity at both the thematic and the lexical level, while his reading of seventeenth-century poetry pushes him toward the company of T.S. Eliot and A.J.M Smith. *The Prophet's Man* reveals the diversity of the Ryerson Poetry Chap-Books, which, notwithstanding Roberts's general influence, should not be summarily dismissed as predictable.

MORE EXPERIENCED AUTHORS were less amenable to Pierce's terms of publication. One of the ghosts of the series is Frederick George Scott's *Selected Poems*, which was advertised on the inside back cover of other Chap-Books in 1926, first as "in preparation" and then as available for $0.75.[67] Ryerson would ultimately print *Selected Poems* but not for another seven years and not as a Chap-Book, both because Scott objected to self-publication and because he took a dim view of the slight form.

At sixty-five years of age, Scott, the Anglican archdeacon in Quebec City, was a public figure, known not only for his association with Roberts and the other Confederation Poets in the 1880s and '90s — even if he was routinely ranked least among them — but also for his distinguished service as an overseas army chaplain during the First World War.[68] He was a veteran and a veteran author: he knew the international terrain of literary publishing firsthand and had a dozen books to his credit, including a novel published in New York in 1892 and four books of poetry published in London, most recently *Poems* (Constable, 1910) and *In the Battle Silences: Poems Written at the Front* (Constable, 1916).

The Canadian issue of this last work had been mostly destroyed in a fire at the Musson Book Company in Toronto, which prompted Scott to contact Pierce in December 1925, as the first Chap-Books were making their way across the country, to suggest that Ryerson republish them along with several new poems under the title "In War and Peace." Scott's canonical stature, classical technique, clerical collar, and nationalism made him the ideal contributor to the series, but when Pierce suggested this, Scott replied brusquely, "Thank you for your letter. I don't care very much however for the style of the Chapbooks. It is not permanent enough & a pamphlet form soon gets lost. Will you therefore kindly return the poems & I will think out some other plan of publishing them."[69] However, the inclusion of another Confederation Poet would counteract precisely this plain weakness of the series — its ephemerality — so Pierce shrewdly rephrased his offer: "We should like to have a selection from your poems in our Chap Book series, as we believe that before many months we would be justified in reprinting them in cloth, in a more permanent form. This would enable us to sell the cloth bound edition at a much reduced rate which we believe would meet your approval."[70] Scott held his ground, insisting, "I still prefer to have my poems printed here, so will you kindly return the ms."⁷¹ Pierce reluctantly complied and Scott followed through, privately hiring Dussault & Proulx of Quebec City to print what became *In Sun and Shade* (1926). The result is a handsome little book, starkly printed in red and black ink on heavy paper, its five gatherings properly stitched (not stapled) and bound (with endpapers) in white-paper-covered boards with a spine that made it visible on a shelf.⁷² Scott dedicated it to the memory of his son, Henry H. Scott (an older brother of F.R. Scott), who was killed in action during the First World War.

The opportunity to join a canon-building effort must nevertheless have tempted Scott, for with his war and peace poems disposed of he saw Pierce's second offer in a new light. Roberts's *The Sweet o' the Year* had been, through and through, a republication of old work, and Scott now sent Pierce's letter back to him with an inquiry scrawled at the foot: "Do you wish me to prepare a selection of my poems for the Chap-Books series? How many lines do you want?" His qualms over the design of the Chap-Books, however, remained: "I wish instead of a chap book you would publish a little volume. It lasts better. If you would take a volume, I could send some more selections to make it up. However here are my selections for the Chap book. You have a volume of mine, I think [i.e., *Poems* (1910)], & can get them printed from it. I hope you like the selection." A postscript presented the apple of discord: "I take it that I get 10% royalty for the Chap book."⁷³ From his experience with specialist publishers in London and New York, Scott knew the difference between a trade publication and a private edition. He expected the flow of money between publisher and author to accord with what were, outside of Canada, norms of the book trade, especially since his contribution to the series had been Pierce's idea. A week later he repeated his assumption, slightly more warily: "Yes: I am in favour of the Chap Book idea, since you cannot see your way to the other ... I take it you give me ten per cent on the sales as usual. Let me know if this is agreeable."⁷⁴ Pierce was evidently loathe to cross him, for he delayed his answer for three months. When at last he sent Scott the Chap-Book publishing agreement, conflict broke into the open. "I see that by the contract you have sent me to sign, I am to make myself responsible against loss on your part," Scott replied. "I thought I told you the last time you spoke about the Chap Book idea, that I could not do this. I haven't got this money & it simply is equivalent to my publishing the poems myself. If my poems are not worth your while handling, they had better be left where they are."⁷⁵ With this letter he included a copy of *In Sun and Shade* as if to say, see, *this* is a book. Given that he was able to self-publish if he chose, his crying poverty was more a matter of principle than fact, but his resistance to Pierce's terms was not any less strenuous. Six weeks later he remained obdurate: "Are you absolutely determined not to publish my poems in Chap Book form unless I guarantee the expenses will be met? If so, will you kindly return me the list of poems I sent to you. I want to preserve it in case of future publications."[76] In essence the struggle was over what it meant *to publish* – what action did this denote, and who was the acting subject? – and Scott, drawing on standards from abroad, permitted himself to teach Pierce his trade. The dispute repeated the row between Fallis and Pierce the year before, with Pierce now awkwardly wearing the printer's hat. Both quarrels were instances of the public debate that the 1920s copyright reform had ignited over the nature and conditions of Canadian authorship. In November 1926, as the negotiations dragged on, Pierce seems to have attempted to arrange a royalty, for Scott in turn expressed himself "very glad you are publishing my poems in the Chap Book series"[77] – but the project faltered. Scott wrote again at the end of the month to ask when he should expect the proofs, but none were sent and the following year his book was dropped from the series.

Although Pierce did eventually return to Scott's *Selected Poems*, the case demonstrates the centrality of author financing to the Ryerson Poetry Chap-Books, a mode of publication that not only limited the books to their pamphlet-like form, but also favoured the brevity of the literature within them. Scott's ire reveals a clash of literary-economic expectations. The specialist literary publishing that was normal in London and New York conflicted with the agency publishing that prevailed in Toronto. The Ryerson Poetry Chap-Books should be interpreted in light of this disparity.

Howsoever Pierce may have regretted such struggles, they were the fire in which a policy was forged. By 1928, he was able to articulate it brusquely to another Chap-Book poet, Susan Frances Harrison: "owing to the difficulty of disposing of even a limited edition of these little books we have had to ask authors to pay the printing costs. During the last year we have accepted manuscripts for the Chap-books on this basis only." When she, like Scott, refused to pay, Pierce nevertheless proceeded with her *Later Poems and New Villanelles*.[78] He thus appears to have made an exception for her as a distinguished elder Canadian writer, but it is an exception that proves what had otherwise become the rule of self-publication.

THE THIRTEEN RYERSON POETRY CHAP-BOOKS printed in the first two years of the series tend to articulate an idealism grounded in the experience of Canadian places. They express desire for a national literature; overall, they tend to celebrate the beauty and goodness of nature, morality as a hard-won spiritual treasure, and nationality – Canada – as a cultural promise arising from the land. The romantic influence of the Confederation Poets was one factor in this idealism. First publication in Canadian newspapers and church magazines, in which the general reader expected to find straightforward, buoyant visions that could be enjoyed without being studied, was another. The difficulty of persisting as one's own publisher was a third. As privation whets desire, as suffering increases faith, so the austerity under which their books were produced augmented the anti-materialistic values that the Chap-Book poets strove to proclaim and enshrine. Little, resilient works that fix precepts worthy of public admiration, the poems should be construed as artful surfaces that belie the personal effort through which they were made, as bright little achievements of what were, overall, fragmentary and faltering writing careers.

Lilian Leveridge typifies the poet who fit the Chap-Book mould. She was born near Norwich, England, in 1879, came to rural Ontario as a child, attended normal school in Winnipeg, and after a brief teaching career moved to Toronto, where she wrote poetry. She became a regular contributor to the *Christian Guardian*, the flagship magazine of the Methodist Book and Publishing House, and its successor, the *New Outlook*, the magazine of the United Church of Canada. As explained in chapter 1, she wrote "Over the Hills of Home" when the First World War claimed her brother's life, and it became the title work of her first collection, published by E.P. Dutton in New York and by McClelland & Stewart in Toronto. She would author four more collections, three of them Ryerson Poetry Chap-Books, before her death in 1953.[79]

While preparing *A Breath of the Woods* (no. [13], 1926), Leveridge acknowledged the Confederation Poets as a formative precedent. "Some weeks ago," she wrote to Pierce in January 1926, "Mrs Woodrow showed me the Foreword that Dr Roberts had written for her book, and it occurred to me that if Bliss Carman would do a similar favor for me it would add very much to the attractiveness and success of my book. He is my favorite Canadian poet. I met him some years ago, and have had a letter or two from him; he has a copy of my published book."[80] The foreword did not materialize, but the explicit literary indebtedness to Carman may be descried in the nature imagery of the poems, in their apprehension of a divine essence, and in their polished stanzas and rhythms.

Another Canadian poet of the previous generation makes her influence felt, too. In Leveridge's poem "The Loon," the call of the waterfowl lures the speaker into an imaginative flight across a lake, past swaying trees, over rippling waves, through sailing winds, under the laughing sun, into the healing bosom of nature:

> The low winds murmur about the eaves,
> And rustle the standing corn;
> There's a glint of dew on the clover leaves,
> For day is but newly born.
> List! List! From the silver mist
> Enshrouding the blue lagoon,
> There's an echo that floats in weird, wild notes –
> The shrill, strange laugh of the loon.[81]

The journey across water, the wind imagery, the iambic tetrameter with frequent anapestic substitution, and above all the peculiar internal rhyme in the middle of the stanza recall Pauline Johnson's "Song My Paddle Sings":

> West wind, blow from your prairie nest,
> Blow from the mountains, blow from the west.
> The sail is idle, the sailor too;
> O! wind of the west, we wait for you.
> Blow, blow!
> I have wooed you so,
> But never a favour you bestow.
> You rock your cradle the hills between,
> But scorn to notice my white lateen.[82]

The auras of Tennyson and of Shelley are perceptible in these passages, but the repeated monosyllabic verb also affirms a Canadian poetic link, which aligns *A Breath of the Woods* with the Chap-Books' nationalistic purpose.

"Give to me," writes Leveridge in another poem in this book, "A sweet, enduring friendship, true and pure; / The lifelong, loved companionship of books; / The inspiration of a high ideal / ... / To others you may give your minted gold" ("To Life" [13, ll. 6–9]). The same letter that praises Carman also admits the relative poverty in which Leveridge's muse left her. "I have been wondering if you ever have any extra stenographic work that you need to send out," she asked Pierce. "I have no regular office position, and am glad of anything of that kind that can be done at home. McClelland & Stewart have frequently given me some work, addressing envelopes, copying, etc. I would call, if necessary, for any work you might care to entrust to me at any time. I shall appreciate it if you will kindly keep my name in mind in this connection."[83] Despite her tight financial straits she continued to write, and her next letter records the energy she drew from Pierce, from the example of fellow Canadian poet Marjorie Pickthall, and from the readership of the *New Outlook*: "Thank you so much for your very kind letter of May 1st, in which you expressed your appreciation of my poem. It gave me much pleasure and encouragement to receive this good word from you. A few days ago I also received a delightful letter from a stranger in Saskatchewan, Mrs Seaman. It was sent in care of the New Outlook. She wrote to tell me how much she liked my poem 'To Marjorie Pickthall' ... Mrs Seaman says she keeps all of my poems that she finds, and knows most of them by heart; she particularly mentioned a few that have appeared in the Christian Guardian and the New Outlook."[84] The satisfaction of reaching an appreciative public was no doubt sweeter for the financial worries that Leveridge staved off in order to do so.[85] Her remarks reveal the centrality of the church magazines to her formation as an author, as well as the important purpose her Chap-Book would serve in collecting her otherwise scattered work. What is of greatest value in her comments, however, is that they enable us to see her writing in a fitting light. The letter pinpoints a social location for poetry that differs from the academic setting where many assume poetry belongs today. Readers such as Mrs Seaman wanted lucid, morally inspiring verses that could be memorized, expressions of pleasurable and dignified sentiment for rare moments of quiet, and textual mirrors in which they could trace their own best potential selves – and this is what many of the Chap-Book poets attempted to give them.

Poetry, in short, should be a breath of the woods – a fresh inspiration that transports the reader away from life's tiresome pressures. Leveridge's layering of poetic vision onto a Canadian landscape in "Sunset in the City" is representative of the early Chap-Books:

Full many a glorious sunset I have seen,
The splendid pageant of departing Day
That, clad in radiant robes of shimmering sheen,
Her royal banners waved and passed away,
Trailing her garments, crimson, gold and blue,
O'er dimpled wave and fields of glimmering dew.

I've heard the mellow music of the thrush
Piping at vespers; and the fitful cry
Of nighthawks wheeling through the warm rose-flush
In spacious, airy regions of the sky.
I've heard the cuckoo, and the loon's wild note
In lyric laughter on the wood-winds float.

To-night the sun sinks down behind a spire
That terminates the long, grey city street.
A myriad windows catch the crimson fire,
And dun grey roofs are bathed in beauty fleet:
But who among the throngs that come and go
Lift up their faces to the glory glow?

No piping song across the twilight calls,
Nor drowsy chirp of birdlings in their nest;
But never-ceasing, never-resting, falls
The clamor of the city's fevered quest.
Yet through the sounds discordant float to me
Low, vibrant strains of life's great symphony.

There's music, music pulsing on the air –
The lilt of laughter and of happy song,
And homeward-turning footfalls everywhere,
Mingling in rhythmic cadence full and strong.
Perchance the tremulous minor chord of pain
Blends in the Great Musician's perfect strain.

The world is homing in this clamorous hour,
While lights flash out and softly star the gloom.
Like rosebuds opening in a garden bower

A thousand tender thoughts burst into bloom.
Behind closed blinds I dream of lips that meet,
And love's low tones ineffably sweet.

And I am happier for that joy unknown.
Its essence is distilled like precious balm
From fragrant herbs on gales of heaven blown,
Or wafted from some far-off vale of calm.
When, blossom-wise, the heart is lifted up,
The dews of blessing fill its empty cup.

All faded now the sunset's golden light,
The crowds thin out along the echoing street.
The city folds me in its arms to-night,
And croons me wonder-songs, elusive, sweet.
From Love's thought-gardens perfumes steal to me
'Mid poppy-blooms of dream and memory.[86]

The poem is unified, from its recurrent music imagery to its chiselled stanzas. Rhythmic deviation from the iambic pentameter is reserved for select verses: for example, "And love's low tones ineffably sweet" is one syllable short of the requisite ten, employs a spondee ("low tones"), and ends with an anapest. This interruption of the metre signals the special role that the poet reserves for common affection, which in this poem turns out to be as much the ordering principle of the modern urban life as the traditional pastoral one. The person who wishes to be at home at the end of the workday is a blossoming country rosebud; the city lights that herald the evening commute are as precious as stars. Much like Thomas Gray's *Elegy Written in a Country Churchyard*, which also has a crepuscular setting, "Sunset in the City" approaches the unknown masses of humanity with humility and sympathy. Echoes of Lampman's "The City of the End of Things" suggest themselves as well in the images of unceasing, unresting noise, but Leveridge redeems the metropolis from the unnatural abysm to which Lampman consigns it. The specific birds listed reinforce the Canadian setting. Finally, the lyric's crucial action is explicitly imaginative and hence poetic. The speaker sees husbands, wives, and children kissing, but only with her mind's eye through "dream" and "memory." Like Roberts's "Tantramar Revisited" or Wordsworth's "Lines Composed a Few Miles above Tintern Abbey," this poem cherishes the meaning of a place imaginatively and retrospectively. Not mere love but the love of poetry is what allows Leveridge to fold her ordinary Toronto into a transcendent musical embrace.

IN LIGHT OF THEIR publishing history, the poems in the initial Ryerson Poetry Chap-Books come into focus as "significant little offerings" in two senses, both as small poetic achievements, each with its own particular occasion and aura, and also as personal sacrifices to an impossible ideal. They were shaped directly and indirectly, first, by the birth of the modern chapbook form amid the little magazine explosion at the end of the nineteenth century and, second, by Roberts's decisive touch. They were generally designed to be intelligible aurally – that is, to work for listening audiences, as the tribute of some readers' memorizing them bears witness. Many of them are the work of novices pleased by the prospect of getting into print and willing to pay to do so. They were produced cheaply with no offer of remuneration. These financial circumstances were poor soil for a real writing career. If the poems seem little, however, this minority only accords with the publishing structure through which they passed, which was characterized by an editor who was equally idealistic in that his wish to be a specialist Canadian literary publisher exceeded his actual capacity to be one. In their proper place, the poems demonstrate the marginality and the provisionality of literary publishing in early-twentieth-century Canada and, inversely, the resolve of those who nevertheless attempted it. At their origin, the Ryerson Poetry Chap-Books reveal much about the conditions in which Canadian literature was striving to take shape.

THREE

Modern Romantic

Nathaniel A. Benson

THE PRECEDING CHAPTERS have described the establishment of the Ryerson Poetry Chap-Books as a national publishing initiative in Canada in the 1920s, focusing largely on the motives of the editor, Lorne Pierce. The attention will turn now more squarely to case studies of individual authors. What effect did a Chap-Book have on their development and career? If Pierce went against agency publishing and instituted a program of publishing poetry that regarded the Confederation Poets as a vital standard, how did this series affect the life and work of the younger poets whom he aimed to attract? The question seeks not only a literary answer, but also a historical one with reference to the field of Canadian cultural production. As discussed in the introduction to this volume, it is the conjunction of the two dimensions – the writer's work, and also their life – that will enable a new appreciation of the creativity that ran through these little pamphlets. Despite their high national goal, the Chap-Books offered at most a narrow opportunity through which contributors might find an economic niche in the North American book trade. Therefore, it is all the more remarkable that so many people took up the invitation to use these little books to practice poetry.

This chapter will trace the career of one Ryerson poet, Nathaniel A. Benson (1903–1966). The goal is to show in detail both the romantic idealism that the series encouraged in Benson's poetics and the compromises that this romanticism ultimately had to negotiate as he strove to make a living and raise a family in the decades before and after the Second World War. When the literary-aesthetic and the historical-material aspects of a career such as Benson's are combined, the culture of twentieth-century Canadian poetic romanticism grows clearer. Benson represents a deep strain in Canadian poetry centred loosely in Toronto that drew on nineteenth-century models and ultimately helped to nurture the romanticism of post-1960 writers such as Al Purdy. At the same time, it hardly needs to be said that nineteenth-century styles of verse, regardless of their intrinsic value, came under increasing pressure not only to change poetically but also to cede to other forms of modern culture such as television. A young man like Benson could not simply don Bliss Carman's mantle. Instead, he had to negotiate his poetic vocation from a crush of new circumstances. In one sense, romantic poetry broke in Canada in the middle decades of the twentieth century, as modernist poetry spread to influential creative, critical, and academic positions, deliberately and by definition thriving on its breaking. In another sense, intermediaries like Benson brokered new roles for romantic poetry in the decades around the Second World War – in the classroom, in the glossy magazine column, in the private letter, in the television ad, as well as in verse itself – adapting and spreading it to a broad variety of cultural forms. The story of authorship reconstructed here is therefore not one of a minor poet's failure, as tempting as that paradigm may be, but rather one of fruitful contamination. Benson spent his creative talent in a number of practical, compromised ways that, in various aspects of both success and failure, helped to pass romantic poetry forward through twentieth-century Canada, especially through his preferred mode: elegy.

Benson does not appear in anthologies of Canadian poetry today. During his lifetime, however, he earned a degree of public significance that is worth noting. One hundred and seventy people attended his funeral in July 1966.[1] Letters of condolence arrived from some distinguished quarters, including a telegram from John Robarts, the premier of Ontario, and a note of deep sympathy from Ken Thomson, son of Roy Thomson, on his way to becoming a newspaper magnate and Canada's wealthiest person. Bill Davis, then the provincial education minister, wrote to Benson's widow, "Please accept my sincere expression of sympathy at the passing of one who made a very real contribution to the education system and to the cultural life of this Province as poet, journalist, and teacher."[2]

These tributes recognize important life work and committed service in the field of Canadian letters. Benson published six books of poetry, edited an anthology, and wrote a biography of James G. Gardiner, the Canadian agriculture minister. He was the protégé and close friend of Charles G.D. Roberts, leader of the Confederation Poets, during Roberts's sunset years in Toronto. He was a key supporter of E.J. Pratt, writing advance reviews of Pratt's books and helping to position him as Canada's unofficial poet laureate. In 1947, Benson's lengthy interview with Prime Minister William Lyon Mackenzie King was published in *Forbes*.[3] If Benson began his career as an unknown poet, he ended it as a public figure of some standing.

It is not, however, anything extraordinary about Benson that recommends him for examination here. Rather, it is the average character of his literary activity, his running in the middle of the pack, that is especially valuable. The ordinary wreckage of his creative career reveals the thick layer of romantic idealism that lies within twentieth-century English Canadian poetry. Passionate but conservative, this poetic culture is not easily visible to literary criticism in search of historical watersheds and avant-garde revolt, but its existence is important because, as a norm, it fed into the basic practice and concept of poetry from which many more distinctive and original talents sprouted. Pianists grow through many sweet and simple pieces of music, and many will stop before they ever play Ravel's *Tombeau de Couperin*. The case of Benson helps us to see the romantic dream stretching out from the nineteenth century like a river in flood and fertilizing a common ground from which later Canadian poets such as Dorothy Roberts, Anne Marriott, R.E. Rashley, and Douglas Lochhead would rise.

NATHANIEL ANKETELL MICHAEL BENSON was born at home, at 224 Manning Avenue near Trinity Bellwoods Park in Toronto, on 11 October 1903. His father, Thomas Benson (1870–1937), was a postal worker and, in his off hours, a semi-professional baseball pitcher who helped to promote the sport in Canada. His mother, Katherine Sheehan (1870–1950), was the daughter of a woman who had immigrated from County Fermanagh,

3.1 / Nathaniel A. Benson, circa 1907. Courtesy of Julian Benson.

3.2 / Poets at the Muskoka Assembly, undated photograph (circa 1930). Charles G.D. Roberts is in the first row on the right. Nathaniel A. Benson is in the middle of the group, wearing a dark jacket and light tie. Courtesy of Julian Benson.

3.3 / Nathaniel A. Benson, *Twenty and After*, Ryerson Poetry Chap-Books [no. 17] (Toronto: Ryerson Press, 1927), 1.

Ireland, to Toronto in 1866.[4] Benson attended nearby Grace Street Public School, followed by Harbord Collegiate. He then entered University College at the University of Toronto, where he earned his bachelor's degree in modern literature in 1927 and his master of arts the following year, with a thesis on the poetry of Thomas Hardy and A.E. Housman.

In 1926, Benson won the Jardine Memorial Prize for poetry, the same University of Toronto prize won by Robert Finch (1924) and Dorothy

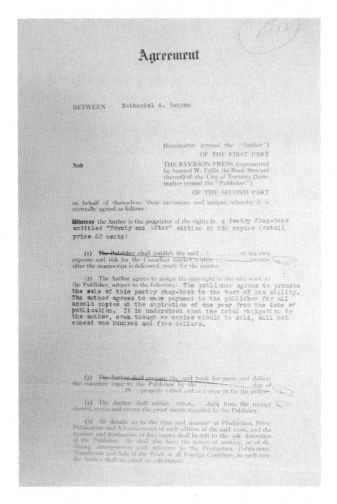

3.4 / The publishing agreement for Nathaniel A. Benson, *Twenty and After*. The second clause obliges the author to pay as much as $105 to the press for any copies not sold within a year. The signatures of Benson, his father Thomas Benson, and the Ryerson book steward Samuel Fallis appear on page 2 of the agreement (not shown). Courtesy of Ryerson University Library.

Livesay (1929). With this laurel on his brow Benson proceeded to publish his first two books of poetry. *Poems* (1927) was a twenty-four-page chapbook printed by F.W. Robertson in Toronto. *Twenty and After* (1927), twenty pages long, was published as a Ryerson Poetry Chap-Book, the seventeenth in the series (see figure 3.3). The title poem, "Twenty and After," was the one that had won the Jardine. At the age of twenty-three, then, Benson joined Pierce's campaign to recover and create a canon of Canadian poetry.

The publishing agreement for Benson's *Twenty and After* breaks down the engagements and liabilities (see figure 3.4). Ryerson would print 250 copies to sell at a retail price of $0.60 (or had already done so when the contract was signed). Ryerson would promote the book "to the best of [its] ability." Benson would assign the copyright to Ryerson and in return would receive six complimentary copies of the book. Most importantly, he would reimburse Ryerson up to a maximum of $105 for all copies remaining unsold after one year.[5] What these terms reveal, again, is a mode of operation that left the financial burden of the edition on the author's shoulders.

Appended to the contract is a letter from Thomas Benson that confirms his willingness to foot the bill, if necessary, on his son's behalf:

> My son has requested me to give you assurance in writing that I realize the terms under which I have given my signature on the contract drawn up between your publishing house and himself, which guarantees that you shall not be at a financial loss should his chap-book not sell as expected. I hereby assure you that my signature is given in full realization of the terms of your contract with my son, and that I shall be ready, if necessary, to reimburse your house in case of financial discrepancy.[6]

These arrangements divided the publishing of *Twenty and After*. Ryerson designed, edited, printed, and to some extent marketed the book, but the author and his family bore its financial risk.

"Twenty and After" is an elegiac romance. Equal parts confession and fantasy, it is a narrative long poem of nearly six hundred lines that reworks the Greek myth of Hippomenes and Atalanta into a lyric exploration of erotic love. In Ovid's telling, Atalanta is a virgin huntress who refuses to marry any man but the one who beats her in a footrace. Hippomenes, who loves her, prays to Aphrodite for help. The goddess equips him with three golden apples, which he throws in front of Atalanta once the race is underway, distracting her enough to win. They set off for his home to marry, but en route they take shelter in a temple and make love. Angered by this sacrilege, the goddess Cybele (or Rhea) transforms them into lions.

Benson subtly adapts this classical source into an oneiric meditation or dream vision on the ecstasy of love and its consequences. In blank verse, from a first-person point of view, he unfolds a romantic awakening:

> With slow-believing eagerness
> I closer came and found I truly fed
> On all that love and loveliness had stored
> For one who never knew such precious food
> Grew elsewhere than in fond and fleeting dreams,
> In fair imaginings, in faery woods
> That guard the first Ideal.[7]

Repetition enhances the emotional crescendo of this passage. Alliteration (seven *f*s), the polyptoton that mingles subjective "love" with objective "loveliness," the paronomasia that links "fair imaginings" to "faery woods" – all of these rhetorical techniques herald the romantic sublime.

Vague hints of danger attend this discovery and attainment of love, however. Benson recuperates a topos of early-modern literature, the syncretic tension between pagan and Christian paradigms, to warn against mere indulgence of the senses: "The gods of Greece were beauty, but our God / Is truth when firmly templed in the mind" (4, ll. 133–4). An allusion to the English romantics similarly asserts a firm reminder that feeling, even feeling as exultant or torrential "As Shelley's spirit pleading to the wind," must remain "In bonds of verse" – specifically, within the "narrow line" of iambic pentameter (5, ll. 166–77). A single troubling word pollutes a series of images of perfect pleasure. Love, possessed, is described as:

> A light outshining sun and moon and star,
> A music dulcet lute shall never give,
> A peace that poppied warmth may not unfold,
> The glory *maddening*-sweet a mother gains
> To feel her first-born nursing at her breast.
> (7, ll. 249–53, emphasis added)

The use of "maddening" cautions against the insanity that can infect sensuality. It also foreshadows the conclusion of the plot in loss and grief. The speaker and his lover's Ovidian race down the happy beach changes abruptly into a flight from pain through a hellish landscape. A storm breaks; they are separated. The next day, the speaker walks on, forlornly searching for his lover. Desperate and exhausted, he finds his way back, at last, to paradise:

>   I reached
> The mighty portal, and the flaming sword
> One moment ceased to swing. I lay within.
>   In all its glory Eden shone again,
> Unending summer, flowers infinite
> Of beauty, scent, and hue. Soft mossy ways
> Caressed my feet, and breezes lingering,
> Upraised my hair, while velvet-leavèd boughs
> Brushed faint my passage down the verdant aisles.
> Unfading amber lilies bathed the sense
> With odours earthly roses never gave,
> Light emerald brooks streamed swift with joy intense
> While sunlight sparkled on each laughing wave;
> Jonquils and daisies nodded from the grass
> That wore the colour of immortal June,
> Rose-wingèd figures lightly floated past
> With flower-petals on their samite strewn.
> The bough in leaf eternal arching high
> Gave perfect coverture, while foliage
> Hid pleasant dells, and ferns like tapestries
> Made setting rich for every joyous tree ...
> And now mine eye remarked within the heart
> Of all the happy woodland round about
> One slim black cypress needling to the sky
> And, drawn inevitably as wind to leaf,
> I neared the quiet space where mystic gloom
> Stirred strangely forth from all the cypress' boughs.
> I saw beneath, half-sensing ere I saw,
> A narrow mound that rose above the sward,
> And there, beside that pitiful small hill,
> Grass-clad, and silent in its sacred peace,
> I slowly knelt and watered with my tears
> The place where angels laid in tenderness
> The loveliness and beauty that were you.
> (14–15, ll. 560–93)

At its end, this poem accounts for itself: like other elegies, it springs from the poet's tears and prayers over his lover's grave. In "Twenty and After," if the age "twenty" signals the discovery of full adult love, the "after" is poetry. The poem culminates with the elegiac renewal of love in death, through memory and art.

Poetically, Benson understood himself to be the disciple and heir of Charles G.D. Roberts. He was also his friend. The two men first met "on a hot, humid night in August 1926."[8] Roberts, whose *The Sweet o' the Year and Other Poems* (1925) had been the inaugural Ryerson Poetry Chap-Book, may thus have been the one who introduced Benson to Pierce. Either way, it is clear that Benson's poetics accorded deeply with Roberts's own romanticism. In Benson's next long poem, "The Wanderer," which constituted the core of his second Chap-Book, he explicitly honours Roberts as his mentor: "He termed me poet and has granted me / Friendship and understanding sympathy."[9]

Naturally it was through Roberts that Benson met Bliss Carman. Benson's first Ryerson Poetry Chap-Book played a decisive role in the introduction. On a spring night in 1927, Roberts invited Benson to accompany him down to Union Station to meet Carman's train as it arrived from the West. Benson was unprepared for "the moose-tall, ambling figure who appeared beyond the glass doors ... wearing a light fawn broad-brimmed Stetson, a light fawn whipcord-type of ulster, the first pair of 'toreador' pants I had seen, and easy-looking dark brown gaiters." The celebrated author of the Vagabondia poems looked as though he "preferred the wooded outdoors to crowded cities, apartments or studios; [and] his kindly, gentle dark eyes seemed to dream behind his spectacles." Pausing on the sidewalk before the taxi, Carman turned to Benson and said, "That poem of yours that won the prize at 'Varsity' was over 500 lines long, wasn't it, Nat? *Some* marathon effort for a young fella still in college – and it was good stuff, too." The memorable consecration occurred because Roberts had sent his cousin a copy of Benson's chapbook.

Benson's gratitude and admiration expanded through the rest of the evening during the party that Roberts hosted at his apartment. "To me [Carman] seemed almost an incredible person, entirely unlike all other people I had ever met," Benson observed, "a wandering spirit, a furtive Pan, an unreal lovable dreamer who was in all of his dreams a high priest of truth and beauty, a singer of the God in Nature, a classical scholar, something of a scientist and very much a mystic." What made the deepest impression on the young man was Carman's reflection on the poet's living: "I remember best of all his last words of encouragement concerning the loveliest of all trades, the poet's: 'It's a good thing to devote yourself to. It's well worth all it costs.'" Approval, wisdom, and admonition mingle in this statement. Benson would remember it for the rest of his life.[10]

One of the shorter poems filling out Benson's second Ryerson Poetry Chap-Book is a tribute to another of Roberts's circle. In "The Lampman Cairn at Morpeth," Benson eulogizes Archibald Lampman as a national poet. Implicitly, the sonnet also shows Benson considering the costs of devoting himself to poetry:

> Build high this cairn, for here was Lampman born,
> Here fell that silver seed of high endeavor,
> Here first he raised that echoing golden horn;
> Beauty his creed, and truth his sign forever.
> Here he first heard the secrets of the Spring
> Whose white feet passed between the early flowers,
> And listened as the April winds would sing
> The lyric of a poet's childhood hours.
> Little he gained of gold, that lustrous sign
> Of all the world's acclaim – yet in the mind
> He was a Crœsus of pure song, whose arts
> To poets' hands the wandering winds resign.
> These touched him and he is forever enshrined
> Imperishable in Canadian hearts.[11]

Crossing Shakespearean quatrains with a Petrarchan sestet, Benson romantically defies the economy and contends that poetry is its own form of wealth. Crœsus, king of Lydia in the sixth century BC, was the putative inventor of the gold coin and hence a proverbial figure of riches. Benson's allusion metaphorically figures Lampman as one who is rich not in purse but in "pure song": he is "silver" in his generative example of poetic achievement, and his musical writings are "golden." The poem is an occasional address written for the unveiling of the Lampman monument in Morpeth, Ontario, in September 1930, but the first line's deictic command also self-reflexively indicates the present poem as a textual "cairn." The implication is Benson's own youthful vow to follow

3.5 / Charles G.D. Roberts, E.J. Pratt, Pelham Edgar, and Nathaniel A. Benson judging the Toronto *Daily Star*'s Royal Family Poetry Contest, March 1939. Courtesy of Julian Benson.

in Lampman's footsteps and work not for the dollar but for the "lustrous sign" of "Imperishable" art.

Benson's friendship with Roberts was the prime relation in what he felt to be a broad movement of Canadian poetry centred in 1920s Toronto. In an unpublished memoir from the 1960s, Benson explained Roberts' return to Canada after more than two decades in the United States and Europe thus: "At 65 he had felt the irresistible call of his native land, and returned, not to his own Maritime Province of New Brunswick, but to prosperous, humming Toronto, the centre of the book and magazine publishing business and gathering place of most of the writers in the Dominion. Here the distinguished exile was to settle and make his headquarters for the last profitable seventeen years of his life."[12] In 1937, Hugh Eayrs, president of the Macmillan Company of Canada, solicited an article on Roberts on behalf of W.P. Percival, secretary to the Protestant

School Board of Quebec, for Percival's magazine, the *Educational Record*. Benson was more than happy to supply the desired text. Again praising Roberts as mentor, he writes that "three generations of poets have tried to sit at his feet and been hoisted from obscurity by [his] strong comradely hands."[13] With Roberts, E.J. Pratt, and Pelham Edgar, professor emeritus of English at Victoria College, Benson judged a poetry contest run by the *Toronto Daily Star* in March 1939. On the back of a photograph of the judging (see figure 3.5), Benson wrote that the four men gathered "to judge the last 125 poems in the Toronto Daily Star's Royal Family Poetry Contest, before sending the best 25 to John Masefield, England's Poet Laureate + final judge. It was a great night of royal food + drink, hard work, and great fellowship. Charles G.D., Pelham E. + I left in a taxi at 3 am all royally illuminated."[14]

Roberts was the best man at the wedding of Benson and Emma Wright at Hart House at the University of Toronto on 4 October 1930. The bride, a graduate of Victoria College, was given away by Pratt because her strict parents disapproved of the match and refused to attend.[15] Benson's banner year as a young writer was 1930. Besides his chapbook, *The Wanderer*, he had two other books appear: *Three Plays for Patriots*; and *Modern Canadian Poetry*, an anthology that he hoped would prove "the first utterance of a new Romantic Movement in Canadian literature" (10). All of this is to indicate that Benson embarked on his career with high ambitions and good connections, at the centre of a busy Toronto literary scene, as the very flower of Canadian romanticism.

❧✝❧

AUTOFINANCING POETRY CHAPBOOKS was not in itself sustainable; less still was turning to one's father for a guarantee. How then did Benson make a living? How did the unfolding of his life define a course of authorship? Following his consecration as a romantic poet circa 1930 through his Ryerson Poetry Chap-Books, Benson underwent a further process of socialization as a Canadian author, a process in which he exchanged his creative potential for a wide variety of paid work, including writing in an array of genres. He never lost sight of his ideal identity as a poet, but he did subordinate and sublimate it into a number of imperfect manifestations in order to negotiate an income. Following him down the various unlikely channels of his creative activity discovers not only the corruption of his talent, but its infiltration of a broad middle stratum of culture, a stratum in which children and students first encounter poetry and decide if it will have any meaning for them.

After completing his master of arts in 1928, Benson embarked on a career as a freelance writer, finding work at one of the pillars of Canadian print culture since the eighteenth century: the newspaper. He spent a year from 1929 to 1930 at the *Manitoba* (later *Winnipeg*) *Free Press* as an editorial and feature writer, where he worked with the influential journalist John Wesley Dafoe. Then the Canadian Pacific Railway hired him as a promotional writer on an assignment to travel the country and describe the various railway-sponsored Folklore Festivals. He contributed articles to *Saturday Night* magazine in Toronto and prepared the three books that would appear in 1930. With the onset of the Depression, Benson turned from full-time writing to teaching high school and completed a certificate at the Ontario College of Education with specializations in English and French in 1932. His first year, at Weston Vocational School in 1933, was "grim." His responsibilities increased that year with the birth of his first son, Julian. In 1934, Benson transferred to Danforth Collegiate and Technical Institute (near Greenwood Avenue in Toronto), where he taught English and drama until 1937. He directed the Danforth Theatre Guild during this period, the Electra Theatre Players, and the Toronto Drama Guild, writing one-act plays such as "Dark Footlights," a gothic murder mystery with a *Hamlet*-inspired play-within-a-play. His papers also contain an unfinished fragment from 1937 entitled "Fortinbras: A Tragedy."[16]

Benson's turn to teaching explains his fourth book of poetry, *Dollard: A Tale in Verse* (Toronto: Thomas Nelson & Sons, 1933). It is a history lesson that recounts the story of Adam Dollard des Ormeaux, the seventeenth-century commander of the garrison of Ville-Marie (Montreal) in New France. According to volume 45 of the Jesuit Relations, Dollard led a military party up the Ottawa River to the Long Sault (near present-day Carillon, Quebec) in 1660. There he engaged a much larger Iroquois force and perished in the battle. Benson embellishes his source text with a romantic motive, suggesting that a tragic love affair back in France spurred Dollard to sail to the New World and lose his life heroically. Otherwise, his poem is faithful to the details of the missionary record. His digging through the Jesuit Relations brought him into contact with the Jesuit martyrs – Jean de Brébeuf, Gabriel Lalemant, and Isaac Jogues – and their appearance in Benson's poem may have prompted his friend Pratt to

III

Around the Island came the swift canoes,
Before them rose the wooded Royal Mount
Crowned by the heavy Cross of Maisonneuve.
Dollard had heard of this same valiant cross
Vowed unto God, when He turned back the flood.
The river had o'erfoamed its natural banks
And brimmed the ditch, lapping the low stockade.
Then at that pregnant hour rose Maisonneuve
Made strong his covenant, and took the vow
That should the perilous river by God's hand
Be overstemmed, the Governor himself
Would bear aloft a ponderous cross until
Christ's symbol crowned the Mount of Montreal.
The torrent ceased. The soldiers hewed a road,
And Maisonneuve, the great Rood on his back,
Climbed step by step, and on the summit fixed
The Tree austere, high over the brawling flood.

3.6 / Nathaniel A. Benson, *Dollard: A Tale in Verse*, illustrated by Walter J. Phillips (Toronto: Thomas Nelson & Sons, 1933), 14. The image depicts Dollard, second from left, approaching Ville-Marie in a brigade of canoes.

retell their story in another English Canadian epic of New France, *Brébeuf and His Brethren*, which won the Governor General's Award for poetry in 1940. The main conceit of *Dollard* is the shining example: the hero plunges forward into darkness, but casts backward light that others may see and follow. "Tell the tale of Dollard," the prologue begins, "evermore / Linked in remembrance with this holy place, / Upraised forever, a crusading flame / That burns about our night, and lifts our race / With the proud sound of his Canadian name" (1). In *Dollard*, the narrative through-line is stronger than in Benson's prior long poems. The language is more straightforward, more literal, less symbolic and less allusive, and there are pictures (see figure 3.6). Its success as a book to teach both poetry and history to a Canadian student audience is measured by its going into a second edition in 1958.

Benson ranged further into the popular book market in 1936 when he teamed up with Fred Hall, president of the Canadian Amateur Ski Club, to write a handbook on downhill skiing, published by Dodge in New York.[17] He continued to write poetry, but never returned to the genre of the long poem. He contributed lyrics to a number of newspapers, such as the *Mail and Empire* and the *Regina Leader-Post*, and to the *New Outlook*, the magazine of the United Church of Canada. Many of these were collected in his 1937 book *The Glowing Years*, which also republished selections from *The Wanderer*. One reviewer, Jacob Markowitz, faulted Benson for his conservative technique yet admired his emotional sincerity and his accessible lines: "In Bede's Ecclesiastical History is made the statement that Caedmon learned the art of poetry not from men but from God; and professors have often maintained that it needs an especial Grace to write poetry. No one who reads this volume will doubt the genuineness of the inspiration, even if at times the tune seems a bit familiar." He went on to chastise Benson for minor negligence and borderline plagiarism: "It is true that an occasional sonnet crumbles in his hand; and we grant that two poems have a disturbing resemblance to Brooke and Wilde. But in general the level is surprisingly high, the quality consistently good. The poems are neither trite nor recondite, are replete with memorable lines, are witty, are ironic, are sentimental, and are bitter."[18] Markowitz accurately contextualized Benson's writing in fin-de-siècle and Georgian precedents, while approving of his navigation of a way for poetry between banality on the one hand and obscure difficulty on the other.

In the summer of 1937, Benson jumped into the world of advertising. W.A. Deacon, literary columnist at the *Globe and Mail*, reported Benson's hope that, by taking a position at the Baker Advertising Agency, "he may find more time for creative writing. However that may be, the appreciation of literature will not be helped by Mr Benson's exit from the teaching profession."[19] For the next five years, through the outbreak of the Second World War, he worked as an ad writer for Foster Advertising and Young and Rubicam in Toronto and Montreal. At the same time, he expanded his service to the literary community. He served a two-year term as president of the Canadian Literature Club of Toronto in the latter part of the decade.[20] He was elected to the executive of the Toronto branch of the Canadian Authors Association in 1940, chaired its poetry group, cycled through the offices of branch vice-president and president from 1941 to 1943, and was national vice-president from 1943 to 1944. He was managing editor of *Canadian Poetry Magazine* from 1937 to 1943 and also served as the secretary of the Canadian Writers' War Board from 1940 to 1943.[21]

In his poetry, Benson responded to the crisis of the war through his proclivity for elegy. He was quick to support Canada's standing with Britain from the outset in 1939, commemorating, in "The Ballad of the 'Rawalpindi,'" the first naval action of the war involving Britain, the sinking of a merchant cruiser by the German battleship *Deutschland*:

> There lay the huge grey sea-wolf
> That whelped the wolves of the sea
> Who dream of a great World-Kingdom
> Where never a heart is free;
> Dread was the dark Atlantic,
> Icy and drear and vast
> And dead ahead in the northern dusk
> The fight that would be her last.[22]

The focus of the ballad is the fatal moment, when the outgunned crew of the British ship decides to engage the enemy. In 1959, Benson's fellow teacher, Keith Bissell, arranged the poem in the Dorian mode, for unison or two-part voice and piano, and it was performed in Benson's Remembrance Day pageant, "Take up This Torch," at R.H. King Collegiate on 10 November (see figure 3.7).

3.7 Keith Bissell, *The Ballad of the Rawalpindi*, for unison or two-part voice and piano, text by Nathaniel A. Benson (Toronto: Gordon V. Thompson, 1959), 2–3.

❧✠❧

IN ANOTHER BALLAD, "Cincinnati Lounge," Benson satirized the American business elite for their country's refusal to join the Allies through the first years of the war: "Better a flaming plane, / Than these who forget their heritage / And laugh in this day of pain!"[23] Under the bitter critique is a lament for a nobler past. In addition to these ballads, which are elegiac in tone, Benson employed the elegiac form directly in such poems as "Elegy for Icarus," which he wrote for his friend Robin Godfrey, a Royal Canadian Air Force pilot killed in action in February 1942:

> Hardly could he abide our sluggard ways
> Where swift hearts slacken, and brightest hopes fall cold;
> Not his to be chained in life's middle common days –
> His was a spirit bold!

Benson adopts the stanza of Gray's *Elegy* – four lines of iambic pentameter with an abab rhyme scheme – but shifts the pentameter to trimeter in the fourth line, creating a leap into the void. This technique of conspicuous rhythmic silence, fitting for an elegy, is common in Archibald Lampman's poetry, which Benson knew well. "Elegy for Icarus" raises a eulogy for the deceased hero, whose high station contrasts with that of the speaker "chained in life's middle common days."[24]

One of Benson's most stirring war elegies is his "'Marseillaise' for a Penny Flute," a poem that focuses on the layers, both rich and tawdry, of a symbol. Looking out over Montreal, the speaker hears someone playing the French national anthem on a tin whistle. It is September 1941, over a year after France fell to the Axis powers. The thin tune seems to the listener to interweave threads of destruction and immortality:

Something has died in this,
Something greater than a nation,
A vision that in the hearts of men lies dead,
And this is its requiem ...
Yet over all, that strange, awakening, pulse-hastening glory of summons
Still sounds, still sings and hovers,
Over the roofs of this ancient, wonderful city
More like shadowed Paris than any in the world.

Sharp and commanding now, the little flute shrills
Over these still-unbeleaguered roofs,
Over these yet-free shores
A reproach in the ears of men
And in their tense hearing
The crash of one of the great Lamps of freedom!

"Aux armes!" from the ringing glorious past
To the dumb inglorious present.
"Aux armes!" – but the arms are shattered;
"Citoyens!" – but the city is fallen;
"Formez!" – but the battalions are broken
And the march is ended.
For an impure blood has overflowed our furrows.

Something deeper than we know reposes here,
Too sad for epitaph, and, aye, too deep for tears.

Still the little flute shrills,
Rising and falling over these old gables.
And here I stand stock-still
Wondering at the empty sunlit day.[25]

Several techniques of adumbration cooperate in the poem. The anaphora of the opening manifests an inarticulate significance, the "Something" that the speaker struggles fully to illuminate. The first three lines build toward the noble rhythm of iambic pentameter through three, four, and five stresses, respectively, only to disintegrate into a grave silence in the fourth line, with the remainder of the poem failing to uphold the high metre. The alternation that is the hallmark of the elegy appears formally in the half-rhyme of the final stanza, but also thematically in the two cities of the poem. Montreal tempts comparisons with Paris, but it takes some inspiration to stand in the former and see the latter. Meanwhile, the City of Light is, and perhaps forever will be, "shadowed."

The difference between "the ringing glorious past" and the "dumb inglorious present" grows keenest in the fourth stanza in the contrasts between French and English, between italic and roman type, and between the song's call and the speaker's contradictions of it. This difference, however, is a conjunctive layering, in so far as that which is present and that which is absent poignantly demonstrate each other. Moreover, in the same way as a symbol calls to what is beyond it, allusion bridges the gap between works. When rhyme finally appears in Benson's poem, his couplet recalls Wordsworth's "Intimations" ode, a *locus classicus* for the elegiac assertion of eternal glory through grief over its temporal loss: "To me," Wordsworth concludes, "the meanest flower that blows can give / Thoughts that do often lie too deep for tears."[26] Through these alternating layers of light and sound, of sign and significance, "'Marseillaise' for a Penny Flute" fills "the empty sunlit day" with wonder and asks us to hear a melody through the type, a symphonic chorus through the melody, and the "crash" of both city walls and cymbals.

Roberts's death in 1943 occasioned another elegy belonging to these years. In "The Last Parting," Benson transmutes a goodbye, "my old friend's last farewell to me," into a welcoming of Roberts into the canon of poetry.²⁷ The poem begins with death freezing trivial details with unexpected finality: a chilly autumn night, the yellow streetlights, the signature black ribbon of Roberts's pince-nez fluttering in the breeze, his open coat, and his casual curbside parting constitute the speaker's last view of the elder poet. Lines of pentameter and hexameter intermingle randomly in the first stanza, which voices grief using figures of repetition:

> And I saw him standing there. And now no more,
> Not any more, not in the longest day,
> Nor on the longest street, save in my long, long thoughts,
> Will he come back and walk our ways again ...
> (ll. 12–15)

Blank verse takes the rest of the poem firmly by the hand, as this sadness cedes to images of Roberts's faring onward into new and farther countries. The second stanza imagines his dust going back to "his deep-loved and long-lost Tantramar" (l. 19) but then traces his life, "Not always good, not always wholly wise" (l. 21), yet always uncommon, through other landscapes, such as "The rare dim crags where greatness climbs alone" (l. 34). The third stanza follows Roberts into the worlds of his writing, and alludes, for example, to the 1934 poem "The Iceberg," which Benson marked as one of his favourites in his copy of Roberts's *Selected Poems*.²⁸ The themes and thoughts of Roberts's poetry "were his provinces, his wonted trails, / His long-familiar paths, his trodden ways" (ll. 50–1), Benson asserts, continuing the imaginary geography with images of the poet rowing out to sea. The final stanza envisions Roberts arriving in the country of poets:

> Forth has he gone, before his peers to stand;
> On that far beach I doubt not he can hear
> The eldest Genius of his god-like line
> Say: "Welcome, worthy heart! Come, stand with us;
> To be a Poet is to laugh to scorn
> The last fell thrust that darkling Fate can give."
> (ll. 80–5)

Alliteration completes the elegiac reversal of leave-taking and makes poetry an apocalyptic land where tears and partings are no more.

Six weeks before Roberts's death, Benson had moved to a new country himself.[29] In 1943, Young and Rubicam transferred him to its New York office to compensate for the loss of personnel as the United States entered the war. One of the company's clients was Borden Dairies, and Benson was assigned to work on advertisements involving Elsie the Cow, the marketing mascot invented for the dairy producer in 1936. Of all Benson's creative exertions, this was probably the one with the widest appeal and impact. Elsie's happy smile and butter-yellow daisy collar would become synonymous with a glass of milk for the Baby Boom generation. Commercial success of this sort translated into middle-class prosperity for the Bensons. Nathaniel and Emma's second son, Charles, was born in 1945. Julian, aged twelve then, still remembers outings to the theatre with his father, as well as seeing the triumphant procession of US warships in the Hudson River on Navy Day (27 October) 1945.[30] Benson worked at three other advertising agencies in New York – Lawrence C. Gumbinner, BBDO, and Biow – until 1949.[31]

Through this busy period in advertising, Benson continued to write in a variety of genres, maintaining both his versifying and a side-career in journalism. His routine was to snooze after supper and then work late into the night.[32] *Saturday Night* (Toronto) appointed him its New York drama critic, and Benson reviewed more than forty Broadway productions for the magazine. He also wrote a feature article on Eaton's, tracing the founding of the department store in Toronto in 1869 by Timothy Eaton, an Irish immigrant, through its growth into a national chain with 32,000 employees by 1943. "There are two ... enormously important reasons for the company's growth," Benson argued, idealistically: "for nearly 75 years Torontonians have felt very sincerely that Eaton's was a trustworthy and advantageous place to shop and a generous-minded place to work."[33] He described Sir John Eaton, Timothy's son and the company's second president, as generous to a fault, and cited his reduction of the store's opening hours (and hence the employees' work week) to five-and-a-half days. Fact-finding and patriotism intermingle in this optimistic account of a Canadian institution.

After the war, Benson interviewed the seventy-three-year-old William Lyon Mackenzie King for *Forbes*. Remarkably, the article turns from the privileged one-on-one conversation with the prime minister to King's 1918 book, *Industry and Humanity*, published almost thirty years earlier. Pointing to a sun dial as a symbol of the order of the universe, King had asked, "'In the chaos which envelops human relations throughout the world today, has the time not come for search after such an order? ... Is not all that Humanity has been called upon to endure, evidence of a wanton departure somewhere from the purpose of God among men? We know whence the deviation has arisen. It is in our industrial and international relations. We have turned the dials of human conduct to commercial uses when they were intended as guides to the divinity which lies everywhere about us.'"[34] Through his quotation of this passage, which refers to the First World War, Benson recuperates a Biblical, mystical paradigm forged in King's youth in the 1890s and applies it to postwar 1947.

Benson returned to Toronto with his family in the fall of 1949, and he spent his last two years in advertising at the Hayhurst Agency. Toward the age of fifty, he returned to teaching, finishing his career at Central Secondary School in Hamilton (1952) and then at R.H. King Collegiate and Sir Winston Churchill Collegiate, both in Scarborough (until 1966).

Benson knew first-hand the vicissitudes of the Canadian author's career, and vividly and self-reflexively rendered them in a 1953 feature on his fellow alumnus of University College, Arthur Stringer (1874–1950). The piece is one of many that he wrote for the *University of Toronto Alumni Bulletin* in this decade,[35] and is an extended obituary – another form of elegy. Benson's time in New York had overlapped with Stringer's last decade, and the two had been friends. They had founded a New York branch of the Canadian Authors Association together.[36] In the article, gorgeous portraits of the photogenic Stringer accompany Benson's extraordinarily warm and candid biography. Benson constructs "a literary enigma," a paradoxical portrait of an author who "was at the same time a self-confessed literary hack and the writer of many volumes of fine, imaginative poetry" (10). This conflict, of course, interested Benson keenly. He begins with two disarming anecdotes that Stringer himself liked to tell on his reading tours and that capture his literary humility:

> One concerned a school boy in Calgary who asked him to sign an autograph book at a Canadian Authors' meeting. Arthur duly obliged and was somewhat taken aback when he heard the lad exclaim to his mother, "Have you a rubber? I thought he was Charles G.D. Roberts." The other story was about a pert young lady of twenty or thereabouts who listened intently while an actor first introduced Stringer and then read one of his poems at a literary gathering near

Mountain Lakes, New Jersey. It was a particularly delicate reading of one of his love lyrics, and the young lady was afterwards heard saying to a friend beside her: "That was such a beautiful poem – so sensitive! I don't believe that big brute ever wrote it."
(10)

The humility is not only charming but also indicative of the problem that Benson recognizes in Stringer, namely, the incongruity of lofty dream and animal vitality, of artistic delicacy and economic power.

The analysis goes on to examine the many facets of this incongruity. Benson judges that "much of his [Stringer's] work actually suffered from a glib fluency which often precluded his loading every rift with ore. But to live in the comfort he desired he had to think, write and work at top speed all his life" (10). "Comfort" was a mansion in the beautiful New Jersey countryside, where Stringer spent the last third of his life with his wife and three children. He acquired it by working like a horse for the slickest of American mass-market magazines, the *Saturday Evening Post.* If Stringer was 60 per cent "human fiction-factory," however, some fraction of him remained a poet. "He wished to make his name respected and honoured along with those of Lampman, Carman, Charles G.D. Roberts," and others (11). He failed to do so, but Benson hallows the failure: "That he almost succeeded is almost a literary miracle. To use his own rueful phrase, muttered one night in 1940 when we were baring our unshirted literary souls in the ruddy glow of his living room fireplace, he admitted he was 'the best paid of all the famous Canadian hacks.' Then he added, quite unaffectedly, 'I write my fiction as you do advertising copy – to make a living at it. But I have tried to save enough of myself out of the hurly-burly to do the stuff that counts in the end'" (11). The career comparison brings Benson's identification with Stringer to the fore. He, too, cleaved to the hope of doing "stuff that counts in the end," despite the press of other work – stuff like Stringer's *Woman at Dusk and Other Poems* (Indianapolis: Bobbs-Merrill, 1928), which Benson admired.

The threads of poetry, money, love, and society grow increasingly tangled as the article turns to a biographical explanation of the enigma. Benson traces Stringer's childhood on the Thames River in Southwestern Ontario, his first poems in Goldwin Smith's the *Week* in 1892, his travels in Europe, his work for a railway in Michigan, his apprenticeship as a journalist at the *Montreal Herald*, his recruitment by New York magazine editors, and his unhappy first marriage to actress Jobyna Howard. Through all of these disparate experiences, Stringer held on to his calling as a poet, or some shred of it. Two years before his death, he saw his *New York Nocturnes* published as a Ryerson Poetry Chap-Book (no. 132, 1948). Ultimately Benson returns to the moment about which he had written his 1930 sonnet quoted above – the unveiling of the Lampman Cairn – this time treating it not with youthful bravura but with melancholy wisdom. Stringer delivered an address that day, and Benson quotes it at length: "All our work and accomplishment are nothing if we are without poets to elucidate them and preserve them in song. I shall not say that we can never be a strong nation without strong poets. But I do say that our strength will be the brute strength of a second Dark Continent, unilluminated and unrecorded and unremembered. For it is the poet who interprets us, not only to our own souls, but to those who come after us" (13). Stringer avails himself of a Gothic figure, suggesting that twentieth-century Canada might prove no more literary than (imaginary conceptions of) seventh-century Europe or nineteenth-century Africa, but the critique's thrust is reflexive. Moreover, with the repetition of the word "brute," Benson's article gashes itself, breaking into a sober confession of the strength that has ensnared and corrupted not only Stringer but Benson, too.

The elements of the entanglement remain at the end of the article, standing unreconciled in four anaphoric statements: "Arthur had lived a good life, a full rich life, filled with romance, success, love, art, prosperity ... He wanted to be a genuine poet, and he was. He wanted to be a highly paid fiction writer, and he topped most of his contemporaries. He wanted a fine family, and he had a lovely wife and three sons. He wanted his own people of Canada to admire and remember him, and they do" (13). Poet, businessman, father, Canadian: the categories repel each other and cohere. Benson's ability to articulate this complexity with poetic figures in a prose article is evidence of his own familiarity with it.

A similar complexity structures another text that Benson wrote in the 1950s. "By-Line Bill" is the draft outline for a television musical.[37] Although never produced, it constitutes further evidence that Benson spread out into different media and genres of writing. The plot centres on Bill Gale, a reporter in New York, and Loveday Shane, an aspiring singer. They meet on the deck of the Staten Island Ferry one summer evening and, with a kiss, seal a deal to help each other reach the big time. Bill promotes Loveday in the newspapers, helping her rise from club to club. Loveday comes to the attention of Harold Herringbone, a wealthy talent scout who invites her to sing at the Constellation, a high-society supper club. After that, she ascends to the prestigious By-Line Ball. Bill grows increasingly bitter as Loveday leaves him behind. The grand finale takes place at the ball: "Loveday offers to sing Bill's song 'I Saw Your Picture in the Papers'. He says, 'No, don't sing it. Nobody reads yesterday's newspapers tomorrow – least of all you, with the tomorrow you've got coming up. Give 'em the old whoopdedoo – the old Vishinsky.' So she and the chorus boys sing 'You're in the BIG-time', a fast wacky mow 'em-down song with lots of ya-ta-ta" (4). During the final number, Bill tosses back drink after drink and then jumps into the orchestra. He "gives the drummer a sawbuck [ten dollars] and says: 'Get lost, son and let a *man* take over! I wanna get in this redhot Moddun Tempo – but Good!'" (4) The curtain falls as Bill ruins the music with his furious cacophony.

"By-Line Bill" shows Benson thinking about the ways in which romance collides with modernity. The writer loses hold of his muse, and young love loses out to ruthless money. At the same time, the romantic protagonist triumphs in so far as he embroils the modern finale in his own emotion and drags it with him into self-immolation. It is not mere defeat, but tragedy. There is also the intriguing similarity between the name of the final ball and that of the protagonist. Does this make for an allegory, in which all elements of the conflict, from hopeful dream to business deal to personal catastrophe, represent conflicting desires within the individual? This draft outline for a television musical seems to constitute further evidence that Benson searched to understand the poet's purpose and place in society. It also reveals the confirmed romantic trying out new genres for romance: the television musical, the dance routine, and the pop song.

In the 1950s, Benson was commissioned to write several biographies. As mentioned earlier, James Garfield Gardiner hired him to write his, which was published as *None of It Came Easy* in 1955. It is a national story written for a broad public:

> The Gardiner Story tells with a wealth of dramatic detail the career of an indomitable Ontario farm-boy who used the precious tool of an education obtained step by step, the hard way, to rise from hired man to country teacher, to high school principal and political leader,

to Provincial Premier, and lastly to a position of national eminence as Canada's Minister of Agriculture, which he has occupied with unchallenged distinction for twenty years. Farmer, humanitarian, spokesman of the wheatlands and friend of the history-making leaders of our time: Laurier, Mackenzie King, Sir Winston Churchill, Prime Minister St Laurent – James Gardiner's story from 1883 to 1955 is one that every reader will enjoy.[38]

A similar manuscript was completed for Roy Thomson, but never published. Benson worked as a ghostwriter for other public figures of the day; their identities remain undisclosed, out of the family's wish to respect the terms of the writing contracts.

The fact of the ghostwriting is a reminder that Benson's writing habits went beyond his various publically sanctioned roles as an author. Beneath the surface of the poetry and the journalism, the advertisements and the high-school plays, was an extensive private writing practice glittering with the pleasure and the discipline of recording experience. A trace of this practice survives in the form of a long letter that Benson wrote to his favourite aunt in the summer of 1957, describing a family trip to Prince Edward Island.[39] Fragmentary and close to the flow of the lived life, the letter is essentially an unedited journal intent on capturing events and impressions without regard to style.

It reveals a past Canada, at once strange and familiar. At the end of July, Benson, aged fifty-four, set off with Emma and their two sons, Julian (twenty-four) and Charles (twelve), in Julian's car. Over the next six days, they drove 1,200 miles east, through Ontario, Quebec, and New Brunswick, to Prince Edward Island. Their progress was frequently hampered by a "bad mucky road." Highway 401 did not yet extend past Oshawa, and Highway 50 between Gatineau and Montreal did not yet exist, but Highway 7 from Peterborough to Ottawa offered them its picturesque segments (Havelock, Kaladar, Silver Lake, Perth). They spent their first night at Fritz von Allmen's farm at Carillon, Quebec (now a municipal park), and enjoyed a "lovely breakfast of fruit juice, and bacon, eggs, coffee, toast, kirsch." Montreal, then as now, was clogged with "heavy traffic," but they were thrilled with St Joseph's Oratory: "Chuck and I in rain drove up to Westmount View place, went to Wax Museum Tour. Crossed street, climbed 250 steps to Oratory. Saw Frère André's tomb, lit candles, said prayers, took escaliers to half-finished basilica. Very impressive lower chapel, crypt, altars, magnificence of it all. Stranded in rain atop Oratory for hour." In Quebec City, they admired the historic view from the Citadel cannon but not their mediocre dinner at the "posh-phoney overcrowded Kerhulu Restaurant." Like Susanna Moodie over a century earlier,[40] and like the average traveller today, they were awed by the North Shore east of Quebec: "Left Montmagny at 10 am, got gas, drove east along St Lawrence, saw most superb scenery of clouds, mountains over river, mists, southern hills." Other features of the landscape have changed. They walked in the beautiful Pokiok Gorge west of Fredericton, a decade before it was submerged by the construction of the Mactaquac Dam (1965–68), and at Cap Tormentine they boarded the *Abegweit*, a "huge heavy CNR diesel ferry," to cross the Northumberland Strait. The Confederation Bridge would not be built until the 1990s. (As Benson notes, *Abegweit* is the Mi'kmaq name for Prince Edward Island.) The passage of time is also palpable in the prices they paid. At Woodstock, New Brunswick, where they spent their fourth night, they "got 2 nice rooms at Motel Haven for $16."

The middle-class family holiday was literary in two dimensions. First, as was his habit, Benson wrote each day. He records that in Woodstock, for example, he woke at 3:30 a.m. and spent the next two-and-a-half hours writing in his diary. On other mornings, he wrote letters. Second, Canadian writers and literary landmarks were goals for certain legs of the journey. In Carillon, their host "escorted us down to site of Dollard stockade on Ottawa River," a place defined by the Jesuit Relations and by Benson's own 1933 long poem, *Dollard*. While in Ottawa, he telephoned his friend and fellow Ryerson Chap-Book poet Arthur Bourinot. In Fredericton, "in the quiet cloudy afternoon at 3 p.m. of July 31/57," they visited the graves of Bliss Carman, Charles G.D. Roberts, and Theodore Goodridge Roberts, Ryerson Chap-Book poets all. "Chuck copied down Bliss's inscriptional verse + I did the others. Julian took pictures. Custodian told him how Hurricane Hazel had toppled Bliss's stone over. After an hour we left. I bought floral tribute for Charles G.D's grave + asked to be notified every July 1 for same." Through transcriptions, photographs, and laying flowers, the cemetery visit was the ritual equivalent of the elegiac commemoration for which Benson strove in so much of his poetry. In Prince Edward Island, they "drove out to Cavendish Beach, scene of LM Montgomery's labours." The letter-journal thus provides evidence of Benson's habits as a writer and as a reader.

The long letter is most valuable, ultimately, for its innocent, uncalculating portrait of a personable man. Benson experienced a recurrent irritation of some kind in his eye, but does not dwell on it, writing only "eye bad" from time to time. He played the piano when one was to hand, especially *con brio* if his sonatina could also serve as a family alarm clock: "Up at 7.30 am. Musical piano bugle call for Emma." He "watched TV + midget wrestlers," enjoyed a "nice milk shake + choc sundae," and swam with his twelve-year-old son in the sea. He struck up conversations with strangers, in French and English. He watched with good-natured astonishment as a Wally Byam caravan overtook the line-up for the ferry.[41] The embarcation was delayed an hour by this "beret-wearing bevy of gregarious Americans of more-than-ample means, all Cadillacs, Chryslers, etc, from Florida, Arkansas, California + all points of the US Compass, showing amazingly nomadic characteristic of my beloved 'adopted' people the Americans." Nevertheless, Benson affably "talked on boat to tall greying American industrial-type, WM Matthews[?] of Schick Rd., Bartlett, Illinois. We exchanged addresses. How those female caravaneers yallocked together. Like a hive of guinea hens. The men were quiet + very friendly."

The end of the letter reveals the purpose of the voyage, which also further discloses Benson's character as a father: "We had beautiful discussion as I tried to cheer up my Beautiful [Emma]. She dressed beautifully, so did Chuck as we picked up to move to beach cottage. Taxi at 1.30. Got red rose boutonnieres for C[huc]k + me which J[ulian] made us discard for routine white carnations. Marriage 2.30 ... David [best man] + Julian [groom] + Sheila [Clark, bride] performed nobly. Reception at Summerlea, 60 people, nice minister Rev. Webben. Took pix outside. Happy couple took off at 5.30. We returned to rest at beach cottage on Bedeque Bay." It was a watershed trip, organized and undertaken in order to see his son Julian wed. Two days after the wedding, Brenton Clark, the bride's father, gave Benson a tour of Malpeque Bay in his oyster trawler, and Benson recorded his respect for his counterpart: "B.C. earns a good living the hard way indeed." Emma's sadness at giving away her son is tangible in the letter, as is Benson's wish to console her. They knew that it was the last time they would travel together with their two children as a family of four. They did not know that Emma would be a widow within a decade. In sum, this extended letter deepens one's sympathy for Benson. In granting one like him full, red-blooded humanity, we discover a way into appreciating not only the bibliographical fact of his poetry, but also its literary beauty. In crossing his life with his work, we enter into his perspective.

In July 1966, at the age of sixty-two, Benson set off alone on his last voyage. He wanted to see California. For one reason or another, Emma did not accompany him. In Detroit, he stayed with old friends, George and Helen Pierrot. "Nat looked exhausted," Helen later wrote to Emma, "but he revived after a shower and was full of conversation about his trip." They drank a toast and had dinner. The next morning (19 July), after the Pierrots had gone to work, Benson had a heart attack while leaning over the wash basin to brush his teeth. Helen found him in bed when she returned from the office mid-afternoon: "He said he was sure he'd be all right in a day or two – that he'd had an attack like this 12 years ago – and he'd just stay quiet." She telephoned for a doctor, and had some trouble securing one because of summer holidays. "Nat didn't want any of the pills he had with him – and he didn't want me to call you [Emma] because he didn't want to worry you. While we were chatting he put his foot out from under the covers – and it was dark purple." This discovery prompted Helen to call emergency, but before the ambulance arrived, Benson "started to sit up to change his position – then suddenly fell back – and half turned over." The paramedics arrived five minutes later and "felt he had gone." They tried artificial respiration and transported him to hospital, but the emergency room doctor "indicated Nat had probably died almost as soon as he fell back on the pillow."[42] The Pierrots then faced the terrible task of informing Emma that her husband had died at their house. This they must have done, but four months would pass before Helen could bring herself to write her friend a full account in a proper letter. Benson's body was transported back to his native Toronto for the funeral, which took place a few days after his death at the Newbigging Funeral Home, then located at 733 Mount Pleasant Road. Among those in attendance were Fred Swayze (another Ryerson Chap-Book poet), and Claire, the daughter of E.J. Pratt. Benson was buried in Mount Pleasant Cemetery.

※✝※

NARRATIVE AND HISTORICAL long poems, sonnets, ballads, satires, elegies, high-school dramas, concert reviews, feature articles, advertising logos, an outline for a television musical, biographies, letters, diaries: Benson's practice as a writer extended into all of these various genres over the course of his life. Collectively they reveal the socialization of his creativity. Symbolically they represent the middle culture of authorship in which he participated. He was a romantic poet who found all of these ways to practice his vocation in mid-twentieth-century Canadian and American modernity. In addition to these genres, there are also his longer occasional poems, such as that written for King George V's silver jubilee in 1935, or the volume *In Memoriam Principis* (1951) to commemorate Mackenzie King on the first anniversary of his death. There are also Benson's scripts for radio, including a pageant, "What Shall I Tell My Son?" written for the approaching 1967 Centennial. Benson's potential as a poet translated itself into all of these genres, high and low, more or less as his society demanded. His original talent dispersed itself down all of these various formal channels, in a process that this chapter has endeavoured to present as one of fruitful contamination. He set out to be "a Crœsus of pure song"; he became, at least, a singing Crœsus.

The Chap-Books lured Benson with their gleam but did not amount to a solid place where he could stay and build. They defined an ideal of authorship that he espoused in his twenties but that did not suffice for the colourful practice of authorship that he experienced over the rest of his life. Earning a comfortable salary and supporting a household with children took him far beyond the limited financial range of the Chap-Books. At the same time, it must be acknowledged that they made him the poet that he was – a modern romantic who remained loyal to the tradition of poetry inherited through Lampman, Carman, and Roberts. The Chap-Books allowed Benson to combine the unstable elements of poet, businessman, father, and Canadian, and they served a similar purpose for his friends, Arthur Stringer and Arthur Bourinot.

For as long as he lived, Benson never stopped writing poetry. His sixth and last collection, *One Man's Pilgrimage*, was published in 1962. It contains lyrics from the whole of his adult life, reaching back to 1924 before his first chapbook was published. Several of the poems show him working in his strongest mode, elegy. "An Actor's Soliloquy," a dramatic monologue toward the end of the book, undated but placed among others written in 1960, reflects on the hopes and disappointments of authorship:

So this is I! This is what I've become –
A master-mummer, a mere sounding board
For great men's thoughts, I who aspired so high,

Ev'n to the highest: alone, on that rare level
Where I alone would make the words I spoke!

Such talent was not mine – too soon I knew
My niche of true performance lay far lower –
Yet, was it so? For who's to judge? Not I.
Not mine to visualize His scheme entire,
But to portray the moving power of all:
The depth, the grandeur, the essential mime:
That was my role – and who's to say it's base?
So few have stood upon the mountain-top,
A splendid handful, an unearthly few
To whom 'twas given to know the tongues of God.

Mine be the lesser plane: the power to study,
To reach, to know, and last, to sift out clear
The subtlest shadings of the deepest words;
That, 'tis enough – no mean, but a mighty feat,
To encompass thus the cycle of slow time,
The tortured hours, the cataracts of mirth,
And last, the sombre peaks of tragedy.

To "portray the moving power of all"; "to sift out clear / The subtlest shadings of the deepest words"; "To encompass thus the cycle of slow time": if this dramatic monologue is a self-portrait, the authorship to which Benson ultimately felt title was not the pure creativity of the high poet-priest. He saw that the action of life had given him various scripts, and he had performed them, cherishing a pure ideal of poetry even as he dirtied his hands with paid work in line with various socially sanctioned forms of creativity. He is an example of the breaking and the brokering of Canadian romanticism in the twentieth century. Perhaps he failed to affect the literary tradition with his own original gravity, but he succeeded in airing and exercising that tradition. His creativity dispersed itself in many genres and shows not the end of romanticism but the absorption of romanticism into a wider cultural atmosphere – an atmosphere in which poetry would continue to need emotion and dream.

FOUR

Broadcasting Authority
Anne Marriott

THE PRIOR CHAPTER offered a study of Nathaniel A. Benson of Toronto in order to provide a detailed case of the culture of authorship that the Ryerson Chap-Book poets facilitated, arguing that he inherited and adapted Charles G.D. Roberts's poetics to the mid-twentieth century. Over half of the Chap-Book poets, however, were women. The next three chapters, therefore, will reconstruct the experiences of important women contributors in order to show how they found their voices through Pierce's national poetry series. Moreover, all of them knew each other as residents of the West Coast. Looking at them sequentially will suggest the function of the Chap-Books in developing poetry in regions of the country far from Toronto.

One of the most important poems published in the Ryerson Poetry Chap-Books was Chap-Book no. 80, Anne Marriott's *The Wind Our Enemy*. Printed in the winter of 1939 and frequently anthologized since, *The Wind Our Enemy* is, according to most critics, a groundbreaking, realist account of the 1930s drought on the Prairies and an early example in Canada of the modernist long poem. Much has been made of the poem as a Canadian manifestation of the influence of T.S. Eliot.[1] By contrast, it is rarely placed in the context of the series in which it was first published.

Without discounting Eliot's influence, this chapter will paint a broader picture of Marriott as an author, one focused on her development as such in and through Lorne Pierce's series. What sort of authorship did the Chap-Books permit her to experience, and what produced the authority that attached to her name? As in the prior chapter, the emphasis will fall on the construction of authorship through social processes both personal and institutional. Members of the Canadian Authors Association, themselves Chap-Book poets, guided and supported the young Marriott as she declared her talent. At a crucial moment, a well-connected mentor validated her poetry and became the de facto literary agent that she needed to negotiate favourable terms for her first book, thus establishing the relationship with Pierce that was at once prestigious and insufficient. Marriott helped to found a little magazine dedicated to poetry, which was significant, but all the while she was writing in other genres for other media, most notably radio and film. In later years Marriott reaffirmed her vocation as a poet through small-press publication, a practice (by that time supported by the Canada Council) that returned her to the authorship that she had experienced first through the Chap-Books. However, the diversity of her writing experience overall, like Benson's, bespeaks her responding to a public with a shifting set of political demands and a guarded appreciation for pure poetry. In her response, Marriott realized a heterogeneous practice of authorship, making a lasting mark on Canadian poetry while making ends meet in other ways.

FROM A YOUNG AGE, Anne Marriott (1913–1997) was determined to be a writer – "a determination which started out when I was about eight. I had been ill in bed for some time and then something occurred which was even worse than the sickness – I ran out of books. Nothing to read! So in an old ledger I proceeded to write another book for myself – and this turned out to be almost as much fun as reading one."[2] She attended Poplars School and then Norfolk House, both girls' private schools in Victoria, and in her adolescence began to write poetry. "I was so caught up – possessed, almost – by the beauty of the natural world, and also by its sometimes dramatic ugliness – that I simply was under a compulsion to write about it."[3] After graduating, she took a correspondence course in general writing from the London School of Journalism, and by the summer of

1934, when she travelled to England, she had published several poems in newspapers and magazines in Canada, the United States, and England.[4]

The Victoria poetry group of the Canadian Authors Association (CAA) was the fertile environment in which Marriott's poetry took root. "The Victoria and Vancouver poetry groups of the CAA and of *Contemporary Verse* were the motivating forces behind her poetic production for roughly two decades – from the mid-1930s through the early 1950s," writes Dean Irvine. "Her history and her poetry call attention to the vital cord that connects the poet to her community and that, if severed, may lead to alienation, invisibility, even silence."[5] In later life, Marriott repeatedly affirmed that the association supported her as she discovered how to be a writer. "Poets in Victoria (I can't speak for Vancouver) in the 1930s pretty well belonged to the Canadian Authors' Association, mainly because of Doris Ferne's group. I had won several prizes in CAA contests around 1934, and became sort of the child prodigy of the CAA! I met Alan [Crawley] at Doris Ferne's – I *think* their mothers knew one another and that was how Doris heard of him. He came to a poetry group meeting."[6] Alan Crawley (1887–1975) was the discerning critic who first pressed Marriott to attempt a long poem, *The Wind Our Enemy* being the result. It was he whom Dorothy Livesay, Ferne, Floris Clark McLaren, and Marriott would choose to be the editor of *Contemporary Verse* when they founded it in 1941 as a Canadian equivalent to *Poetry* (Chicago).

The Victoria poetry group also furnished the occasion through which Marriott met another influential supporter of the arts, Ira Dilworth (1894–1962). In 1938, Dilworth was teaching English at the University of British Columbia, conducting the Vancouver Bach Choir, and beginning a distinguished career with the CBC. He would soon befriend the artist Emily Carr and help her to publish her well-known book of stories *Klee Wyck* (Toronto: Oxford University Press, 1941).[7] Marriott acknowledged him for introducing her to *The Waste Land*: "One of the CAA ladies (most were ladies!) had a meeting at her house at which Ira gave a reading of T.S. Eliot's 'The Wasteland'. The Keats and Shelley et al I'd had at school fell away into the past and I sat there truly enthralled. I thought 'The Fire Sermon' the most wonderful piece of writing I had ever heard."[8] These encounters with Crawley and Dilworth at CAA meetings are prominent in prior accounts of Marriott's career.[9]

Who, however, was Ferne? The "ladies" whom Marriott mentions were clearly the ones who sustained the Victoria poetry group as an institution.

Frances Ebbs-Canavan, Hermia Harris Fraser, M. Eugenie Perry, Ferne – all of them sold poems to newspapers, all of them appeared in the *Canadian Poetry Magazine*, and all of them published Chap-Books shortly before or after Marriott. "The first time I remember hearing of the Ryerson Chapbooks was [when] one of the CAA [members], Frances Ebbs-Canavan, had 'Harvest of Dreams' published in that series," Marriott later recollected. "It was considered a great accomplishment."[10] The publications by these women constitute the primary context in which Marriott learned her art.

Doris Maude Ferne (1894–1986) was, in Marriott's words, "an excellent leader of the Victoria Poetry Group (CAA) in the 30s."[11] She had been born in London (Richmond) but had spent most of her life in Canada, living for a time in Fort McLeod, Alberta, before settling definitively at 380 King George Terrace in Oak Bay, Victoria. Her husband, Ernest George Ferne, was a storekeeper, and they had at least two children. The family attended the Christian Science church.[12] Newspapers and magazines on both sides of the Atlantic published Ferne's poetry. She won prizes in national competitions and appeared in the pages of *Saturday Night* magazine, *Canadian Forum*, *Canadian Poetry Magazine*, and, later, *Contemporary Verse*.[13] One poem – "Memory," a Shakespearean sonnet – caught the eye of anthologists and became Ferne's international calling card. Alan Crawley chose it for the 1936 *Victoria Poetry Chapbook*, the yearbook self-published by the Victoria poetry group. It then found its way into *New Harvesting*, a national anthology published in Toronto by the Macmillan Company of Canada in 1938, and also into the massive, deluxe *Muse Anthology of Modern Poetry*, which Carlyle Straub published in New York with the support of several wealthy patrons in the same year.[14] Despite such accomplishments in periodicals and anthologies, only two slim books of her own would be the yield for posterity: *Ebb Tide*, a Ryerson Poetry Chap-Book (no. 93, 1941), and *Paschal Lamb* (Toronto: Macmillan Co of Canada, 1946). Nevertheless, Ferne's activity as a poet in the 1930s and '40s helped Marriott to orient herself as a writer.

Opening Ferne's *Ebb Tide* quickly reveals the poetics shared between the older and the younger woman.[15] The title poem, "Ebb Tide," like Marriott's *The Wind Our Enemy*, is an unflinching look at the darkness of current events. The speaker remembers sitting at the death bed of her husband, a veteran of the First World War, shortly after the outbreak of the Second. In the second half of the poem, she finds that she cannot countenance the hope implicit in his last words:

> When the night grew pale as a moth you raised your head
> And gave me one clear look. "The dawn" you said.
> The dawn for you? For us the sky is grey
> And desolate yet, heavy with sullen thunder
> Of hungry guns you thought you helped to still
> Just two decades ago. You lived to wonder
> What was the use of those tormented years
> If all's to do again? Body and will
> To be cut to the age-old pattern of blood and tears
> Designed by war. It is false dawn,
> Faint as the line of foam on this ebb tide,
> Quiet as your silent heart. When at your side
> Stood our growing lad the light grew dim.
> I did not grieve for you. I wept for him.[16]

What blots out her faith is fear for their son. He should be the gleam of new life and his mother's comfort at this moment of generational transition; instead, thunderheads are gathering to extinguish his light. The central metaphor of the poem, the light of hope, recalls Psalm 112: "Even in darkness light dawns for the upright, for those who are gracious and compassionate and righteous." The title of the poem points to the ebbing of this light from a woman's life and from Canada generally in the early years of the Second World War.

The Wind Our Enemy treats the prior catastrophe of the Dust Bowl with equal grimness. Each section enacts a reversal, delivering a fresh sting of disappointment. A promising field of wheat is the last in years.[17] A woman's daydreams about a new dress are dispelled by her husband's announcement of a failed crop (part 3). Reassuring predictions of rain next year decay into bitter jokes about empty clouds (part 4). Recollections of galloping colts cede to the image of a mare, bloated with thistle, stumbling to her death (part 5) – and so on. A pessimistic realism thus pervades Marriott's poem as it does Ferne's, lending gravity to both as descriptions of the modern world.

At the same time, both poems leave open a possibility of hope. "Ebb Tide" is a dramatic monologue, voicing the speaker's anguish in a way that leaves one wondering about the other characters. What did her husband see? What does her son feel? Its metaphorical terms imply balance. Dawn must follow night, as high tide follows low. *The Wind Our Enemy,* similarly, interprets the characters' suffering through a religious subtext, as Anne Geddes Bailey traces.[18] The characters may be "Dust-blinded to the staring parable," but the impersonal narrator sees "Each wind-splintered timber like a pain-bent Cross" (6, part 8, ll. 9–10). The penultimate section inverts the pattern of disappointment:

> The sun goes down. Earth like a thick black coin
> Leans its round rim against the yellowed sky.
> The air cools. Kerosene lamps are filled and lit
> In dusty windows. Tired bodies crave to lie
> In bed forever. Chores are done at last.
> A thin horse neighs drearily. The chickens drowse,
> Replete with grasshoppers that have gnawed and scraped
> Shrivelled garden-leaves. No sound from the gaunt cows.
> Poverty, hand in hand with fear, two great
> Shrill-jointed skeletons stride loudly out
> Across the pitiful fields, none to oppose.
> Courage is roped with hunger, chained with doubt.
> Only against the yellow sky, a part
> Of the jetty silhouette of barn and house
> Two figures stand, heads close, arms locked,
> And suddenly some spirit seems to rouse
> And gleam, like a thin sword, tarnished, bent,
> But still shining in the spared beauty of moon,
> As his strained voice says to her, "We're not licked yet!
> It must rain again – it *will!* Maybe – soon –"
> (7, part 9, ll. 1–20)

In the emotional texture of both poems, hope needs only a sliver of possibility to assert itself.

Beyond their nuanced realism, Ferne's and Marriott's poems are similar in their technique, deploying metre and rhyme comparably. Both take iambic pentameter as an appropriate basis for their solemn topics but consciously depart from it for pointed effect. "Ebb Tide" uses tetrameter and caesura to emphasize the insight that "It is false dawn." Lines of trimeter create silence, accenting "death" (1, l. 8) and "the embracing sea" (1, l. 12). In the same way, *The Wind Our Enemy* distinguishes the "Two figures stand[ing], heads close, arms locked," the tetrameter of that line contrasting with the surrounding pentameter. Part 5 also works its contrast through rhythm. Whereas the thrill of riding a two-year-old colt is rendered in lines of anapestic tetrameter, the listless feeding of the sickly horses returns to a slow pentameter. In part 9, caesura and enjambment may obscure the end rhyme, but it is there in every second line, underlying the forlorn statements in a gentle order. "Ebb Tide" begins with the same effect, and alternates lines of rhyme, but hardens into decisive couplets at its mid-point and its end to convey the speaker's grief.

The shared techniques in Ferne's and Marriott's poems suggest the poetic understanding that flourished in the Victoria poetry group of the Canadian Authors Association. Both *The Wind Our Enemy* and "Ebb Tide" eschew lyric fantasy to engage major issues in the news realistically. Both give voice to human suffering in a perceptible if subtle Biblical framework. Neither uses end rhyme automatically: rhyme structures both poems by design, and many lines are left unrhymed. Both explore the relation between beat and rhythm in metrical lines of varying length. These similarities manifest a shared poetics. In holding meetings at her house, arranging readings, discussing form, and introducing people to one another, Ferne sustained conditions that were favourable to poetry. She encouraged and promoted Marriott as an author.

THE WIND OUR ENEMY remains Marriott's best-known poem and still defines her as an author in the eyes of most today despite the calibre of later, longer works, such as "The Rose and the Dagger" in *Aqua* (Toronto: Wolsak and Wynn, 1991). It is therefore all the more striking that the success of Chap-Book no. 80 derived from much more than Marriott's genius. The poem's publishing history invites us further to grasp the ways in which its – and hence Marriott's – authority was constructed socially through a series of interactions. After Ferne's, another pivotal contribution was J.F.B. Livesay's. He consecrated the poem as an authentic and political portrayal of the Prairies despite the fact that Marriott had not been born or raised there. Assuming the role of literary agent, Livesay added the value of his sympathetic reading to Marriott's text, enhancing it and securing its publication on terms that were unusually favourable to the novice writer.

Marriott herself summarized the writing and publishing of *The Wind Our Enemy* in a retrospective letter in 1974. Her account goes right to the heart of the matter of the poem's authority. Marriott explains that, although her home was in Victoria, she witnessed the drought on the Prairies first-hand during a visit to her extended family at their farm near Wiseton, Saskatchewan, a small town 150 km southwest of Saskatoon:

> Anyway – briefly, the poem happened this way: I was born and raised in Victoria, an only child who [w]ent to a private school and lived in quite comfortable circumstances. In the late 1930s I had an illness of several months' duration and afterwards went to my aunt's farm in Saskatchewan to convalesce in the more bracing atmosphere – and was confronted by the drought and its attendant poverty. After the greenness of Victoria, the barren prairie and the blowing dust were a tremendous emotional shock.
>
> I wasn't really aware of this shock at the time, however; I felt very distressed by the hard times my relatives and their neighbours were having – but on the other hand, I was having such a wonderful time in a large, young family group that my main feelings were great enjoyment and happiness. And it was a time of "making your own fun" – dances in the school houses, horseback rides, picnics, local stampedes – all new and delightful to me.
>
> However, when I got home to Victoria, my subconscious reactions to the drought scenes surfaced, I guess. – Also, I was very frustrated by the indifference of people on the coast, and in eastern Canada (as I learned from letters and newspapers) to the <u>human</u> situation on the prairies. Anyway, when I'd been home three weeks or so, one day just as we (my mother and I) were sitting down to lunch "The Wind –" began to form in my mind and I wrote most of it right then, on odd bits of paper – I still remember my mother cautioning me not to get ink on the clean white tablecloth!
>
> Within the next day or two I had added more stanzas, mainly I think the horse section and the dance section – the latter a deliberate attempt to add variety with a different metre – and did very little revising. In fact, what I did change in a minor way I regretted later.
>
> I belonged to a poetry group at that time, led by Doris Ferne, and Dorothy Livesay's father, J.F.B. Livesay came to Victoria and Mrs Ferne, knowing his interest in poetry, showed him "The Wind –" and he took it back to Toronto with him and showed it to Lorne Pierce of the Ryerson Press who published it as a chapbook.[19]

The details of this account are irresistible: colliding with the reality of the drought, brooding on the poem subconsciously, giving into a rush of inspiration, ignoring the domestic concerns of meals and linens. Still, one notes Marriott's emphasis on her immersion. Her visit to the Prairies was "a wonderful time in a large, young family group." The "atmosphere" was not only "bracing" but embracing. Before long, she was at home there enough to feel "very frustrated" by the rest of the country's political impassiveness to the hardship on the Prairies. Did Marriott have the authority to write about the Dust Bowl on the Prairies? The account addresses this question.

Correspondence from the 1930s confirms Marriott's recollection that Doris Ferne's providing J.F.B. Livesay with a copy of the poem was instrumental in the publishing of *The Wind Our Enemy*. Marriott had submitted it to the Macmillan Company of Canada and the *New Republic* in New York, but both rejected it. Its fortunes changed when Ferne read the poem aloud at a Saturday evening meeting of the Victoria poetry group in the fall of 1938.[20] The author herself was not in attendance, but two of the listeners were J.F.B. Livesay, the general manager of the Canadian Press, and his daughter, Dorothy, and their enthusiasm for the poem was so great that Ferne was moved to give the former the typescript at the end of the meeting. What appears to have struck them so favourably was its political potential. On his way back to Toronto, J.F.B. Livesay wrote to Marriott and offered to find a publisher:

> I am sorry indeed you were not there that Saturday evening as I was much interested to see the author of so fine a piece of work. Have you done anything more of this epic kind – lyrics no doubt?
>
> I take it I can talk it over with some of our publishers and Ned Pratt – I fancy he would like to have it in the [Canadian] Poetry Mag[azine]. It's very little longer than Dee's [Dorothy Livesay's] "Day and Night." Things are bad in the publishing world – but would you consider a chap-book, tho' it's the sort of impermanent compromise one doesn't like. I'll let you know of any prospect. My interest lies in 17 years on the prairie – the good years when we'd never heard of drought – and yours seems to me the most authentic voice we've heard out of the drought years. It is a voice the people of Ontario and the Maritime[s] must be made to heed. If it is propaganda, it is no doubt undeliberate and that makes it the more valuable.[21]

As the word "propaganda" makes clear, what J.F.B. Livesay saw in *The Wind Our Enemy* was the capacity to stir the nation to action to redress the farmers' suffering across the West. The value he grasped in the text was prospective and utilitarian: it would help to shape policy by spreading a message that Canadians in other regions "must be made to heed." When she recalled this moment ten years later, Dorothy Livesay likewise expressed her gratification in discovering an author oriented, like her, toward social justice: "Here was a writer setting down in unfaltering, vivid language all that the long years of drought had meant to the Canadian prairie folk. Here moreover was a Canadian writer interesting herself, not in maple trees or trilliums, but in a sociological study of the people."[22] Both Livesays recognized *The Wind Our Enemy* as a good poem in political terms.

J.F.B. Livesay's letter also manifests the reader's power in arbitrating the truth of a text. Without knowing the measure of Marriott's link to the region, he invested the typescript with his own life, his "17 years on the prairie," including his daughter's birth in Winnipeg in 1909. He later asked, "how and when did you get your experience[?]" and still later, "You know I'm interested to know how you came to write it, having lived many years on the prairie,"[23] but Marriott was not yet ready to provide a full explanation. On the strength of his own reading of the poem, then, J.F.B. Livesay decided that Marriott's was "the most authentic voice we've heard out of the drought years." Falling back on his own judgment, he helped to authorize Marriott's poem.

If J.F.B. Livesay had not appraised *The Wind Our Enemy* as potent and authentic, he would never have taken the next step – that of becoming the poem's champion in Toronto. He had helped his daughter self-publish her first book with the Macmillan Company of Canada, and with this experience in mind he intended now to hold the trade to the standard of financing and marketing Marriott's edition, a mode of publishing from which the Ryerson Press and other Canadian publishers had a tendency to slip away: "As to a Ryerson Press chapbook, quite the wrong idea. I'm dead ag[ain]st any 'guaranteed' publication – it's immoral. The publisher must take the risk if the thing is to be authentic."[24] Here again emphasis falls on the authenticity that derives from other people besides the author: in lieu of the writer buying her way into print, the publisher must buy into, and the public must buy, her book for it to be true.

On 12 December 1938, J.F.B. Livesay negotiated the publication of *The Wind Our Enemy* on a royalty basis:

> Dr Lorne Pierce read your poem today and as I expected was immensely struck with it and said at once he would publish it. He is writing to you.
>
> He is quite deaf and I did not probe deep what he had in mind, but any way the Ryerson Press will take the risk. He agreed chap books are ephemeral and he has in mind a respectable sized little book. He observed rightly that a first book of poetry is apt to fall flat unless the poet has become fairly well known through periodical publication and her friends will push it. Young poets approach a publisher with a bunch of lyrics, freshly decorating well worn themes (trailing arbutus!) and we cannot throw away $500^{00} bringing out a book of that kind – but here is something authentic, in touch with the realities of this day – something like that was his comment.
>
> So his approach to you will be from a standpoint of real enthusiasm, prepared to do a good job. If you care to let me know what he says I may be able to give you a bit of advice.[25]

The royalty arrangement was not unprecedented in the Chap-Books, but until now it had been rare. For reasons of prestige or favouritism, Pierce had offered it to a handful of other poets, such as Charles G.D. Roberts and members of his family, Lilian Leveridge, and Susan Frances Harrison (see table 4.1). Something seems to have changed in 1938, however, for Ryerson began much more frequently to offer contributors a royalty of 10 per cent and six free copies, and this pattern lasted for the war's duration. (In 1946, the norm shifted again, to the offer of complimentary copies in lieu of all royalties.) J.F.B. Livesay's urging Pierce to "take the risk" seems to have been effective against the latter's protests that "we cannot throw away $500^{00} bringing out [every novice poet's] book." Whether or not this conversation was what changed the terms of publication for subsequent Chap-Book poets, it worked for Marriott. The publishing agreement specified that "The Publisher will pay to the Author a royalty of ten per cent. on the retail price of all copies sold," with no reference to any payment or financial guarantee by the author.[26] Pierce, an advocate for authors from the first, needed little reminding but some nudging to offer a better contract. J.F.B. Livesay's "bit of advice" to Marriott – that is, his informal work on her behalf as her literary agent – delivered that nudge.

A "respectable sized little book" may have been briefly contemplated, but plans were soon in place for a Chap-Book. "It is a great thrill to get the news that the Ryerson Press will publish my long poem," Marriott wrote to Pierce; "I gather from your letter that you are planning to publish just the one long poem in the Chapbook. But on the chance that you might care to see some of my shorter verse I am sending you a selection under separate cover."[27] *The Wind Our Enemy* was neither the first nor the last Chap-Book to consist of a single poem. R.D. Cumming's *Paul Pero* (no. [29], 1928) preceded it, as did H.L. Huxtable's *The Fountain* (no. [40], 1929), a verse drama performed by the Women's Art Association of Canada in Toronto in 1929. M. Eugenie Perry's *Hearing a Far Call* (no. 102, 1943) came a few years after, and in later years there followed Dorothy Livesay's *Call My People Home* (no. 143, 1950) and Fred Cogswell's *Testament of Cresseid* (no. 168, 1957), translated from Robert Henryson's Middle English. J.F.B. Livesay continued to encourage Marriott to aim for a longer book with a variety of poems – "a chap book isn't so hot and I'm glad you've sent along some more stuff"[28] – but his opposition to a Chap-Book ceased with Ryerson's promise to finance it, and Pierce was clearly favourable to publishing long poems in the series. Although cut from her first Chap-Book, several of the shorter poems that Marriott submitted ultimately appeared in her third, *Salt Marsh*.

The Wind Our Enemy was typeset in January 1939, and through the proofreading stage Marriott was obliged to negotiate with the others now involved in the publication in order to have the poem appear as she wished. After going through the galleys, she wrote, "I see that my original manuscript has had some changes made in it, one of them being the shifting of the italicized first and last sections of the poem from the centre to the left of the page in line with the other sections. Personally I feel that it looks more effective in the centre and have so marked the proofs."[29] Against this request, the press maintained the left justification of sections 1 and 10, albeit with an indent. "In the twenty-third line of [section 5] I originally had two dashes, one of which has been deleted in the typewritten copy," Marriott continued. "I am deleting the other, as in the present form the meaning of the line is confused. It should now read, 'Nellie the kid's pet's gone, boys.'"[30] The editor further corrected this line to read "Nellie the kids' pet's gone, boys" (4, part 5, l. 23). Marriott

TABLE 4.1
Terms of publication for the Ryerson Poetry Chap-Books

Year	Series no.	Author	Title	Terms of publication	Print run	Price
1926	3	Munro, Kathryn [Tupper]	*Forfeit and Other Poems*	Author guarantees press against loss after 1 year ($85). Royalty (10%). Free copies (12)	500	$0.50
1926	6	Newson, W.V.	*The Vale of Luxor*	Author guarantees press against loss after 1 year ($70). Free copies (12)	250	$0.50
1926	8	Stevenson, Lionel	*A Pool of Stars*	Author guarantees press against loss after 1 year ($85). Free copies (12)	250	$0.60
1926	9	Brewer, Alice	*Spring in Savary*	Author guarantees press against loss after 1 year ($85). Free copies (12)	250	$0.60
1926	10	Cox, Leo	Seventeen Poems [*Sheep-Fold*]	Author guarantees press against loss after 1 year ($55). Royalty (10%). Free copies (6)	250	$0.50
1926	11	Riddehough, Geoffrey B.	*The Prophet's Man*	Author guarantees press against loss after 1 year ($70). Royalty (10%)	250	$0.50
1926	12	Joynes, Agnes	*The Shepherd of the Hills*	Author guarantees press against loss after 1 year ($55). Royalty (10%). Free copies (6)	250	$0.50
1926	13	Leveridge, Lilian	*A Breath of the Woods*	Advance royalty (10%). Free copies (6)	400	$0.60
1927	14	Watt, Frederick	*Vagrant*	Author guarantees press against loss after 1 year ($105). Royalty (10%) payable if edition sells out. Free copies (6)	250	$0.60

Year	Series no.	Author	Title	Terms of publication	Print run	Price
1927	15	Hanlon, John [Mitchell]	*Songs*	Author guarantees press against loss after 1 year ($125). Royalty (10%) payable if edition sells out. Free copies (6)	250	$0.75
1927	17	Benson, Nathaniel	*Twenty and After*	Author guarantees press against loss after 1 year ($105). Free copies (6)	250	$0.60
1927	18	Fraser, Alexander Louis	*By Cobequid Bay*	Author guarantees press against loss after 1 year ($70)	250	$0.50
1927	19	Mason, Guy	*The Cry of Insurgent Youth*	Author guarantees press against loss after 1 year ($85). Royalty (10%). Free copies (6)	250	$0.60
1927	20	Coleman, H.T.J.	*Cockle-Shell and Sandal-Shoon*	Author guarantees press against loss after 1 year ($125). Free copies (6)	250	$0.75
1927	21	Isles-Brown, Esme	*Honeysuckle and Other Poems [Twelve Poems]*	Author guarantees press against loss after 1 year ($55). Royalty (10%). Free copies (6)	250	$0.50
1927	22	Roberts, Gostwick [Dorothy]	*Songs for Swift Feet*	Royalty (10%). Free copies (12)	250	$0.50
1927	23	Catley, Elaine M.	*Ecstasy and Other Poems*	Author guarantees press against loss after 1 year ($55). Royalty (10%). Free copies (6)	250	$0.50
1927	24	Hanlon, John [Mitchell]	*Other Songs*	Author guarantees press against loss after 1 year ($155). Royalty (10%). Free copies (12)	250	$0.75
1927	25	Newson, W.V.	*Waifs of the Mind*	Author guarantees press against loss after 1 year ($185). Royalty (10%). Free copies (6)	500	$0.75

1928	32	Harrison, Susan Frances	*Later Poems and New Villanelles*	Royalty (10%). Free copies (12)	250	$0.50
1931	53	Guise, Mary Ellen	*Blown Leaves* [*Pennies on my Palm*]	Author pays ($20). Author guarantees press against loss after 1 year ($55)	150	$0.50
1931	54	Hughes, Aubrey Dean	*Argosies at Dawn*	Author pays ($20). Author agrees to purchase at cost all unsold copies after 1 year	150	$0.5
1938	78	Casey, Michael T.	*Sonnets and Sequence*	Author guarantees press against loss after 1 year ($75.60). Royalty (10%). Free copies (6)	250	$0.60
1938	79	Smalacombe, John [Mackay, L.A.]	*Viper's Bugloss*	Royalty (10%). Free copies (6)	250	$0.60
1939	80	Marriott, Anne	*The Wind Our Enemy*	Royalty (10%). Free copies (6)	250	$0.50
1939	82	Leveridge, Lilian	*Lyrics and Sonnets*	Author pays ($185). Royalty (53% = 40¢/copy)	500	$0.75
1941	89	Marriott, Anne	*Calling Adventurers!*	Royalty (10%). Free copies (6)	250	$0.50
1941	90	Matheson, Mary [Nasmyth]	*Out of the Dusk*	Author pays ($30 = 100 copies @ 30¢). Royalty (10%) thereafter. Free copies (6)	250	$0.50
1941	92	Carsley, Sara	*The Artisan*	Royalty (10%). Free copies (6)	250	$0.50
1941	93	Ferne, Doris	*Ebb Tide*	Author pays ($30 = 75 copies @ 40¢). Royalty (10%) thereafter. Free copies (6)	250	$0.50
1941	95	Wensley, Amelia	*At Summer's End*	Author pays ($24.90 = 83 copies @ 30¢). Royalty (10%) thereafter. Free copies (6)	250	$0.50

Year	Series no.	Author	Title	Terms of publication	Print run	Price
1942	98	Edelstein, Hyman	Spirit of Israel	Author pays ($45 = 150 copies @ 30¢). Royalty (10%) thereafter. Free copies (6)	250	$0.50
1942	99	Colman, Mary Elizabeth	For This Freedom Too	Royalty (10%). Free copies (6)	250	$0.60
1942	100	Marriott, Anne	Salt Marsh	Royalty (10%). Free copies (6)	500	$5.00
1943	101	Eaton, Evelyn	Birds before Dawn	Royalty (10%). Free copies (6)	250	$0.60
1943	102	Perry, M. Eugenie	Hearing a Far Call	Royalty (10%). Free copies (6)	250	$0.60
1943	103	Benson, Irene Chapman	Earthbound and Other Poems [Journey into Yesterday]	Royalty (10%). Free copies (6)	250	$0.60
1944	104	Laurence, Elsie Fry	Rearguard and Other Poems	Royalty (10%). Free copies (6)	250	$0.60
1944	106	Call, Frank Oliver	Sonnets for Youth	Royalty (10%). Free copies (6)	250	$0.50
1944	107	Campbell, Austin	They Shall Build Anew	Royalty (10%). Free copies (6)	250	$0.50
1944	108	Sister Maura	Rhythm Poems	Royalty (10%). Free copies (6)	250	$0.50
1945	109	Fraser, Hermia Harris	Songs of the Western Islands	Royalty (10%). Free copies (6)	250	$0.60
1945	110	Chalmers, Monica Roberts	And in the Time of Harvest	Royalty (10%). Free copies (6)	250	$0.60

1945	113	Howard, Dorothy	When I Turn Home	Author pays ($50 = 200 copies @ 25¢). Free copies (12) in lieu of royalty	300	$0.50
1946	115	Rashley, R.E.	Voyageur and Other Poems	Free copies (30) in lieu of royalty	250	$0.75
1946	116	Whalley, George	Poems: 1939–1945	Free copies (30) in lieu of royalty	250	$0.75
1946	117	Campbell, Marjorie Freeman	Merry-Go-Round	Free copies (30) in lieu of royalty	250	$0.75
1946	121	Hedges, Doris	The Flower in the Dusk	Free copies (60) in lieu of royalty	500	$0.50
1946	122	MacDonald, Goodridge	The Dying General and Other Poems	Free copies (30) in lieu of royalty	250	$0.50
1947	123	Perry, M. Eugenie	Song in the Silence	Free copies (60) in lieu of royalty	500	$0.75
1947	125	Hedges, Doris	Crisis	Free copies (60) in lieu of royalty	500	$0.75
1947	126	Howard, Dorothy	As the River Runs	Author pays ($50 = 200 copies @ 25¢). Free copies (12) in lieu of royalty	300	$0.50
1947	127	Nichols, Ruby	Songs from Then and Now	Free copies (30) in lieu of royalty	250	$0.50
1948	128	Pratt, Lenore	Midwinter Thaw	Free copies (30) in lieu of royalty	250	$0.60
1948	129	Bartole, Genevieve	Figure in the Rain	Free copies (33) in lieu of royalty	250	$0.50
1948	130	Coulby, Margaret	The Bitter Fruit and Other Poems	Free copies (30) in lieu of royalty	250	$0.60
1948	131	Levine, Albert Norman	Myssium and Other Poems	Advance royalty (10% on 200 copies)	250	$0.60

Year	Series no.	Author	Title	Terms of publication	Print run	Price
1948	133	Stringer, Arthur	*New York Nocturnes*	Author guarantees press against loss after 1 year ($114). Royalty (10%)	500	$0.75
1949	134	Campbell, Marjorie Freeman	*High on a Hill*	Author pays (20 copies @ wholesale price). Free copies (30) in lieu of royalty	250	$0.75
1949	135	Edelstein, Hyman	*The Last Mathematician*	Author pays ($100 = 200 copies @ 50¢). Royalty (10%) thereafter	250	$0.75
1949	136	Saunders, Thomas	*Scrub Oak*	Free copies (30) in lieu of royalty	250	$0.75
1950	138	MacDonald, Goodridge	*Beggar Makes Music*	Author pays ($70 = 100 copies @ 70¢). Free copies (30) in lieu of royalty	300	$1.00
1950	139	Tupper, Kathryn Munro	*Tanager Feather*	Free copies (30) in lieu of royalty	300	$1.00
1950	140	Bourinot, Arthur S.	*The Treasures of the Snow*	Free copies (30) in lieu of royalty	250	$1.00
1950	142	Hale, Katherine	*The Flute and Other Poems*	Free copies (50) in lieu of royalty	500	$1.00
1950	143	Livesay, Dorothy	*Call My People Home*	Free copies (50) in lieu of all royalty	500	$1.00
1951	144	Thomson, Theresa E.	*Silver Shadows*	Free copies (30) in lieu of royalty	250	$1.00
1951	145	Brewster, Elizabeth	*East Coast*	Free copies (30) in lieu of royalty	250	$1.00
1951	146	Souster, Raymond	*City Hall Street*	Free copies (30) in lieu of royalty	250	$1.00

1952	147	Dudek, Louis	The Searching Image	Royalty (10%: paid in 25 free copies and lump sum of $15)	350	$1.00
1952	148	Farley, Tom	It Was a Plane	Royalty (10%: paid in 25 free copies and lump sum of $15)	350	$1.00
1952	149	Hazelton, Ruth Cleaves	Mint and Willow	Royalty (10%: paid in 25 free copies and lump sum of $15)	350	$1.00
1952	150	Lazechko-Haas, Myra	Viewpoint	Royalty (10%: paid in 25 free copies and lump sum of $15)	350	$1.00
1953	151	Rashley, R.E.	Portrait and Other Poems	Free copies (30) in lieu of royalty	350	$1.00
1954	153	Brewster, Elizabeth	Lillooet	Free copies (18) in lieu of royalty	150	$1.00
1955	157	Purdy, Alfred W.	Running Colours [Pressed on Sand]	Free copies (18) in lieu of royalty	250	$1.00
1955	158	MacDonald, Goodridge	Compass Reading and Others	Free copies (18) in lieu of royalty	250	$1.00
1955	159	Thomson, Theresa E., and Don W. Thomson	Silver Light	Free copies (18) in lieu of royalty	350	$1.00
1955	162	Adams, Myrtle Reynolds	Remember Together	Author pays ($100 = 100 copies @ $1). Free copies (18) in lieu of royalty	250	$1.00
1956	163	Henry, Marion Kathleen	Centaurs of the Wind	Free copies (18) in lieu of royalty	250	$1.00
1956	164	Cogswell, Fred	The Haloed Tree	Free copies (18) in lieu of royalty	250	$1.00
1956	165	Bunner, Freda Newton	Orphan and Other Poems	Free copies (18) in lieu of royalty	250	$1.00

Year	Series no.	Author	Title	Terms of publication	Print run	Price
1956	166	Nichols, Ruby	*Symphony*	Free copies (18) in lieu of royalty	250	$1.00
1956	167	Pratt, Lenore	*Birch Light*	Free copies (18) in lieu of royalty	250	$1.00
1957	168	Cogswell, Fred (trans.)	*The Testament of Cresseid*	Free copies (18) in lieu of royalty	250	$1.00
1957	169	Fraser, Hermia Harris	*The Arrow-Maker's Daughter and Other Haida Chants*	Free copies (18) in lieu of royalty	250	$1.00
1957	170	MacDonald, Goodridge	*Recent Poems*	Free copies (18) in lieu of royalty	250	$1.00
1957	171	Thomson, Theresa E., and Don W. Thomson	*Myth and Monument*	Author pays (100 = 200 copies @ 50¢). Free copies (20) in lieu of royalty	350	$1.00
1957	172	Finnigan, Joan	*Through the Glass, Darkly*	Free copies (18) in lieu of royalty	250	$1.00
1957	173	Bayer, Mary Elizabeth	*Of Diverse Things*	Free copies (18) in lieu of royalty	250	$1.00
1957	174	Brewster, Elizabeth	*Roads and Other Poems*	Free copies (18) in lieu of royalty	250	$1.00
1957	176	Reynolds, Ella Julia	*Samson in Hades and Other Poems*	Free copies (18) in lieu of royalty	250	$1.00
1958	177	Adams, Myrtle Reynolds	*Morning on My Street*	Author pays ($100 = 100 copies @ $1). Free copies (18) in lieu of royalty	250	$1.00
1958	179	Saunders, Thomas	*Something of a Young World's Dying*	Free copies (18) in lieu of royalty	250	$1.00

Year	No.	Author	Title	Notes	Copies	Price
1958	180	Swayze, Fred	*And See Penelope Plain*	Free copies (18) in lieu of royalty	250	$1.00
1959	181	Bayer, Mary Elizabeth	*Overture [Faces of Love] Poems*	Free copies (18) in lieu of royalty	250	$1.00
1959	182	Collie, Michael	*In Her Mind Carrying*	Free copies (18) in lieu of royalty	250	$1.00
1959	183	Harden, Verna Loveday	*The Heart Is Fire*	Free copies (18) in lieu of royalty	250	$1.00
1959	184	Lockead, Douglas	*River & Realm*	Free copies (18) in lieu of royalty	250	$1.00
1959	185	Thomson, Theresa E., and Don W. Thomson	*The Crafte So Longe to Lerne*	Free copies (18) in lieu of royalty	250	$1.00
1959	186	Purdy, Alfred W.	*Moon Lake and Other Poems*	Free copies (18) in lieu of royalty	250	$1.00
1959	187	Rashley, R.E.	*Poems*	Free copies (18) in lieu of royalty	250	$1.00
1959	188	Wyle, Florence	*The Varsity Chapbook*	Free copies (18) in lieu of royalty	250	$1.00
1959	189	Colombo, John Robert (ed.)	*It Is All Around*	Free copies (22: 1 each to 14 contributors, 4 to designer, 4 to editor) in lieu of royalty. Publisher pays designer $10	500	$1.00
1960	189	Lockead, Douglas	*The McGill Chapbook*	Free copies (18) in lieu of royalty	250	$1.00
1959	190	Kaye, Leslie (ed.)	*Skirmish with Fact*	Free copies (22: 1 to each of 13 contributors, 4 to designer, 5 to editor) in lieu of royalty	500	$1.00
1960	192	Collie, Michael	*Skirmish with Fact*	Free copies (18) in lieu of royalty	250	$1.00
1960	194	West, Paul	*The Spellbound Horses*	Free copies (18) in lieu of royalty	250	$1.00

Year	Series no.	Author	Title	Terms of publication	Print run	Price
1960	195	Matheson, Mary Nasmyth	*Autumn Affluence*	Free copies (18) in lieu of royalty	250	$1.00
1960	196	Swayze, Fred	*In the Egyptian Gallery*	Free copies (18) in lieu of royalty	250	$1.00
1960	197	Adams, Myrtle Reynolds	*To Any Spring*	Author pays ($100 = 100 copies @ $1). Free copies (18) in lieu of royalty	250	$1.00
1960	198	Bayer, Mary Elizabeth	*The Silver Swan: An Epithalamion*	Free copies (18) in lieu of royalty	250	$1.00
1960	199	Acorn, Milton	*The Brain's the Target*	Free copies (18) in lieu of royalty	250	$1.00

This table compiles information from the agreements between Chap-Book authors and the Ryerson Press preserved in the Ryerson Press Collection, Ryerson University Library.

suggested that the cover be grey, feeling it suited the tone of the poem, but Ryerson chose a shade of red. Most importantly, Marriott struggled to control the lineation at the end of the poem: "In the last section, number ten, the person who edited the original manuscript moved the last word, 'wind' up on to the previous line. It is important that 'wind' should be on a final line to itself, both for emphasis and to complete the pattern of the stanzas."[31] This request was respected.

J.F.B. Livesay also received a set of proofs, and his involvement in the poem continued. He asked his daughter to write a review, which he then distributed over the Canadian Press mail service.[32] According to Marriott, it created a stir: "A review of THE WIND OUR ENEMY appeared in the Victoria Daily Times last night, by Dorothy Livesay Macnair. I expect this is the one which Mr Livesay told me was to go out over the Canadian Press. A number of people whom I know noticed it, and I have had a lot of enquiries as to how soon the book will be in (one even from a policeman who gave my father his driver's test today!) so I hope that means that it will sell well."[33] Her words convey the excitement of being published and reviewed through a national print network. It was a step beyond Ferne's poetry circle, and a step short of the energy she would soon discover in radio.

At this point, Marriott began to run up against the Chap-Books' structural limitations. The Livesays' publicity efforts, generous though they were, were not coordinated with the publisher's, and the author soon discovered that marketing and sales were the weak link in the production cycle. "How are these Chapbooks sold?" Marriott asked. "Will it [*The Wind Our Enemy*] be handled in the usual way through the stores? ... Also, what about review copies? Do you send them to all the newspapers and magazines or do I assist with that?"[34] She was pleased to receive her six complimentary author copies in March 1939 but increasingly concerned about distribution:

> How soon will copies for sale be in Victoria? Do you know which stores will handle them? I am being asked continually where they can be got – the review in the local paper by Dorothy Livesay Macnair has raised a lot of interest and I believe quite a lot of books could be sold here if they arrive before that interest has died down.
>
> I was wondering if it was customary for the author to have some copies for sale to friends, etc. – I know one local writer [Frances Ebbs-Canavan] who had a Chapbook brought out by you who sold

all the copies herself and had none in the stores. But she paid for publication of the book herself, which of course makes it quite a different situation from mine. Would you let me know just what you are going to do about selling the book locally? I do feel it will be to our mutual advantage to get it here as soon as possible.[35]

Ultimately Marriott would go around to local booksellers herself to ask them to stock her book. Victoria Book and Stationery refused to order any copies on their own account but offered to display any that Marriott might care to leave with them. Diggon-Hibben, the firm that printed the *Victoria Poetry Chapbook*, agreed to order some copies, as did Spencer's, a department store.[36] In the first six months, Ryerson sold eighty-eight copies, yielding a royalty payment to the author of $4.26, and in addition Marriott sold forty copies privately.[37] Overall, the cost of printing the edition was fifty-five dollars and the full run of 250 copies sold out in 1942. Twenty-four promotional copies, including the six author copies, were given away. Of the remaining 226, 108 sold in 1939, 112 in 140, and the remaining six in the next two years. Per copy, the printing and binding cost was $0.22, the royalty $0.05, the wholesale price $0.375, and the retail price $0.50. The selling out of the edition thus implied a revenue of $23.73 for Ryerson and $11.30 in royalties for Marriott.[38] Even with the Livesays' extraordinary support and Marriott's considerable lengths to ensure maximum sales, the venture was a poor one in financial terms. The publication process, a mixture of honour and adversity, yielded a lasting poem but little money to either publisher or author.

Over the next six years, Marriott published three more books of poetry with Ryerson – two Chap-Books and a forty-two-page collection, *Sandstone* (1945), which reprinted poems such as *The Wind Our Enemy*. Notwithstanding little profits and weak marketing, the number of titles indicates that a relation of convenience and trust developed, and this relation must be counted as another factor in Marriott's social formation. Through its lyricism, variety, and especially its geographical imagination, her third Chap-Book, *Salt Marsh* (no. 100, 1942), shows best the convergence of her writing with the broader character of Pierce's series.

Only three poets authored more Ryerson Poetry Chap-Books than Marriott, and only eight as many as her.[39] This recurrence of contribution argues a pronounced compatibility between Marriott's and Pierce's poetics. Clearly, Ryerson offered an avenue of publication that worked for her.

TITLE	THE WIND OUR ENEMY				DATE March 1, 1939.				
AUTHOR	ANNE MARRIOTT								
LIST PRICE	50¢	DISCOUNT	25		ROYALTY	10 %			
DATE	PRINTED	BOUND	SHEET STOCK	BOOKS ON HAND		SALES			
					1938	1939	1940	1941	1942
May.1939	250	250			JAN.		105		
28/7/39				226	FEB.		5		
					MAR.		35	1	
					APR.		24		
					MAY		13		
					JUNE		16		
					JULY		3		
					AUG.		1		
					SEPT.		6	1	
					OCT.		5		
					NOV.				
					DEC.		5		
					TOTAL		108	112	0	0

TITLE:
AUTHOR:
AUTHOR CONTRACT: O.K.   ARTIST CONTRACT: VITA: Yes
FORMAT.: Chap-book
CLOTH: ....   PAPER: Paper binding
EDITION: 250   BIND: 250   PAGES: 8 + cover   ART:
MS. TO FACTORY: PUB'N DATE:
GALLEY PROOFS: PAGE PROOFS:

COSTS
PRINT: $55.00   REPRINT:
BIND: ART:
JACKET: PLATES:
EXTRAS: COPY'TS:

LIST PRICE
RETAIL:_____   .50
TRADE:____25%_____   .37½
  PRINT:)
  BIND:) .22
  ART:
  TAX:
  ROY.: .05
  EDIT.:
  PROM.:
         .27   .10

4.1 / (top) Front of the production card for *The Wind Our Enemy*, Ryerson Press Collection, Ryerson University Library.

4.2 / (bottom) Back of the production card for *The Wind Our Enemy*, Ryerson Press Collection, Ryerson University Library.

"The Ryerson chapbooks didn't set a very high standard (it seems now) and were certainly not too contemporary," wrote Marriott in 1984, "but they were a good way to get published, and get reviewed." This assessment is worth highlighting, because it is somewhat at odds with Marriott's involvement in *Contemporary Verse* during the same period. She helped found the magazine and contributed a number of poems to its pages, from "Prayer of the Disillusioned" (September 1941) to "Holiday Journal" (fall-winter 1950). Irvine is right to emphasize Marriott's ambivalent relationship to the little magazine: "Marriott's memory of her relationship with Crawley represents a clear difference from other women's memoirs of the editor of *Contemporary Verse*: McLaren, Livesay, and Ethel Wilson each contribute to the enduring portrait of his 'open and supportive manner' ... Apparently, however, Crawley shared with [John] Sutherland a certain distaste for ... Marriott's early attraction to the imagist lyric."[40] Marriott herself summed up her position in *Contemporary Verse* as a marginal one: "I was always on the fringe of the group (a lifetime position – never quite inside any group, I think)."[41] Counterbalancing Crawley's demands for another Eliotic long poem was Pierce's approval of the lyric of place, which *Salt Marsh* manifests in full colour.

Salt Marsh was printed in an edition of 500 copies, the maximum number for any Chap-Book. The collection demonstrates Marriott's interest in portraying Canadian landscapes, which for Pierce was one of poetry's prime functions. Of the thirty poems, over a third prioritize local descriptions. "Night Travellers," a miniature portrait of Canadian society during the Second World War, captures the experience of travelling immense distances by train. "Still I Cheat Myself" is chiefly a love lyric, but it operates through the speaker's emotional interpretation of landscapes: "Then in the futile hammering of the sea / Against iron headlands, heard my hopeless words / Beating against the stern cliffs of your will" (2, ll. 8–10). Moving freely in and out of iambic pentameter, "Woodyards in the Rain" imagistically describes a West Coast lumber yard, which the lyric speaker claims through her desire:

> The smell of woodyards in the rain is strong
> like six-foot lumberjacks with hairy chests
> and thick axe-leathered hands.
> The scent is raw, it slices through
> pale drizzle and thin mist,
> biting the sense.

I like to watch piled wetness dripping off
the yellow-brown stacked shingles, while behind
the smoke churns up in black revolving towers
from lean mill chimneys.
(3, ll. 1–10)

"City" is less geographical than its title implies, being a wry observation of the licentiousness attached to cities everywhere, but "Storm over a Garden" is more so, in that it equates the speaker's peaceful Canadian home with the cultivated space of poetry, both of which are threatened by the war:

So all this place, rich-leafed, quick-coloured, seen
Against a blackened world that madmen make
Ravaged with blood, seems thin and falsely sweet,
A brittle beauty one least touch would break.
(6, ll. 5–8)

"Tide Spell," "River Mouth," "Frozen River," and "Station" are all likewise based on the first-hand observation of specific points in Marriott's Victoria orbit, while the final poem in the collection, "Prairie Graveyard," depicts a place "lone / in the centre of the huge lone land and sky."

Most geographical of all is the poem that opens the book. "Salt Marsh" describes a Pacific coastal scene, and through this description it imagines the resurgence of art out of the land. The poem gives fresh expression to the literary nationalism that motivated Pierce, and harmonizes with the symbolism of the series cover with its interwoven pine tree and lyre (see chapter 2). Through colour imagery, Marriott heightens the life and colour of the place described:

Octopus-sprawls from tight-mud cliffs
held in strained root-hands of pine
to flat rumbling, rain-pitted sea
this half-caste child of shore and brine.

Twisted grey-slimed channels snake
through sedge-thick borders, silt, reeds,
bleary with grated leaves, spent foam
of distant rock-strong creeks, churned weeds

4.3 / Anne Marriott, *Salt Marsh*, Ryerson Poetry Chap-Books no. 100 (Toronto: Ryerson Press, 1942). In 1942, Thoreau MacDonald updated his father's design. This front cover shows the new design, which the series used until 1950 and then again between 1953 and 1955.

tide-forced back winding gullets. Clouds
crumble suddenly, rampant sun
strides the colour-roused salt marsh. Black-
threaded green pines, cliffs' grey-dun

back spread of rusty tuft-topped reeds
running bent-spined from low sea-gale.
Salt-grey knot-jointed grasses writhe
hissing queer echoes of waves' tales.

Mud-green crabs scuttle sideways – in – out –
slit-caved burrows. A flung-string clutter
of washed weed shines – orange wire – on rush tops,
marsh buttercups' flat yellow. Strayed bees mutter

sounds in sea-pinks, purple-red clover
bordering white shells' sparkle on dark sand.

Strange bitter beauty lies over the salt marsh
strange bitter beauty of mixed-blooded children
part but not one with sea or land.[42]

The poem begins in grey. A difficult syntax emphasizes the dullness: is "Octopus-sprawls" the verb, divided by three lines from its subject, "this half-caste child" (which is itself a circumlocution)? In the third stanza, however, the sun comes out and rouses the colours of the salt marsh (now named clearly). Grey divides into gradations: "grey-dun" cliffs, "rusty ... reeds," "Salt-grey ... grasses," "Mud-green crabs." By the poem's end, we see an explosion of colours in the "orange" seaweed, the "yellow" marsh buttercups, the "sea-pinks," the "purple-red clover," and, brightest of all, the "white shells" on the "dark sand," which throw back the sun's light. To a lesser extent there is a parallel progression in sound. Whereas the poem begins with the inanimate "flat rumbling" of the sea, it proceeds to the sounds of living things – grasses hissing, crabs scuttling, the natural music of bees, and ultimately this rhyming poem, which is one with the "strange bitter beauty" of the salt marsh.

The poem's nationality is understated but can be inferred from the key metaphor, the representation of the marsh as a "mixed-blooded" child. In later years Marriott fretted that the racial conceit would be objectionable, and wrote, "its justification and purpose is that it *is* a Salt Marsh, with its own particular beauty. The same applies, in still more force, to the now repugnant reference to the children."[43] Is it necessary, however, to take the hyphenated adjective as pejorative? Marriott, like Pierce, promoted a concept of modern Canada as not only descended from French and English colonization, settlement, and the fur trade, but also, especially after Laurier, open to immigration and ethnically diverse. Practices such as the infamous Chinese head tax and the Japanese internment were at odds with this concept, but they do not cancel contemporary attempts to articulate it. In fact, beyond colour and sound, the poem exploits hyphenation as one of its central techniques, declaring beauty to be hyphenated. "Salt Marsh" celebrates an interstitial space and symbolizes Canada hopefully as the land of mixed-blooded children, the land with an emerging artistic identity. It represents the process of culture that will produce a heritage, rousing colour from country. The coastal salt marsh where formless ocean becomes landform is a place where a nation may be formed.

Alan Crawley disapproved of geographical poetry and tried to steer Marriott away from it: "I used the coastal scene a great deal (prompting Alan to tell me that a catalogue of natural wonders didn't constitute a poem)."[44] Dorothy Livesay also deplored what she saw as Marriott's abandonment of politics and reversion to "adolescent verse."[45] Pierce, by contrast, approved, and because of him *Salt Marsh* took up a place in the record as Marriott's third book.

※✢※

AN AFFINITY FLOURISHED between Marriott and Pierce, but the financials were too little to support a writing career on their own. It was clear that no quantity of Chap-Books could provide the living that Marriott was eager to earn from her typewriter. The publication of her second Chap-Book, *Calling Adventurers!* (no. 89, 1941), shows that she had already begun to turn to another practice – writing for radio. Like Nathaniel A. Benson, she adapted her poetics to the better-paying opportunities that society offered her.

What planted the seed to write for radio was another approbative reading of *The Wind Our Enemy*. In December 1939, Margaret Kennedy of Winnipeg found Marriott's address through M. Eugenie Perry of the Canadian Authors Association and wrote to Marriott with praise: "The intention to write you was born in me after I had read your 'The Wind Our Enemy.' I bought your little chapbook a few months ago, shortly after it was published, I believe, and when I'm not handing it around to my friends to read, I find myself rereading it. I must congratulate you on your very fine poem, and I hope it won't be long until I'm reading more of your work. 'The Wind' is the finest verse I have ever read that has been written by a Canadian on a Canadian theme."[46] Again, authentication by a reader would prove pivotal for the turn Marriott's authorship would take. Like J.F.B. Livesay's, Kennedy's thoughts flew to giving the "very fine" text the widest possible exposure, but this time the suggestion went beyond print. She requested Marriott's permission to adapt the poem for radio – to add dialogue to Marriott's verses and extend the text to a thirty-minute segment. "Your poem could stand, almost as is, for radio, and with additions, keyed to radio, could be made into a very good script ... I have some on mine [Kennedy's proposed part] done – it is the same type of verse, rhythmical, but not nearly so colorful as yours. The finished radio version would probably be a combination of the two, but mine, less rich, would serve to help the public digest yours more easily."[47] Kennedy, working to deadline on her first CBC production, explained that original music would be composed. She offered to split the proceeds fifty-fifty and indicated that Marriott would have full credit as the primary author. Kennedy's request was organized, assertive, and knowledgeable. It is what introduced Marriott to a new class of publication.

The radio adaptation of *The Wind Our Enemy* was slow in coming to fruition, but the two writers were soon at work on what would become "Payload" and *Calling Adventurers!*. Marriott explained that she could not acquiesce to Kennedy's initial request because the Ryerson Press owned the copyright to *The Wind Our Enemy*: "I am afraid by the time I had got more information from you about the production and could write to them for possible permission it would be too late to meet your deadline."[48] She was, however, intrigued, prompting Kennedy to pursue the project over a longer time frame. "I might add," Kennedy replied, "that two ideas I have right now that I feel rather strongly about are first that radio is the very logical and certainly the broadest medium for verse, and secondly that Canadian radio isn't getting the best efforts of our writers."[49] These principles, sketching out a new genre of Canadian poetry ("verse for radio"), were enticing, as were Kennedy's remarks on payment: "Although C.B.C. doesn't pay a fortune for plays, they are very fair, and certainly encouraging. There is plenty to be criticized about their methods, (and some of their programs) but I think they are making tremendous strides against tremendous odds, in providing entertainment and education etc. for such a scattered population."[50] Marriott was persuaded to try this new way to reach the Canadian public.

"Payload" is as geographical a text as "Salt Marsh" and as interested in public issues as *The Wind Our Enemy*, but more than either it shows Marriott deliberately veering toward the political interests of a national audience. It dramatizes history, represents social groups, and describes landscapes in a clear effort to address a topic of current importance in the 1940s, namely, the opening of the North to modern economic development. It shapes itself to Canada's interest in realizing the Arctic's vast potential, much like F.R. Scott's poem "Laurentian Shield." What unlocks this potential in Marriott and Kennedy's work is the technology of flight.

The first northern pilots in the 1920s and '30s build transportation and communication routes on the traces of the fur trade, routes that open the northern backcountry to industry – above all, to mining – and in so doing deliver to the nation the payload of a prosperous future.

Generically, "Payload" is "a documentary drama in verse and prose, written especially for radio ... with original music."[51] Verse choruses set the scenes and guide the audience's interpretation in a way that is reminiscent of Ancient Greek drama. Fifty-six passages of music by the composer Barbara Pentland punctuate the script, elaborating moods and drawing out key moments, while additional sound effects suggest scene details such as crowds, wind, waves, and propellers. There are approximately ten scenes of prose dialogue that dramatize various achievements in the history of northern aviation. Some passages are a medley of overlapping scenes with voices that fade in and out. One character is Harold Anthony "Doc" Oaks (1896–1968), a First World War flying ace.[52] Marriott and Kennedy portray him hitting on the idea in December 1926 of flying freight, mainly lumber and dynamite, to a backcountry mine northeast from Winnipeg, taking with him enough turkeys and ice cream to surprise the miners with "a real Christmas" dinner. Another character is Clennel Haggerston "Punch" Dickens (1899–1995), the first pilot to fly an airplane to Aklavik, 2,900 kilometres north from Edmonton. The significance of his achievement is underscored by his arrival on Dominion Day, 1929. The final scene is a roll call of winners of the McKee Trophy for aviation, in which the Canadian defence minister, Charles Gavan Power (1888–1968), catalogues the flying heroes who have opened the North.

The climactic scene narrates the discovery of pitchblende (uraninite), an ore for radium, by the prospector Gilbert LaBine (1890–1977) at Great Bear Lake in 1930. His pilot is Wilfred Leigh Brintnell (1895–1971). With Brintnell's help, LaBine connects his mine at Port Radium, Northwest Territories, to his refinery at Port Hope, Ontario, linking the nation's hinterland to its industrial heart and thereby allowing Canada, by 1939, to become the leading producer of radium worldwide. At "two million dollars an ounce" (22), radium is the most valuable of the literal payloads that the text instances. Marriott and Kennedy represent it as the means for Canada to enrich itself, to deliver medical miracles, to fulfill its traditional colonial promise, and to prove its worth on the world stage. "The British Empire needs radium, and I'd like to be the man to find it," declares LaBine (20):

LABINE: We're willing to put every cent we have into a new Eldorado. That's why I'm so anxious to get up to Great Bear.
BRINTNELL: I hope you won't be disappointed, Gilbert – and I hope you find pitchblende.
LABINE: Gold – silver – copper – sure! But pitchblende, – maybe!
BRINTNELL: It's always just maybe for pitchblende.
LABINE: Do you want me to sign an order, or anything?
BRINTNELL: Not necessary – I'll just make a memo. (SLOWLY, AS IF WRITING QUICKLY) Gilbert LaBine, special flight from Winnipeg, via The Pas, McMurry, Simpson, to Great Bear Lake. August 1929. Return to pick up prospector late in September.
LABINE: ~~Strictly between us, Leigh – as far as possible.~~
~~BRINTNELL: Of course.~~
LABINE: Thanks. My brother Charlie is the only other person in on it – and wouldn't I like to be able to send him a wire saying I'd found pitchblende, at last – Charlie thinks radium is the most
MUSIC NO 31
GIRL'S VOICE: [*handwritten:*] FILTER (READING SLOWLY AND PLEASANTLY) October 3, 1929. Telegram to Mr Charlie LaBine, Toronto. We have a new Eldorado. Everything is there and now it's up to us to get it out stop will arrive Toronto on the 8th with samples. Signed Gilbert. Telegram to Mr –
MAN'S VOICE: (QUICKLY) – and if Gilbert LaBine found pitchblende around Great Bear Lake I'm going up there tomorrow. Can you stake me? It would only –
MUSIC NO 32 TO CONTINUE UNDERNEATH CHORUS. [*handwritten:*] up + under
CHORUS:
   Pitchblende, black in the earth and heavy in the hand
   Radium essence of light never touched by the hand.
(21–2)[53]

The two lines of poetry, which recur throughout the scene, cap the genial prose of the business conversation and translate the men's excitement into eloquence. If two syllables are elided (*-vy* and *in*), then the couplet's rhythm is pentameter. Repetition/rhyme ("hand") accentuates the paradox in these joined lines, namely, that a "black," "heavy" rock contains the "essence of light never touched." The paradox points to the inestimable value of this mineral, which a subsequent chorus calls a "marvellous miracle, old as the world, / Most precious treasure of all this land can hold, / Powerful to heal the bitterest sores of men" (25). This interweaving of choric chant and plain speech into a kind of diaphony is representative of the ways that Marriott and Kennedy found to make "verse for radio."

Their venture was a successful one. The CBC broadcast the work on 8 November 1940 and paid the two authors one hundred dollars (fifty each). It was rebroadcast in Britain and the United States; the BBC paid the authors a total of £30.00, and the American Broadcasting Company $105.09, both sums to be divided among Marriott, Kennedy, and Pentland.[54] Here was a larger income for an author, ten times more than the $11.30 that she earned from her first Chap-Book.

Calling Adventurers! is a vestige of this venture. It is the trace of a successful performance in another dimension, like the inaugural Ryerson Poetry Chap-Book, which was printed for Charles G.D. Roberts's recital tour. *Calling Adventurers!* contains only the choruses from "Payload," which it cuts and arranges into a long poem of twelve sections, dropping all of the prose dialogue and reducing the thirty-three-page radio script to an eight-page Chap-Book. Marriott was content to print these passages as they had been broadcast. She made only a dozen revisions, consisting at most of a single word here and there. The theme remains intact: the voice of the North calls to "Men ... / Who long for a land too large for them" (1, part 1, lines 19–20). The realistic illustration of the theme, however, suffers without the dialogue. Pierce published *Calling Adventurers!* in a print run of 250 in 1941 and the booklet served to keep the topic of northern development in the public eye. The Canadian Authors Association awarded it the Governor General's Literary Award, in approbation of its optimistic nationalism in wartime. Ryerson books had won the award before, but the distinction was a first for the Chap-Books and adorned Marriott's curriculum vitae through the rest of her career.[55]

A storm of objections would greet the poem today. Where *Calling Adventurers!* proclaims the medical value of radium, the post-1945 reader cannot help but trace the advent of the atomic bomb. Where the poem celebrates modern transportation, we must criticize carbon emissions and mining pollution. The Inuit appear only as a pre-modern race amazed by the technology of the airplane: "Eskimos stand, sloped eye-slits / Widened as the noisy bird comes" (4, part 5, lines 24–5). It should be added that Marriott herself disapproved of *Calling Adventurers!* in later years, as she wrote in response to a friend's request for a copy: "I'll copy 'Calling Adventurers' from a school text – its only reprinting, I am not proud of it even if it did get the G.G.! It's very artificial – the only thing I ever wrote to order."[56] Far from burying the poem, however, these judgments only further illuminate its visceral connections to the Canada of 1941. It is palpable that Marriott wrote "to order" on several levels, forming herself as an author in response to compelling demands and opportunities. The pressure to write another political long poem on a topic of national interest, the desire to document Canada's modernization, the innumerable compromises made with a coauthor, the sense of wartime duty to a mass audience, the allure of a more substantial payment: all of these factors shaped the little book that Marriott left to posterity in *Calling Adventurers!*. It may be catalogued as a poem, but what it reveals most vividly is Marriott's finding her way toward a more thoroughly socialized order of authorship beyond poetry.

Thus began a sustained practice of writing for radio. Marriott and Kennedy's collaboration continued in 1941 with "Who's Johnny Canuck," a "series of questions and answers in dramatic verse form provid[ing] an idealistic and multifaceted definition of the Canadian citizen."[57] They also wrote "We See Thee Rise" together, a light comedy for Dominion Day 1943, but it led to a disagreement over money that interrupted their partnership, as Marriott alleged that she never received her share (fifty dollars) from Kennedy.[58] Having taken a summer course in radio-script writing at the University of British Columbia in 1942, Marriott carried on alone.[59] She wrote six other thirty-minute works for general broadcast on the CBC in the 1940s, among them serious dramas, light comedies, and an adaptation of Keats's "Eve of St Agnes." The CBC paid one hundred dollars for each production (see table 4.2).

The summer course also introduced her to the opportunity to write educational scripts for local radio broadcast (still by the CBC) to school audiences. In 1942, Marriott "got some work writing school broadcasts, and moved out to Sooke to support myself. I figured I could do it on $35.00 a month (my staple, hamburger, was .13¢ a pound at the village store). But school broadcasts – local ones – only paid $15, so eventually I had to give up and go home."[60] After dipping her toe into educational writing, she plunged in: "In 1943 I had a tour of the *nine* provinces, doing a school broadcast series ('My Canada' (!) [*sic*] I got around $300.00 for

TABLE 4.2

Works by Anne Marriott broadcast on CBC Radio

With Margaret Kennedy. "Payload." Music by Barbara Pentland. Produced by Rupert Lucas, Montreal. CBC National Network. 8 Nov. 1940. 30 min. Rebroadcast by British Broadcasting Corporation and by American Broadcasting Company. Drama in verse and prose.

With Margaret Kennedy. "Who's Johnny Canuck?" Produced by J. Frank Willis, Toronto. CBC National Network. 19 Sept. 1941. 30 min. Questions and answers in verse.

"The Twenty-Third." *Theatre Time.* Produced by Andrew Allan, Vancouver. CBC Western Network. 13 Jan. 1942. 30 min. Light comedy.

"Wedding March." *Theatre Time.* Produced by Andrew Allan, Vancouver. CBC Western Network. 9 June 1942. 30 min. Light comedy.

With Margaret Kennedy. "We See Thee Rise." Feature for Dominion Day. Produced by J. Frank Willis, Toronto. CBC National Network. 1 July 1943. 30 min. Light comedy.

"O for the Wings." *Winnipeg Drama.* Produced by Esse W. Ljungh, Winnipeg. CBC Western Network. 24 Aug. 1944. 30 min. Drama.

John Keats, adapted by Anne Marriott. "The Eve of St Agnes." *Producer's Workshop.* Produced by John Barnes, Vancouver. CBC Western Network. 20 Jan. 1945. 30 min. Poetry.

"The Black Horse." *Winnipeg Drama.* Produced by Esse W. Ljungh, Winnipeg. CBC Eastern Network. 26 July 1945. 30 min. Drama.

"Mary." *Winnipeg Summer Theatre.* Produced by Esse W. Ljungh, Winnipeg. CBC Western Network. 22 Aug. 1945. 30 min. Rebroadcast 20 Feb. 1948 on *Maritime Theatre.* Produced by Stephen Ker Appleby, Halifax. CBC Eastern Network. Rebroadcast 26 Apr. 1951 on *Prairie Playhouse.* Adapted by Wakefield H. Maunsell. Produced by James Kent, Winnipeg. CBC Eastern Network. Drama.

With Margaret Kennedy. "The Wind Our Enemy." *Wednesday Night.* Produced by J. Frank Willis, Toronto. CBC Trans-Canada Network. 20 Sept. 1950. 30 min. Drama in verse and prose.

"The City Cousin." 27 Oct. 1950. Short story.

"The Party." 1951. Short story.

"The Ice Forest." 7 Mar. 1951. Short story.

"The Death of the Cat." 6 Dec. 1953. Short story.

"Mrs. Absalom." *Anthology.* Nov. 1954. Short story.

4.2, continued

"The Carillon." Short story.
"The Ladies." *Anthology*. 1957. Short story.
"Star Bright." *John Drainie Tells a Story*. 7 Dec. 1964. Rebroadcast 14 June 1965. Short story.
"A Day Like Spring." *Anthology*. 1968. Short story.
"The Ladder." *Canadian Short Stories*. 1969. Short story.
"The Ride." *Anthology*. May 1971. Short story.
"Stella." *Anthology*. 1974. Short story.
"Suitable Employment." *Anthology*. 31 Jan. 1976. Shorty story.
"Letters from Some Islands." *Anthology*. 1982. Rebroadcast on *Audience*. Poetry.
"A Military Man." *Anthology*. 14 Jan. 1984. Short story.

Compiled from Fink, "CCBS Bibliography"; and Anne Marriott, curriculum vitae [1984], A.1.2, Marriott Fonds. Broadcast dates and program titles are spotty in the curriculum vitae. Arranged chronologically.

those so that set me up for a while – at Sooke again."[61] Over the next three decades, Marriott would write "some 75 school broadcasts for CBC and the Department of Education" on topics that ranged from creative writing to Canadian history.[62] Her productivity in this genre was substantial.

It was Marriott's success in radio that led to her being hired by the National Film Board in 1945: "After various moves, attempts to join the Air Force or the C[anadian] W[omen's] A[rmy] C[orp]s as a writer, and so on, I finally achieved what seemed to be the most a writer or artist or film-maker who wanted to earn a living could hope for at that time, and in March 1945 went to work at the National Film Board in Ottawa as a scriptwriter."[63] If the job brought her a regular pay cheque, it also shifted the political and documentary function of her writing into its highest gear. Many of the films she worked on can be seen as a direct extension of "Payload," pushing the theme of northern development. When she left the National Film Board in 1949 to move back west with her husband, Gerald McLellan (whom she married in 1947), she was weary of this propaganda: "I'm just not interested in doing documentaries – I have written so many – and the mere thought of ever doing another at this point (for any medium) makes my brain feel knotted! I have specially done an awful lot of writing about the new developments and significance of the north – in films, at any [rate], it's a subject that's been done to death – and I'm written right out on it."[64] Her fatigue indicates the extent to which she had stretched her creativity to meet the public demand for nation building.

At the end of the 1940s, Marriott and Kennedy retrieved their partnership sufficiently to realize their original idea, the radio adaptation of *The Wind Our Enemy*. The broadcast both concentrated Marriott's reputation in the text of her first Chap-Book and furthered her radio career. Back on the West Coast and out of work, Marriott looked up Kenneth Caple, the CBC's regional director in British Columbia, and he proposed that she "re-submit The Wind Our Enemy right away."[65] She and Kennedy had completed a script years earlier, which, like "Payload," weaves scenes of prose dialogue into Marriott's poetry. Now Marriott dusted it off and asked Kennedy for permission to proceed. In the aftermath of the Second World War, she was intent not to cast any aspersions on immigrants from Eastern Europe and wished to change the name of the malefactor who brews moonshine in his barn: "I'd like to make one or two very minor changes," she wrote to Kennedy, "particularly substituting an Anglo-Saxon name for that of the villain of the piece Pete Masik. Prejudice not being dead yet, alack, it doesn't seem fair to tie a 'foreign' name to him."[66] The bootlegger became "Pete Hill."[67] Pierce soon added his support to the undertaking: "If the CBR of Vancouver would like to use the script then we are very pleased indeed, and you have our permission without question to make the adaptation for production. I should like to have a copy of the adaptation if it is possible, but if that is not possible, let me have the time and date and we will listen in."[68] Ultimately the production moved to Toronto, where a cast of ten rehearsed and performed the piece under the direction of J. Frank Willis. Original music by Philip Simmons, conducted by Samuel Hersenboren, enhanced the text. *The Wind Our Enemy*, adapted for radio, aired on the national program *Wednesday Night* from 8:30 to 9:00 p.m. on 20 September 1950, and the authors were paid one hundred dollars (fifty each).

Enhancing the poem and rendering it more accessible, the radio adaptation channelled the state broadcaster's power into multiplying the poet's authority. A world war had taken place since the Dust Bowl, and the announcer begins by looking back across the gulf of the past decade: "Ladies and gentlemen, CBC WEDNESDAY NIGHT presents a poem from the great western plains by Anne Marriott, inspired by the dark day of wind and drought and dust that clouded the 1930's." The preamble thus gives the poem a historical authority, and adds to the regional authenticity that its original circumstances of publication had bestowed on it. The ten actors, performing thirteen different anonymous speaking parts, suggest society in general. As in "Payload," the dialogue pieced into the poem reinforces and illustrates its theme dramatically. The plot traces the conflict between a farmer and his wife as the historic drought dashes their visions of prosperity, and perhaps the most remarkable change in the adaptation occurs toward the end, when the sliver of hope the man voices in the original poem is expanded into a moral fortitude centred in the woman. Confronted by his wife, the farmer confesses going out each night to drink: "I can't stop myself. You don't know – you can't know what it means to me. A man can go on for three-four years, maybe even five years, putting everything into his land and getting nothing in return. Then something's got to happen. Working on it, loving it, praying over it – he'll give his life to it – but it's got to give him something in return. It's not enough for him to sow his land and get nothing but a cloud of dust" (22). His wife fends off this despair:

> THE WOMAN: You do care. Some night you'll walk to that door and when you open it you'll know that spring is here again – you'll feel it just like you used to. From the land.
> THE MAN: I don't know. Sometimes, over at Pete's, I think I do get the feeling of spring again. Something happens inside of me – just like it did when I used to know that spring had come and we'd be sowing again. Sometimes I can even smell it in the air. But it always drifts away again. It never stays. – That's why I go over to Pete's. It's the only way I know to forget the wind – sometimes I even forget about the dust. I wish I could make you understand. I wish you knew.
> THE WOMAN: I know. But there are some things you used to understand. And you've forgotten them. It's not for you to go to Pete's, alone. Everything we've had we've shared. We used to be like one person – we worked together – we worried about the kids together – we went to church and prayed together. And when the wind first came we fought it together. You've forgotten – how it was always the two of us.

THE MAN: Yes. I had forgotten, I guess. Oh, I don't know. I don't know what to do.
THE WOMAN: (GENTLY) It's alright. Go to Pete's if you have to. But – come home early.
THE MAN: I – oh, I don't know. I guess I don't have to go. I'll stay home with you tonight. We do need to be together.
MUSIC: HAS FADED IN GENTLY AND SOFTLY FROM THE WOMAN'S LINES "YOU DO CARE."
(23–4)

The inserted dialogue thus strengthens the moral lesson that hope and virtue can stand up to suffering. It lightens the text for a mass audience. In these ways, the radio production of *The Wind Our Enemy* augmented Marriott's standing as a Canadian poet, intensifying her canonization as such even as she grew into her accomplishments in diverse genres.

In 1950, Marriott branched into fiction with "The City Cousin," which the CBC broadcast in October. In all she would have fourteen stories performed over the next four decades, most often on Robert Weaver's program *Anthology*. Her third story broadcast on the CBC, "The Ice Forest," was also accepted for print publication by the *Canadian Forum* in 1951, after which Marriott pursued a strategy of publishing her work both on the air and in print. Fiction's economic pull is palpable in Weaver's offering her, for example, $700 for a single story, "Suitable Employment," in 1975.[69] By 1983, twenty stories by Marriott had appeared in print. She considered her most successful to be "On a Sunday Afternoon," an uncanny pageant in which teenagers embody a primal sexuality that interrupts a family picnic. It was published in *Queen's Quarterly* in 1971, republished in Rudy Wiebe and Andreas Schroeder's *Stories from Pacific and Arctic Canada* (Toronto: Macmillan Company of Canada, 1974), and translated as "An einem Sonntagmittag" for the German collection *Die Weite Reise: Kanadische Erzählungen und Kurzgeschichten* (Berlin: Volk und Welt, 1974). Eight of her short stories, including "On a Sunday Afternoon," were collected in her book, *A Long Way to Oregon* (Oakville, ON: Mosaic Press, 1984). Marriott also drafted a novel in the 1970s. It was not published, but she won two Canada Council grants to work on it and described it enthusiastically in her correspondence: "And now I'm doing what I've always most wanted to do – writing a novel (about Victoria in the Depression! Especially the 'distressed English gentlewomen' whom I encountered)."[70] Although rarely associated with fiction, Marriott wrote a fair amount of it, adding it onto what by then had undeniably grown into a multifaceted writing practice. This practice was based on the name that she had made for herself – and that others had made for her – in her Ryerson Poetry Chap-Books, both as they appeared in print and as they propagated themselves on the air.

❧✝❧

MARRIOTT'S WRITING CAREER eventually grew into a supple tree, neither especially tall nor especially brittle. It had many leaves and branches, which spread out from her Ryerson Poetry Chap-Books and her vital interactions with Pierce and others in the 1930s and '40s. In addition to her work in radio, film, and fiction, she wrote newspaper columns – a poetry column in the Victoria *Daily Citizen* in the 1940s, and the women's page in the Prince George *Citizen* from 1950 to 1953.[71] In 1958, 1959, and 1962, she and her husband adopted three babies. Like Ferne before her, she found ways to nurture literature despite not having much time to write: "The three children, Celia, Marya and Jerome, remember their mother's passion for camping trips and bridge and her wildly varied garden and pets (mice, guinea pigs, turtles, rabbits, dogs, cats, sometimes all at once ... Not writing regularly, [Marriott] went on every possible reading tour, hosted teas for writers, attended their readings. 'She was tremendously supportive of her fellow poets,' said the poet Marya Fiamengo."[72] In the 1970s and '80s, Marriott worked in libraries, an educational role that developed out of her experience as an author and parent, and her school radio broadcasts. She taught poetry-writing workshops for elementary and secondary students at the North Vancouver City Library from 1971 to 1975.[73] She volunteered in her children's school libraries and coauthored a textbook on creative writing.[74] During the National Book Festival in 1982, she led ten workshops in Vancouver public libraries in which participating children composed over a thousand poems.[75] Being a published, prize-winning poet was of course a key component to Marriott's leading these creative writing workshops with authority, but the equation can be flipped around equally well: teaching poetry to diverse student audiences was an excellent way for her to continue to be a national poet.

Marriott's authorship ramified into many practices. She herself confessed the verdant spread of her career without embarrassment or regret: "Actually, poetry had been almost an accident – I wanted to be a *writer*, not just a poet so I wrote scripts for CBC, then went to work at the National Film Board, then on a weekly newspaper; got married, adopted three kids, and wrote short stories when I had time!"[76] It is a summation that is genial, frank, and true to life. It helps us to reverse Dorothy Livesay's 1949 assessment, which disciplined itself critically to discount all but Marriott's purest poetry: "Like so many other Canadian writers of talent, Anne Marriott has had to sacrifice the most creative side of her nature for the economics of living. She has not had the leisure nor the solitude to devote herself solely to poetry."[77] The purpose of this chapter has been to acknowledge the truth of Livesay's judgment the other way around, to analyze this "sacrifice," to characterize and colour the transaction between "talent" and "the economics of living," and to appreciate the ways in which she broadcast her creative energy beyond the "leisure" and "solitude" of printed poetry in order to trace her existence as a writer in society.

Finally, although Marriott's practice as a writer went far beyond her Chap-Books, they remain the trunk and centre of her literary identity and authority. This centrality is apparent in her last book, *Aqua* (Toronto: Wolsak & Wynn, 1991). A product of the small press written and published with support from the Canada Council, it returns to the prestigious but unlucrative form of her first books. Toward the end of it, in a poem entitled "After a Meeting of Poets," Marriott seems to acknowledge at once the emptiness and the vitality of poetry – its little resilience – when the speaker proclaims to vacated lecture halls that it has been her "life's essential act":

> Everyone's gone.
> Rooms gape
> huge melancholy yawns.
> Everyone's gone
> from lobbies, corridors
> but not from in my head;
> a noisy frieze
> you faces, eyes
> are clearer than these walls
> and doors
> indelibly inscribed.
> Going homeward

all your planes can crash
yet you'll still smile and scowl
make motions, argue
each face outlined with light
inside my restless skull.

My forebears all
ripened into long old age
so predictions are quite good
I'll keep you going for years
my sharpest memory marked *reserved*
your names heaped on my tongue.

For myself? All that I ask
is that when I have to leave
there'll be a survivor
with a space for me
talking and scribbling in his brain
insisting he recall
my life's essential act:
I wrote poems
as
did all of
you.[78]

FIVE

Chap-Book, Deafness, Sacrifice
M. Eugenie Perry

LIKE DORIS FERNE, Martha Eugenie Perry was one of the women in the Victoria poetry group who inducted the young Anne Marriott into writing verse. Perry's letters offer a good view of the character of the Ryerson Poetry Chap-Books in the 1940s, at the mid-point of their publication. The rich correspondence that survives between Lorne Pierce and Perry reveals the formation of an author who, like Benson and Marriott, persisted against unfavourable conditions enough to negotiate the complex opposition between romanticism and modernism and find her own poetic voice. Perry had a good record writing for newspapers and magazines and had self-published two books by 1940, but in Pierce and his series she discovered a supportive framework in which to legitimate herself as a serious poet. Mutual respect flourished between writer and editor, engendering two Chap-Books and a full-length collection. Few readers will know Perry's poetry, but it is technically accomplished, conversant with the poetic issues of its day, ground-breaking in its representation of a minority, and accessible. Moreover, Perry thoroughly became a Ryerson poet, to the point of tailoring her creativity to the forms that Pierce was able to produce. In contrast to Benson's and Marriott's, her writing career culminated with Pierce and his Chap-Books. Examining her case thus gauges the dimensions of the series differently, emphasizing its continuing attractions as a channel of Canadian literature. Writers like Perry found it to be a space in which to deepen their vocation as poets, to surpass their own prior efforts, and to offer their best poetry to the country and to posterity.

Meanwhile, the perseverance of the series into its third decade and Perry's gravitation to it as an artistic home suggest that Pierce had indeed found the way to publish Canadian literature: sparely, at a loss covered by other revenue, and relying on the micro-agency of a handful of people. Effectively piloting a small press at the heart of a big publishing house, Pierce enabled Perry to write herself out of the silence and into the chorus of Canadian poetry. In return, she held up an intimate, accurate mirror to his profile as a publisher.

PERRY'S LONG POEM "Song in the Silence," published in 1947 in the second of her two Ryerson Poetry Chap-Books, is a realistic rural coming-of-age narrative.[1] Linnet, the daughter of a Manitoba farmer at the turn of the twentieth century, is in love with her cousin Alan, but during his first term away at university in the East, not only does he fail to write the letters she expects, but she is struck by an illness that leaves her deaf. At Christmas, Alan's greeting her like a sister amounts to abandonment, and the house of love planned with him collapses. Against the doctor's cautious prescription of rest indoors, Linnet's grandmother advises her to face the weather and go for a walk. Outside, on the wintry riverbank, she meets Jarrod, the deaf boy who works on the neighbours' farm, chopping wood. Whereas she has lost her hearing, he was born without his. Once when they were younger, he astonished her by pointing out, in the cedar tree, a beautiful bird – a linnet – which he could not hear. Now his recommendation of a hearing aid and, later, his studying to teach at a school for deaf children show her the path forward. Still smarting from her unrequited love for Alan, she is attracted to the "Genius, or power – how name it?" that Jarrod possesses (10, l. 352). As the poem ends, she stands outside on a spring evening, waiting for Jarrod to come in his car, thinking about the Biblical story of Ruth.

"Song in the Silence" asserts an ideal of service but interlaces it with realism. Ultimately Linnet finds a noble purpose through her trouble:

With Jarrod – ah! Here lay her hope of serving,
Serving him and his kind.
That aura was not the sinister thing of her dread,
But strength instead, some following of the Gleam,
And greater even than his love for her.
(10, ll. 360–4)

Romantic idealism is palpable in a word like "Gleam." At the same time, "Song in the Silence" is a love poem, in the same way that Alice Munro's "Mischief," "A Queer Streak," and "Tricks" are love stories: in lieu of the anticipated dream, plausible disaster arrives, trailing a lifelong disappointment that itself becomes the measure of the protagonist's capacity for love. "*Now through each day of empty silence wove / The strange, the devastating power of love*" (7, ll. 225–6). This couplet, made memorable by diacope, emphasizes that "love," for all its allure, is a term for deception and pain. The following lines are similar: "*She learns that what is held for love may prove / The thoughtless flourish of a javelin*" (6, ll. 199–200). The ambivalence of the poem's final mention of Alan reveals a realistic mingling of repudiation and longing:

Alan? Ah! that was self; self and the charm,
The primeval warmth he wore so carelessly.
From Alan though the privilege, pain-hooved,
Never in life forgotten, of having hopelessly loved.
(10, ll. 353–6)

Such details indicate that Perry was in touch with the current of twentieth-century realism. She worked to make her writing both realist and idealist, and inscribed lived experience and peripety into an overall moral design.

Perry attested to the truth of this experience for her when she submitted the manuscript to Pierce: "One's own life must always influence any writing one does, I think, and so apart from the character of Jarrod, and the inclusion of the deaf and hard of hearing complication, the poem is built up from my own experiences of life, and my girlhood home in Manitoba, (near the town of Dauphin), supplied the setting."[2] Perry, who never married, knew an Alan. In the spring of 1909, when she was twenty-seven, she had received a long letter from a lover that broke off their relationship of several years:

And now I suppose we have got to face the situation as it now is. And the sky is still obscured with clouds. I trust they have silver linings but I have as yet been unable to penetrate them to find out; and therefore if affairs cannot go on any longer as they are I shall be glad to do anything to make it as easy for you as possible – will go away for an indefinite period – or [?] you [?] a trip of extended duration – or anything else. I don't want to leave you or have you leave me. And I would be not a little lonesome but as you intimated I have probably a good deal more to take up my attention than you and in that way I might have a slight advantage.

If I had only got off the scene some time ago you could have been happy with some one else – and it doesn't make so much difference about me. But I didn't want to go. You have been so good to me that during the last couple of years I seem to have drifted away from practically every place else where I had been previously in the habit of calling occasionally. You thought – or rather you pretended to think – that I didn't desire to go to your place afterw[?]. That wasn't it but rather that I thought I was perhaps really already going too often considering the way your folks felt about it – and that they would much prefer that I stayed away.[3]

In writing "Song in the Silence," Perry came to terms with a pivotal experience in her own life thirty-five years earlier.

Another realist aspect of the poem (again comparing with Munro) is its double point of view. Most of the poem is narrated from young Linnet's perspective, but a number of passages leap to a much older voice, as in the last example above. Part 4 opens with a reflection on the primacy of birdsong to poetry since time immemorial, but then abruptly shifts to an image of the Second World War, which obviously lies beyond the turn-of-the-century setting of Perry's girlhood (9, ll. 318–19). Perry moves easily between these two points of view – her own and Linnet's, or old Linnet's and young Linnet's – and this facility indicates not only a grasp of psychological realism but a readiness to adjust it frankly to include the writing mind. "Whenever I have found it necessary to write lines a little out of character – Linnet's character – I have italicized them," Perry explained to Pierce, smoothing the way for him to appreciate the poem.[4] The alert reader sees the difference without explanation.

The form of "Song in the Silence" also reveals a poet who knows both the poetic tradition and her own sovereignty. Metrically, the poem moves freely under the light pressure of blank verse, an appropriate choice for a serious narrative poem, with canonical precedents in Milton's *Paradise Lost* and, closer to home, Isabella Valancy Crawford's "Malcolm's Katie." The unstrained metre is evident from the opening passage:

> She paused, then ran a little, light and swift,
> Ran as a bird runs, curious to see
> What Jarrod saw,
> So still beneath the cedar's emerald fringe.
> A flash of black and yellow through the tree,
> And so she knew one of her namesakes here,
> The goldfinch linnet.
>
> His hand held out, though not with any thought
> Of touching her, the tall boy turned –
> He always seemed to know when Linnet came –
> "The bird – the sweet – song": his studied speech
> Was difficult and harsh.
>
> Slowly, as drawn by some uncharted urge,
> Nearer and nearer she came until his eyes,
> Flecks of green-gold firing their grey, now burned
> Deep into hers with their young brown-pansy tinge;
> And so, poised as for sudden flight, she heard –
> Lovely and special as in spring the first warm rain –
> The beaded thread of song
> Spaced from the quivering throat of the small bird.
>
> Then, and it could have been his eyes' strange light,
> Or thinking how his heart had heard the sound
> His ears would never hear, a fluttering fright
> Held her; and now she flew back through the trees.
> (1, ll. 1–24)

Enjambment, a simple prose-like syntax, a paucity of end rhyme, and frequent recourse to shorter or longer lines half-conceal the iambic pentameter on which the poem is woven. In this passage, Perry introduces the main conceit – the listening heart – with irregular rhythmic threads, beginning with the dimeter of line 3 and climaxing with the hexameter of line 18 and the trimeter of line 19. At this climax, one sense leaps into another. The spondee on "warm rain" asks for pause in which to contemplate the simile that hearing birdsong is like feeling a spring shower. The next metaphor (the song, a beaded thread) likewise explains a sound in terms of touch or vision. Figure and rhythm cooperate to lead the reader, with Linnet, to the insight that Jarrod is not disabled, despite his disability. This is the theme of the poem. Alliteration and half-rhyme and near repetition immediately reiterate it, in a clause that the poem will return to verbatim in its closing lines: "his heart had heard" (10, l. 370).[5]

The four parts of "Song in the Silence," each named for a season of the year, correspond to Linnet's progress from love, through shock and survival, to hope. Each part harbours a sonnet, italicized and thus spoken by the older narrative voice, that acts as a chorus to the unfolding drama. The Petrarchan sonnet in part 1, "Summer," describes a love that is full but still, like the mature leaves of a tree or "the white kid of a wedding glove / Yellowing in a chest" (101–2). The Shakespearean sonnet in part 2, "Autumn," figures the loss of love as a military invasion at night, including the javelin metaphor quoted above, and culminating bitterly with day's return as only a *"mocking panoply"* (6, l. 202). In part 3, "Winter," a second Shakespearean sonnet sets romantic passion in its place, stepping back to see providence continuing in the rhythms of the land – in the harvest, in the birds feeding in the fields – which Linnet's father, "a man who knew and loved the birds," taught her to see (7, l. 248). (Notably, Perry dedicated *Song in the Silence and Other Poems* to her father.) "Spring," the final part, opens thus:

> *Since the first poet carved a runic lay*
> *The bards have harped on simple strains – the may*
> *That carmines in the spring, the fielded drove*
> *Of cattle, the sea's harvest, and man's love*
> *Of woman; yet through their revealing words*
> *Always has pulsed the pearl-clear song of birds.*
> *When the first woman wept in Paradise,*
> *Was there a rippling solace from the skies?*

> *The maimed in Normandy praying soon release*
> *Would smile to hear the linnets presage peace;*
> *And when the poet weaves the world's last rune*
> *Something of a bird-song will be in that tune.*
> (9, ll. 310–22)

Technique is manifest in the graceful rhyme, in the anthimeria that turns "carmine," a colour, into a verb, in the play on "may," in the juxtaposition of mythical Eden and war-torn France, and in the metaphorical description of birdsong as pearls, which returns to the "beaded thread" of the opening. One might also puzzle over the elusive sketch of literary history. The real question for this passage, however, comes from the formal momentum already established. Why are these lines not quite a sonnet – or are they? The implication could be that Linnet has found something beyond the eros that is the Renaissance lyric's hallmark. It could be that her last phase, her life with Jarrod, is not yet achieved. It could be that these twelve italicized lines, which make a hopeful amalgam of the protagonist, birds, and poetry, are not complete without the last two, and only other, italicized lines of part 4, which confess Linnet's animal desire for Alan and describe it as a *"pain-hooved"* "privilege." Taken with the dozen lines above, this couplet would make a set of fourteen, with rhymes that run from *aa* to *gg*.

The most interesting quality of Perry's "Song in the Silence" is its self-reflexive concept of poetry as a silent song. Through it, Perry places her poem in dialogue with Keats's "Ode on a Grecian Urn," which formulates the same paradox: "Heard melodies are sweet, but those unheard / Are sweeter; therefore, ye soft pipes, play on."[6] In Perry's poem, Jarrod's love for a woman named for a bird, and Linnet's willingness to marry a deaf man, cross the boundary of the senses. The plot thus delivers "the beaded thread of song": the symbol plays out in the narrative, and the narrative dissolves back into synaesthesia. "Song in the Silence" reconceives of poetry as a deaf-mute song that is heard through the eyes. Every poem is a bird; every reader is a listening heart. Perry was not herself deaf, but her achievement should not be misconstrued as an illegitimate appropriation. The publishing history of her Ryerson Poetry Chap-Books will explain why.

MARTHA EUGENIE PERRY (1881–1958) was born in Kirkfield, in the Kawartha Lakes region of Ontario, and grew up in nearby Cannington and Eldon, one of several children of Matthew Perry, a general merchant, and Elizabeth Cowan. Her parents, also born in Ontario, were Scots-Irish Anglicans. Perry attended high school in Lindsay but as a young woman moved with her family to Dauphin, Manitoba, where her father became the manager of a farm that bred railway workhorses. He was successful enough to leave his children an inheritance at his death in 1910, which enabled Perry to pursue a writing career. In 1916, she settled with her mother in Victoria, where she lived for the rest of her life.[7]

Like Lilian Leveridge's (see chapter 2), Perry's writing career was rooted in the periodical press. In 1909, she contributed to the *Dauphin Herald* under the pseudonym "Guinevere." By 1926, she had a regular children's column in the *Toronto Evening Telegram*.[8] She contributed poems, short fiction, children's features, and plays to "scores of magazines and newspapers in Canada, the British Isles, and the United States,"[9] including the *Manitoba Free Press*, the *Canadian Bookman*, *Canadian Poetry Magazine*, *Chatelaine*, *Maclean's*, the *New Outlook*, and the *New York Times*.[10] Under the pseudonym "Perry Page," she wrote the "Home Chat" page of the *Western Recorder*, the magazine of the United Church of Canada in British Columbia, and was a friend of the editor, J.P. Hicks.[11] A late biographical sketch stated that she had "published in almost a hundred magazines."[12]

Having a book published was not as easy. Perry followed the narrow path of self-publication to produce her first two, *The Girl in the Silk Dress and Other Stories* (Ottawa: Overbrook Press, 1931) and *Hero in Ermine and Other Poems* (Victoria: Clarke Printing Company, 1939). Her first book of poetry reflects her economic position as a successful newspaper and magazine writer. As its acknowledgments indicate, *Hero in Ermine* collects poems first written for an array of periodicals, among them *Love Story Magazine*, *Independent Woman*, and the *Vancouver Sun*.

Accordingly, the poems in *Hero in Ermine* present a variety in content and form. They range from world politics to private sentiment, from sonnets to free verse. The title poem expresses gratitude to George VI for ascending the throne after his brother abdicated. There is a satire of Hitler's annexation of Memel (Lithuania) and a critique of the Canadian lumber industry first published in the March 1937 number of *Canadian*

Poetry Magazine. "Old Lace" celebrates the beauty of an old woman's face, "Roof Dancers" captures the weird ebbing of a nightmare, and "Laurel" is a witty lesson to those who would cut down a tree. Perry's next work, *Hearing a Far Call*, appears here in embryo under the title "Doro-Lynd Comes Home." The eclectic assembly of poems in *Hero in Ermine* reveals a talent in search of a form. Perry wished to rise above the fugitive piece trafficked by the popular press.

As the prior chapter makes clear, Perry was part of an active literary community in Victoria and nearby Vancouver. She was a member of the Canadian Authors Association; she served as president of the local chapter (Victoria and the Gulf Islands) and convened its poetry group, which was "long under [her] capable leadership."[13] Perry knew Marriott well, followed her career supportively, read aloud from Marriott's work at poetry meetings, and shared in the pleasure of seeing Marriott reviewed well over tea with Marriott's mother.[14] She regretted Marriott's departure in 1945: "Anne Marriott has gone to Ottawa to take a position in the film department. Her loss will be a severe one to our literary group here, as well as to her many friends."[15] Because of her "friendship for Mr [Alan] Crawley," she helped to publicize an "interesting" talk he gave on modern Canadian poetry at the Empress Hotel in the last week of January 1946: "The poems he gave – being blind he has to learn all the poetry by heart – were all familiar to me; and I felt that the effect he gets – he has a great deal of personal magnetism, and can sell modern poetry to almost anyone – was a little dulled by the space and distance in the big room ... He gave Dorothy Livesay, who is one of his most admired intimates, and came over with him for the occasion, a particularly good advertisement, but also 'did right' by Anne Marriott, Pat Page, and Earle Birney."[16] P.K. Page was in Victoria from 1944 to 1946. Her mother, Rose, bought a house (1626 Wilmot Place) across the street from Perry in the fall of 1945, and the two writers, thirty-five years apart in age, were briefly neighbours.[17]

Perry's circle also included other Ryerson Chap-Book poets: the "lovely" Frances Ebbs-Canavan (*Harvest of Dreams*, no. 69, 1935); the "peculiar" Audrey Alexandra Brown (*V-E Day*, no. 120, 1946) ("I tried to make friends with her, but she has always been very unresponsive"); and Hermia Harris Fraser (*Songs of the Western Islands*, no. 109, 1945; *The Arrow-Maker's Daughter and Other Haida Chants*, no. 169, 1957), whom Perry comforted when her son died in the Second World War:

I have not yet seen Hermia Fraser's Songs of the West Coast Islands, but shall get a copy as soon as she has any for sale. I was very glad that she has this collection published in book form, as she has been one of our hardest literary workers here for many years, and like myself has had reams of material published in magazines etc. where it then disappeared forever, not in any way helping one's literary advance. And any lift is a help to her now, when she has to try and rise above the shockingly sudden death of her lovely eldest son – one of the most attractive and finest boys I have seen grow up in Victoria. We were *all* shocked and depressed by Nicky's death.[18]

Both Harris Fraser and Perry sold their writing to magazines. Both sought a more lasting place in books. Perry could not alleviate her friend's ordeal, but her sympathy is a measure of their proximity. Victoria was no New York, but it did possess a number of poets with whom Perry socialized.

The modernist/romantic binary too readily erases a writer like Perry. It is more productive to understand the two literary modes as combining and overlapping in her work. If the preceding list of acquaintances projects a complex position in the literary field, then her mixed feelings about the local CAA only stake it out further. As a past president, she was loyal to the association, but she grew more than a little frustrated when idle conservatism got the upper hand. Still, when Earle Birney, newly appointed to the Department of English at the University of British Columbia, became the editor of *Canadian Poetry Magazine* in 1946, succeeding prior editors like Nathaniel A. Benson, Perry greeted the "drastic" change with some trepidation:

> At the C.A.A. Poetry Group meeting, last Thursday, the subject came up; and the convener said, "Well, there will probably not be one of us who will be able to place a poem with the C.P.M. now, except Miss Perry." That amused me. I said: "My work is hardly modern enough to appeal to Earle Birney." But the fact that I am considered the only admirer, and practicer of "Modern" poetry in the group will give some idea of how far we have fallen from the days when Dr [E.J.] Pratt said we had the best working poetry group in Canada ... I go on attending the meetings, and trying to keep "Modern" poetry on the map in some small way. By "modern" I mean not only free verse, but the quite different approach to a subject which the moderns practice

as compared with that of the early Victorian poets. As four of our older men all now having some influence in the local Branch C.A.A., dislike and make no effort to understand the new poetry, it is as a voice crying in the desert to try to make any impression on the group at present.[19]

Birney was known for his leftist contributions to the *Canadian Forum*; his two Governor General's Literary Awards; and his dense, learned, bold style. Perry's ambivalence toward modernism is palpable in her distinguishing herself from him while simultaneously criticizing the local CAA for its reactionary attitude. In any event, Birney would prove receptive to her work. He accepted her poem "Nettle-Shy," a free-verse dialogue that distills something of the Book of Job, for *Canadian Poetry Magazine*, and a fruitful editorial relationship soon ensued between them. Perry met Birney when he gave a talk at a Victoria CAA meeting on 30 November 1946. Pierce wrote approvingly of their connection: "When you have pleased him [Birney], you may be sure your work is very good."[20]

The most important figure in Perry's literary community, however, was Pierce. He was the editor through whom she published her books. Sandra Campbell describes Pierce's complex turn to modernist poetry in the 1940s, and it is the proper context in which to locate Perry's poetics. Campbell's account is multifaceted, but one salient aspect is that Pierce's turn was less a conversion than an accommodation, brokered partly by congenial critics such as E.K. Brown (who, with a foot in the university, saw an academic rather than a popular function for poetry). Pierce accumulated new poets for the Ryerson list – Birney, Dorothy Livesay, P.K. Page, A.J.M. Smith, F.R. Scott, Patrick Anderson, and John Sutherland – without abandoning old ones – Archibald Lampman, Bliss Carman, Marjorie Pickthall – whose work he continued to keep in the public view through both new editions and school books. His notorious edition of Carman's *The Selected Poems of Bliss Carman* (1954), which severely abridged several poems in an attempt to tailor them to a new taste, symbolizes his conflicted loyalties. Idealism and beauty continued to define real poetry for Pierce, but realism and shock were true to a Canada that had come through the Great Depression and the Second World War: "As he saw it, the modernists were both expressive of and ravaged by the grim forces of the contemporary world. As a result, before the war was out, he felt the need to publish them."[21]

This need appeared in his correspondence with Perry. "The tendency in verse today is toward ultra-modern, hard-bitten and realistic," Pierce advised her, adding, "I think perhaps it will have a salutary effect for the Canadian artist in both words and paint is reluctant to look into the faces of the people about him." Pierce deplored the "strident," "adolescent," and "astonishingly crude" tones of some contemporary self-expression, but he saw the virtue in shaking up the establishment, in particular "the Canadian Authors' Associations and Poetry Clubs across Canada, which for so long have narrowly escaped being mutual admiration societies."[22] After reading an issue of *Contemporary Verse*, he continued, "I am bound to confess that I cannot appreciate some of the modern stuff." Yet in the same letter he praised Perry thus: "I like your work because it is modern, and by that I mean contemporary. I think everything that can be said has been said about 'The Song of the Throstle' and 'The Lily Asleep on the Pool in the Moonlight.'"[23] The editorial message was difficult: be modern, but not ultramodern.

Perry proved equal to negotiating this challenge. "One does not want Canada to be behind in any of the contemporary trends, even if they turn out to be only temporary ones," she replied. She pointed to Brown's *On Canadian Poetry*, which Pierce had published in 1943, as a recipe for the right blend of tradition and originality:

> You will have noted that although E.K. Brown praised, and gave much room to, the so-called "moderns," he went back to Lampman and D.C. Scott for the masters of Canadian poetry. You, I know, would do likewise. I am sure that Brown, even as you and I, wishes to have Canada keep abreast of the times. There is no doubt that Canadian writers are still self-conscious to the extent of shying away from the ugly, and so-called "realistic" themes, or treatment of themes. I am myself. Our communities in general are small, and we feel that if we wrote something that some people living close to us, even if only prudes, thought improper, we should have unkind things said about us. People do say unkind and untrue things about us, of course, but we have a horror of being called "offensive."
>
> But that is not to say we might not be original in our chosen forms, and treatment of forms; and I agree with you that the time has come when Canadian writers should branch out, and that the purely lyric poem should not be specialized in as it has been in the past.[24]

Perry situated her poetics in a Canadian tradition rooted in the Confederation Poets. She saw the poet's goal to push the edge of tradition, but rejected ugliness, irresponsibility, or gratuitous transgression as the means. Perry had written lyrics and valued their expression of sentiment. This much is clear from lines like "The bud is lovelier than the rose, full-blown; / But barren is the path I tread alone."[25] In stepping away from the confessional mode, maintaining a certain propriety, keeping abreast of the times, and drawing on Lampman and D.C. Scott, she studiously traced Pierce's principles and aligned herself with him.

Perry's reading, like her social circle, positioned her to appreciate both tradition and change in poetry. She attended the Pacific Northwest Writers' Conference in Seattle in August 1945 and read the poetry of the keynote speaker, John Gould Fletcher. She admired his early imagism but noted that he had exchanged it for a Southern regionalism, and she was interested to learn of his respect for Pratt.[26] She read Yeats and critical studies of his poetry, such as Louis MacNeice's *The Poetry of W.B. Yeats* (Oxford, 1941): "I enjoyed every word of it, and chortled over the fact that [MacNeice], who was such a great d[is]ciple of T.S. Eliot, has in this book more or less repudiated him and his poetry."[27] Joseph M. Hone's biography, *W.B. Yeats: 1865–1939* (Macmillan, 1942), left her feeling the gap between the Irish poet's cultural milieu and her own: "his opportunities to mix with artists and writers from his earliest years gave him contacts which never ceased to be useful and important in forwarding his career."[28]

The depth of her reading was due in part to her participation in the Victoria Literary Society, a general interest reading group to whom, in the 1940s, she gave an annual talk on recent Canadian literature. She was impressed with Elsie Pomeroy's *Sir Charles G.D. Roberts: A Biography* (Ryerson Press, 1943) for its lifting of a poet out of the checkered reputation of a man: "Because Roberts for a number of years was so approachable, and so much in evidence, (and for some other less virtuous reasons), he had suffered to some extent from that contempt which familiarity is said to breed. We needed to be reminded that he was a really distinguished writer when only middle-aged ... [who] did so much to help Canadian literature advance to its present position."[29] D.C. Scott and E.K. Brown's edition of previously unpublished poems by Archibald Lampman, *At the Long Sault, and Other New Poems* (Ryerson Press, 1943), created a stir, and Perry reviewed it for the *Western Recorder*.[30] Before Birney accepted her work, Perry praised *David and Other Poems* (Ryerson Press, 1942), which had won the Governor General's Literary Award. However, she judged Audrey Alexandra Brown's *Challenge to Time and Death* (Macmillan Canada, 1943) to be "disappointing as compared with [her] former works."[31] She did not like the Canadian modernist anthology *Unit of Five* (Ryerson Press, 1944), "nor found a great deal of poetry in it, but it does illustrate what you said about the writer or artist 'looking into the faces of the people about him.'"[32] Dorothy Livesay's *Day and Night* (Ryerson Press, 1944) affected Perry. She saw quality and difficulty in it, but to her it also embodied the receding of poetry from popular culture: "Behind my remarks, and thoughts [on *Day and Night*], I think there was a feeling that it was not worth while to write any more simple, or lyric poetry, as the newspaper and magazine market for that type of material at least in Canada – indeed for any kind of poetry – has almost vanished ... That would be an odd reason for the improvement or elevation of Canadian poetry, wouldn't it? The possibility that one could no longer get a cheque for the simpler types of verse?"[33] Perry's reading was extensive, scrupulous, and current. She grew up on a farm and never attended university, but through community organizations, literary magazines, and books (often borrowed from the Victoria Public Library), she applied herself to discover what was happening in the world of poetry.

After having "reams of material published in magazines etc. where it then disappeared forever," Perry found a somewhat better toehold on the cliff of literature through the books that she published with Pierce. Although the Ryerson Press offered her terms only marginally better than those of self-publication, Perry embraced them eagerly. She bought and distributed copies of her books, promoted the Ryerson Press, shaped her creativity to the Chap-Book form, and shrewdly cultivated a poetic vision as close to the editor's heart, perhaps, as any writer could reach.

Hearing a Far Call (no. 102, 1942 [1943]) marked Perry's entry into the Ryerson Poetry Chap-Books, which had recently broken the threshold of one hundred titles. Perry took the sixty-two-line dramatic monologue "Doro-Lynd Comes Home" from *Hero in Ermine* and added an introduction and four sections to precede it, expanding it sevenfold to 456 lines that weave in and out of iambic pentameter and rhyme. In it, she tells the story of a woman who leaves husband and child behind in Canada to pursue an acting career in Europe. The plot is tragic. The protagonist, Doro-Lynd, becomes the Juliet she plays to such acclaim, but like Shakespeare's tragedies the effect is not simply didactic: one sympathizes

TABLE 5.1
Chronological list of books by M. Eugenie Perry

The Girl in the Silk Dress and Other Stories. Ottawa: [self-published], Overbrook Press, 1931. Short fiction, 144 pages.
Hero in Ermine and Other Poems. Victoria: [self-published], Clarke Printing Co., 1939. Poetry, 31 pages.
Hearing a Far Call. Ryerson Poetry Chap-Book no. 102. Toronto: Ryerson Press, 1942 [1943]. Poetry, 12 pages.
Canteen. Victoria: [self-published], Clarke Printing Co., 1944. Poetry, 19 pages.
Two Hundred and Fifty Thousand Strong: A Survey of the Deaf and Hard of Hearing Organizations in Canada. [Toronto: Lorne Pierce, 1946]. Amateur history, vi, 49 pages.
Song in the Silence and Other Poems. Ryerson Poetry Chap-Book no. 123. Toronto: Ryerson Press, 1947. Poetry, 16 pages.
Green Timbers and Other Poems. Toronto: Ryerson Press, 1955. Poetry, 57 pages.

---

with Doro-Lynd as she reluctantly leaves a loveless marriage, tastes the loneliness of fame, seeks rest with a second husband in Vienna, and witnesses his killing by Nazi soldiers. The poem ends with her leading a group of Austrian refugees to a new life in Canada. Allusions to Shakespeare (*As You Like It, Romeo and Juliet*) tilt the mood gradually from comic pastoral to urban tragedy, and the protagonist's name seems chosen for its rhythmic equivalence to both "Rosalind" and "Juliet," an effect stressed by the repetition of a refrain involving the names that does not scan: "Doro-Lynd, Doro-Lynd, Juliet! / She is the realest Juliet of them all!"[34] It is a war poem, in so far as it allegorizes global catastrophe in one woman's ruinous journey. It is also a Canadian poem, and uses images of pines to symbolize the fresh start that the country offers to prodigal and immigrant alike.

The contract for *Hearing a Far Call*, dated 29 December 1942, specifies professional terms of publication. Perry did not have a literary agent. Most Canadian writers in the 1940s still did not, although exceptions like Sara Jeannette Duncan can be traced as far back as the 1890s.[35] What she signed adhered to the new standard adopted about the time of Marriott's *The Wind Our Enemy*. Perry's agreement offered a royalty and a half-dozen complimentary copies in exchange for a flat-out copyright transfer, and the author was not required to guarantee the press against loss: "The Author agrees to assign his copyright in the said work to the Publisher subject to the following: HEARING A FAR CALL will be published as a Ryerson Poetry Chap-Book to retail at 60¢ a copy, the Author to receive a royalty of 10% on the list price of all copies sold."[36] As the inside front cover states, it had the usual print run of 250 copies. The book probably appeared early in 1943: the contract was signed in the dying days of 1942; Evelyn Eaton's *Birds before Dawn*, the Chap-Book (no. 101) immediately prior to Perry's, is dated 1943; and both Chap-Books have the identical series advertisement on the inside back cover. Over the next year and a half, thirty-two copies were given away for promotion and review and 138 copies sold, leaving eighty in stock. This was a "better record than some of the chap books have achieved."[37]

The contract was professional, but behind the scenes Perry still had to intervene in the financing. Based on the sales figures, one might calculate a gross revenue of $82.80, royalties to the author of $8.28, and a remainder of $74.52 to cover printing. This calculation would not be far off, except that many of the sales were to the author. It is clear that, after receiving her six free author copies, Perry purchased a good number more: "As for *Hearing a Far Call*, I am enclosing an order in this letter for twenty more copies, and I think I may say that if within a reasonable time you still have more copies on your shelves than future orders for the complete Chap-book series are likely to take care of, I shall send another considerable order."[38] As stipulated in her contract, the author bought copies of her book at the "trade price," rather than the retail price.[39] Nevertheless, these transactions were more than enough to cancel out any royalties that she might have earned. After seventeen years of Ryerson Poetry Chap-Books, authors were still effectively subsidizing publication.

Perry not only helped to finance her book, but also took an active part in distribution and promotion, like Kathryn Munro twenty years earlier (see chapter 2). Pierce was trying to move the series to a subscription basis in the spring of 1943: "May we suggest that you put your name down to receive the chap-books as they are published. The expense is negligible! ... send in your standing order today for future chap-books as they appear."[40] Nine months later, Perry shared his chagrin "that in a population of about 12,000,000, at least a hundred could not be found who would be willing to stand behind this series." When Pierce informed her that "we spend far more than the manufacturing price on these chap books, trying to promote them," Perry exerted herself to remedy the problem. She indicated "people with money" who were known to buy Canadian books in order to support domestic authorship – Robert Reid of Vancouver, Judge Fred Martin of Victoria, Lady Amy Redpath Roddick of Montreal – and promised to supply "a list of Victoria people who could afford to buy" if Pierce committed to sending each a personal invitation to support the series.[41]

An internal memo indicates that the Ryerson Press responded seriously: "Could Miss Perry send the list she suggests – of Victoria people who can afford to buy. Could you ask other Chap-Book authors to do the same thing? Then we could put on a campaign for our 100 subscribers."[42] The plan made little headway, however. In the fall of 1945 Pierce was still toying with "the hope of building up advance orders from collectors and institutions for at least 100 each edition."[43] Such tactics – subscription publishing and tasking authors with finding buyers – were more than familiar to the Methodist Book and Publishing House in the days of William Briggs (see chapter 1).[44] The reversion to them is a sign of the poor economic conditions for Canadian literary production, against which, nonetheless, the Chap-Books persisted through the editor's commitment and the authors' willingness to assume the business aspects of publication.

In effect, Perry worked as an unpaid promotional agent for the Chap-Book series and the Ryerson Press as a whole. As noted above, she reviewed Ryerson books for the Victoria Literary Society, advocating especially for the Chap-Books:

> I explained that they played a useful part in putting forward Canadian poetry. Publishers, however willing to help Canadian writers, I explained, were opposed by the public apathy to home-grown poetry. So, feeling not quite justified in taking the risk of publishing a larger, cloth-bound book, which would cost at least $250.00, the Ryerson Press, at your suggestion, invented these smaller chap-books, which, costing perhaps from $75.00 to $100.00, did not involve so much expense, yet gave less-known writers an opportunity of getting their work before the public, and perhaps of going on from there to real prominence, as, I cited, in the case of Anne Marriott who won the Governor-General's prize with one of these chap-books.[45]

Perry wished to see Ryerson books displayed better in Victoria bookshops, observing that the department store Spencer's was the only local place to carry the Chap-Books.[46] During a plenary session of the Pacific

Northwest Writers' Conference, when the discussion turned to the difficulty of getting poetry published even in the United States, Perry stood up and recommended the Chap-Books – inexpensive, national, cumulative – as a solution: "I think a lot of people were interested as they spoke to me about the matter afterwards, and asked questions."[47] When she wrote about fellow Ryerson authors for the newspapers, she sent Pierce the clippings, and eventually he could not help but thank her: "You have been doing good work for a long time in connection with Canadian books and this House appreciates your loyalty to its authors and books as time has gone on."[48] Canadian literary culture undoubtedly drew strength from the enthusiastic support of women like Perry.

These efforts were not wasted. *Hearing a Far Call* received favourable reviews. *Canadian Poetry Magazine* called it "a distinguished and mature piece of work, rich in drama, in lyric beauty, and in human understanding." *Saturday Night* praised its "originality" and its "sharp, vivid description."[49] In his annual national poetry survey, E.K. Brown ranked Earle Birney's *David and Other Poems* first, followed by Ralph Gustafson's *Lyrics Unromantic* and Anne Marriott's *Salt Marsh*, and continued, "Among the smaller collections of the year the Ryerson chapbooks were outstanding." Brown praised Perry's versification and story, but challenged her to enrich her characterization: "The characters in Miss M. Eugenie Perry's *Hearing a Far Call* do not come alive and the situation is not so treated as to disguise its essential commonplaceness, but there are passages in the narrative which have a pleasing music and in pure narrative Miss Perry is notable."[50] The reception extended into the United States. J. Berg Esenwein, in the November 1943 issue of the *Writer's Monthly* (Springfield, Massachusetts), called *Hearing a Far Call* "a striking narrative poem ... [that] is especially effective in its shorter lyrical passages." On 22 February 1944, Ellen Cubitt gave a dramatic reading of *Hearing a Far Call* at a meeting of the Boz Club, a Toronto literary society. Perry's sister attended and reported that Cubitt delivered the poem beautifully to an audience of seventy-five people. Perry also adapted the poem into a radio play and submitted it to the CBC. The broadcaster did not accept it, because "the sound of the pines, which was the principal sound effect called for, would be difficult to reproduce," but encouraged her to submit something else.[51] As important as these public reactions were the judgments the author received privately, such as from Floris Clark McLaren: "she considered *Hearing a Far Call* to be one of the best chapbooks [Pierce] had published. She said that might have been in part because it was one long poem, and so gave a much better idea of a writer's talent than could a dozen or so short poems which often did not have a noticeable thread of connection between each and each. She called it a sustained piece of work."[52] This last phrase particularly resonated, but all of the attention to her first professionally published book brought Perry legitimation as a serious poet.

The contract for *Hearing a Far Call* gave Ryerson the right of first refusal on Perry's next manuscript, but Pierce declined Perry's *Canteen*, a collection of poems inspired by her volunteer work at the Three Services Canteen on Broad Street in Victoria during the war. She pitched the book appealingly. Currency and accessibility were two of its deliberate qualities. In her words, it was "much more objective tha[n] H.A.F.C., and so might appeal to more people, especially as it is so timely."[53] Moreover, she offered to underwrite production: "I have previously stated that I would buy one hundred copies – intending to give fifty outright to be sold for the Three Services Canteen. The hundred would cost me fifty dollars, and that is all I feel I can put into the book. I could have a book done locally for that."[54] The comment is illuminating, first for disclosing the cost of having a chapbook printed privately, and second for revealing the Chap-Books as a structure still perched on the practice of self-publication without being either totally equivalent to or entirely separable from it. Although Perry had correctly discerned so much, Pierce turned down this submission, citing the overabundance of war verse – it "has become a drug with us and we cannot sell it" – and larger operating troubles. "Our poetry is reduced to the minimum," he stated. "The number of Chap-Books we publish and formal collections of greater length are even now giving us trouble."[55] Campbell explains that publishing poetry, difficult enough in 1940 due to "appalling" sales, was "even more problematic" now, toward the end of the war, because the Canadian government, reacting to material and labour shortages, compelled publishers to reduce their paper consumption and prioritize textbooks.[56]

Consequently, Perry "went down to the Clarke Printing Company's office" on a day in July 1944 "and made arrangements to have them print 250 or 300 [copies] – not sure which yet – of *Canteen*." The edition was ready in September, and Perry sent out review copies to local newspapers, which gave it good notices. CKMC Radio in Vancouver even broadcast a reading of some of the poems. As far as Perry was concerned, however, "it was printed about a year late. I seem to have got beyond most of the material included, and one's thoughts about the war kept on changing each year, so that some of the earlier-written stuff seemed to have been done in a former life. But then writers are like that, I think, and keep finding when they have completed new work, that what they did before has grown a bit shadowy."[57] Bare self-publication was now disappointing, not only because of Perry's satisfaction with her first Ryerson Chap-Book, but also because she was gunning for her next one.

❧✝❦

IN THEIR HOUSE IN OAK BAY (1627 Wilmot Place), Perry lived with and supported her sister, Gertrude Elizabeth Perry, as the latter progressively lost her hearing. Gertrude had a hearing aid, still very much a new and unwieldy technology in the 1940s, and Eugenie would help her "struggle" to use it comfortably.[58] This was precisely the situation that Pierce was in: "Both Pierce children remember the nightly formality of dinner, where each child in turn was expected to be an intelligent and cultured conversationalist with their witty father. His hearing aid was set to catch their words as much as possible."[59] Pierce had been a key player in the chartering of the National Society of the Deaf and Hard of Hearing in Toronto in 1940, which sought to coordinate the many municipal and regional associations that predated it.[60] The Canadian deaf advocacy movement now had a president and a secretary-treasurer. Pierce believed that what it needed next was a historian. Overworked himself, he turned to Eugenie Perry with the idea, and to her credit she took charge of it.

Perry devised a questionnaire to gather information and mailed copies of it to deaf advocacy groups across the country. Over the course of 1942, the responses trickled in, most, however, describing an association's present members and projects rather than its past. Perry, as she compiled her findings, began to adjust her planned history into something more of a descriptive survey of work being done for the deaf in Canada. Then came the epiphany:

> Until I started to collect material for the Deaf and Hard of Hearing History, I had never come in contact with any of those whom the public speak about as "deaf and dumb." When Miss Paulson – then of Montreal, now of Portland – came out here in 1942 she came to see me, and brought Mrs George Riley of Victoria with her. Speaking of Mr G. Riley, Miss Paulson said: "You'll fall for him." She had to

write it down, as her speech was too difficult for me to understand. When I met him I agreed with her that he was very attractive, and indeed meeting those three gave me an entirely new picture of the really "deaf." No doubt they are unusually clever, but they made me feel that there was no insuperable barrier between those who speak, and those who write, or just use sign language. I merely felt that I was trying to communicate with people whose language I did not understand, as foreigners, and I had no feeling of superiority at all.[61]

The scare quotes indicate the pressure of Perry's insight. She forces words that until then she had seen as pejorative to denote her new understanding of the full humanity – the beauty, even – of deaf-mute people. The conversion narrative is respectful, political, and sexual. Perry was already a friend of people with hearing loss, but at this moment she felt her perspective change.

The history/survey was obstructed and would be self-published, but not by Perry. She had a draft ready by 18 July 1943 and dedicated it to her sister. Upon receiving it, Pierce forwarded it to the National Society executive for review. The placement officer, E.B. Lally, who had been a teacher at the Ontario School for the Deaf in Belleville for more than twenty years, agreed to correct the text, especially to fill in the gaps regarding the society's founding. This important step never happened. Whether he was opposed to Perry's text, unable to revise it, or simply too busy, Lally did not advance the project. Perry suspected that her not being deaf was the reason: "I know the attitude they are possibly taking. 'Why wasn't I, or why weren't we asked to [do] this instead of an outsider?'" Pierce, however, had chosen her precisely because of this disinterest. She was not inclined to over-represent either those born deaf or those with hearing loss. As time went by, even the patient Perry grew upset over her stalled manuscript: "Have those people at headquarters not yet released it? Why leave it with them any longer."[62]

Pierce was equally exasperated when at last the national executive returned the work, untouched. "I think you will have to spend a holiday in the East," he wrote to Perry, "and bring your gun ... I have asked these people regularly, month after month, to get me material that will fill in the blanks in your records ... I don't think Mr Lally is very much interested in the venture, although, in my judgment, it is [of] very good value and I told him that I was going to make this material available to institutions for the Hard of Hearing and the Deaf as well as educational institutions and libraries all across Canada, if I have to do it at my own expense."[63] In the end, Pierce personally financed an inexpensive edition of 250 copies. The text was mimeographed on 8½ × 11" paper; only the cover and title page were printed. Early in 1946, Pierce received *Two Hundred and Fifty Thousand Strong: A Survey of the Deaf and Hard of Hearing Organizations in Canada* from the Ryerson bindery. He sent the first dozen copies to Perry and distributed most of the others for free to interested institutions and individuals.[64] The episode reveals once again Pierce's alacrity to operate in the manner of a small press. He desired a writer's work, hit obstacles in others' apathy, forged ahead impetuously at personal sacrifice, and achieved a product that was as paltry in form as it was dignified in character. It also reveals the sympathetic collaboration that had exploded between Pierce and Perry concerning deafness.

Their bond over hearing loss is what generated Perry's excellent, second Ryerson Chap-Book, *Song in the Silence and Other Poems*. Perry conceived the title poem in the fall of 1943, after writing *Two Hundred and Fifty Thousand Strong*, and made headway with it the following spring at a time when it was also growing clear to her that, whereas *Hearing a Far Call* had made a mark, her collection of short war poems might languish. Her first reference to "Song in the Silence" presents it as "another narrative poem which might appeal to you more than Canteen, and which will perhaps be ready, with several quite good shorter poems, not about the war – the narrative poem is not about the war, either – by next year when you say you will be ready to consider another collection."[65] The remark that a story about hearing loss "might appeal" to Pierce is modest. In fact, Perry was in the midst of discovering that Pierce's deafness was, like Beethoven's, a spur to accomplishment.

She finished the first draft of "Song in the Silence" early in the fall of 1944, and permitted herself to name it for the first time to Pierce, formally. She had written much of it outside:

> In the rather unusual late spell of summer weather which we had in September, I sat out on the porch or in the garden ... and read, and wrote. Wrote slowly, sometimes only a line or so a day, but even so I managed to get the first rough copy of the narrative poem – Song in the Silence – on which I had been working for a year, finished. It seems to me to be quite good, but as no one else has seen it yet,

> I am not sure whether I have anything of value, or not. I want to read it to a few friends whose opinion I value, and then put on the finishing touches.⁶⁶

Perry drew creative strength from her garden, from the trees of Wilmot Place, and from the birds. Her correspondence from this time captures the beauty of her surroundings: "As I sit now, typing on the front porch, I look north over two gardens to the end of the blind street, with great trees all around rising against the sky, and realize as on every summer day, how fortunate we are in our situation."⁶⁷ Perry was reading Lampman that August, and one feels her writing adhering to his favourite pattern, the mind's renewal in nature. She joined the local Natural History Society and went on excursions (to Goldstream for instance) to learn about flora and fauna. What she writes of Linnet was true for her writing self: "Now, all around her Nature's impulse stirred: / Fragrance of bud, breath from the turned earth, / Simmer and sound of bird and insect breed" (357–9). Moreover, Perry knew that her images of gardens would appeal to Pierce, for he, too, had one he adored at his home in Toronto.

Perry revised her long poem over the next year, according to the reactions she received from the friends in her literary circle, and added the shorter poems that would fill out the chapbook. "Tanager," a virtuosic exercise in the sprung rhythm of Gerard Manley Hopkins, commemorates her rare sighting of this species in her garden. Alan Crawley accepted this poem for *Contemporary Verse*.⁶⁸ "The Mainspring" she carried over from *Canteen*, and it became the last poem in the next book. She wrote "Whom You Must Fear" (originally titled "Whom We Must Fear"), a free-verse riddle about ethics and conscience, in July 1945 and first shared it with Pierce by letter.⁶⁹ "Fall of the Mighty," a late addition to the collection, won the 1946 national CAA Canadian Poetry Contest. Perry had submitted it under the pseudonym "John Oxford," and after studying it the judges guessed that the author must be A.J.M. Smith.⁷⁰ The long poem was her chief concern, but Perry was set on including the others, too, to show both the breadth of her style and her record of success with magazine publications and prizes.

When Perry submitted the manuscript of *Song in the Silence and Other Poems* to Pierce in October 1945, she explained the extent to which the Chap-Book form had guided her writing:

> Today I spent hours counting lines, and apportioning *so* many lines to each printed page, so that what I am forwarding might be compassed in a sixteen-page chapbook. When I first started the long poem, Song In The Silence, I aimed to have it fit into eight pages, with a number of other poems added to make a twelve-page book. But the poem just wouldn't be cramped into that space, and the fugitive poems kept piling up. As I have arranged it the pages will not be any more crowded than in Hearing a far call, and I did not hear any one call it crowded. As a matter of fact buyers grumble if the small books contain any empty pages, or pages half-filled – I have heard them.[71]

Using her first Chap-Book as a measure, Perry laid out and trimmed her second. She knew how many pages made a book (sixteen) and how many lines fit on a page (fifty, maximum). Her original arrangement ended with "Tanager," because Pelham Edgar had judged it "better than first rate" and "readers should be left with a good send-off." Another poem in the submission, "Lovely Birds," would be cut to make room for "Fall of the Mighty" after the latter won the CAA prize.[72] Otherwise, the book was printed very nearly as Perry submitted it. She had written to the available form with exactitude.

Still, Perry made her submission with trepidation. She knew that she was running a great risk in submitting a story about deafness to a deaf editor. This was one of the reasons for the year's delay: "Perhaps I wondered how you would like it."[73] Any anxiety she felt about offending Pierce, however, was quickly allayed, for he accepted *Song in the Silence and Other Poems* immediately: "We like your manuscript very much." Initially, there was some discussion about whether the text would indeed fit into the sixteen allotted pages. Pierce also could not promise when the book would appear – "Unfortunately, we see [no] chance of our being able to bring it out before the Autumn of 1946 as we are swamped with work now and can hardly see our way ahead at all"[74] – but on the whole, Perry had delivered a winner.

She acknowledged the acceptance with delight: "Received your letter of Nov. 10th, last week, and was both pleased and relieved that you liked my manuscript. I had been so close to Song In The Silence that it was difficult to know how it would appear to anyone else, although a great deal of work, and thought, and emotion had gone into the making of it."[75] Pierce's approval of poem and poet is manifest in his generous decision a few weeks later to self-publish her *Two Hundred and Fifty Thousand Strong*. His evaluation was, and remains, crucial to the validation of "Song in the Silence" as a genuine account of disability, albeit one from a non-disabled writer.

The truth of the poem may stem from the fact that Perry identified with some of the disadvantage within the deaf person's experience. It was not easy to be an aging, unmarried woman in 1940s Canada, a society on the brink of the Baby Boom. Perry's letters are full of graceful cheer, but occasionally she let down her guard. Describing another friend with hearing loss, Archdeacon Robert Connell (former president of the Natural History Society), Perry turned the analysis on herself: "I feel that same poignance for myself, so much less worthy, but facing towards the sunset years with so little accomplished, such an unfulfilled life."[76] These feelings are captured in her poem "Hummingbird":

> Darting from flower to flower the hummingbird
> Gleams in his feathering of red and green.
> The lady, darting too, quaintly absurd,
> Cuts fragrant branches from her woodbine screen
> To carry to a neighbour's ailing child.
> She wears gay silks to mock the spinning years –
> Love, has it passed while little cares beguiled
> Her days? She laughs to still her clutching fears;
> And hums a measure of lost melody
> Timed to the waltz; then patterns in her mind
> A gold gown for the dance for charity:
> Her fading youth and beauty loath to find
> A mirror in the bird-sprite flashing by –
> So bright, so lovely, and so soon to fly.[77]

She felt herself to be a spinster, easily overlooked: "My mind *has* roamed continually afield, and I have traveled a lot, too, physically; but most people do not realize that, because I am a very unimpressive person."[78] She reluctantly agreed to have her photograph in the newspaper when *Two Hundred and Fifty Thousand Strong* was published, and was vulnerable to judgments of it: "I asked her [a neighbour] what she thought of the photograph. She said: 'Well – it had your smile, and I liked that; but Hubby said it didn't flatter you'. My friends, and even acquaintances here all seem to have agreed with

'Hubby.'"[79] Of course, gender, age, and physical appearance do not constitute a disability. "Song in the Silence" furnishes the wisdom that everyone must deal with one kind of disadvantage or another, and, on the flip side, that disabled people harbour more abilities than one might assume.

Perry had helped to publish her first Chap-Book and worked to promote the series as a whole. She had reoriented her writing according to the criticism implicit in a rejected follow-up collection. She had collaborated with Pierce to serve the Canadian deaf community, had meticulously fitted her next manuscript to the Chap-Book's material constraints, and had won his approval in her treatment of what for him was a very personal matter. When, after all this, another year elapsed, casting the realization of her second Chap-Book into doubt, Perry launched a final effort to achieve the desired result. She reminded Pierce that, although it had not sold out, *Hearing a Far Call* "did get more press notices almost than any chapbook which has been published that year or since," second only to Anne Marriott's *Calling Adventurers!* (no. 89, 1941). She stressed that publication "means so very much to me." She appealed to Pierce's nationalism, knowing that "you have continued the publication of the chapbooks, not from any idea of earning money for Ryerson's, for they are not big enough, in edition, to mean much either in outlay or profit, but to help along the cause of Canadian poetry." Finally, she once again made the key offer to support publication financially: "The new collection, also, contains a long poem which may be considered a sustained piece of work, though in a different vein from *Hearing a Far Call*, and in the event of its publication, I shall of course buy a good percentage of the copies, as in the former case."[80]

This final appeal was effective. Pierce promised to push her Chap-Book through the queue and bring it out by the following spring. Perry signed the contract, dated 16 January 1947, for an edition of 500 copies (double the normal print run) and accepted the new terms that Pierce had instituted: "sixty free copies of the book in lieu of all royalty."[81]

※✢※

SONG IN THE SILENCE AND OTHER POEMS, like many a Chap-Book before it, was published through a complex process of sympathetic cooperation and material adversity, mingling romantic and modern influences, bringing the author credit but not profit, and starkly pointing Canadian literature on its way forward toward the small press. In it, Perry not only fulfilled her potential as a serious poet worthy of a national readership, but also delivered a transformative discourse on the dignity of the deaf and hard-of-hearing community. Working intimately with her editor, she blended romantic and modernist themes and techniques into a poem of true social responsibility. Her work, almost unknown today, represents the tissue of the Ryerson Poetry Chap-Books in the 1940s. Moreover, the qualities that Perry experienced in her collaboration with Pierce – small-scale printing, sympathy, and spirituality – would soon play a key role in careers as diverse as Dorothy Livesay's and Al Purdy's.

SIX

A Responsible Home

Dorothy Livesay

TO PORTRAY LIFE IN CANADA was one of Lorne Pierce's prime purposes in editing the Ryerson Poetry Chap-Books. M. Eugenie Perry's Chap-Books had responded to it, as had many others written across the country. As the series entered its final decade, it achieved another landmark representation of Canada in *Call My People Home* (no. 143, 1950) by Dorothy Livesay (1909–1996). In an influential review, Northrop Frye singled it out for praise soon after it was published. Livesay herself for a time considered the title poem her best work. It is foundational to the genre of the Canadian documentary long poem that Livesay later theorized, and it was probably the first work of imaginative literature to engage with what has since been recognized as a major event in Canadian history: the internment of Japanese Canadians during the Second World War. It deals explicitly with gender and racial inequalities, and seems in hindsight a forerunner of the swelling politicization of Canadian poetry after the 1960s, predicting the social-justice poetics and hence the careers of writers such as Dionne Brand and Margaret Atwood. If Livesay demonstrated that Canadian poetry could be at once lyrical and leftist, "Call My People Home" represents a major step in her doing so.

This chapter will interpret the poem in the context of its publishing history in order to argue that its chief quality, both politically and aesthetically, is responsibility. Prior chapters have argued that the Ryerson Poetry Chap-Books played an important role in the making of many poets in twentieth-century Canada, focusing on the material conditions of Canadian literature, which generally remained so difficult that these tiny books published at a loss were nevertheless pivotal to the average writer's career. This chapter will maintain the theme while demonstrating in the first instance the political work that Livesay undertook in "Call My People Home." In writing it, Livesay knew that she was speaking for an ethnic community to which she did not belong. It was therefore paramount to ascertain and report the facts of their experiences as accurately as possible. Her goal was not to write the last word on the Japanese Canadian internment or the redress movement, which Ken Adachi, Joy Kogawa, and others have since treated extensively,[1] but to make the internment a matter for national literary attention.

Even thus justified by the priority of her intervention, Livesay did not view it lightly. On the contrary, she took on the challenge of political representation artistically, and probed the twin problems of difference and belonging through theme and form. What emerges is a poem of responsibility in two senses. First, "Call My People Home" advocates for a constituency (Japanese Canadians) with a sense of duty and accuracy, much as Perry had done for the deaf and hard-of-hearing community in 1947. Second, it emphasizes responsiveness – the flux of relation across an interval of difference – as a national, human, and spiritual virtue. In this double responsibility, there was a deep correspondence between Livesay's views and Pierce's. The socialism of the former and the nationalism of the latter shaded into each other. Pierce, a son of the Social Gospel, recognized the value of Livesay's reformist activism, and his nationalist inclusivity cooperated with hers. "Call My People Home" thus manifests an aspect of the Chap-Books, a potential for social commentary, that drew strength from the editor's deep-seated interest in a catholic and diverse representation of Canadian experience.

⚜︎

THE COMPATIBILITY between Pierce and Livesay can be traced back to their respective upbringings. Both were raised in Protestant families. From his earliest years, Pierce's mother had ambitions for him to become a Methodist minister. For her part, Livesay was raised in the Anglican tradition by an "extremely traditionally religious" mother and confirmed at the age of fifteen.[2]

Pierce began to cultivate an editorial relation with Livesay shortly after the appearance of her first book, *Green Pitcher* (Toronto: Macmillan Company of Canada, 1928). These were the busy years during which Pierce courted dozens of authors for inclusion in his series. His appreciation for specific poems in *Green Pitcher* must have encouraged Livesay: "You have the gift of real song. I may be a little old fashioned, but I warm to poetry that sings to me as yours does. Then you have ideas, and very beautiful word-pictures to paint them with. Sometimes, as in 'The Invincible,' 'Impuissance,' 'Explanation,' 'Chinese,' and others you approach almost to magic, certainly to the memorable. So go on and up and out and over and crown the promise of your first book."[3] Pierce's admiration for the music, intellect, and imagery of Livesay's poetry indicates that he had no aversion to her style.[4] Then Livesay won the Jardine Memorial Prize in January 1929 for her poem "City Wife," the same University of Toronto prize that Nathaniel A. Benson, whom she knew, had won three years prior for "Twenty and After."[5] Pierce was open to Livesay's poetry, and his praise amounted to a tacit offer to print her next book.

Perhaps he also felt that he should have printed her first, for its production seems to owe much to Ryerson's precedent. *Green Pitcher* is a Ryerson Poetry Chap-Book in all but name. It is a little pamphlet of eight leaves (sixteen pages), saddle-stitched (stapled) in an inexpensive but tastefully designed paper cover. The Livesays paid Macmillan $57.50 to print an edition of 250 copies ($0.23 per copy, including the cover). The retail price was $0.50, and Macmillan invited the author to involve herself in the sales: "This book should sell for 50¢ retail, allowing one third off to the bookseller (17¢) and 15% of the net price to us for handling (5¢) will return you 28¢ per copy, or a profit of 5¢ per book (L6% [i.e., 10 per cent] of the list price). Whatever books you sold yourself at the list price (50¢) would give you a profit of 27% per book, as we do not take the commission when we supply the books to the author."[6]

These terms are close to those that Pierce had developed for his series in the late 1920s (see chapters 2 and 3). To offer a further example for comparison, in 1926 Ryerson printed Leo Cox's *Sheepfold*, a Chap-Book (no. 10) of four leaves (eight pages), likewise in an edition of 250 copies to retail at $0.50 each with a royalty of 10 per cent for the author. The conditions were as follows: "The author agrees to guarantee us against loss at the end of one year from the date of publication. It is understood that the total obligation to the author, even though no copies should be sold, will not exceed fifty-five dollars."[7] Considering that Cox's book was half as long as Livesay's, Ryerson's cost ($55.00 for eight pages) seems higher than Macmillan's ($57.50 for sixteen pages). On the other hand, Macmillan's conditions were harder, in that it demanded the full payment up front, in contrast to Ryerson's more flexible practice of reckoning what the author might owe after a year. Thus, following quite closely the model of a Ryerson Poetry Chap-Book, Livesay and her parents published *Green Pitcher* on their own initiative, financing the printing and taking charge of the sales.

By the time her second book, *Signpost* (Toronto: Macmillan Company of Canada, 1932), appeared, Livesay had converted to socialism and embraced "first, social work as a career and then communism as a belief."[8] Her year in Paris at the Sorbonne (1931–32) was transformative both for her increasing "alienat[ion] from the elitism and obscurantism of such poets as [T.S.] Eliot" and for her exposure to workers' demonstrations and police brutality.[9] Upon returning to Canada, she studied social work, took placements in Montreal (1933–34) and Englewood, New Jersey (1935), joined the Young Communist League and the Progressive Arts Club, and contributed a few poems to the radical Marxist periodical *Masses* (which published 1932–34).[10] "I want to think and belong to, work for, the proletariat," she wrote to her friend Jean Morton in July 1932.[11] It was in New Jersey that Livesay first came across the poetry of Cecil Day Lewis, Stephen Spender, W.H. Auden, and Louis MacNeice, which she joyfully embraced for its determination to represent society to itself in a direct and lucid style, combining public reform and personal lyricism.[12]

The strain of her work led to a collapse in the summer of 1935, and she returned to the family home at Clarkson, Ontario, to recuperate. While there, she wrote her well-known socialist poem "Day and Night," which E.J. Pratt snapped up for the inaugural number of *Canadian Poetry Magazine* in 1936.[13] After the demise of *Masses*, she found a new publishing outlet in another leftist magazine, *New Frontier* (1936–37), which was attached to the broad reform alliance, the Popular Front. Livesay became a western editor for *New Frontier* and through it met her husband, Duncan Macnair. They married in 1937 and settled in Vancouver, where Livesay found a job in family welfare. She gave birth to her son, Peter, in 1940, and to her daughter, Marcia, in 1942.

Through the early years of motherhood she kept her face turned toward her society, writing poems about Vancouver during the war. As mentioned earlier, she helped found the important little magazine *Contemporary Verse* (1941–52), edited by Alan Crawley. Crawley encouraged Livesay to write for radio (as Margaret Kennedy had done for Marriott), and in the spring of 1939 she joined him in reading poems aloud on the air.[14] The further medium of film also began to plant a seed in her imagination, as it had for Marriott. At the National Film Board, John Grierson, the first commissioner, was overseeing the production of a host of films about Canada and the Second World War. They were neither newsreels nor drama, but rather a hybrid genre – the documentary – rooted in ethnography. Grierson defined the documentary as the "creative treatment of actuality."[15] Livesay acknowledged Grierson's influence years later when she formalized her concept of the *documentary poem* as the "conscious attempt to create a dialectic between the objective facts and the subjective feelings of the poet," adding that it is "based on topical data but held together by descriptive, lyrical, and didactic elements ... the story is a frame on which to hang a theme."[16] Livesay was thus thinking about responsibility on many levels, from mass media to raising children, when at last, twelve years after *Signpost*, she looked to Pierce and the Ryerson Press to publish her third book.

Pierce was no communist, but his formative young-adult experiences entailed an education in social responsibility analogous to Livesay's, making allowance for generational differences. His Irishness predisposed him to a skeptical view of British imperialism and the sense of privilege that it inspired in some quarters in English Canada. He grew up in the small town of Delta, Ontario, sixty kilometres northeast of Kingston, was raised in a strict denomination of Christianity that was "reform-oriented in both individual and social terms,"[17] and absorbed idealism during his undergraduate degree at Queen's University.[18] He put these values to work as a probationary minister in Saskatchewan. From 1912 to 1914, he lived in a few different railway settlements on the Prairies and ministered to destitute immigrant farmers and their families, most of them from Eastern Europe. Sect and doctrine quickly faded before the sheer challenge of helping people get by. As Campbell writes, "Like many probationers in the region, Lorne Pierce was radicalized by his experiences, coming to reject the rigidity and conservatism of the eastern Methodist establishment in the face of the enormous social and organizational problems confronting the church in the west."¹⁹ He was appalled by the lack of schools, hospitals, libraries, and government offices in the towns, and responded by organizing literary societies, raising money, and becoming a community leader. He worked on the farms of the families on his circuits and shared their hardship shoulder to shoulder. The most searing of his experiences was perhaps the funeral of a three-year-old girl. During a winter storm in which the temperature dropped to −45°C, Pierce conducted the service in the family's shack and then helped the father take the coffin twenty-three kilometres through the snow to the cemetery. When they arrived, they found that the grave was too narrow. Pierce had to chop at the frozen earth so that the little casket would fit. Before the ordeal was over, his face and his ears were frozen so badly that, when they later thawed, they cracked and bled.²⁰ Such were the experiences that informed Pierce's nationalism. Through the rest of his career he maintained that Canada must know the reality of its inhabitants' lives and that a representative literature would be the vehicle of this knowledge. As Campbell notes, "Pierce's sense of the country and its social and spiritual needs was transformed by his western experiences."²¹

Because of their parallels working for the vulnerable and disenfranchised, it is fitting that Pierce ultimately became Livesay's publisher. One person who helped bring them together – posthumously – was the gifted imagist Raymond Knister (1899–1932). Livesay, like Pierce, was shaken by Knister's unexplained drowning in Lake St Clair during his habitual afternoon swim one summer day. As his friend, she admired Pierce for publishing Knister's novel, *My Star Predominant* (Toronto: Ryerson, 1932), despite the trouble involved in liberating the manuscript from the Graphic Press of Ottawa, which had gone bankrupt after accepting it. A decade later, in 1943, Pierce approached Livesay to edit a collection of Knister's poems, an initiative that bore fruit in *The Collected Poems of Raymond Knister* (Toronto: Ryerson Press, 1949).²² Meanwhile, Pierce had begun to collaborate with A.J.M. Smith, granting him several key copyright permissions for Smith's landmark anthology *The Book of Canadian Poetry* (Chicago: University of Chicago Press, 1943), and publishing Smith's own first collection, *News of the Phoenix* (Toronto: Ryerson Press, 1943), which won the Governor General's Literary Award for poetry. Smith gave Pierce a list of talented modernist poets to pursue and urged the latter group in turn to put aside their prejudices against a church-owned publishing house and publish with him. Livesay's name was on that list.²³ Thus it was that Ryerson published Livesay's next books: *Day and Night* (1944), *Poems for People* (1947), and *Call My People Home* (1950). *Day and Night* and *Poems for People* both won the Governor General's Literary Award for poetry,[24] and in 1947 the Royal Society of Canada bestowed its gold medal for literature – the Lorne Pierce Medal, which Pierce had created in 1924 – on Livesay, too.[25] By the late 1940s, Livesay and Pierce had come together as author and editor.

THE WRITING AND PUBLISHING of "Call My People Home" began in response to the Japanese Canadian internment, with a stretching and expansion of Livesay's own home. "For some time," she later wrote, "I had had the idea of writing a tribute to the endurance and tolerance of the Japanese-Canadians who so roughly and so violently, in the year 1941, were uprooted from their fishing-villages and fishing-boats, on the west coast of British Columbia, because it was believed they might be spying for the Japanese – our enemies."[26] According to her account in *The Documentaries*, Livesay's engagement with the issue of the Japanese Canadian internment began through a committee formed to protest it on which her husband, Duncan, served. The committee attempted to resist the expropriations through legal action. Then, in the summer of 1942, the pacifist and social worker Mildred Fahrni invited Livesay to help organize an evacuation centre and school for the internees in New Denver, British Columbia. Livesay, adjusting to the birth of her baby daughter only six weeks earlier, regretfully declined. However, when Ottawa relaxed its restrictions later in the war, allowing Japanese Canadian children to return to Vancouver for schooling, Dorothy and Duncan offered to billet a high-school student, Amy Tabata, who "stayed for a year, attending North Vancouver High School and helping me with the children. Perhaps she was of more help to me than I was to her!"[27] Livesay thus witnessed the public issue privately by opening her home to a teenager. Livesay also met Amy's brother, Susumu, an oceanography student at the University of British Columbia. His story of growing up in Steveston, learning to fish, and suddenly being separated from his family affected Livesay deeply.

Livesay started to draft her poem in the summer of 1948, the year after the publication of M. Eugenie Perry's *Song in the Silence and Other Poems*. On 15 June, Canada passed an act to restore the federal franchise to Japanese Canadians, and Livesay joined the momentum to press British

Columbia and its various cities likewise to repeal voting restrictions against them.[28] A direct invitation to begin writing something substantial arrived through Malcolm Lowry. Humbled by Livesay's persistence as a poet while mothering two young children, he offered her the use of his cabin at Dollarton on Burrard Inlet during his vacation in Europe. Livesay later noted: "Ideas were tumbling about in my head on the way to Dollarton. Would this project be a prose documentary or a lyrical, poetic interpretation? I already knew the title: 'Call My People Home.'"[29] It was there on a Friday evening, "with an orange August moon rising directly before me over the soft-soughing sea,"[30] that she began to write "A Young Nisei," which would become section 3 of her poem, derived from Susumu Tabata's story. After that first weekend, she set out to gather more information and other perspectives on the internment:

> I realized that a considerable amount of research would be needed to corroborate my personal impressions of the Japanese-Canadian evacuation. I spent several afternoons reading back files of the Nisei newspaper, to obtain the material for the long section of the documentary, "The Fisherman." My son, who has himself fished halibut up that coast, tells me that my description is authentic: but I owe that fact to the letters of Japanese fishermen who wrote to the paper describing their personal uprooting. From the same source I obtained the details for "The Wife." Material for "The Mayor" came to me after I had made a visit to the Similkameen where the then mayor of Greenwood, B.C., showed me around that "ghost" town and told me most movingly of his experience with the Japanese evacuee families.[31]

Thus, through a program of research in both printed documents and interviews, Livesay applied herself to convey as responsibly as possible the facts of the historic evacuation.

Accuracy was all the more important because she was aiming for a national radio audience comprising both former internees and people across the country whom the war had generally disposed against Japan. In January 1949, nearing completion of the manuscript, she wrote to Pierce to raise the possibility of publishing the poem in his series: "I have been working to finish my epic poem on the Japanese Dispersal, hoping the CBC will put it on. May send you a copy soon: you might think it to be good chapbook material."³² She believed her work complete until she read it aloud one evening to Earle Birney and his wife Esther. Esther pointed out that Livesay had omitted the dehumanizing detention of women and children in livestock stables at the Vancouver exhibition grounds in Hastings Park. After investigating this aspect of the internment further, Livesay added section 4, "The Letter" ("Mariko"), which she thus wrote last.³³

Once the writing was complete, the publication of "Call My People Home" began, through performance ahead of print, partly thanks to the good graces of Earle Birney. A successful reading took place at the University of British Columbia, where Birney was a professor of English. When Livesay submitted the manuscript to CBC Toronto, she was initially rebuffed, but in March 1949 Birney wrote her with the good news that CBR Vancouver (an AM radio station operated by the CBC) would broadcast the poem: "I told him [Ken Caple] he ought to grab it for CBR because it had proved itself most effective to a large aud[ience] at UBC, because it was a very good poem, and because the news of the Japanese getting B.C. voting rights today made the whole thing very topical. I dont know whether it was coincidence or not, but five minutes later he rang back and left a message for me as follows: 'Dorothy Livesay's poem on the Japanese will be read over CBR on March 28th at 7.45 p.m.'"³⁴ Birney's "today" may have been 7 March, the day the government of British Columbia introduced a bill to amend the Elections Act to include Japanese Canadians.³⁵ As the time slot suggests, the CBR production was "a short version ... less than fifteen minutes in length."³⁶

Five months later, Raymond Whitehouse at CBC Montreal produced a thirty-minute version, which aired on the show *Listening Room Only* on 2 August 1949 on the Trans-Canada Network.³⁷ It featured musical accompaniment by the Montreal Symphony Orchestra; in fact, Whitehouse conceived of the production as "in the nature of a tone poem" and did not go to air until he had secured all of the desired musicians and instruments. "We are so anxious to do a first-rate job on this, that we have put the quality of the production before everything else," he explained to Livesay.³⁸ His comments represent perhaps the first instance of a reader grasping the musical dimension of Livesay's poem. Certainly, it was a compliment to the author to classify her work under the same heading as Richard Strauss's *Ein Heldenleben* (1898). On 4 March 1954, CBC Winnipeg broadcast another thirty-minute version, this one produced by Emrys Jones, on *Prairie Playhouse* on the Eastern Network.³⁹

"Call My People Home" first appeared in print in *Contemporary Verse*. Livesay had submitted the poem to two other magazines – *Saturday Night* (Toronto) and *Poetry* (Chicago) – but when neither accepted it, Alan Crawley devoted the entire summer 1949 issue to Livesay's poem.[40] In an editorial note, he expressed satisfaction at being able to publish a "worthy" poem "which by reason of content or length [was] unlikely to get printing elsewhere." He also approved of the wider play that Canadian poets were receiving on the radio, but deprecated Whitehouse's musical interpretation of this particular work: "the Montreal producer allowed his readers to interpret and intensify Miss Livesay's words and when incidental music was added the broadcast became a turmoil of sound in which the force and feeling of the poems were often confused and obliterated."[41] However, the adaptations for radio pleased the author: "Livesay herself, having heard it broadcast, was inclined to consider *Call My People Home*, as both radio and written work, perhaps the best piece she had ever done."[42]

Given Livesay's rapport with Pierce, his acceptance of "Call My People Home" for the Ryerson Poetry Chap-Books might have seemed a foregone conclusion, but he was not able to take up her offer until the following spring. Apologizing for his delay, he confirmed that:

> We have placed you on our fall list with a Chap Book, and we shall want to list it in the catalogue within a month. Suppose you send along *Call My People Home* and a dozen new things you would like to see appearing in the Chap Book, and let me work it out. I will try to give you a very low quotation. As a matter of fact I have been shopping around for better prices on these Chap Books. I would hate very much to retreat from the poetry field since we have spent so much time and so much money trying to retain the position we now hold, but I think that the poet, as well as his publisher, will have to be content for a while with some sort of Chap Book arrangement.[43]

By now a veteran of the Canadian book trade and its longest-serving editor, Pierce was careful not to promise too much. He still couched his offer to publish in cautious language; what he had learned in 1925 he never forgot. Ultimately, he was able to offer Livesay at least neutral terms, a clear improvement over the guarantee against loss that he had required of Nathaniel A. Benson and over the promise to buy a large fraction of the edition that M. Eugenie Perry had been obliged to make. Halfway into his third decade as series editor, he remained as loyal as ever to the cause of Canadian poetry, but as sober about its financial limits and uncertainties.

The periodical text functioned as copy for the first edition. Footnotes glossing the Japanese words *Issei* and *Nisei* were added, spellings were Canadianized, other matters of style such as dashes were changed, and one or two more substantive revisions were made ("seasick and helpless" became "seasick and sore"), but for the most part Livesay republished in Chap-Book form the poem as it had appeared in *Contemporary Verse* (see figure 6.1). She also complied with Pierce's request for further poems. When published, *Call My People Home* comprised, in addition to the title poem, "Departure in November," "December," "Variations on a Tree," "Marcia," "Indian Graveyard," "Tale," "Interval With Fire," and "Invisible Sun," making a booklet of twenty-four pages. The contract transferred copyright in the work to Ryerson in exchange for "fifty (50) free copies of the Chap-Book in lieu of all royalty on the first edition" – a relatively generous quantity that recognized Livesay's status. A pencilled tally at the top of the contract indicates that *Call My People Home* sold well. Of the 500 copies printed in October 1950, only 163 remained in stock by April 1958.[44]

Qualitatively, the reception was equally positive. The occasional reviewer sounded a negative note. The *Toronto Telegram*, reacting to Livesay's generic experimentation, dismissed the title poem as a "cross between Stage 51, an inglorious Milton and News Roundup."[45] Marriott similarly pointed the way back to lyric; she preferred the shorter poems, "Variations on a Tree" and "Interval with Fire," to the "disappointing" main poem, which she castigated for its "prosaic expressions of fact," "dullness," "outworn poetic stuff," and "sentimentality."[46] However, "its potentially toughest critics, the Japanese Canadians, saw themselves truly in the poem and were vocally appreciative of Livesay's art."[47] For example, Mickey Nakashima wrote on behalf of the Japanese Canadian Citizens' Association to thank Livesay and her husband for taking part in their convention banquet in Vancouver on 28 February 1953: "Words cannot express the feeling of gratitude we felt as we realized the many friends we had who understood and shared with us our problems, large and small, which arose from our national origin. Thank you again, Mrs Macnair, and please thank Mr Macnair for his simple, touching reading from your poem, 'Call My People Home', which undoubtedly brought tears to many guests' eyes as it did to mine."[48] In literary circles, the most influential review would

CALL MY PEOPLE HOME

by Dorothy Livesay

TORONTO · *The* RYERSON PRESS

6.1 / Dorothy Livesay, *Call My People Home*, Ryerson Poetry Chap-Books no. 143 (Toronto: Ryerson Press, 1950). In 1950 the series design was simplified as shown here. Subsequent Chap-Books (except for ten published 1953–55) have a similar front cover.

have been Frye's: "The invaluable and dauntless 'Ryerson Poetry Chapbooks' series still goes on, with no fewer than six volumes this year ... The best thing in them by far is Dorothy Livesay's radio play *Call My People Home* ... It is written with close sympathy and a dry, unlaboured irony, and in a taut, sinewy narrative style with no nonsense about it: it will pick up an image as it goes along, but it never stops for any synthetic beautifying."[49] As will be seen below, the poem's qualities go well beyond the objectivity and imagism that Frye touches on.

⚜

"CALL MY PEOPLE HOME" describes the Japanese Canadian internment during the Second World War through the theme of home. Livesay originally conceived of her poem as an "epic," and her achieved work preserves this concept in so far as its central questions recall *The Odyssey*. What must it have been like to lose one's home because of war? What does it mean for anyone to have a home? The poem answers with a bemusing refiguration. Lynda Morrissey discerns that the poem turns on the disturbance of normal ideas of home: "While 'home' is unequivocally the functional word in the poem, the prevailing image is not so much the making of a home, as the repetitive and irretrievable loss of home ... [The] metaphors in the introductory chorus firmly dispel any notion of home as the locus of comfort and security."[50] Livesay does indeed turn the idea of home on its head, but the analysis of the theme can be taken further. She thematically figures home not as a comfortable place, but rather as a call to which one must respond. In "Call My People Home," home is a tension, a difference felt between one's position and a longed-for potential. It is a heartfelt split between what is and what should be. The difference is felt spatially and also temporally: home is a trajectory, a mingling of memory and hope, a suffering in quest of fulfillment. The final stanza of the poem states that "Home is labour, with the hand and heart, / The hard doing, and the rest when done,"[51] and this ultimate definition, decorated with polyptoton, comprises opposites that invoke each other (present "doing" versus past "done"). After all, "labour," for a socialist such as Livesay, designates a complex category that encompasses not only real pain and effort but also the ideal participation in society to which every member has a right. By expanding the idea of home from mere real estate, which is subject to expropriation, into a call of desire, which transcends physical

6.2 / A 1940s musical arrangement of the spiritual "Go down Moses." *Fireside Book of Folk Songs*, selected and edited by Margaret Bradford Boni, arranged by Norman Lloyd, illustrated by Alice and Martin Provensen (New York: Simon and Schuster, 1947), 316.

control, Livesay dignifies the dispersal, including the internees' story in a new narrative of the Canadian national home, while evoking a mythic backdrop of human migration.

The poem's title alludes to prior historic displacements – African American slavery and the exile of Israel in Egypt – by echoing the spiritual "Let My People Go" ("Go down Moses") (see figure 6.2).[52] This song was in the repertoire performed from 1925 on by the great twentieth-century bass Paul Robeson (1898–1976), who was internationally famous through radio broadcasts by the 1940s. In her introduction to a later edition of "Call My People Home," Livesay explicitly identified Robeson as her source.[53] The song itself manifests the tension of the call in many ways. It tells of God calling to Moses from the Burning Bush to lead his people out of bondage (Exodus 3:4, 5:1). It originated among slaves in the Deep South dreaming of escape via the Underground Railroad. Each stanza alternates between the call of distinct verses and the response of the refrain, and musically the refrain quivers on the dominant note of the minor scale and then rises through the tension of the leading note to rest on the tonic. Livesay's title, through parallelism, repetition, and assonance, resonates with that of the song, drawing on its popular tune and narrative in order to counter the anti-Japanese sentiment running high since the bombing of Pearl Harbor and Hong Kong, the fall of Singapore, and other events of the Second World War. Like its original, the adapted sentence "Call My People Home" is an imperative that stretches between injustice and justice, between races, between suffering and salvation, and between individuality and collectivity.

Formally, the tension of difference structures the poem into many dialectical patterns. Paul Denham perceives the interplay between private and public modes as characteristic of Livesay's poetry: "both lyric and documentary are essential aspects of her poetic genius, and ... part of the power and authority of her best work derives from the coalescence of the lyric and the documentary impulses."[54] This technique of "coalescence" leaps out as an ordering principle of "Call My People Home." By assembling a number of private voices and letting them speak their innermost feelings, the poem becomes a parliament, with all the public significance which that term connotes. Throughout "Call My People Home," Livesay's primary focus is the individual character of the witnesses and the nuances of their emotions, rather than the economics and policies that encompass them, which appear only obliquely. To fault the poem for focussing on character instead of system would be to judge it by inappropriate criteria and mistake its design. For example, as one testimony among many, Mariko's letter to Susumu (explaining how trauma has interrupted love) becomes a symbol for the Japanese Canadian internment as a whole. The more private the truth, the more public its significance. The poem's rhetorical gambit depends on this inversion, a fundamental one to literature.

The counterpoint of private and public is only the first of many in "Call My People Home." Each section consists of two parts, like a call and a response, beginning with an announcer and continuing with a witness. The two-part arrangement of host and guest is of course a practical one for radio and is more or less ubiquitous in the medium. The host orients listeners and provides a starting point with which they can identify, while the guest brings special authority and new expertise on a topic. Livesay's announcer plays the role of host both explicitly by introducing each witness and implicitly by speaking from the dominant social position. He refers to Japanese Canadians in the third person, as many in a 1940s CBC listening audience would have done: "This is their story" (1, l. 7). Most of the nine witnesses who, by contrast, speak in the first person, are ethnically Japanese: the chorus of *Issei* (first-generation immigrants); the fisherman; the young *Nisei* (second-generation); Mariko, the author of the love letter; the wife; the renegade; Tatsuo, the philosopher; and the chorus of *Nisei*. (The one exception is the fifth witness, the mayor of the town in the British Columbia Interior.) If the poem thus largely takes shape as an alternation between majority and minority voices, it is surely significant that the announcer vanishes at the end. By then, the work of understanding is complete. The audience should now be able to empathize with the young Japanese Canadians.

Two choruses speak. The poem begins with the older generation, whom the announcer situates in a double landscape of memory and exertion:

> Now after thirty years come from a far island
> Of snow and cherry blossoms, holy mountains,
> To make a home near water, near
> The blue Pacific; newcomers and strangers
> Circled again and shaped by snow-white mountains,
> These put down their roots, the Isseis:
> The older generation.
> (1, ll.1–7)

The first four words signal the temporal complexity of the theme of the poem. The older people put down their roots and speak "Now," in the present moment, but with reference to a lapse of "thirty years" since their emigration from Japan. Their existence is thus split across these two defining moments. Similarly, the repetition of "snow" and "mountains," which is the salient poetic technique in the absence of metre or rhyme, creates a matching geographical complexity. Japan and British Columbia have similar northern alpine and coastal environments, but are seven thousand kilometres apart; nevertheless, the *Issei* inhabit both. Moreover, they receive a twofold designation. They are "newcomers" and "strangers." All of these binary patterns place the people concerned in an in-between state, like listeners harkening to a call from afar.

When the *Issei* speak, they astonishingly claim the anguish of displacement as their home. The old saying goes that "Home ... is where the heart is" (1, l. 8), but they have learned that it is also what the body must endure:

Home was the uprooting:
The shiver of separation,
Despair for our children
Fear for our future.

Home was the finding of a dry land
Bereft of water or rainfall
Where water is cherished
Where our tears made channels
And became irrigation.
(1–2, ll. 19–27)

Tearing a plant up by the roots to transplant it in sorrow, while waiting "For young ones branching, / For our yearning fading" (2, ll. 35–6) – could this be a metaphor of home? Livesay's larger oeuvre reveals the evolution of this idea. Earlier poems show her coupling destruction to regeneration through the figure of an uprooted plant. In "Broadcast from Berlin," she imagines the workers' revolution as "the very storm, / A storm of labour, tearing up old roots, / Bringing to the earth fresh nourishment."[55] In "Seven Poems," she projects the reconstruction that would follow war: "A shell burst in my mind / Upheaving roots since birth, perhaps, confined," and this upheaving is what allows the building of "A city not my own, with others planned / By others dreamed."[56] In "West Coast," she ushers writers and readers of poetry into the war effort, specifically the manufacturing of ships to fight fascism: "We, who lay / in roses and green shade under the cherry tree / we too were rooted up, set loose to beg / or borrow a new roof, accept a poorer view. / The tide had turned."[57] In

"Variations on a Tree," one of the shorter poems in *Call My People Home*, she works an acrobatic reversal. She speaks as a tree in the first person, and begins with the usual idea of being rooted and reaching for freedom, but then suddenly turns on her head so that her hands/roots are rolling the world while her feet/branches are "wading in pools of blue" sky, dancing in the heavens, and playing "football with the moon."[58] Given such precedents, the equation of home with "uprooting" honours the struggle to live and to nurture life through hardship. The first section of "Call My People Home" is therefore a full statement of the theme, and the chorus addresses it with all the wisdom that the internment has brought. Home is less the fact of title than the crooked path of labour toward that end.

The thematic fullness of the first section means that it should not be solved or replaced by the contrasting chorus, that of the younger generation, which concludes the poem. The two choruses are variations on the same wisdom, addressed from two perspectives. Their relation is, again, dialectical. At the end, the *Nisei* learn that "Home is labour ... A wider sea than we knew, a deeper earth, / A more enduring sun" (17, ll. 489–90). As Morrissey notes, Livesay revised the last two lines as follows when the poem was republished in *The Documentaries* (Toronto: Ryerson Press, 1968): "A rougher ocean than we knew, a tougher earth, / a more magnetic sun" (see table 6.1). The creative pressure on the lines is evident in the revision. Livesay enhances them with rhyme ("rougher," "tougher") and alliteration, and "magnetic" captures the gravitational pull of home precisely. Whether in the original or the revised text, however, the poem ends by emphasizing the interval across which home must stretch. Home is the struggle to find a way across the sea, down into the earth, and up toward the sun, and the struggle "is." The present tense of the final section contrasts with the past tense of the first section, but both remain equally true. In fact, they coalesce. The sadness of age finds hope in the promise of youth, while the activity of youth finds guidance in the wisdom of age.

The second section, and the longest, develops the theme of home as a call through narrative, geography, and allusion. The fisherman's story seems at first a straightforward account of dispossession, but if its final effect is pathos, then what it reveals is the inextricability of longing and belonging. Put simply, the fisherman feels his home most keenly when he is deprived of it. Livesay renders this paradox of desire all the richer for the kind of abode she gives him. "Home was my boat," the fisherman begins (2, l. 47). The line exemplifies Livesay's theory of the documentary,

TABLE 6.1
Textual variants in editions of Dorothy Livesay, "Call My People Home"

Editions collated:
    Call My People Home, Ryerson Poetry Chap-Book no. 143
       (Toronto: Ryerson Press, 1950), 1–17.
    Contemporary Verse 28 (Summer 1949), 3–19.
    The Documentaries (Toronto: Ryerson Press, 1968), 34–48.
    Collected Poems: The Two Seasons (Toronto: McGraw-Hill, Ryerson, 1972),
       180–94.
Editions are referred to by date of publication. Unless otherwise indicated, texts follow the first edition (1950), here taken as the basis of comparison. Numerals refer to line numbers in the first edition (*h*: heading).

Section 1: Chorus of Isseis

h	ANNOUNCER] ANNOUNCER *1972 (different style throughout)*	
1	NOW] Now *1949, 1968, 1972*	
6	the Isseis:] *(no Japanese words glossed) 1949;* the Isseis:* *1972 (same footnote moved up to first instance of Japanese word)*	
h	CHORUS OF ISSEIS] *(all speeches by choruses and witnesses are indented in 1968 throughout, further distinguishing them from announcer's)*	
9	copper-coloured] copper-colored *1949 (different style throughout)*	
11	again—] again--- *1949 (different style throughout)*	
16	shack on stilts] shacks on stilts *1949*	
36	fading....] fading... *1972*	

Section 2: The Fisherman

38	Fujiyama's] Fujiama's *1949*	
43	Who pressed the government to give them licences / Before the yellow faces] *(not in 1972)*	
44	So these cut his share] So these men cut his share *1972*	
47	T.K.2930] T.K. 2930 *1949, 1968, 1972*	
54	Tee Kay] Tee Kay *1949 (different style throughout)*	
83	authorities." // Did] authorities." / Did *1972 (no stanza break)*	
85	No, said the voice. Our boats were to be examined [...] for treachery....] "No," said the voice, "Our boats were to be examined [...] for treachery...." *1972*	
86	treachery....] treachery... *1949 (different style throughout)*	

95	We thought: perhaps] *(indented) 1949;* We thought: perhaps *1972 (different style throughout)*	
97	Ucluelet] Ucleulet *1968;* Ucluelet *1972*	
112	"Starpoint"] *Starpoint 1972*	
114	westerlys] westerlies *1972*	
132	Propellors] Propellers *1972*	
134	Seasick and sore] Seasick and helpless *1949*	
142	As we set sail at midnight] So we set sail at midnight *1968*	
145	rocks' end] rocks end *1949;* rocks'-end *1972*	
146	As we set sail for home, the young ones] So we set sail for home: and young ones *1968*	
156	*ofuro*] *ofuro*★ ★Ofuro—the bath. *1972 (footnote added)*	

Section 3: A Young Nisei

165	British Columbia home] British Columbia home, *1972*
168	*We lived unto ourselves*] *We lived into ourselves 1968*
170	harbour] harbor *1949 (different style throughout)*
174	Sometimes at remote midnight / With a burnt-out moon / An orange eye on the river / Or rising before dawn / From a house] Sometimes at midnight— / A burnt-out moon / An orange eye on the river— / Or before dawn / We rise from a house *1968*
184	Till morning steals over, sleepy] Till morning steals on us, sleepy *1968*
189	Hiding the unannounced prayer / Resounding in the heart's corners] Hiding the unacknowledged prayer / At the heart's corners *1968*
194	*Locked in the harbour*] *Locked in the harbour. 1968*
199	learning— // (And learned] learning---- / (And learned *1949 (no stanza break)*

Section 4: The Letter

234	Hastings Park] Hastings Park, *1949*
256	kimono] kimona *1949*
263	my mother. / It is hard] my mother. // It is hard *1949 (stanza break)*

SECTION 5: The Mayor

282	even a mayor.] a mayor *1972*
289	"The first contingent] "The first contingent: *1968*
291	funneled] funnelled *1972*

300   neighbours] neighbors *1949 (different style throughout)*
331   And saw the Issei mother. / *(verse continues on next line of type)* Putting out my hand] And saw the Issei mother. / *(new verse, indented)* Putting out my hand *1968*
336   I took them into the store, the post-office, / Showed them the ropes, then headed for the school,] *(not in 1968)*
339   I knew her / Inside out, like a book—the Principal.] I knew her well: / The high school principal. *1968*

Section 6: The Wife

353   choose: But choices loom / Two iron doors beyond which lie more doubt, more gloom.] *(not in 1972)*
361   government granted huts—] government huts *1972*
362   the family parted. // Or] the family parted, / Or *1968; 1972 (no stanza break)*
365   labour] labor *1949 (different style throughout)*
400   neck] necks *1949*
416   Dneiper] Dnieper *1968*
421   you heard] we heard *1972*

Section 8: The Philosopher

h   THE PHILOSOPHER] THE STUDENT *1968*
455   (I had looked out] *(next twenty lines indented) 1949; (indented without parentheses) 1968*
464   A book again in my hand] A book in my hand *1968*
475   So must I remember. It cannot be hid / Nor hurried from. As long as there abides / No bitterness; only the lesson learned / And the habit of grace chosen, accepted] To be alone is grace; to see it clear / Without rancour; to let the past be / And the future become. Especially to remember / The habit of grace; chosen, accepted. *1968*

Section 9: Chorus of Niseis

482   B.C.] B. C. *1972*
489   A wider sea than we knew, a deeper earth, / A more enduring sun.] A rougher ocean than we knew, a tougher earth, / a more magnetic sun. *1968*

for it combines the plainness of fact with the paradoxical interests of the theme, specifically here the jostling between mobility and fixity. In one sense, it is impossible that a boat, moved by winds and waves, should be a home; in another, this is an apt metaphor for the human journey through time, recalling again the vicissitudes of Odysseus and perhaps also the Old English elegies. The boat appears first as a number, "T.K. 2930" (2, l. 47), and then, after thirty years of labour have allowed the fisherman to purchase his freedom from the cannery, as a wife, "*Tee Kay*, the Gillnetter / The snug and round one, warm as a woman" (3, ll. 54–5). This humanized, named home, however, evaporates into heartbreak, because the story ends with the arrival of the arrested boats in Vancouver and the impounding of the *Tee Kay*:

> Others of us, like me, who knew no one,
> Who had no place near the city's centre
> Stood lonely on the wharf, holding the *Tee Kay*'s line
> For the last time, watching the naval men
> Make a note of her number, take my name.
> That was the end of my thirty years at the fishing
> And the end of my boat, my home.
> (6, ll. 157–63)

In seizing his boat and returning it to a mere "number," the authorities "take" away the "name" that the fisherman has made for himself in his adoptive country. However, this moment of loss is also the climax of longing and sympathy, when the fisherman and the reader realize most starkly the boat's status as a home. Holding the tense "line" of the poem, we see the *Tee Kay* floating opposite us, too, and feel her being pulled away.

Having the fisherman spend "Christmas at sea. The bitterest for me / That any year had given" (5, ll. 136–7) produces a similar sentiment. In such ways, Livesay's poem, like Robeson's song, creates sympathy between the national audience and the persecuted racial minority. Reading (or hearing on the radio) the fisherman's story in security at home, one should reach out to him, homeless. In other ways, the poem reverses this ethical call, by revealing the depth to which the witnesses are at home in Canada. The fisherman's unhappy odyssey, for example, reveals a vast coastal environment that he knows well but that most readers would find alien and unfamiliar. The convoy of boats goes from "Skeena," to "Inverness," "Tusk,"

"Rupert," "Lowe Inlet," "Milbanke Sound," and "Alert Bay," before passing "Point Grey" and arriving at "Steveston, 'Little Tokio'" (4–5, ll. 97, 91, 91, 110, 116, 117, 139, 150, 153). How many of these places, across approximately six hundred nautical miles of British Columbia's Inside Passage and the Strait of Georgia, does the reader know from experience? Even other lifelong inhabitants of Vancouver without the fisherman's experience might not be familiar with any but the last two. Some are now historical names only. Inverness, for example, was a salmon cannery fourteen kilometres south of Prince Rupert at the mouth of the Skeena River. Livesay did not know the Inside Passage firsthand, but took her information from a Japanese Canadian newspaper, as illustrated above. The geography of the second section thus achieves a surprising reversal. If nationality ultimately reposes on a lived connection to the land, then it is the fisherman who is Canadian, and the author who is a stranger to this Canada. It is the fisherman who is "naturalized," who "smel[ls] the wind / Wetting my face," who "churn[s] off up the river" Skeena to earn his living (3, ll. 64–6, 73). It is his "authentic" story that has the power to call us home.

In addition to these geographical references, Livesay employs literary allusion to identify the Japanese Canadian fisherman directly with Canada. "How speak about the long trip south, the last / We ever made, in the last of our boats?" (4, ll. 104–5), he asks. The rhetorical question is a cautious approach to sublimity, and Livesay uses it to acknowledge that no words can fully capture the grief of expulsion. Moreover, these lines allude to one of the most popular Canadian poems of the twentieth century, Earle Birney's "David," which also treats the sublime. Terrible experience and isolation inform the memorable final flourish of "David": "And none but the sun and incurious clouds have lingered / Around the marks of that day on the ledge of the Finger, / That day, the last of my youth, on the last of our mountains."[59] Through a parallel repetition of the phrase "the last," Livesay aligns the fisherman's ordeal with that of Birney's narrator. The comparison endows the fisherman with the rhythm of a celebrated national poem.

Similarly, the image of the fishing boats "Smashing like blind birds through a log-strewn sea" (5, l. 127) brings to mind the scene of danger in Isabella Valancy Crawford's "Malcolm's Katie" in which the heroine, Katie, tries to cross a lake jammed with floating logs and nearly drowns. Livesay not only admired Crawford's poem – "That poem has become a classic to which I am deeply indebted" – but used it to theorize the documentary poem, so the echo again invests the Japanese characters with national-literary value.[60] Perhaps there is even a reference to Hugh MacLennan's *Two Solitudes* in the next section (the third) of "Call My People Home." The *Nisei* teenager remembers "rising before dawn" to fish as a child (6, l. 177): "We go out toward misty islands / Of fog over the river" (7, ll. 183–4). In MacLennan's novel, the protagonist, Paul, eight years old, gets up before dawn to go fishing with Captain Yardley and his granddaughters on the St Lawrence River, and "because there was a mist over it they couldn't see the other shore."[61] Dawn, boats, rivers, and mist are common elements in any fishing excursion, but the point of both passages is also childhood bliss. Again, therefore, Livesay's character seems to don the aura of a well-known work of Canadian literature. Through these intertextual references, her poem summons the national canon and joins it.

The third section, the first drafted, renders the *Nisei* teenager's reflections on the internment in further patterns of duality. The narrated experiences contrast ironically and therefore operate dualistically. The speaker remembers going out in a boat to "Set the nets" (7, l. 188) in hopes of catching salmon, but it turns out that he will have "the stifled feeling / Of being caught" (8, ll. 218–19) in the Mounties' net himself. The typography is dual, too, alternating between the italics of a chorus that expresses a general innocence – "*We lived unto ourselves / Thinking so to be free*" (6, ll. 168–9) – and the roman of the individual speaker who recalls specific details – "I remember the schoolhouse, its battered doorway" (7, l. 195). The point of view is also dual, in that it fluctuates between the speaker's present and past ages. On one hand, he recognizes racism, wryly observing that his older sisters went off to school "Deliberately bent on learning – // (And learned, soon enough, of / The colour of their skin" (7, ll. 199–201). On the other, he recognizes sweetness, "out on the hillside / Reaching high over my head for the black ones / The first plump berries of summer" (7, ll. 207–9). The deferral of the accurate term, *blackberry*, reveals a five-year-old who knows first through colour, shape, and undoubtedly taste. Finally, the imagery of the lost home is dual. The speaker's testimony culminates with two parallel, anaphoric, rhyming statements:

> Never again did I go
> Blackberry picking on the hillside.
> Never again did I know
> That iron schoolbell ringing.
> (8, ll. 225–8)

The lure of the blackberry that cannot be picked, the signal from the school that cannot be attended — these two images and symbols of unattainability summarize this witness's feeling of home. Through these dualities, Livesay explores the split state of being called.

The letter that constitutes the fourth section of the poem incarnates the tension of desire, in that it reaches out to a lover through the written word. Mariko writes from a degrading place, the stables in Hasting's Park in Vancouver, which served as a temporary detention centre. She strives to hold on to her deported lover, with only a vague knowledge of his being on a train somewhere in the British Columbia Interior. Against proliferating doubts, she struggles to keep the vision of the fulfilling place that her lover promised her: "It is hard for me to believe, myself, / How you said the words, how you spoke of a garden / Where my name, MARIKO, would be written in flowers" (9, ll. 264–6). That writing, rooted and beautiful, contrasts poignantly with Mariko's letter, sent from a horse stall. Compounding the problem is the fact that her mother's vision is running the other way, back to Japan, where she would choose her daughter's husband. Mariko thus strains for her home graphically, across sexual and filial chasms.

When Livesay turns to her lone non-Japanese witness in the fifth section, she models progressive courage. A significant challenge, which the poem must negotiate, is the representation of racism. One line of reasoning is that identifying racism is the first step in eliminating it; another, that accusations of racism return insult for insult, provoke defensive reactions, and compound antagonism. Both arguments have validity; essentially, they divide over preferring negative critique or positive encouragement. The poem's textual history reveals the author's vacillation regarding this challenge. The 1950 text includes a direct charge of racism: explaining the fisherman's hardship, the announcer points to:

The uncertain temper of white fishermen
Who hungered also, who had mouths to feed
Who pressed the government to give them licences
Before the yellow faces. So these cut his share
From half to one-eighth of the fishing fleet.
(2, ll. 41–5)

In the 1972 text, by contrast, the passage is shortened:

> The uncertain temper of white fishermen
> Who hungered also, who had mouths to feed.
> So these men cut his share
> From half to one-eighth of the fishing fleet.⁶²

Eliminating the phrase "yellow faces" casts the white fishermen in a better light, in that the racism is softened.

If an older Livesay thus chose even further to eschew a politics of recrimination, her revision accords with her portrait of the mayor of the town in the British Columbia Interior in the poem's fifth section. Rather than repelling the internees transported into his jurisdiction, the mayor decides to do what he can to accommodate them. In the manner of the second section, which worked a geographical reversal between domestic and foreign, the fifth confesses that the mayor needs the migrants as much as they need him, because his town has been in decline since the gold rush. Anticipating the ultimate definition of home by the *Nisei* chorus, this section enacts a constructive collaboration. The mayor commandeers a bilingual boy at the train station to translate his call of welcome to the crowd: "This is your home. Can you tell the people that?" (11, l. 320). He does not wait long for a response:

> Their conference began. I waited, tense;
> Then plunged into the job of lifting crates
> And scanty furnishings, getting local lads
> To pile it up on trucks; until I felt
> A timid touch upon my arm; I turned
> And saw the Issei mother.
>   Putting out my hand
> I felt hers move, rest for a moment in mine –
> Then we were free. We began to work together.
> (11, ll. 325–32)

If the mayor succeeds in housing the displaced people that night, if he conspicuously leads a group of the children through town to a school classroom the next day, his initiatives toward community pivot on the moment of mutual kindness above. Technically, the splitting of a verse across two lines of type is unique in the poem, and this layout draws special attention to the passage as poetry and signals its high dignity. Livesay's belief in humanitarian understanding is most visible here. It is also most vulnerable to cynical mockery, and this is surely the reason why she forges identification not through speech, which is easily discredited, but through gestures such as labour ("the job of lifting crates," "We began to work together") and touch ("my hand / ... felt hers move, rest"). She also protects the mayor through double levels of meaning. His vow, "those people would be mine!" (12, l. 347), at first appears self-interested, but by connecting with the title of the poem ("My People") it invites a second reading, one in which the work of empathizing with the oppressed becomes self-transforming. The larger implication is that Canada as a whole is called to achieve this belief in interracial collaboration.

The witness of the sixth section is a wife who is sent with her husband and children to the Prairies to farm. "It was harder than hate," she attests. "Home was a blueprint only" (13, l. 384). Like the fourth section, this one juxtaposes prospective and retrospective images of home. Their neighbour is a Ukrainian farmer, less fluent in English, who identifies with the wife and husband's efforts to make a home for their children. Encouragingly, he calls the Prairies "clean and big / And gentle with the wheat. For children too, / Good growing" (14, ll. 418–20). Parental hope and cross-cultural understanding look forward, while an unlooked-for simile looks backward, nostalgically. Fireflies appear one evening and dance "Like lanterns of Japan on prairie air" (14, l. 408). Both the neighbour and the insects unexpectedly grace the hateful farm with the beauty of home. Calls from the future and the past lighten suffering and enable perseverance.[63]

The chief characteristic demonstrated by the Japanese Canadian internees, as Livesay imagines them in this poem, is grace. Far from being a superficial romanticization of experience, grace is what makes up the poem's moral and rhetorical fibre. Notwithstanding the injustice of their trials, the witnesses generally forego indignation and rebellion in favour of obedience and passion. The seventh and eighth sections emphasize this self-discipline through a contrast between two young men. On one hand, the "renegade" who "wanted the world / In his two hands" (14, ll. 423–4) narrates his friend Shig's descent into the criminal underworld and inevitable incarceration: "There were only a few of us such as he / But he blackened our name / Shut the gates to the sea" (15, ll. 444–6). On the other, the "philosopher" Tatsuo who "wanted the world / For others"

(15, l. 447–8) lives with the turmoil and pain of loss – the "burning rain in the eye" obscuring all lovely and familiar shapes (15, l. 458) – but nevertheless asserts "No bitterness; only the lesson learned / And the habit of grace chosen, accepted" (16, ll. 477–8). Whether figured as a practice or a piece of clothing, grace appears here as something external to the self, a call that the self can approximate. The last two participles, especially, marked by asyndeton, suggest movement from there to here, and hence a coming and a becoming. Tatsuo indicates the distance to be travelled to arrive at peace – to arrive home – as well as the travelling of it. Once again, however, textual collation reveals this expression of a high ideal to be marked by the pressure of revision. In 1968, Livesay dropped the phrase "lesson learned," perhaps because of a flavour of insensitivity or didactic cliché, and retreated to repeating the wisdom of "let the past be / And the future become" from Tatsuo's earlier stanza. All versions of the poem, however, have him donning "the habit of grace."

In fact, grace is threaded throughout the texture of the poem. The fishermen celebrate a humble "Christmas at sea" (5, l. 136). Mariko writes a love letter while her mother "lies in a manger" (9, l. 261). The mayor goes out "to find some carpenters / To build a village in a single day" (12, ll. 344–5), echoing Matthew 26:61 ("I am able to destroy the temple of God, and to build it in three days"). The Ukrainian farmer "lift[s] up his hands, his praise" (14, l. 421) in an attitude of devotion. Once the young philosopher has explicitly spoken the word – the occurrence of "grace" at l. 478 is unique in the poem – no justification for the segregation of the internees from the body politic of Canada remains. It is at this moment that the announcer vanishes and the poem turns to the brief concluding chorus.

☙✠❧

THE ESPOUSAL OF GRACE in the title poem of *Call My People Home* makes it the summa of social responsibility that the Ryerson Poetry Chap-Books possessed. Underpinning Pierce's labour for a national literature was his belief that all literature, at its best, extends from the salvific word that touches people in their need. As an ordained minister, he never relinquished his conviction that poetry should guide and uplift everyone. Livesay's graceful humanitarian advocacy for a wronged constituency harmonized perfectly with the tenor of Pierce's nationalist poetry series, for nationalism was to Pierce merely the first of many forms of ethical commitment. Livesay's poem highlights values of inclusivity and responsibility that the editor's character made run through the series. These values shine out in the poetry of other contributors, too. Kathryn Munro depicted destitute women. Agnes Joynes described urban slums. William P. McKenzie wrote in Scots dialect. Hyman Edelstein spoke for Jews. Hermia Harris Fraser studied Haida culture. Mary Elizabeth Colman represented diverse newcomers sympathetically.

It would be worthwhile to trace political responsibility through all of these writers, not only to better understand the demographic representation and social justice that the Ryerson Poetry Chap-Books enabled but also to chart the centrality of these concerns diachronically to the very concept of Canadian literature. The endeavour by some Canadian poets to represent marginalized voices begins long before Atwood's "This Is a Photograph of Me" (1966). There is a modal connection between Livesay's account of the Japanese Canadian internment in the 1940s and Daphne Marlatt's portrait of Japanese Canadian fishery workers in *Steveston* (1974), George Elliott Clarke's exposé of racism in the Maritimes in *Execution Poems* (Wolfville, NS: Gaspereau Press, 2001), Di Brandt's critique of ecological crisis in *Now You Care* (Toronto: Coach House, 2003), Sachiko Murakami's inquiry into Vancouver's missing women in *The Invisibility Exhibit* (Vancouver: Talonbooks, 2008), and Susan Elmslie's defence of autistic children in *Museum of Kindness* (London, ON: Brick Books, 2017). Religious and socialist idealisms have combined in strange and various ways throughout the twentieth century and into the twenty-first, moving social responsibility to the fore in the assessment of poetic value.

The preceding publishing history and thematic analysis has striven to provide one example of this combination. Livesay's 1991 dismissal of her poem should therefore be taken with a grain of salt: "Another twenty years went by before the Canadian public began to realize what had happened; my play had failed in its aim to rouse the wrath of the people. It was ahead of its time."[64] "Call My People Home" did not fail to inspire Ken Adachi, who quotes a passage from it as the epigraph to chapter 8 of *The Enemy That Never Was*. Moreover, is Livesay not implying that, if the "time" of social responsibility had not yet come to Canadian poetry in the 1950s, it indubitably had arrived with the feminism of Canadian literature in the 1970s or the multicultural pluralism of the 1990s? If so, her Chap-Book helped to lay a foundation on which many others would stand as they continued to build the Canadian literary home.

SEVEN

Romantic Modern
Al Purdy

IF THE RYERSON POETRY CHAP-BOOKS offered a receptive environment for Dorothy Livesay's political poetry, they also provided an essential framework for Al Purdy's development. In fact, their deep romanticism helped to legitimate his own. As prior chapters have intimated, the works in the series opened themselves gradually to modernism without renouncing the literature that had preceded it. This diversification partly composed the rich ground on which Purdy learned to combine two poetics. He grafted techniques of formal innovation, realism, modern diction, urban-industrial imagery, and arcane allusion onto the practice of sincerely approaching sublime topics through recognizable stanzas. Chiefly by producing effects of paradox, this grafting allowed Purdy to infuse into his poems a fluctuation or dynamism that made them enticing to a wide readership. The Chap-Books comprise Bliss Carman and Raymond Souster; Charles G.D. Roberts and Fred Cogswell; Marjorie Pickthall and Elizabeth Brewster; Susan Frances Harrison and Louis Dudek. Dreamy beauty and cutting realism accumulated as the series grew over three and a half decades, with no clear break between the two. Convention and experiment drifted through the same print-cultural field, competing with and pollinating each other.

In concluding with Purdy's contributions, this study aims to open the Chap-Books up to modes of evaluation capable of registering the ways in which romantic and modernist poetics were combining and recombining in mid-twentieth-century Canada, in emulation of Alexandra Harris's work on "romantic moderns," including Virginia Woolf, in 1930s England.[1] This recombination was the matrix in which Purdy found his voice as a poet. By the late 1950s, nearing their end as a series, the Chap-Books embraced political critique and intellectual difficulty yet reserved a place for nature poetry and high spirituality. Purdy grasped this equivocation, especially the fluctuation between idealist transcendentalism and realist skepticism. He forged it into his signature intermingling of the sacred and the profane. Purdy's two Chap-Books – *Pressed on Sand* (no. 157, 1955) and *The Crafte So Longe to Lerne* (no. 186, 1959) – are not failed attempts at poetry preliminary to his real arrival as a writer in the 1960s. They are the books in which he discovered his creative power as a romantic modern.

✻

MANY READERS OF PURDY, while acknowledging his modernist identity, note his poetry's deep romanticism. Sandra Djwa acknowledges that he learned much from the Montreal modernists, and identifies Dudek as the chief influence, but she goes on to trace the broad overlap between Purdy and a prior national poet, E.J. Pratt, who was at his peak while Purdy was coming of age. The similarities, Djwa argues, range from the smallest details to the largest convictions. Both use the rare term *quagga* (an extinct species of horse) and spell *Samarcand* with a *c*. Both recurrently write about time on the evolutionary scale and some form of love "that raises man and gives meaning to his life." She concludes: "I see Purdy in the same line of new Romantics with whom Pratt identified: that is, with those who combined both romanticism and realism in their poetry. In his impulse towards romantic myth-making and his insistence on the primacy of the human imagination (especially on the function of poetry in creating the world we live in), Purdy, like Pratt, is a modern romantic, but one who invokes realism, irony, and humour in his stance as a national poet."[2] Classifying Purdy as a "modern romantic" leads Djwa to position one of his most famous poems, "Lament for the Dorsets," squarely in the tradition of Keats's "Ode on a Grecian Urn."

D.M.R. Bentley explores the influence of the romantic tradition, and of Carman in particular, on Purdy's formation as a poet in the years leading up to the publication of his first book, *The Enchanted Echo* (Vancouver: [self-published], 1944). It was Carman, Bentley notes, who first prompted Purdy to write, as Purdy acknowledged: "writing poems began for me at age thirteen, when I read Bliss Carman."[3] Recalling how little modernist poetry was published in Canada in book form before the Second World War, and how dismally it sold when it was, Bentley reveals a newspaper editor's pivotal role in encouraging Purdy through his twenties. Joan Buckley, a polio survivor and a "great admirer of the Confederation poets,"[4] edited the *Vancouver Sun*'s weekly poetry page. She accepted forty or fifty of his poems for publication, paying a dollar per poem, and awarded prizes to several. Purdy and Buckley discussed poetry when he visited her at her parents' farm in Langley, British Columbia, and they agreed on many things: the use of "natural English" rather than antiquated poeticisms (more on this below); the psychotherapeutic benefits of poetry; phonoaesthesia, or the affective value of word sounds; the richness of metre; and beauty and music as the poet's goals. *The Enchanted Echo* manifests all of these principles. It is also full of allusions to Carman (one poem is entitled "Summons to Vagabonds"), *symboliste* suggestiveness, romantic trajectories of escape and return, and wanderer personae. "Great poetry this most certainly is not," Bentley states, "but it is nevertheless a rudimentary *ars poetica* that anticipates the combination of raffishness and tenderness – 'salty, robust ... language' ... and sweet, even sentimental, emotion – that is so characteristic of Purdy's later work."[5] Having unearthed a prior paradigm of success for the poet, before his success in the modernist paradigm (or a prior position in the field of literary production, to use Bourdieu's terms[6]), Bentley argues that Purdy learned from Carman and Buckley principles of sound and sensitivity that he never discarded. On the contrary, he folded them into his later style, which combined "raffishness" and "tenderness." It is a compelling analysis, one well worth extending beyond Purdy's first book.

I.S. MacLaren discusses the various literary frameworks in which critics have placed Purdy's Arctic poems, especially his eighth collection, *North of Summer: Poems from Baffin Island* (Toronto: McClelland & Stewart, 1967). Modernism, one such framework, may be suggested by the A.Y. Jackson paintings included in the book, but it alone does not satisfactorily account for the poetry: "One *could* – and critics *did* – indulge in a modernist rupture by isolating the solo, modern, male artist, and making him, as it were, a hero as an aesthetic arctic explorer. This is a misreading of what *North of Summer* offers in its totality."[7] Instead of the strong individual, the poems focus on people and the places they inhabit (i.e., communities), human vulnerability, comedy and farce, and flora and fauna (especially dogs). Above all, they enact a tension between centrifugal forces pulling out to the grandeur of the earth (escape) and centripetal ones pulling into the smallness of life (return). The visionary climax of the book comes in "Still Life in a Tent," which finds its way to the sublime precisely through the trembling speaker's weakness: "His fevered physical being having been reduced to inaction, his imagination can begin to recreate. It ventures across the entire North, sees it in theocentric dimensions, including existence beyond life, before returning Lazarus-like to the interior of the tent-infirmary. Out of weakness and vulnerability comes some strength of northern vision, broken by strength and still strong. The sublime and epic issue from the diurnal and prosaic."[8] The allusion to A.J.M. Smith's poem "The Lonely Land" allows for a modernist element in "Still Life in a Tent," but the core of this reading is the romantic transcendence that Purdy's poem admits. It is an analysis that remarks on the fusion of modernist, romantic, religious, and popular elements in Purdy's poetry, driving home the point with a demonstration that, as late as 1981, Purdy was not above invoking Robert Service, the author of "The Cremation of Sam McGee," in his own "Across the Mary River ..." (*The Stone Bird*, Toronto: McClelland & Stewart, 1981).

Sam Solecki's discussion of the "shadow" that Carman cast over Purdy's development is perhaps the greatest testimony to his romanticism, because it is so grudging. Solecki seems to be exasperated by the fact that Purdy was genuinely enchanted with the Confederation Poet, along with Byron, Browning, Tennyson, G.K. Chesterton, Hilaire Belloc, W.J. Turner, and other writers outside the Pound-Eliot nexus. His irritation comes from a critical unwillingness to give any quarter to different modes of Canadian poetry, different positions in the field of cultural production, different periods, or different scales of evaluation. It boils over in delightful remarks such as the following, which tries to cast Purdy's persistence as a poet in terms of Nietzschean heroism: "In retrospect, it is no exaggeration to call the achievement heroic, though during the lonely years of living in rental housing and in periods of mind- and body-numbing labour there must have been weeks and months of quiet desperation in the struggle to earn a living and to become a poet rather than a versifying dummy under the sway of a ventriloquist named Carman."[9] Gratuitous arrogance aside, Solecki does acknowledge the way in which this "sway" manifested itself not only in *The Enchanted Echo* but throughout Purdy's oeuvre. One manifestation is metrical: "the occasional presence of quatrains as well as lines with an iambic base in Purdy's poetry – his commitment to open form and [D.H.] Laurentian free verse is never complete – are a residual legacy of the poets he admired in his youth and who wrote much of his first book for him."[10] It is perceptive to observe that Purdy saw how much would be lost with the jettisoning of regular rhyme and rhythm: "Purdy is one of the few contemporary poets writing predominantly in free verse who is nostalgic for the past, saddened by the fact that his poems – because of free verse – cannot be memorized and recited and therefore cannot be literally as memorable as the poems of his first model."[11]

Another sign of Carman's lasting influence on Purdy is generic. Solecki reads "Bestiary [II]" (*Piling Blood*, Toronto: McClelland & Stewart, 1984) alongside Carman's similar poetic catalogue, "The Green Book of the Bards" (*Pipes of Pan*, vol. 2, *From the Green Book of the Bards*, Boston: L.C. Page, 1903). A third similarity is thematic. Both poets write about the beauty of spring, Arcady and other flotsam of Greek mythology, vagabonds and transients, and Canada.

The most interesting commonality to which Solecki gestures – subtly but, to his credit, substantiated through example – is conceptual. Purdy, like Carman, understood poetry to be an oneiric experience conducive, in its own way, to truth. It is a conviction distinguishable from the political concept of poetry championed by Dorothy Livesay, discussed in the prior chapter, but no less sustaining. Despite his frequent recourse to modernist tapinosis, Purdy shared with Carman a concept of the poem's gravitation to dream, and the dream's gravitation to God. In his reading of "Inside the Mill" (*Sundance at Dusk*, Toronto: McClelland & Stewart, 1976), Solecki gives an example of this concept at work:

> The opening line's present tense creates the momentary illusion that the "men are still working," an illusion to be gradually and reluctantly undone by the rest of the poem ... And yet for three unpunctuated stanzas the hypnotizing song-like lilt created by the rhythm and the metre – a deft mix of iambs and anapests – keeps whole and real the first stanza's dream image from the past. The reader's complicity

in the dream image is also secured in part by the deliberately ambiguous "you" running through the third stanza, which is simultaneously the speaker, a synonym for "one," and, as so often in Purdy, an address to the reader.¹²

The same poem, Solecki argues, implies a "pillar of fire," a phrase it does not use, through two phrases that it does, "pillar of shadows" and "birds fumed into fire." The invocation of the God of Exodus 13:21 is as vivid as it is subtle. The claim, then, that "Carman and the kind of poetry he represents were completely left behind when Purdy remade himself as a writer through the 1940s and 1950s" must be largely rhetorical. What Solecki's discussion really proves is Purdy's inheritance of Carman, which, like any inheritance, was complex and selective, an "act of using from one's past whatever comes in handy in the fashioning of one's own prosody and poetic." The "co-presence of what could be called the Carman and Lawrence strands in Purdy's poetic reminds us, poem by poem, of the two traditions he has brought together and reforged into his own voice."¹³ Solecki's analysis is at its most perceptive here, in its granting that Purdy brought together two traditions.

Tracy Ware places Purdy in a robust line of succession going back through Birney and Pratt to Duncan Campbell Scott, refuting any assumption that nineteenth-century poetry was "moribund" to him.¹⁴ Tim Heath takes Purdy's penchant for downtrodden or obsolete objects – stones, bones, fossils, sewers, dilapidated buildings, old cars, garbage cans, broken bottles, weeds, rot, trains, piss, animals, tramps, prostitutes, grandfathers – and advances the theory that his poems flow from a belief in the oneness of all things, much as Wordsworth's did: "many of his poems conceive of things as a oneness or unity, with such force that God and the universe are aspects of this single substance."¹⁵ Frank Davey attributes both Purdy's work and its canonization to what he pejoratively terms a "generalized irrationalism": "although Purdy's poetics were a part of the 1960s, they were arguably a rear-guard element – both part of the 1940s poets' revisiting of romanticism and part of the 1960s' confused romantic mixing of the occult, individual liberty, heroic masculine resistance to authority, and pure presence with various quite different interests."¹⁶

The critical review could go on, but lining up these studies should be sufficient to make the point that Purdy, although a modernist by virtue of association with D.H. Lawrence, Irving Layton, and others, nevertheless possesses pronounced romantic qualities: a gravitation to the sublime, a concept of poetry as spiritual/prophetic, a reverence for nature, a sincere grasping of love and beauty, a preference for history and tradition over purity, and a retention of the music of "conservative verse." Purdy's first book publisher (after himself) confirmed and strengthened this romanticism, making it not an apprentice's cap to be doffed at the first opportunity but the bone and sinew of his poetics. Purdy has not yet been read in the context of the Ryerson Poetry Chap-Books, because there has been so little scholarship on the Chap-Books as any kind of context at all. They are, however, the imprint under which his second and fourth book appeared, and are one early and important milieu in which he emerged as a national poet.

꧁✢꧂

ROMANTICISM AND MODERNISM struggled and blended with each other throughout the Chap-Books. The former may have had the upper hand in 1925 and the latter in 1960, but as the prior chapters have intimated, contributors across these three-and-a-half decades engaged with this dyad in various ways, some declaring themselves for one side and suffering the incursions of the other, some embracing both sides and trying to manage their interaction, some pushing the binary away in the effort to find other poetic dimensions. It is difficult to name with any certainty a date when the series became modernist – all the more so since abstract terms vary in application with the interpreter. Lionel Stevenson's "British Columbia Vignettes" ponder the problem of modernity (*A Pool of Stars*, no. [8], 1926). Kathryn Munro wrote free verse poems that recall the city landscape of "The Love Song of J. Alfred Prufrock" (*Forfeit and Other Poems*, no. [3], 1926). A.G. Bailey, often described as a modernist, published a luxuriously fantastical arabesque in *Tâo* (no. 51, 1930). Carol Coates wrote haiku-like poems about Japan in the 1930s (*Fancy Free*, no. 85, 1939).

Modernist voices increased in strength and number in the Chap-Books of the 1950s, without, however, drowning out romantic ones. Elizabeth Brewster's three books reflect this polyphony. *East Coast* (1951), her debut collection, assembled modernist poems that she had previously placed in *Poetry* (Chicago), *Canadian Poetry Magazine*, *Northern Review*, *Contemporary Verse*, and the *Fiddlehead*. "Paper Flowers," one of the poems in *East Coast*, is a stinging critique of the shallow feminine arts of Victorian convention. In this poem, a maiden lady sits inside under a portrait of the imperialist Lord Kitchener, making lilies and daffodils out of crinkled paper, oblivious to the real flowers outside: "The house was full of false flowers, spilling from bulging vases / And lying in tangled heaps on the tops of desks." Assonance and consonance emphasize the falseness, as does the play on "lying," which implies that the modern author's present free-verse poem is a truer paper flower.[17] Other poems, such as "Jamie" and "Anna," are realist character sketches in the vein of Edwin Arlington Robinson's "Reuben Bright" (*The Children of the Night*, 1897), and anticipate those in *The Stunted Strong* (1954) by Brewster's friend and *Fiddlehead* cofounder Fred Cogswell. The title poem of Brewster's first Chap-Book, "East Coast – Canada," nods to iambic pentameter and end rhyme in its first six lines and then abandons them for a ragged form appropriate to a lyric about the overwhelming wind and the loneliness of Maritime life. The effect is comparable to A.J.M. Smith's "The Lonely Land," but the nearer model is probably Marriott's *The Wind Our Enemy*, especially given that Brewster's poem, like Marriott's, has people turning on the radio in hopes of escaping the wind's assault; both poems begin and end with bleak images of the wind.[18] Anti-Victorian, unsentimental, ruthless with falsehood, plainspoken, and metrically irregular, *East Coast* adds to and highlights the modernist character of the Chap-Books.

Brewster's second book resists such quick classification. *Lillooet* (1954), a long poem in heroic couplets, is a satire of small-town Canada. The first joke is on the reader: the village described is not Lillooet, British Columbia, but Chipman, New Brunswick, the author's birthplace. The deliberate confusion is a strategy to generalize the account to every small town across the country. There are modern images – paperbacks, a jukebox, a department store, a movie theatre – but also colonial ones – churches, lumber camps, singalongs. A realistic exposure of vice animates the poem, but it is more Horatian than Juvenalian. The author pokes fun at the community in a manner that, like Stephen Leacock's in *Sunshine Sketches of a Little Town* (1912), is ultimately good-natured and affectionate. The heroic couplets suggest an ironic invocation of a prior Canadian long poem about a town in the Maritimes – Oliver Goldsmith's *The Rising Village* (1825) – but if there is any model for *Lillooet* it is surely Byron's *Don Juan* (1819–24):

A poem you have asked – a long one, too.
No trifling, tiny lyric verse will do;
No sonnet to an eyebrow or a whiffletree,
No elegy to an enemy dying of sniffles he
Acquired from the cold glance of an icy eye –
In short, no small potatoes poetry,
But something grand, impressive and sublime
And guaranteed to use up years of time
In writing, if not reading.[19]

Brewster's intrusive narration, poetic self-ridicule, triple rhymes, and line-bursting rhythms recall Byron's mock epic (especially its famous opening, "I want a hero"). One could call *Lillooet* modernist, then, with the proviso that it is an imitation of one of the greatest poems of the English romantic period.

Brewster's third book, *Roads and Other Poems* (1957), continues this bemusing mingling of tones and styles. The untitled first poem ("Only the subtle things") is a manifesto for realism. "Roads" records the hopelessness of a hobo looking for work during the Depression. "Canon Bradley" unfolds the intimate tragedy of an Anglican priest confounded by his daughter's death. "Louisa" is a bleak portrait of a woman's life in a small town, and alludes in its last line to T.S. Eliot's *The Waste Land*. Then there is a surprising turn to lyric penitence ("Eviction"), a demonstration of the subjunctive essence of faith ("Supposition"), and finally this:

Poem for Good Friday

O HOLY cross,
O gracious tree
That casts so sweet a shade
On me,

Once you grew tall
In a green wood;
Rustling in new green leaves
You stood.

They chopped you down
Where tall you grew;
Birds from your frightened
Branches flew.
Two plain brown boards
They made of you.

Yet what green leaves
Could round you twine
More gently than this
Sacred Vine?

What fresher flowers
Could grace your wood
Than rosy blossoms
Of His blood?

What fruit more Eden-sweet
Could be
Than this dear flesh
That died for me?[20]

One would be hard pressed to find a more genuine meditation on the Passion of Christ. The six stanzas of rhyming iambic dimeter form a humble path, straight and symmetrical, into the "shade" and "fruit" of mystery: three statements indicate the death of the body; three questions wonder about the spirit's life. Brewster's 1957 Chap-Book thus culminates with a hymn comparable to George Herbert's *Temple* (1633) in its faith and to Wordsworth's Lucy poems (1800) in its simplicity.

The Chap-Books certainly got a modernist boost with Dudek's *The Searching Image* (1952), which he dedicated to Pound. Brian Trehearne reads it as a pivotal moment in Dudek's development, in which he embraced that which he had formerly rejected – the dense aestheticism of the *Preview* poets, P.K. Page and Patrick Anderson especially – and so granted and helped to crystallize a distinctive 1940s style of Canadian modernist poetry. More specifically, Dudek, who debuted in *First Statement* in a number of traditions of English verse, including love lyrics, nature poems, and dandyism, immersed himself in Marxist social realism in *East of the City* (Toronto: Ryerson Press, 1946) in the manner of Livesay. Remarkably, he then turned to Poundian imagism in *Twenty-Four Poems* (Toronto: Contact Press, 1952) and stylized formalism in *The Searching Image*. This heightened engagement with the pure problem of poetic form ultimately helps to explain the difficult long poems of his maturity, from *Europe* (Toronto: Laocoön [Contact], 1954) to *Continuations I* and *II* (Montreal: Véhicule Press, 1981, 1990), for in these he pursues, centrally, the challenge of representing the living mind through bolder and bolder forms of fragmentation.[21]

Assessing *The Searching Image*, Trehearne judges "The Pomegranate," "The Bee of Words," "Christmas," and "Old Music" to be self-reflexive poems dripping with metaphor, fascinated with decoration, and reckless of obscurity.[22] All four of them rhyme, or half-rhyme, and all four are written in quatrains, but there is nevertheless a distinguished formal daring that bespeaks a confident manipulation of tradition. "The Bee of Words," for example, chooses its metre for a metaphorical reason:

> I am the hot hive to which those bee words come,
> my palace floors swept clean for their sultry wings;
> out of the light into my dark cave each one brings
> its sweetness that it stores in the mind's honeycomb.
>
> There, of that clear honey, love like a queen bee wives
> in dark fertility; and of her honeyed streams
> unborn bees of mine rise up in their cells from dreams
> of a myriad shining wings whirled out to a million hives.[23]

The iambic hexameter makes rhythmic room for lavishness, as it does in Spenser's *Faerie Queene*, but in this case it also showily plays into the conceit of the poem, appropriately reflecting the hexagonal cells of the honeycomb. As if in confirmation, a few pages later, "The Pomegranate," also written in alexandrines, compares the fruit's seeds to "hexagons of honey."[24] That beauty gives rise to poetry is the premise of any love lyric, but here the figuration is not only self-conscious but gloriously in love with itself. Involuted and dazzling, it measures up in its own way to the wit of the Renaissance sonneteers. The woman's voice is a buzzing bee that brings sweetness to the speaker's mind and body; visions of creation and procreation intermingle; the poem rises from him like an apiarist's smoke enveloping a hive; the bee, like the poem, is a sound, thus playing on the letter *b*; and there is even the sense of a social gathering where communal work – in this case, not a quilting bee or a logging bee, but the literary work – is performed. The point of the poem becomes its technique, and the technique is virtuosic.

The technical concentration on form is all the clearer for the contrasting shapes of other poems. "Line and Form," with which *The Searching Image* closes, represents the collection's furthest departure from rhyming quatrains:

> The great orchestrating principle of gravity
>   makes such music of mountains
> as shaped by the mathematical hands
>   of four winds, clouds
>   yield in excellent and experimental sculpture;
> mushrooms, elephants
>   and women's legs, have too their form
>   generated within a three-dimensional space
>   efficiently.
>
> And so the emotions
>   combine into exquisite
>   counterparts of mind and body
> when the moving principle and the natural limits imposed
>   work against each other,
>   give in, and resist.[25]

In this poem, gravity, wind, parabola, ocean, and ideas are the pure "line" of a "moving principle," which, when it collides with "natural limits," creates the real "form" of mountains, clouds, finite integers, ripples in the sand, and poetry. The case is put discursively as well as stanzaically, in that the free-verse sections appear as clouds on the page. "Line and Form" supports the argument that Dudek was pivoting in 1952 toward a poetics oriented to the task of finding forms to mirror thought, forms as original and fluid as thought itself. It needs only be added that the title of the collection, itself a poem that stands apart from all the others, signals this quest. The "image" is both object and subject; "searching" both adjective and participle. The poet's telos is the usual one, to present capacious and memorable images to the reader, as well as the radical one, to free the image or idea from convention so that it may discover its own, appropriate form. The elevation of stylistic decision over emotional expression as the prime cause of a poem makes *The Searching Image* a modernist accomplishment, although romantic themes of love, beauty, divinity, and nature certainly make their presence felt.

For every Dudek pushing the series toward modernist innovation, however, there was a Ruth Cleaves Hazelton (1902–1961) pulling it toward romantic tradition. Her Chap-Book, *Mint and Willow* (1952), appeared in the same year as his and amounts to a counterweight. Like him, she adapts form to content and broaches contemporary topics, but her manner is much more one of working with formal expectations rather than defying them, while her goal remains above all to suggest a fleeting emotion. Hazelton is more accessible than Dudek. Like Perry, she published in regional newspapers (*Niagara Falls Evening Review, Cass County Democrat, Times-Herald Newport News*) and mid-scale magazines (*Canadian Poetry Magazine*) and was a member of the Canadian Authors Association.[26] "Ishtar," imagining superstition and astrology in ancient Sumer, is a short dramatic monologue in free verse but employs archaic diction: "Ishtar was wroth!" Another poem, "Hope," expresses a woman's longing for her husband's (or brothers' or sons') safe return from the war, and is exactly as common and as grave as that 1940s experience. In the form of a Petrarchan sonnet, "No Whispers in the Grass" grieves the invention and testing of the atomic bomb, and condemns humanity for this historic transgression against nature. "His Crime" employs dignified stanzas of iambic pentameter to narrate the sublime suffering of a Holocaust martyr. "The Night" conflates the desire for freedom with the desire of acting in a drama: "For me, the Night is blessed / With magical devices, and the fire / Of all romance, and wizardry, and love!"[27] "Manhattan Towers" dismisses modern skyscrapers for structures that tower far higher, namely, the Book of Genesis and Keats's "On First Looking into Chapman's Homer." "Shard" attests, as does Coleridge's "Kubla Khan," that perfection can only be glimpsed in fragments. "To You" is a solemn, realistic tribute in blank verse to a life partner:

> Because of love we found together once –
> I know a room could be a regal place;
> A chair could hold a dream; and ecstasy
> Could swirl within a cup of simple brew.

That useful things could still partake of that
Exquisite idiom of beauty, won
When we sat down content with simple place![28]

The inhering of wonder in mundane things is a common theme of romance. The title poem, "Mint and Willow," is perhaps the most romantic of all, for its mix of antiquarian mystery, the trope of the noble savage, the idealization of art, and the exotic combination of trochaic tetrameter and anaphora:

Shall I tell you where I found it?
In a shop where souvenirs were
Piled in myriad heaps and clusters
Shell, and bark; and ancient carvings,
Wood, and wampum; bone and leather.
There it hung upon the high wall
Worked in grass, and beads of silver,
Worked with loving care, and fashioned
Scene a dryad might have longed for,
Scene a poet must have dreamed of,
Scene two lovers saw, and lingered.
Surely none more fair than this one,
Sky as rose as dawn could offer
Tree so tall that stars might shelter
In its topmost branches resting,
Brook so clear it was a mirror
For a fawn to see its likeness,
Pebbles there of pearly whiteness –
Worked in grass of scented sweetness,
Worked on leather soft as satin,
Worked with beads of shining silver,
Painting called the Mint and Willow!
Painting, by an Indian maiden
One who dreamed a matchless vision,
One who dwelt with metal magic;
Skilled in art, and loving nature,
Working beauty into leather,
Painting gently, mint and willow![29]

Mythology, nature, art, and love intertwine to suggest beauty and its evanescence. The bright taste of "mint" and the death symbolism of "willow" are chiefly affective, and the poem varies with the reader's willingness to respect the sentiment expressed.

These representative examples indicate the syncretic character of the Ryerson Poetry Chap-Books in their final decade. Modernism grew sharper and more conscious, but it did not supplant romanticism, which persisted in whole or in part in the work of many contributors. E.K. Brown and others persuaded an older Pierce to open Ryerson's publishing program to a younger generation of writers, but he never relinquished his loyalty to the poetry of his youth, and his catholic and parliamentary approach to publishing ensured that it would persist as long as he: "By the end of the Second World War, Pierce had begun to publish modernist poets in quantity. His heart still lay with the romantic traditionalists, but a pragmatic drive to stay at the centre of literary publishing in the 1940s and 1950s – coupled with a recognition that a newer, starker poetry had undeniably emerged in the crucible of economic depression and war – spurred him to publish writers like A.J.M. Smith, F.R. Scott, Louis Dudek, Patrick Anderson, A.M. Klein, and P.K. Page."[30] If bibliographical objectivity gives a clear view of the cohabitation of different books and authors in the House of Ryerson, the corollary is a literary history that is willing to perceive the cooperation of their styles and purposes. What if the spirituality and accessibility of romanticism and the formalism and experimentation of modernism converged in the last phase of Canada's longest-running poetry series? The result might be a flexible, athletic poetry giving both uplift and jabs to a readership that it refused to circumscribe too academically, a poet as ready to anoint the humble (including himself) as to humiliate the anointed (including himself). The result, in short, might be Purdy, who entered the Chap-Books on the heels of Brewster, Dudek, and Hazelton.

※☩※

PIERCE FIRST ENCOUNTERED PURDY in the pages of the *Fiddlehead*.[31] Purdy had published a poem, "Landscape," in the literary magazine in February 1954, and another Chap-Book poet, Arthur Bourinot, brought it to Pierce's attention as the latter was revising and enlarging his anthology,

Canadian Poetry in English (Toronto: Ryerson Press, 1954). Pierce admired it enough to write to Purdy in Vancouver for permission to include it. Immediately the two began to discuss a Chap-Book, as Purdy's reply of 5 July indicates:

> I am very pleased to hear that you are including my poem "Landscape" in your anthology, but am also a trifle puzzled. "Landscape" was not among the six submitted for the anthology. Is it the poem that appeared in "The Fiddlehead" a short time ago, beginning "The snow fell slowly over the long sweep of mountain ... "?
>
> If that is the poem I think it is a good one but not the best. However, I have long recognized that a different perspective from my own generally makes a better choice than I make myself. I am often enthusiastic on first writing a verse, but in most cases the first enthusiasm dies and is replaced with something approaching disgust that the verse is not better.
>
> I should also be very pleased to submit a manuscript of my verse for chapbook appearance. I hope to have the work on it completed and send it to you within a month. If there is no special time limit I hope that will be convenient.[32]

The letter indicates the poet's willingness to take editorial direction.

Pierce answered with a justification of his choice, a characterization of his literary position, and encouragement of the submission that would become *Pressed on Sand* (1955):

> We felt that "Landscape" was not only an excellent poem but the right poem with which to close the anthology. In a sense it carried out the spirit of the entire collection. Other anthologies have been prepared which are left of centre. We are a little if anything right of centre, for we feel that our best work has been done in that area. The rest seems too experimental and requires more time to see it in proper perspective.
>
> We should be very happy to see your 60-page booklet which you printed privately [*The Enchanted Echo*]. We will also be pleased to see your manuscript with a view to publication on our spring list. It will be a great help if you can have the manuscript in our hands by the first of October.[33]

Purdy fairly leapt at the opportunity. Ten days later – well before October – he submitted the manuscript, provisionally entitled "Running Colours." ("I had in mind a water colour running in the rain.") He indicated particular pride in "Far Traveller," which had won a prize when published in *Canadiana*, and in "Meander," which had appeared in *Canadian Poetry Magazine* and been reprinted in the *New York Herald Tribune*.[34] Pierce accepted it immediately – "We have you down for a Chap-book on our Spring list" – and reflected gratefully on "the fact that you were introduced to us by Arthur Bourinot."[35]

Purdy wrote again in August, and his letter shows increasing trust both in himself and in Pierce: "Thank you for your letter and your kind words about my poems. As a matter of fact, I have for so many years dreamed of having a book come out and have imagined the enjoyment vicariously for so long that the actual event is anti-climax. It would seem that I have become cynical which may reflect favourably in my work but is undoubtedly bad for my digestion. But then to be cynical demands a certain calmness and serenity of spirit and blood pressure, which condition is probably unfavourable to ulcers. Which is certainly paradoxical." He offered a few new poems for substitution, including the title poem "Pressed on Sand," and then asked Pierce's advice on the title for the book:

> I have also been wondering about the title *"Running Colours."* It is a dreamer's title, to which tribe I suppose I belong, and subscribe to the doctrine that writing a poem in the first place is the thing that matters. But still I am not enough of the dreamer to be entirely true to that ideal and would like the book to sell fairly well too. I suppose that is unreasonable, but I am disturbed by thinking that another title would serve as well a commercially minded dreamer. A phrase from the enclosed poem seemed suitable but not final, *"Pressed on Sand."* It suggests impermanence and perhaps cynicism, but is not memorable. And I thought of *"Thirteen Poems"* which is rather English and states the case fairly, but perhaps too fairly. And I thought of *"Thirteen"* which seems to me better. It is ambiguous, conveys no information except a number which might relate to anything and it is odd enough to be memorable.

I should appreciate any comment you might care to make on this, since no doubt, you would like any book issued by Ryerson to sell fairly well too.[36]

Ultimately fifteen poems were included, ruling out the last two suggestions, so Purdy and Pierce settled on *Pressed on Sand*. The most important detail of this letter is Purdy's paradoxical identification as a "commercially minded dreamer," which would have struck a chord with Pierce.

A contract was signed late that month, specifying for the author "eighteen (18) free copies of the book in lieu of all royalty."[37] Although published with the date 1955, the poet received his first copies of *Pressed on Sand* toward the end of December 1954. He was pleased with everything "with the exception of the cover design" – Pierce had briefly restored the Macdonald woodcut – and noted only "one place where my punctuation missed fire" (a period missing from the last stanza of "Pressed on Sand").[38] The rapidity with which the collaboration occurred, and its repetition within five years for Purdy's second Chap-Book, *The Crafte So Longe to Lerne*, which was published on the same terms, are a sign of relative satisfaction on the part of both author and editor. Each recognized and approved of something in the other.

TURNING TO THE POETRY that Purdy published in these two collections, one finds the splicing together of romantic and modernist impulses that would later come to characterize his best-known work in the judgment of Djwa and the other critics discussed earlier. The cross-pollination is evident in poems that Purdy carried forward for republication and revision in subsequent books. It is equally apparent in poems that he left untouched after their publication in his Chap-Books. What this suggests is that the conversion narrative, whereby Purdy "failed" at poetry until he suddenly succeeded with his "breakthrough" book, *Poems for All the Annettes* (Toronto: Contact Press, 1962) – a narrative that Purdy himself helped to spread in later years – is a function more of modernist literary criticism than of fact. The reality is that the poet's blend of romantic modernism resonated deeply with Pierce's series, which helped form him.

"House Guest," for example, is an important Purdy poem, which he gestated in his first Chap-Book. It belongs to the corpus that commonly defines Purdy as an author. One of the reasons for its broad appeal is doubtless that it bears witness to the achievement of building the Purdy A-frame near Ameliasburgh – an achievement that verges on national myth, because the A-frame was and remains a house of Canadian poetry. In 1957, Al and his wife, Eurithe, bought the plot of land for $800 and began to build with the help of Eurithe's father, Jim Parkhurst, reusing wood from the Canadian Pacific Railway.[39] Al and Eurithe's hospitality to fellow writers made the A-frame a hub of literary creativity. "Even while the A-frame was being built, it became a meeting place – for poets, for poetry lovers, for those aspiring to be poets" – from Earle Birney, Milton Acorn, and Patrick Lane, to Margaret Atwood, Michael Ondaatje, and Steven Heighton. Today, a writer-in-residence program aims to maintain the A-frame as place where poetry is written.[40] "House Guest" is also a record of Purdy's friendship with fellow poet Milton Acorn.[41] In 1974, Mike Doyle admired the poem's "finely realized concreteness" and singled it out as one of Purdy's best in his critical review of the oeuvre to date.[42] "House Guest" was one of the seventy-five poems selected for *Rooms for Rent in the Outer Planets: Selected Poems 1962–1996* (1996), the slim volume that aimed to put Purdy's lifetime-best work in the hands of the general reader, an aim that was to some extent realized when Susan Musgrave defended it in the 2006 Canada Reads competition. "House Guest" is one of the handful of poems featured prominently in Brian D. Johnson's documentary film *Al Purdy Was Here* (2016). If Purdy succeeded in rebuilding the house of Canadian poetry with salvaged materials, "House Guest" has come to stand for this feat.

"House Guest" figures quarrelling as constructive. The speaker and his guest bicker about everything under the sun as they work together on the house that shelters them each night:

> For two months we quarreled over socialism   poetry   how to
>   boil water
> doing the dishes   carpentry   Russian steel production figures
>   and whether
> you could believe them and whether Toronto Maple Leafs would
>   take it all
> that year and maybe hockey was rather like a good jazz combo

never knowing what came next
  Listening
  how the new house made with salvaged old lumber
  bent a little in the wind and dreamt of the trees it came from
  the time it was travelling thru
  and the world of snow moving all night in its blowing sleep
  while we discussed ultimate responsibility for a pile of dirty dishes
  Jews in the Negev   the Bible as mythic literature   Peking Man
  and in the early morning looking outside to see the pink shapes of wind
  printed on snow and a red sun tumbling upward almost touching
     the house
  and fretwork tracks of rabbits outside where the window light had lain
  last night an audience
  watching in wonderment the odd human argument
  that uses words instead of teeth
  and got bored and went away[43]

Host and guest are equals: they both know enough about poetry, for example, to fight over it. Their relationship is antagonistic yet cooperative. They labour together "with saw and hammer at the house all winter afternoon / disagreeing about how to pound nails / arguing vehemently over how to make good coffee" (ll. 22–4). In fact, their hostility is a measure of their intimacy, for their friendship stands clear at the end. After leaving his guest at the highway, the speaker admits his own error in the last dispute (how to cook eggs), and by doing so admits his guest into that innermost room of the home, his own heart. On a further level, the structure built by the argument between the two men is the poem itself, for like the physical building, the verbal one is made from any old material lying at hand ("bedbugs in Montreal   separatism   Nietzsche   Iroquois horsebreakers on the prairie" [l. 46]). Both buildings make sound and invite "Listening" (l. 6); both dream (l. 8); both endure, "travelling thru" "time" (l. 9). Every poetic house is an instance of "the odd human argument / that uses words instead of teeth" (ll. 17–18); every poem is built by a quarrel between author and skeptical reader, whose skepticism softens only when the struggle to discover the meaning (the form) is finished. If "House Guest" begins with a quarrel, it ends with the transformation of that quarrel into poetry. The binary character of this quarrel between host and guest, between writer and audience, is manifest in the particular highway named ("#2"), the period of time spent together ("two months"), the transition between two seasons (from winter to spring), mention of the Cold War (capitalism versus communism), suggestions of Canadian biculturalism ("Toronto," "Montreal," "separatism"), the two-word title, and the arrangement of the poem on the page in two sections of free verse.

Moreover, "House Guest" salvages prior Canadian poetry for reuse, indicating the larger pattern of the national canon. Purdy's poem culminates with "frogs mentioning lyrically / Russian steel production figures on Roblin Lake which were almost nil" (ll. 51–2), a metaphor of the poem springing from the mud of an argument. This metaphor – poet as frog – recalls Archibald Lampman's "The Frogs," a sonnet sequence that uses the same figure to assert poetry's invulnerability to decay. Lampman's frogs are

> Breathers of wisdom won without a quest,
> Quaint uncouth dreamers, voices high and strange;
> Flutists of lands where beauty hath no change,
> And wintry grief is a forgotten guest.[44]

The romantic trope is constant: both poems represent frogs as lyrical voices that naturally express a transcendent spiritual phenomenon, whether "beauty" in imaginary "lands" or an impossibly located "production" that would be reckoned as "nil" if measured only physically. Purdy knew Lampman's poem: in "Bullfrogs," he wrote of "just plain frogs" that "their counterpoint / would move Bliss Carman / to iambic hexameter; // rouse Archibald Lampman / to competitive fever."[45] Frogs are poets for Purdy, as they were for the Confederation Poets. Furthermore, both "House Guest" and "The Frogs" pair winter's passing with a guest's departure. The invocation of Lampman also raises the question of scansion. In Purdy's poem, should we hear three spondees that emphasize the pouring of spring rain "downhill outside all day" (50)? This unusual rhythm would be climactic if, as with Lampman, reading the poem entailed scanning it.

Although the free-verse version of this poem was first collected in the second edition of *Poems for All the Annettes* and is the only text now in print, there was an another. The original "House Guest" was published in *Pressed on Sand*. Lexically it is almost entirely different, but thematically it strongly resembles the second version:

House Guest

I have an artist in the house for one week.
And expect to be discommoded, uncomfortable sometimes,
For I know him – the effeminate child,
With some stigmata of greatness that strikes
Violently at the world's hypocrisy; chill blue gleams
Of pure malignity: love soured and love grown old.

I expect pastels on the floor and numerous friends,
And mincing swear words and tentative
Veiled overtures without commitment;
Mild pronunciamentoes that spend
Gusto like a miser's purse, and save[46]
A bottom potential the mind will not decant.

But what is the relationship? I must know
Why this pale man I have studied for six months,
Why his pictures live, what life returns again.
Is there a difference basically
Underlying mine like a Byzantine plinth,
And growing into another world – a gossamer one?[47]

This poem, like its better-known second version, presents a dynamic between host and guest that begins as conflict and then turns toward sympathy. This speaker seems more patient. Rather than contradicting and mocking his guest, he only "expect[s] to be discommoded, uncomfortable," and the "swear words" are all on one side. The "relationship" at the centre of this poem is not obviously one of equality. The speaker is not, or is not yet, an artist, whereas the guest possesses (genuinely or sarcastically) "some stigmata of greatness" that marks his prophetic vocation. There is no mention of cooperatively building the A-frame, as that undertaking still lay two or three years off in the future. Nevertheless, this first version of the poem, like the second, culminates with one admitting the other into his heart. Their antagonism dissolves as the speaker generously reverses their relation, imagining himself inside the artist's house – the art work – with pillars stretching from their bases into a loftier world. The "life" that enfolds the speaker at the end is triply emphasized through two figures of speech — anacoluthon ("Why this pale man I have studied for six months, / Why his pictures live") and polyptoton ("live"/"life") — as well as through the difficulty of the pronoun "mine," which must stand for *my life*. Moreover, the final effect is metapoetic, for as the speaker has entered into the picture, so the reader has entered into the poem. Like the second version, the first version of "House Guest" self-reflexively figures poetry as the act of hosting.

Recovering the 1955 text of "House Guest" thereby allows us to recover Purdy's creative combination of poetic tradition and experiment. The diction ("discommoded," "malignity," "plinth," "gossamer") is refined and elevated, chosen as much for the rare sound as the sense. A neologism that blends *pronunciation* and *mementoes* pushes this interest in the aural artifice of poetry still further. Similarly, the rhythm twists away from any conventionally predictable metre toward unique emphasis, such as the three consecutive stresses of "chill blue gleams" or the anapest with which the poem finishes. Moreover, the poem subtly fulfills a six-line stanza with half-rhymes (*abcabc*): "week"/"strikes," "sometimes"/"gleams," "child"/"old," etc. (Line 16 enacts its "difference" by breaking from the rhyme scheme.) Internal rhyme ("hypocrisy"/"malignity") and alliteration ("pale man"/"pictures," "growing"/"gossamer") further enhance the aural design. These details are evidence of a mode of poetry still centred on the original assembly of sounds. The first version of "House Guest" thus allies itself with poets of Charles G.D. Roberts's generation and positions Purdy as their heir. His "Byzantine" pillar "growing into another world," for example, brings to mind Yeats's "Sailing to Byzantium," in which the speaker has "sailed the seas and come / To the holy city of Byzantium."[48] Purdy's "gossamer" world of art recalls the climax of Roberts's "The Tantramar Revisited," in which poetry metaphorically replaces old fishing nets:

> Then, as the blue day mounts, and the low-shot shafts of the sunlight
> Glance from the tide to the shore, gossamers jewelled with dew
> Sparkle and wave, where late sea-spoiling fathoms of drift-net
> Myriad-meshed, uploomed sombrely over the land.[49]

If romanticism cherishes the musicality of poetry and its adumbration of the sublime, then the first version of "House Guest" shows a poet steeped in it, turning to modern effects such as irregular rhythm and experimentally subtle rhyme.

"Short History of X County," the opening poem of *The Crafte So Longe to Lerne*, presents a similar case. In it, Purdy worked out the theme of what would become his most celebrated poem, "The Country North of Belleville" (*The Cariboo Horses*, 1965). Comparing the two poems again reveals that the heavy lifting was done for the former, although it has since been totally eclipsed. "Short History of X County" constructs the story, sketches out the key imagery, makes room for a paradoxical beauty, implicates the lyric speaker, and, as the title indicates, grapples with the challenge of knowing space through time. These accomplishments laid a foundation upon which to build. Paradox and history, especially, are so recurrent in Purdy's oeuvre as to be more or less essential to his voice. The refrain of the famous poem, "This is the country of our defeat," which may be as well-known as any line of Canadian poetry, is not in the 1959 precursor, but the germ of desolate patriotism certainly is, and it is clear that Purdy wrote his great poem, which would be published by McClelland & Stewart, by revisiting what he knew to be a good one already lodged in his second Ryerson Poetry Chap-Book.

The theme is defeat. Purdy portrays the process of rural settlement that established modern Ontario, and by extension Canada, as a series of setbacks and reversals descending into futility. However, this futility becomes a gauge of character. "Short History of X County" unfolds its theme through a story of urbanization, of which "The Country North of Belleville" retains only the contours. A farmer loans money to his neighbours, effectively buying their vote for his son, who runs for a seat in the provincial legislature. The son prospers, the neighbours default on their repayments, and the father seizes their farms one by one. When he dies, however, the land begins to slide back into wilderness, for the son, ironically the only "farmer" left, has long since become a city man:

So the farmer, rich man,
M.L.A. at Toronto;
Owns more than a thousand acres
Of once cleared land again
Going to woods and weeds and long
Foreshadowing shapelessness.[50]

Enjambment and alliteration here underscore the images of reversion and decay upon which Purdy will subsequently elaborate. The story continues with the son returning to the family farm one day, nostalgically. Instead of rediscovering his childhood, he finds only the strangeness of his own guilt. His ninety-six-year-old mother is still alive, but hates him. They cannot decide anything except in the presence of a lawyer. Within half an hour of arriving, the "fifty year old young farmer" (30) drives away again. The story is thus one of romantic return in which, as in Roberts's "The Tantramar Revisited," true return is impossible. It is also a story of success and failure – or, to keep the paradoxical figure that Purdy here prizes, a story of the failure of success – and Purdy's poem thus follows in the thematic line of Roberts's "Unknown City" in the first Chap-Book, which also celebrated "high failure" (see chapter 2). "The Country North of Belleville" dispenses with the details of plot but keeps the forlorn effects: "the farms have gone back / to forest ... Old fences drift vaguely among the trees ... this is a country where the young / leave quickly ... we may go back there / to the country of our defeat ... But it's been a long time since / and we must enquire the way / of strangers."[51] Both poems explore the paradox of belonging to a land that has been lost, and the exploration is both pessimistic and reverent.

The passage that grips the first-time reader of "The Country North of Belleville" is the one in which beauty appears. After the allusion to Sisyphus and the images of abandoned homesteads, the speaker imagines a man looking up from his plowing "to watch for the same / red patch mixed with gold" (48–9) that adorns the hillside every autumn. The vision of sublime colour stands out against the dull hardship of the rest of the poem. D.M.R. Bentley describes how form lends its support to content to distinguish this passage. The scrambled layout suddenly gives way to "a rectilinear, field-like box of lines," of which the indentation corresponds to the sublime translation that the imagery achieves at exactly this moment. Once this correspondence has become apparent to the reader, the poem's staggered layout becomes a typographical metaphor of the defeated farmland's encroaching shapelessness. The spacing of the lines "can literally be *seen* as a reflection of the emergence and disappearance of 'farms' in the 'Bush land.'"[52]

Purdy hammered out both of these important effects – the irruption of the sublime and the reflexivity of the form – in his prior poem. In "Short History of X County," the speaker sets the politician's ruinous career on a rural ground that is pastoral:

> Fifty years back small holders
> Sowed timothy and buckwheat there;
> Kept bees, boys, grew daughters
> Profitably as young colts,
> Opening themselves in fertile air
> To celebrate no men or pause –
> (13–18)

Before mortgages and cars, there were crops and horses, not to mention children; they, and the democratic plurality of the many "small holders," signal the pastoral ideal. Purdy's own parents had been farmers before his father's early death in 1920. His mother sold the farm a few years later, but childhood memories of their gorgeous apple orchard stayed with the poet his whole life:

> But the springtime apple blossoms! As if the sky had fallen, with immense fleecy pink and white clouds blanketing earth between trees for miles. Seen for the first time in your life, it was breathtaking and breathgiving, for waves and waves of perfume seemed vividly perceptible to the senses. Everything small and of little importance: the apple blossoms, three black snakes under a fallen door, Grandfather and myself, a few trivial moments in the 1920s, they were gathered together at exactly the right time for memory to hold them – in a synchronization of little separate etchings and images beyond time.[53]

Both the memoir and the poem render beauty in terms of atemporality: pastoral perfection appears as a "pause." The moment "beyond time" is a recurrent element of Purdy's poetry, from the oft-revised "Spring Song" (first collected in *Poems for All the Annettes*, 1962), to the late "On the Flood Plain" (*The Woman on the Shore*, 1990). In "Short History of X County," the word and the accompanying dash indicate a step sideways out of chronology and into purity – the purity of profit without greed, of blossoming without sex. At this point, the stanza also tumbles into an impossible altruism, in so far as to "celebrate" a life without men is, for the male poet, to offer a sacrifice to a feminine perspective. Beauty thus appears unexpectedly in this poem, too.

Its contradictory dimensions only heighten it, as is evident in Purdy's locking on to paradox through irony and wordplay:

> That's how he got the farm,
> And everybody's vote except
> Long memoried tale bearers
> Spreading calumny and slander
> Pollen around polling booths – yclept
> The fifty year old young farmer.
> (25–31)

Old-timers (including the speaker) know the truth about the farmer-politician's rise to success, and their tales ("calumny and slander") are rendered imagistically as "pollen." In this image, the alliteration, which is almost rime riche, juxtaposes the fertilization of flowers with the machinations of politics, bringing together natural beauty and scheming opportunism into one paradoxical line that sees the former being defeated, yes, but endlessly – like Sisyphus. Is beauty ever fully lost if tales of its retreat keep "spreading"?

Finally, "Short History of X County" suggests a fading purity through its reflexive form. The opening and closing stanzas self-consciously frame the narration by commenting on the speaker's and the reader's involvement. We are immersed in the tale, despite our misgivings. It has "No beginning and no end, / Pick the tale up in the middle / And draw conclusions or keep mum" (1–3). "Holding the mirror up" to the farmer-politician has made the lyric speaker as "guilty" as he (45, 44), and reading the poem has done as much for the reader: "You can't complete your moral absence, / Your finger's in the puddle – / He's involved you somehow" (4–6). If history is a fall from innocence, then character, poet, and reader fall together, "flaunting / Mock morals and dropping acid / On reputations" (45–7) every time the poem is read. The stanzas parallel this complicity. Metrically, the lines mostly fall short of the tetrameter that is now and then suggested ("Sowed timothy and buckwheat there"). A rhyme scheme of *abcabc* is perceptible in every stanza, but the rhyme has mostly rotted into an assonance that only half-fulfills it ("holders"/"colts," "there"/"air," "daughters"/"pause"). The poem thus presents a defeat of innocence not only at the narrative level, but also at the lyric and stanzaic levels.

"The Country North of Belleville" substitutes a more visual, lineated reflexivity for the accentual-syllabic, rhyming one analyzed above, but the goal is the same. Moreover, the later poem is in many ways simpler than its 1959 predecessor. The 1965 poem reduces the narrative of urbanization, removes the irony around the main character, collapses the lyric subject from "you" and "I" into "we," and transfers beauty from an ineffable feminine freedom to the colours of fall. What it keeps, through a confident selection, are the theme of defeat, the view of the land over time, the pattern of paradox, and the probing reflexivity of form. *The Crafte So Longe to Lerne* does not differ from the award-winning *Cariboo Horses* due to any quantum leap in poetic ability, let alone a thunderbolt conversion to modernism. On the contrary, if anything, there is a relaxation from the one book to the other, an increased self-assurance, a filling sail. Purdy saw that he was free to combine the romance on which he had been reared and the modernity that the profession of poetry now required.

Purdy reworked many of the poems in his Chap-Books. In addition to "House Guest" and "Short History of X County," he revised "From the Chin P'ing Mei" and "Love Song" for subsequent books. "Onomatopoeic People" strongly resembles "Remains of an Indian Village" in theme. "About Pablum, Teachers, and Malcolm Lowry" became "Malcolm Lowry." "If Birds Look In" evolved into "Whoever You Are."[54] These textual connections indicate a continuity in the poet's development.

Republished poems, with no or little revision between editions, are even stronger evidence that what Purdy achieved in his Ryerson Poetry Chap-Books was integral, rather than preliminary, to his mature poetics. "At Roblin Lake," for instance, is an early example – and the first to be collected in a book – of the many poems that were inspired by a view from or incident at the poet's home near Ameliasburgh. It is thus a forerunner of the oft-anthologized "Wilderness Gothic" from *Wild Grape Wine* (Toronto: McClelland & Stewart, 1968). Milton Wilson first published "At Roblin Lake" in a survey of contemporary poetry for *Queen's Quarterly* in 1959.[55] After *The Crafte So Longe to Lerne*, Purdy republished it in the second edition of *Poems for All the Annettes*, and the consistency of the text across the three editions is evidence of his continuing satisfaction with the original. With a few exceptions, the variants are limited to punctuation and typographical style (see table 7.1).

"At Roblin Lake" starts with a jocular irony and then suddenly curves toward an asymptote of beauty. Croaking frogs irritate the speaker and keep him awake one night. The next morning, he catches one, but as he holds it alive in his hands he is stunned to find himself moved by its loveliness. Moreover, it eludes the full grasp of his mind and his heart. The opening stanza, which initially appears rhetorical and sardonic in tone, thus widens into a genuine cosmological question:

TABLE 7.1
Textual variants in Al Purdy, "At Roblin Lake"

Editions collated:
> *The Crafte So Longe to Lerne*, Ryerson Chap-Book no. 186 (Toronto: Ryerson Press, 1959), 17–18.
> *Queen's Quarterly* 66 (1959): 292–3.
> *Poems for All the Annettes*, 2nd ed. (Toronto: House of Anansi Press, 1968), 24–5.

Editions are referred to by date of publication or, where two occur in the same year, by abbreviated title. Unless otherwise indicated, texts follow the first edition (*Crafte*), here taken as the basis of comparison. Numerals refer to line numbers in the first edition.

 1 DID] Did QQ, *1968*
 2 Set] set *1968 (different style throughout)*
 5 nightingales?] nightingales, QQ
 6 Each with a frog] – Each with a frog *1968*
 8 copulation.] copulation? QQ
13 *a mensa et thoro*] *(no italics)* QQ
14 After which, I suppose,] After which I suppose *1968*
16 misogynists –] misogynists? *1968*
17 Frogs are ignorant about the delusion and snare / Women represent] In any case frogs are ignorant / about the delusion and snare women / represent *1968*
20 tangential backyard] tangential, backyard QQ
22 Though] tho *1968*
27 plates).] plates) – *1968*
28 This walking-morning] This walking morning QQ; Next morning *1968*
29 With hands – having no air rifle.] one frog like an emerald breathing, *1968*
30 antibody] anti-body *1968*
38 A nescient, obscure love.] the beginnings of understanding, / the remoteness of alien love – *1968*

> DID any one plan this?
> Set up the co-ordinates
> Of experiment to bring about
> An ecology of near and distant
> Batrachian nightingales?
> Each with a frog in his throat,
> Rehearsing the old springtime pap
> About the glories of copulation.
> If not I'd be obliged if
> The accident would unhappen.[56]

There is an affable surliness to these lines. The scientific metaphor, the incongruous diction (veering from "Batrachian" to "pap"), and the politesse ("I'd be obliged") all seem to mock with choice annoyance the idea of any sort of intelligent design to nature. If there is one irony to the tone, however, there is a deeper one to the structure, because the unanswered question in fact leaves open a magnificent possibility. What created the universe? Could anything have happened differently? What is the origin of love? "Accident" and "unhappen," too, raise these metaphysical questions.

By way of metaphysics, the poem plunges into the sublime. Metaphorically, the frogs are lovers first. They are carolling nightingales and then innocent braggarts, in contrast to the fish of the second stanza, which are calculating adulterers. By the third stanza, when the frogs grow into "theologians, bogged / Down in dialectics and original / Sin of discursiveness" (23–5), the poem's engagement with spiritual questions is obvious. Still, the touch is light: the quoted phrase playfully suggests both the labyrinths of medieval philosophy and the location of the real frogs in a bog by the shore. The eros of the first two stanzas shifts, however, to a different order of love. Finally, the frogs become a chosen race, humbling the speaker, whose irony and pride fall away:

> This walking-morning I make a shore-capture,
> With hands – having no air rifle.
> Hold the chill, musical antibody
> A moment with breath held,
> Thinking of spores, spermatozoa, seed,
> Housed in this cold progenitor,
> Transmitting to some future species

What the wall said to Belshazzar.
And, wondering at myself, experiencing
For this bit of green costume jewellery
A nescient, obscure love.
(29–38)

The moment of "hold[ing]" the frog "with breath held" is set apart. A subtle chiasmus sanctifies it, as does the suppression of the egotistical pronoun *I*. The frog's otherness is tangible in its cold blood and its antitypical body, opposed to the warm-blooded human, but it is an admirable otherness, "musical" and immunogenic. The vastness of evolutionary time comes into view as the speaker's thoughts run to the future, along an alliterative *s*. Primates have somehow evolved from amphibians; will amphibians continue to evolve after primates are extinct?

Moreover, Purdy delivers this possibility of natural selection allegorically by alluding to the Book of Daniel. In Daniel 5, Belshazzar, the Babylonian king, defiles the holy vessels taken from the temple when Jerusalem was conquered. When he and his princes, wives, and concubines use them to drink wine at their feast, a hand appears and writes "MENE, MENE, TEKEL, UPHARSIN" on the wall. The words designate quantities of money. "Then was Daniel brought in before the king. And the king spake and said unto Daniel, Art thou that Daniel, which art of the children of the captivity of Judah, whom the king my father brought out of Jewry?" Daniel interprets the writing to mean that God has judged Belshazzar and divided his kingdom. That very night the king is slain. Purdy's allusion implies that humanity in all its pride may share this fate. The frog, by contrast, although a captive, remains faithful to the laws of nature and will carry the chosen "seed" forward. Through this allusion, the poet ingeniously weaves together two kinds of cosmological thinking, biology and the Bible, to complete his vision of the lowly frog as a divine messenger. In the last lines, the frog is both jewel and Jew.[57]

The few substantive textual variants between 1959 and 1968 reveal Purdy's careful attention to this religious metaphor. More repetition clusters around the sacred moment discussed above, and a new simile enhances it:

Next morning I make a shore-capture,
one frog like an emerald breathing,

hold the chill musical anti-body
a moment with breath held⁵⁸

Breathing now intertwines with holding to mark the speaker's meditative solemnity, and a hyphen augments the play of meanings in "anti-body," but it is the precise comparison of the frog to "an emerald breathing" that is most striking. The simile reinforces the figuring of the frog as "jewellery" in the last lines. It also accelerates the rush of the third stanza into a mystical dimension, since an inanimate stone here becomes animate. On the other hand, the word "nescient" in the final line of the 1959 texts, although it was suppressed in 1968, adds to the evidence that the poem was born out of a spiritual reverence for nature's beauty. Deriving from the Latin *nescire* (not to know), it was originally a synonym for "ignorant," but since the nineteenth century it has taken on the further sense of "agnostic; (asserting that mankind is) incapable of understanding the ultimate constitution of reality" (OED). The suppression of the Latinate word makes the conclusion more accessible and may be another sign of a relaxing style, but its presence in early versions of the poem is a metaphysical flag. It is also, perhaps, a sign that Purdy read other Ryerson Poetry Chap-Books in the 1950s, since Dudek uses the unusual word in "Pomegranate" ("The seeds, nescient of the world outside, or of passionate teeth, / Prepared their passage into light and air"). Finally, revision also clarifies the poem's form. The substitution of a pair of new lines at the end and the breaking of two lines in the first stanza into three fill out the original thirty-eight lines to forty: ten for the first stanza, ten for the second stanza, and twenty for the transformative third stanza. The revised poem thus seems to invoke the tripartite form of the Pindaric ode. It is an appropriate adjustment, given the high sentiment of wonder at which "At Roblin Lake" arrives.

"At Roblin Lake," with its mingling of romantic fervour, twentieth-century science, myth, and backyard muck, is a robust link between the forty-year-old Purdy who was climbing to national prominence and the fifty-year-old who had reached it. The first edition of the poem is worth reading, and this rediscovery of worth corrects the claim that Purdy had to renounce all of his first four books in order to reach true success with *Poems for All the Annettes* (Toronto: Contact, 1962) – a claim that seems to stem from a fear that the good poet might be exposed as bad. The larger point, however, is not critical but historical. Placing Purdy's poetry in the context of the Chap-Books reveals the romantic strains in it that found approval there. There is a thematic consistency between Purdy's "At Roblin Lake" and Alice Brewer's "Spring in Savary" (1926), Leo Cox's "St George de Cacouna" (1926), Lilian Leveridge's "A Breath of the Woods" (1926), Elaine M. Catley's "Fall in the Foothills" (1927), Susan Frances Harrison's "To the Spirit of the West" (1928), Mary Matheson's "Magic Hill," E.H. Burr's "Sunset in Algonquin" (1932), M. Eugenie Perry's "Song in the Silence" (1947), Ruth Cleaves Hazelton's "The Shard" (1952), Theresa E. Thomson's "Silver Light" (1955), and Mary Elizabeth Bayer's "Silver Swan: An Epithalamion" (1960). All of them find a form or trace of the ideal in nature. They hail it as "love" – to take the last word of Purdy's poem – rather than skeptically rejecting it as illusion. Pierce's lifelong openness to nature poetry and religious feeling staked out a plot in the Canadian literary field. Even in its dying years this openness nurtured and emboldened an emerging poet at a formative moment, helping him rise to the peculiar blend of romantic modernism that would prove so fertile for him in the ensuing decade.

Half of the poems in his Chap-Books Purdy did not carry forward into subsequent collections, but even in them his essential traits are quickly descried. "Villanelle [*Plus 1*]" seems to have been written for *The Crafte So Longe to Lerne* alone, given that its publication there is unique. It did not appear in any of the magazines listed in the acknowledgments – *Canadian Forum* (Toronto), *Yes* (edited by Michael Gnarowski, Montreal), *Combustion* (edited by Raymond Souster, Toronto), *Delta* (edited by Louis Dudek, Montreal), or *Queen's Quarterly* (Kingston) – and later selections and collections made by Purdy and his editors also passed it by. Nevertheless, "Villanelle [*Plus 1*]" is a brilliant commentary on the modernity of poetry in postwar Canada:

> *Disdain, my verse, the language of the age ...*
> Heath-Stubbs

> EMBRACE, my verse, the language of the age,
> Coeval sewers of speech that make a poem
> Live argot for the vermifuge of rage.
>
> Of matched mechanic's tools include the spade,
> The crowbar words, the sputnik slang, and so
> Embrace, my verse, the language of the age.

Unless, of course, the foundered Roman state
Invoke in you its dead, contemptuous ghosts'
Live argot for the vermifuge of rage.

And if Catullus once defined bad taste
In pimps and whores – our negative's exposed.
Embrace, my verse, the language of the age,

Eschew four letter words, except on stage,
Or little magazines – a safety zone
(Live argot for the vermifuge of rage!)

Of small self conscious culture needing aid
And grants from regnancy to snuff the rose –
Embrace, my verse, the language of the age,

The verbs that itch like acid, nouns that ache
On human skin and sometimes must explode.
Embrace, my verse, the language of the age –
Live argot for the vermifuge of rage.[59]

As the epigraph and the contrary slap of the first line suggest, this poem poses the question of whether the language of poetry should be traditional or modern. Should poetry mainly draw on the stately measures of its own canon, or rather inscribe common speech, which thumps through life in the present moment? John Heath-Stubbs (1918–2006) took part in the English romantic revival coming out of the Second World War,[60] and the quoted line is from "The Language of the Age":

Disdain, my verse, the language of the age:
Be cold, be hard, impersonal as stone,
Or only use that argot for your rage.

Let Pindar's fire, or Ibycus', assuage
Your lyric want; sing, though it's you alone
Disdain, my verse, the language of the age.[61]

Purdy's first two stanzas thrust aside Heath-Stubbs's Oxonian pedigree and gentle bookishness, and reach instead for "sewers of speech," "crowbar words," and "sputnik slang" (2, 5).[62] Purdy's iconoclastic virility broadly appeals to the avant-garde, to the working class, and even to North American liberty. It would be a short step from this poem to drinking beer in "At the Quinte Hotel" in the second edition of *Poems for All the Annettes*.

However, there is immediately a problem. Is "vermifuge" (3) (a drug that expels intestinal worms) an example of the "language of the age"? At the third stanza, the poem turns to acknowledge the fact that the language of every age has historical as well as current dimensions. Modern English is full of Latin ghosts with which the poet, no matter how rebellious, must be conversant. "Vermifuge," for example, derives from the Latin *vermis* (worm) and *fugare* (to put to flight). "Negative" (11), a term for the reverse images from which photographs (a modern technology) are developed, derives from the Latin *negativa* (a negative word or statement). "Acid" (19) is slang for LSD, a psychedelic drug invented in Switzerland in 1938, but comes from the Latin *acidus* (sour, bitter). Purdy does not reject but adopts two key words from Heath-Stubbs – "argot" and "rage" – for his refrain, and like Heath-Stubbs he turns to the classics. The allusion to Catullus cements the complication. As a first-century BC poet, Catullus obviously belongs to the ancient world; at the same time, he rejected heroic subject matter and wrote instead about common experiences, including sex, with a disarming frankness. The speaker's admiration for Catullus thus "expose[s]" his "negative" (11): it reveals an embracing of the language of a classical age (late Republican Rome) in a manner respectful of, if not consistent with, Heath-Stubbs; and it neutralizes his avant-gardism, since, as it turns out, he is far from the first to develop poetic pictures out of the world of real experience.

Nevertheless, the contradiction is not paralyzing but enormously enabling. Purdy means to practise both modern insurrection and inherited discipline. He will "Eschew four letter words" here and deploy them with relish there. He will claim all "verbs that itch" and "nouns that ache" (19), no matter their connotations or origins. He writes a high poetry that purges the gut of parasites and excrement. The modern/traditional paradox extends into the form of the poem, too. Because Purdy admired Dylan Thomas,[63] Thomas's "Do Not Go Gentle into That Good Night" (1951) suggests itself as the next contemporary model, after Heath-Stubbs's poem, which is of course also a villanelle. The villanelle, however, reaches back in time. Before its vogue in fin-de-siècle and twentieth-century English poetry, there were the influential French examples of Joseph Boulmier (1878), Théodore de Banville (1845), Jean Passerat (1606), and Joachim du Bellay (sixteenth century). The source for the Renaissance French poets, in turn, was the *villanella*, "a trendy Italian style of song that imitated rustic dance tunes from the oral tradition, although its composers were courtly and literate."[64] The villanelle is thus at once a modernist form and a premodern one evocative of medieval folk culture. Susan Frances Harrison recognized this folk character in her *Later Poems and New Villanelles* (Ryerson Poetry Chap-Book no. [32], 1928) when she chose to describe traditional French Canadian culture through a cycle of villanelles. Purdy's villanelle recognizes it, too. Moreover, Purdy's poem is written in iambic pentameter, like the typical English modernist villanelle, but whereas the latter has, strictly, six stanzas (five tercets and a quatrain, for a total of nineteen lines), Purdy's has seven (six tercets and a quatrain, for a total of twenty-two) – an addition that explains the "[*Plus 1*]" of the title and links back to the freer form of the early-modern French precedents. In short, Purdy's manipulation of the form embraces two different ages of poetry.

"Villanelle [*Plus 1*]" also seizes a material paradox of late-1950s Canadian poetry. Modernist little magazines mushroomed after the creation of the Canada Council for the Arts in 1957. State funding abruptly increased the publication outlets and the financial incentives for Canadian poets.[65] If these writers were modernists interested in radical aesthetics and politics, however, the resultant situation was curious, in so far as their rebellion was dependent on the government, which in Canada remains royalist. Whether they fumed in "four letter words" (13) or "snuff[ed] the rose," they were doing so thanks to "grants from regnancy" (17). Purdy's poem shows a canny readiness to find paradox even in the structural conditions that enveloped it, which were inaugurating a new age for Canadian poetry through the age-old practice of royal patronage. "Villanelle [*Plus 1*]" thus splits open the irony in the very idea of literary periodization. It is impossible to define the new literature without invoking the old. Even the poems that Purdy chose not to republish reveal his characteristic allegiance to both.

THE RYERSON POETRY CHAP-BOOKS made a substantial contribution to Canadian literature by giving Purdy two of his first books. Purdy's first productive relationship with a book publisher was with Pierce between 1954 and 1959. Each recognized something valuable in the other. To Purdy, Pierce was the pre-eminent publisher of Canadian poets, from Carman to Birney. To find his own place in the Ryerson list amounted to incorporation into the company of his esteemed mentors. To Pierce, Purdy was a "commercially minded dreamer," a poet ambitious for an audience, who negotiated his way into the experimental little magazines without despising the middlebrow milieu of the newspaper, and who displayed the potential to deepen and extend the main line of poetry in Canada. With Pierce's assistance, Purdy used his chapbooks to announce himself a landscape poet, a lyric historian interested in the layers of time that settle onto a place, a nature poet ready to celebrate the beauty of frogs, a downtrodden bumbler who finds victory in defeat, a love poet, a formalist edging into free verse, a contemporary who admired the tradition, and a realist who affirmed spirituality. Reading Purdy in the context of others in the Chap-Books series reveals that he caught its character fluctuating in the polarity of romanticism and modernism and proved himself able to join the two over and over with electric effect.

CONCLUSION

I BEGAN THIS RESEARCH a decade ago, looking for weakness. Seeing that no international copyright treaty bound Canada and the United States until the Universal Copyright Convention in 1962, I expected to find an early twentieth-century Canadian literary publishing culture that reflected the historic disadvantages of the North American copyright divide – a culture that was inchoate, vulnerable, and hobbled by a lingering inability to sell books in the American market, although American publishers had long been able to sell theirs in Canada.[1] I found what I was looking for – literary critics so often do. However, I also found something I did not expect. Like Al Purdy looking at Arctic ground willows, I found resilience.[2] One editor. Thirty-five years. Two hundred little books of poetry. The numbers command respect by the standard of any life.

In the interval since I began this project, Sandra Campbell's biography of Lorne Pierce was published. The frequency with which the introduction and the seven chapters of the present study cite it indicate the esteem in which I hold her truly commendable opus. Campbell changed my mind about Pierce. Formerly, I discounted his oft-quoted claim of inaugurating Canadian literature: "We were at the beginning of things as a nation and we felt under obligation to assist as many spokesmen of our time as we could ... It was simply that a birth, and then possibly a rebirth, of Canadian letters had to begin somewhere, and it might as well begin with us."[3] Does not every generation of writers and publishers in this country claim as much? Increasingly, however, I am of a mind to agree with Campbell that Pierce achieved something unprecedented. Roy MacSkimming sums up the achievement with nuance (although he reserves the highest "quality" for his own generation):

Lorne Pierce, a Methodist scholar with six university degrees ... joined the Ryerson Press in 1920 and quickly became editor-in-chief. Pierce's ambition was to restore Ryerson to its former eminence as English Canada's leading trade publisher. He never quite fulfilled his aim, but his fervour and idealism had a formative impact on Canadian writing and on public perceptions of it. Convinced that the nation had come of age in the war and was ready to express a new spiritual identity through literature, Pierce ransacked the country for writers on his cross-country tours. Too often he unearthed quantity rather than quality ... but his labours generated a fertilization process that would produce better writing in years to come. Pierce nurtured a notion called Canadian literature.[4]

The argument of this book has been that Pierce's achievement includes the Ryerson Poetry Chap-Books. Through them, he instituted a flexible little model for publishing poetry books in Canada, a model that leaned heavily on the authors' enthusiasm to get into print, without cynically exploiting them. After collaborating on *A Sheaf of Verse* (Ryerson Poetry Chap-Book no. [44B] [1929]), the members of the Writers' Craft Club went on to establish the Carillon Chap-Books. After publishing in Pierce's series, A.G. Bailey joined Fred Cogswell to found the *Fiddlehead* and Fiddlehead Books in Fredericton. Raymond Souster and Louis Dudek did likewise, publishing Ryerson Poetry Chap-Books in the early 1950s and subsequently founding a little magazine (*Contact*) and a small press (Contact Press) in Toronto and Montreal. Coach House Press, the House of Anansi Press, New Press, and others followed in the 1960s. Winding back to 1925, the Ryerson Poetry Chap-Books preceded them all. The series persisted for year after lean year, while other nationalist ventures, like the Graphic Press of Ottawa, went down in flames. Gradually, the accumulating Chap-Books approached a parliamentary inclusivity that brought together the nation's diverse poetic voices to an admirable and unprecedented, if always imperfect, extent. Because of this inclusivity, the series also negotiated rich and productive compromises in the defining literary antagonism of the period, that between romanticism and modernism, and so built a path of influence from one national poet to another. The Chap-Books are the only publishing venture to link the "high failure" of Charles G.D. Roberts with Al Purdy's "country of our defeat" under a single imprint. For these reasons, in addition to those that

Campbell explores, it may indeed be the case that Pierce became a true publisher in the best sense of the term. Canadian writers and publishers of the 1960s and '70s continued where he left off.

If this evaluation of Pierce as a publisher is to stand, however, more readings of the books with which he was involved are required. Counting the titles is not enough. Perceptive and open-minded engagement with the texts is necessary, for that alone reveals their life. To this end, this study has argued that contextual knowledge is indispensable. Knowing how the books were made, who the authors were, and what challenges encircled them throws the writing into new and attractive light. Bibliographical scholarship, construed in the manner of D.F. McKenzie to include all aspects of textual production and reception, must play its part. Prejudice against the assumptions of the past must be suspended. Libraries must hold on to their print collections.

To seal this point about the importance of reading, let me close with a riddle. Here is a poem, entitled "Song to Make Me Still," from one of the Ryerson Poetry Chap-Books:

Lower your eyelids
over the water
Join the night
like the trees
you lie under

How many crickets
How many waves
easy after easy
on the one way shore

There are stars
from another view
and a moon
to draw the seaweed through

No one calls the crickets vain
in their time
in their time
No one will call you idle
for dying with the sun

This poem exhibits Chap-Book themes that have received ample exposition in the preceding chapters. Nature is a scene of insight. Rhythm and rhyme make themselves felt, nodding to the poetic tradition while moving ahead in their own way. The title, "Song to Make Me Still," is an invitation to all readers, even children. Spirituality is underscored: somehow the poem gropes its way through death to life. Now, who is the author — a forgotten nobody, or someone famous? You will find the answer in one of the last dozen Chap-Books that Pierce published, and I urge you to go and seek it. In the meantime, however, can you appreciate the poem without knowing?

APPENDIX
List of the Ryerson Poetry Chap-Books, 1925–62

COMPILING THE FOLLOWING LIST of the Ryerson Poetry Chap-Books has entailed a number of bibliographical problems. First, several of the authors' names vary (for example, Dorothy Roberts published her first book, *Songs for Swift Feet* [1927], under her middle name, Gostwick). The name as it was printed on the Chap-Book has been followed in the list below, with elucidation in brackets. Second, until 1953 the books were published without a title page. Sometimes the title on the front cover differs from that given in the publisher's note, the foreword, or the head-title on the first page of text (for example, W.V. Newson, *The Vale of Luxor / A Vale in Luxor* [1926]). In each case, judgment must be exercised in choosing the better variant. Third, the numbering of the series is faulty. The first Chap-Book to be explicitly numbered at the time of its publication is Lilian Leveridge's *The Blossom Trail* (1932), which bears the number fifty-seven. At some point an effort was made to order the prior Chap-Books, but some were arranged under the wrong year (for example, H.T.J. Coleman, *Cockle Shell and Sandal Shoon* [listed under 1927, but published in 1928]) and one was missed (*A Sheaf of Verse* [1929]). The faulty numbering was set down in appendix C of Frank Flemington, "Lorne Pierce: A Bibliography," typescript circa 1960, Lorne and Edith Pierce Collection, Queen's University Archives Library. Library catalogues follow this faulty numbering and therefore it cannot be discarded, although it distorts the publication history of the series. In the list below it is preserved in parentheses, following the letters RP (Ryerson Press). The series has been reordered by observing the publication year in the copyright statement of each Chap-Book and by collating the series advertisements inside the back cover. For example, Geoffrey B. Riddehough's *The Prophet's Man* (1926) has the faulty number eight (RP 8) and Alice Brewer's *Spring in Savary* (1926) has the faulty number ten (RP 10); the series advertisement in Brewer makes no mention of Leo Cox's *Sheep-Fold* (1926), whereas that in Riddehough does: therefore, Riddehough must have been printed after Brewer. Where two or more books have identical series advertisements (for example, Marie Zibeth Colman's *The Immigrants* [1929] and Mary Matheson's *Magic Hill and Other Poems* [1929]), the book listed uppermost in the advertisement is assumed to have been printed first. The revised numbering is given in square brackets to indicate an inference. With number fifty-seven and thereafter, the series number explicitly printed inside the front cover of each Chap-Book is followed, except where it was mistakenly repeated, in which case the correct number has been taken from the series advertisement and the error noted in square brackets (for example, Arthur Stringer, *New York Nocturnes* [1948]). Fourth, some books, although not explicitly published as Ryerson Poetry Chap-Books, nevertheless belong with them. Pierce published Bliss Carman's *The Music of Earth* in 1931 but did not give it a series number [83] or list it in the series advertisement until 1939. It has been included below under the former year. Joseph Easton McDougall's *Blind Fiddler* (1936), with its cubist cover design, stands apart from the series but was later advertised in it. Ann Boyd's *Spring Magic* (1931) was never advertised in the series but its typography, paper, binding, size, and literary character clearly mark it as belonging with the other Chap-Books; it has been given a subsidiary designation [55B] and included below. The total number of Chap-Books may therefore be given as 202.

1925
[1] (RP 1) Charles G.D. Roberts, *The Sweet o' the Year and Other Poems*
[2] (RP 2) W.H.F. Tenny, *Companionship and the Crowd and Other Poems*

1926
[3] (RP 3) Kathryn Munro, *Forfeit and Other Poems*
[4] (RP 4) Constance Davies Woodrow, *The Captive Gypsy*
[5] (RP 5) Annie C. Dalton, *The Ear Trumpet*
[6] (RP 6) W.V. Newson, *The Vale of Luxor*
[7] (RP 7) Theodore Goodridge Roberts, *The Lost Shipmate*
[8] (RP 9) Lionel Stevenson, *A Pool of Stars*
[9] (RP 10) Alice Brewer, *Spring in Savary*
[10] (RP 12) Leo Cox, *Sheep-Fold*
[11] (RP 8) Geoffrey B. Riddehough, *The Prophet's Man*
[12] (RP 13) Agnes Joynes, *The Shepherd of the Hills*
[13] (RP 18) Lilian Leveridge, *A Breath of the Woods*

1927
[14] (RP 14) Frederick B. Watt, *Vagrant*
[15] (RP 11) John Hanlon [Mitchell], *Songs*
[16] (RP 15) Geoffrey Warburton Cox, *What-Nots*
[17] (RP 26) Nathaniel A. Benson, *Twenty and After*
[18] (RP 17) Alexander Louis Fraser, *By Cobequid Bay*

[19]   (RP 20) Guy Mason, *The Cry of Insurgent Youth*
[20]   (RP 32) H.T.J. Coleman, *Cockle-Shell and Sandal-Shoon*
[21]   (RP 22) Esme Isles-Brown, *Twelve Poems*
[22]   (RP 23) [Dorothy] Gostwick Roberts, *Songs for Swift Feet*
[23]   (RP 19) Elaine M. Catley, *Ecstasy and Other Poems*
[24]   (RP 16) John Hanlon [Mitchell], *Other Songs*
[25]   (RP 21) W.V. Newson, *Waifs of the Mind*
[26]   (RP 24) William P. McKenzie, *Bits o' Verse in Scots*

1928

[27]   (RP 25) Mary Matheson, *Destiny and Other Poems*
[28]   (RP 27) H.T.J. Coleman, *The Poet Confides*
[29]   (RP 28) R.D. Cumming, *Paul Pero*
[30]   (RP 29) Kate Colquhoun, *The Battle of St Julien and Other Poems*
[31]   (RP 35) William P. McKenzie, *Fowls o' the Air and Other Verses in Scots*
[32]   (RP 33) Susan Frances Harrison, *Later Poems and New Villanelles*
[33]   (RP 30) Guy Mason, *Spendthrifts*
[34]   (RP 31) Thomas O'Hagan, *The Tide of Love*
[35]   (RP 34) Nelda MacKinnon Sage, *Fragments of Fantasy*

1929

[36]   (RP 39) F. Elsie Laurence, *XII Poems*
[37]   (RP 36) Regis [R.M. Whylock], *Cosmic Oratory*
[38]   (RP 37) Winifred Stevens, *The Viking's Bride*
[39]   (RP 38) May P. Judge, *The Blue-Walled Valley*
[40]   (RP 41) H.L. Huxtable, *The Fountain: A Dramatic Fantasy*
[41]   (RP 42) Jean Kilby Rorison, *In My Garden*
[42]   (RP 40) Marie Zibeth [Mary Elizabeth] Colman, *The Immigrants*
[43]   (RP 44) Mary Matheson, *Magic Hill and Other Poems*
[44]   (RP 43) John Hosie, *The Arbutus Tree and Other Poems*
[44B] Carillon Group of the Writers' Craft Club, *A Sheaf of Verse*

1930

[45]   (RP 45) William Edwin Collin, *Monserrat and Other Poems*
[46]   (RP 47) Elsie Woodley, *Bittersweet*
[47]   (RP 46) William P. McKenzie, *The Auld Fowk*
[48]   (RP 49) Nathaniel A. Benson, *The Wanderer and Other Poems*
[49]   (RP 48) Edith Beatrice Henderson, *Outward Bound*
[50]   (RP 50) Kathryn Munro, *Under the Maple*
[51]   (RP 51) Alfred Goldsworthy Bailey, *Tâo*

1931

[52]   (RP 53) May P. Judge, *The Way to Fairyland and Other Rhymes*
[53]   (RP 54) Mary Ellen Guise, *Pennies on My Palm*

[54] (RP 55) Aubrey Dean Hughes, *Argosies at Dawn*
[55] (RP 52) Marjorie Pickthall, *The Naiad, and Five Other Poems*
[55B] Ann Boyd, *Spring Magic*
[83] Bliss Carman, *The Music of Earth*

1932
[56] (RP 56) Lionel Stevenson, *The Rose of the Sea*
57 Lilian Leveridge, *The Blossom Trail*
58 Francis Cecil Whitehouse, *The Coquihalla Wreck and Other Poems*
59 Leo Cox, *The Wind in the Field*
60 Sister Maura, *Rhyme and Rhythm*
61 Muriel Miller Humphrey, *Twenty Sonnets*
62 Clara Hopper, *The Emigrants' Stone and Other Poems*
63 Audrey Silcox, *Earthbound and Other Poems*
64 E.H. Burr, *Rich Man, Poor Man*
65 Regina Lenore Shoolman, *Uncertain Glory*
66 George Frederick Clarke, *The Saint John and Other Poems*

1933
67 Murdock Charles Mackinnon, *From the Winepress*

1934
68 Marion E. Moodie, *Songs of the West and Other Poems*

1935
69 Frances Ebbs-Canavan, *Harvest of Dreams*
70 Agnes Maule Machar, *The Thousand Islands*
71 Peggy Pearce, *Wayside Grasses*

1936
72 William Thow, *Odd Measures*
[73] Joseph Easton McDougall, *Blind Fiddler*

1937
74 William Thow, *More Odd Measures*
75 Leo Cox, *River Without End*
76 Charles Frederick Boyle, *Stars before the Wind*
77 Helena Coleman, *Songs: Being a Selection of Earlier Sonnets and Lyrics*

1938
78 Michael T. Casey, *Sonnets and Sequence*
79 John Smalacombe [L.A. MacKay], *Viper's Bugloss*

1939
80 Anne Marriott, *The Wind Our Enemy*
81 Isobel McFadden, *Reward and Other Poems*

82 Lilian Leveridge, *Lyrics and Sonnets*
[83] (see 1931)
 84 Charles Frederick Boyle, *Excuse for Futility*
 85 Carol Coates, *Fancy Free*
 86 William Thow, *Poet and Salesman*

1940
 87 Arthur S. Bourinot, *Discovery*
 88 H. Glynn-Ward, *The Pioneers and Other Poems*

1941
 89 Anne Marriott, *Calling Adventurers!*
 90 Mary Matheson, *Out of the Dusk*
 91 Nathan Ralph, *Twelve Poems*
 92 Sara Carsley, *The Artisan*
 93 Doris Ferne, *Ebb Tide*
 94 Mollie Morant, *The Singing Gipsy*
 95 Amelia Wensley, *At Summer's End*

1942
 96 Ernest Fewster, *Litany before the Dawn of Fire*
 97 Barbara Villy Cormack, *Seedtime and Harvest*
 98 Hyman Edelstein, *Spirit of Israel*
 99 Mary Elizabeth Colman, *For This Freedom Too*
100 Anne Marriott, *Salt Marsh*

1943
101 Evelyn Eaton, *Birds before Dawn*
102 M. Eugenie Perry, *Hearing a Far Call*
103 Irene Chapman Benson, *Journey into Yesterday*

1944
104 Elsie Fry Laurence, *Rearguard and Other Poems*
105 Gwendolen Merrin, *Legend and Other Poems*
106 Frank Oliver Call, *Sonnets for Youth*
107 Austin Campbell, *They Shall Build Anew*
108 Sister Maura, *Rhythm Poems*

1945
109 Hermia Harris Fraser, *Songs of the Western Islands*
110 Monica Roberts Chalmers, *And in the Time of Harvest*
111 Eileen Cameron Henry, *Sea-Woman and Other Poems*
112 Vere Jameson, *Moths after Midnight*
113 Dorothy Howard, *When I Turn Home*

1946

114 Margot Osborn, *Frosty-Moon and Other Poems*
115 R.E. Rashley, *Voyageur and Other Poems*
116 George Whalley, *Poems: 1939–1944*
117 Marjorie Freeman Campbell, *Merry-Go-Round*
118 Verna Loveday Harden, *When This Tide Ebbs*
119 Norah Godfrey, *Cavalcade*
120 Audrey Alexandra Brown, *V-E Day*
121 Doris Hedges, *The Flower in the Dusk*
122 Goodridge MacDonald, *The Dying General and Other Poems*

1947

123 M. Eugenie Perry, *Song in the Silence and Other Poems*
124 Michael Harrington, *The Sea Is Our Doorway*
125 Doris Hedges, *Crisis*
126 Dorothy Howard, *As the River Runs*
127 Ruby Nichols, *Songs from Then and Now*

1948

128 Lenore Pratt, *Midwinter Thaw*
129 Genevieve Bartole, *Figure in the Rain*
130 Margaret E. Coulby, *The Bitter Fruit and Other Poems*
131 Albert Norman Levine, *Myssium*
132 John A.B. McLeish, *Not Without Beauty*
[133] (RP 132) Arthur Stringer, *New York Nocturnes*

1949

134 Marjorie Freeman Campbell, *High on a Hill*
[135] (RP 136) Hyman Edelstein, *Last Mathematician*
136 Thomas Saunders, *Scrub Oak*
137 John Murray Gibbon, *Canadian Cadences*

1950

138 Goodridge MacDonald, *Beggar Makes Music*
139 Kathryn Munro, *Tanager Feather*
140 Arthur S. Bourinot, *The Treasures of the Snow*
141 Geoffrey Drayton, *Three Meridians*
142 Katherine Hale, *The Flute and Other Poems*
143 Dorothy Livesay, *Call My People Home*

1951

144 Theresa E. Thomson, *Silver Shadows*
145 Elizabeth Brewster, *East Coast*
146 Raymond Souster, *City Hall Street*

1952

147 Louis Dudek, *The Searching Image*
148 Tom Farley, *It Was a Plane*
149 Ruth Cleaves Hazelton, *Mint and Willow*
150 Myra Lazechko-Haas, *Viewpoint*

1953

151 R.E. Rashley, *Portrait and Other Poems*
152 William Sherwood Fox, *On Friendship*

1954

153 Elizabeth Brewster, *Lillooet*
154 Anthony John Frisch, *Poems*
155 Arthur S. Bourinot, *Tom Thomson and Other Poems*

1955

156 I. Sutherland Groom, *Queens and Others*
157 Alfred W. Purdy, *Pressed on Sand*
158 Goodridge MacDonald, *Compass Reading and Others*
159 Theresa E. and Don W. Thomson, *Silver Light*
160 A. Robert Rogers, *The White Monument*
161 Thecla Jean Bradshaw, *Mobiles*
162 Myrtle Reynolds Adams, *Remember Together*

1956

163 Marion Kathleen Henry, *Centaurs of the Wind*
164 Fred Cogswell, *The Haloed Tree*
165 Freda Newton Bunner, *Orphan and Other Poems*
166 Ruby Nichols, *Symphony*
167 Lenore A. Pratt, *Birch Light*

1957

168 Fred Cogswell, trans., *The Testament of Cresseid*, by Robert Henryson
169 Hermia Harris Fraser, *The Arrow-Maker's Daughter and Other Haida Chants*
170 Goodridge MacDonald, *Recent Poems*
171 Theresa E. and Don W. Thomson, *Myth and Monument*
172 Joan Finnigan, *Through the Glass, Darkly*
173 Mary Elizabeth Bayer, *Of Diverse Things*
174 Elizabeth Brewster, *Roads and Other Poems*
175 Dorothy Roberts, *Dazzle*
176 Ella Julia Reynolds, *Samson in Hades*

1958

177 Myrtle Reynolds Adams, *Morning on My Street*
178 John Heath, *Aphrodite*

179 Thomas Saunders, *Something of a Young World's Dying*
180 Fred Swayze, *And See Penelope Plain*

1959
181 Mary Elizabeth Bayer, *Faces of Love*
182 Michael Collie, *Poems*
183 Verna Loveday Harden, *In Her Mind Carrying*
184 Douglas Lochhead, *The Heart Is Fire*
185 Theresa E. and Don. W. Thomson, *River & Realm*
186 Alfred Purdy, *The Crafte So Longe to Lerne*
187 R.E. Rashley, *Moon Lake and Other Poems*
188 Florence Wyle, *Poems*
189 John Robert Colombo, ed., *The Varsity Chapbook*
190 Leslie L. Kaye, ed., *The McGill Chapbook*

1960
191 Douglas Lochhead, *It Is All Around*
192 Michael Collie, *Skirmish with Fact*
193 William Conklin, *For the Infinite*
[194] (RP 195) Paul West, *The Spellbound Horses*
195 Mary Nasmyth Matheson, *Autumn Affluence*
196 Fred Swayze, *In the Egyptian Gallery*
197 Myrtle Reynolds Adams, *To Any Spring*
198 Mary Elizabeth Bayer, *The Silver Swan: An Epithalamion*
199 Milton Acorn, *The Brain's the Target*

1962
200 James Reaney, *Twelve Letters to a Small Town*

NOTES

Introduction

1 For an explanation of the numbering of the Ryerson Poetry Chap-Books, see the appendix to this volume.
2 Campbell, *Both Hands*, 8.
3 Ibid., 341.
4 Dudek, "The Role of Little Magazines in Canada" (1958), 205–12 (205, 211).
5 Tremblay and Rose, "The Canadian Little Magazine Past and Present."
6 Macleod, *American Little Magazines*, 94.
7 McKnight, "Small Press Publishing," 308–18 (310–11).
8 Campbell observes that the United Church Publishing House gradually accepted the redirection of agency and textbook profits to specialist publishing: "by the Second World War, with [Book Steward Clarence Heber] Dickinson's support, the Board of Publication regarded Pierce and the publication lists of Ryerson Press as embodying prestige, quality, and patriotism. Moreover, the board, like Dickinson, accepted that some publishing profits from Pierce's textbook publications and from Trade Department head E.W. Walker's wholesaling of American and English best-sellers (books for which the House held agency reprinting and/or distribution rights from foreign publishers) would in effect subsidize Pierce's 'highbrow' Ryerson publications." *Both Hands*, 343.
9 Campbell, *Both Hands*, 18.
10 See the appendix to this volume for a list of the Ryerson Poetry Chap-Books. The editor of an anthology such as *The McGill Chapbook* has been counted as one author.
11 Elsie supported her daughter-in-law through the difficult period of Margaret's divorce. "My mother-in-law was probably the only person in either family who truly understood what I was experiencing and who gave me her total support and love. She knew how much I cared about Jack and our children, but she, and she alone, knew too how much I had to follow, with doubt

and with guilt, but with certainty, the vocation that had been given me." Laurence, *Dance on the Earth*, 129. Elsie's two Chap-Books are *XII Poems* (no. [36], 1929) and *Rearguard and Other Poems* (no. 104, 1944).

12 Judge, *The Way to Fairyland and Other Rhymes*, 2.
13 Campbell, *Both Hands*, 7, 146–7.
14 R.D. Cumming, *Paul Pero*, Ryerson Poetry Chap-Book no. [29] (Toronto: Ryerson Press, 1928), 14. The inside front cover contains a biographical note on the author. The glossary at the back gives the meaning of *mowitch* as "deer meat."
15 Of course, race and ethnicity cannot be determined from the authors' names or pen names alone. It is tempting to look further into the ancestry of Geoffrey Drayton, for example, whose plantation-owning family had been established in Barbados since the seventeenth century and who is now being reclaimed as a Barbadian author. See Thomas Armstrong, "Lifting the Lid on Geoffrey Drayton and His Outsider Role in Barbadian Literature," *Arts Etc.*, 2013, www.artsetcbarbados.com.
16 Campbell, *Both Hands*, 21–4, 46, 48, 101, 116, 162.
17 Ibid., 412. These books were not Ryerson Poetry Chap-Books but full-length collections published by Ryerson.
18 Dudek, "The Role of Little Magazines in Canada," 207–8.
19 There are, of course, many successful studies of publishers' series. I have taken inspiration particularly from Friskney, *New Canadian Library*.
20 Campbell, *Both Hands*, 13.

Chapter One

1 Pierce, *The House of Ryerson 1829–1954*, 3.
2 Ibid., 4–5, 10. Egerton Ryerson went on to become the provincial superintendent of education (1846–76), and founded the Ontario public school system. For a full discussion of the emergence of the Canadian Methodist book trade from the American context, see McLaren, *Pulpit, Press, and Politics*.
3 Friskney, "Towards a Canadian Cultural Mecca," 36–7.
4 Committee report, Conference of the Methodist Episcopal Church in Canada, Aug. 1829, quoted in Pierce, *House of Ryerson*, 6.
5 The figure is a private estimate by Lorne Pierce in a letter to his wife, Edith: see Campbell, *Both Hands*, 145n27.
6 Friskney, "Towards a Canadian Cultural Mecca," 39. See also Wallace, *The Ryerson Imprint*.
7 Ibid., 45.

8 Friskney, "Beyond the Shadow of William Briggs, Part I," 121–63; "Beyond the Shadow of William Briggs, Part II," 161–207; MacLaren, "Living with the 1875 Act," in *Dominion and Agency*, 102–21. For a photo of the Wesley Building, see Parker, "The Evolution of Publishing Canada."
9 Pierce, *The Chronicle of a Century 1829–1929*, 232, 246.
10 Parker, "The Sale of the Ryerson Press, 7–56 (10); MacSkimming, *The Perilous Trade*, 147.
11 This sketch of Pierce's life summarizes Campbell, *Both Hands*, chapters 1–6; Campbell describes Fallis hiring Pierce on 135–7.
12 Pierce, *House of Ryerson*, 46–8.
13 Winship, "The Rise of a National Book Trade System in the United States," 56–77.
14 Parker, *The Beginnings of the Book Trade in Canada*, 255–6.
15 Campbell, *Both Hands*, 313–14.
16 Ibid., 321–2; Campbell, "From Romantic History to Communications Theory," 91–116.
17 Campbell, *Both Hands*, 183–5.
18 Ibid., 207. Estimates in 2019 dollars are taken from the online inflation calculator managed by the Bank of Canada using the Consumer Price Index (measured monthly by Statistics Canada). An average basket of goods and services that cost one hundred dollars in 1925 would cost about $1,484 in 2019 – about fifteen times more. Bank of Canada, "Inflation Calculator," https://www.bankofcanada.ca/rates/related/inflation-calculator.
19 Campbell, *Both Hands*, 248–50, 345.
20 Andrew Haydon to Lorne Pierce, 15 Apr. 1925, box 2, correspondence 1925–27, coll. 2001, Lorne and Edith Pierce Collection, Queen's University Archives. Unless otherwise noted, subsequent archival references in this chapter are to this collection. For a summary of Andrew Haydon's life, see "Behind the Diary: A King's Who's Who Biographies: Andrew Haydon (1867–1932)," Library and Archives Canada, http://www.collectionscanada.gc.ca/king/023011-1050.19-e.html.
21 Andrew Haydon to Lorne Pierce, 18 Apr. 1925, box 2; Andrew Haydon to B. [E.J.] Moore, 30 May 1925, box 2; Andrew Haydon to Lorne Pierce, 25 June 1925, box 2; Andrew Haydon to E.J. Moore, 1 Aug. 1925, box 2; ibid., 4 Nov. 1925.
22 Whereas the first eighteen gatherings are regular, with eight leaves each, the last is composite, with ten leaves and two signatures (19 and 20), indicating that part of sheet 19 was discarded and a new sheet, 20, substituted, to carry the notes.

23   Andrew Haydon to E.J. Moore, 16 Dec. 1925 box. Haydon projected a second volume of *Pioneer Sketches* but never finished it.
24   McRaye, *Town Hall Tonight*, 32–64, 71.
25   Walter McRaye to E.J. Moore, 31 Aug. 1925, box 2.
26   Unsigned copy, Ryerson Publication Dept. to Walter McRaye, 15 Sept. 1925, box 2.
27   Chauvin, "What Others Say of Jack Miner," in Miner, *Jack Miner: His Life and Religion*, xx, xxii.
28   Miner, *Jack Miner and the Birds and Some Things I Know about Nature*, 58, 63, 70, 96–102.
29   Graham, *Where Canada Begins*, 9–10.
30   Chauvin, "What Others Say of Jack Miner," xxii; Manly F. Miner, preface, in Miner, *Jack Miner*, xii; Miner, *Jack Miner*, lxiv; "Jack Miner's Memorial," in Miner, *Jack Miner*, li.
31   Manly F. Miner, preface, in Miner, *Jack Miner*, xii.
32   Manly F. Miner to E.J. Moore, 15 Oct. 1925, box 2.
33   Copies examined: author copy; McGill University, McLennan Library (call no. Redpath Basement Storage QL685 M5).
34   Manly F. Miner to E.J. Moore, 11 Nov. 1925.
35   Manly F. Miner to E.J. Moore, 2 Jan. 1924 [i.e., 1925], box 2.
36   Ibid., 5 Jan. 1925, box 2.
37   "NOTE—This volume is copyrighted, as noted below. Parties are warned against the unwarranted reproduction of photographs or articles from it. Application for permission for such reproduction should be made to Manly F. Miner, Kingsville, Ontario, Canada. PRINTED IN CANADA BY THE RYERSON PRESS COPYRIGHT, CANADA, 1923 BY JACK MINER."
38   "The reason I wrote you so quickly was that in Kingsville Pickard the big retail man gives me orders of 25 at a time and I give him a price of $2.$^{\underline{00}}$ per copy which he retails for 3.$^{\underline{00}}$ When I entered into th[ese] arrangements I gave him sole agency for Kingsville and he does considerable advertising so when I saw this copy in Leggetts you can naturally see what I was thinking about." Manly F. Miner to E.J. Moore, 19 Feb. 1925, box 2.
39   Manly F. Miner, preface, in Miner, *Jack Miner*, xii.
40   Manly F. Miner to E.J. Moore, 5 Jan. 1925, box 2.
41   Manly F. Miner to E.J. Moore, 8 Jan. 1925, box 2. Moore had been a book publishing manager at the Methodist Book and Publishing House since William Briggs's time. Pierce looked up to him initially but soon worked without having to consult him. Campbell, *Both Hands*, 160–1.

42 Manly F. Miner to E.J. Moore, 4 Feb., 19 Feb., 21 Feb. 1925, box 2.
43 Copy examined: author copy; Bibliothèque et Archives nationales du Québec (coll. nationale – coll. St-Sulpi 598.2 M662ja, third impression 1925).
44 Manly F. Miner to E.J. Moore, 19 Feb. 1925, box 2.
45 Manly F. Miner to E.J. Moore, 8 Apr. 1925, box 2.
46 Manly F. Miner to E.J. Moore, 9 Nov., 12 Nov., 11 Dec., 23 Dec. 1925, box 2.
47 For more on copyright in Canada and the United States in the 1920s, including legislative reform and the lobbying of the Canadian Authors Association, see Parker, "Authors and Publishers on the Offensive," 131–85. Parker states that a basic understanding of reciprocal copyright between the two countries was negotiated in December 1923 (155).
48 Mount, *When Canadian Literature Moved to New York*.
49 Spadoni and Donnelly, *A Bibliography of McClelland and Stewart Imprints*, 29. The following account is based on Spadoni and Donnelly's work.
50 Trotter, *A Canadian Twilight and Other Poems of War and of Peace*, introd. W.S.W. McLay. "To the Students of Liège" is the first poem in the book (27). The introduction provides a biography of the author.
51 Thomas, *Songs of an Airman and Other Poems*, introd. S.W. Dyde.
52 Leveridge, "Over the Hills of Home," in *Over the Hills of Home and Other Poems*, 9–12 (12, 11).
53 See, for example, the title poem "The Beckoning Skyline," 13–26 (24).
54 MacKay, "Marjorie Pickthall: A Memory," in *The Wood Carver's Wife* by Marjorie Pickthall, 5–7 (5).
55 Spadoni and Donnelly, *A Bibliography of McClelland and Stewart Imprints*, nos. 660 and 671.
56 In order to concentrate attention on A.J.M. Smith, F.R. Scott, Robert Finch, Dorothy Livesay, and E.J. Pratt, Beattie dismissed other writers of the decade in memorable phrases that will be familiar to many: "By 1920 the romantic-Victorian tradition was at its last gasp. Yet, during the 1920's, its conventions persisted in thousands of mediocre lines published annually in Canadian magazines, on the home-makers' and book-editors' pages of Canadian newspapers, and in the flimsy volumes issued by Briggs or Musson or other Toronto presses." Beattie, "Poetry: 1920–1935," 234–53 (234).
57 Murray, "The Canadian Readers Meet," 150–83 (153–4).
58 French, *The Appeal of Poetry*, 11.
59 Beattie, "Poetry: 1920–1935," 240.
60 Panofsky, *Literary Legacy*, 3–4, 21, 23.
61 Ibid., 105.

62 Ibid., 49.
63 Browne, "The Belgian Mother," in *The Belgian Mother*, 1–2 (1).
64 "Second Edition" is printed on the title page of some copies. Copy examined: McGill Library, call no. PS8453 R64 B4 1917.
65 The following account derives from Whiteman, Stewart, and Funnell, *A Bibliography of Macmillan of Canada Imprints*; see nos. 108–263.
66 Louise Morey Bowman to Amy Lowell, 26 Sept. 1923, in Cameron, "'So Often I Look up at You and Tell You Things, and You Listen!,'" 56–109 (71). The borzoi, a Russian hound, was the ornament of Alfred A. Knopf of New York.
67 Bowman, "The Mountain that Watched," in *Dream Tapestries*, 33–9 (34).
68 *A Book of Canadian Prose and Verse* contains the work of twenty-nine poets, from the eighteenth-century Loyalist Jonathan Odell through the Confederation Poets to Marjorie Pickthall.
69 "Osborne, Marian Francis," SFU Digitized Collections, 2016, https://digital.lib.sfu.ca/ceww-927/osborne-marian-francis.
70 Osborne, "Forest of Mine," in *The Song of Israfel and Other Poems*, 20–1 (21). Copy examined: McGill Library, call no. PS8529 S36 S66 1923.
71 Distad, "Newspapers and Magazines," 294–303 (303).
72 Vipond, "Major Trends in Canada's Print Mass Media," 242–7 (244).
73 In Cameron, "'So Often I Look up at You,'" 76.
74 Yeigh, "The Lake of Bays and Thereabouts," 47–54; Jackes, "The Pearl of Baghdad," 196–205.
75 Masthead, *The University Magazine*, Feb. 1907.
76 Robertson, "Macphail, Sir Andrew"; see also Robertson's biography, *Sir Andrew Macphail: The Life and Legacy of a Canadian Man of Letters*.
77 H.K.G., review of Nova Scotia Chap-Books by Archibald MacMechan, *Canadian Forum*, Aug. 1921, 346.
78 Harrington, *Syllables of Recorded Time*, 15–20.
79 Smith, "Contemporary Poetry"; Beattie, "Poetry 1920–1935," 241–9; Dudek and Gnarowski, *The Making of Modern Poetry in Canada*, 24–7; Trehearne, *Aestheticism and the Canadian Modernists*; McKnight, "Small Press Publishing," 308–18; Smith, *The Book of Canadian Poetry*.

Chapter Two

1 Friskney, "Towards a Canadian 'Cultural Mecca,'" 259–61, 299.
2 Fee, "Lorne Pierce," 51–71 (53–4, 57).

3 Duncan Campbell Scott to D. Dingle, 16 Feb. 1925, box 2, Lorne and Edith Pierce Collection, coll. 2001, Queen's University Archives, Kingston, ON. Unless otherwise indicated, subsequent archival citations in this chapter are to this collection.
4 Duncan Campbell Scott to D. Dingle, 1 Apr. 1925, box 2.
5 Fee, "Lorne Pierce," 62.
6 Quoted in Friskney, "Towards a Canadian 'Cultural Mecca,'" 288, 300. For a full account of this episode see Friskney, 297–301; and Parker, "Authors and Publishers on the Offensive," 131–85 (158–63).
7 Harvey, *Scottish Chapbook Literature*, 12. For hundreds of illustrated examples, see Meriton, with Dumontet, *Small Books for the Common Man*.
8 St Clair, *The Reading Nation in the Romantic Period*, 649–51.
9 Stevenson, *The Ordeal of George Meredith*, 37–41, 248.
10 Tremaine, *A Bibliography of Canadian Imprints*, 271–2; Bentley, introduction to *Abram's Plains: A Poem*, xi–xlviii (xxxix–xliii).
11 Tierney, *The Journeys of Charles Sangster*, 3.
12 MacLeod, *American Little Magazines*, 3–4, 310. See also MacLeod, "The Other Magazine Revolution."
13 Macleod, *American Little Magazines*, 4, 130–1.
14 Ibid., 25–6.
15 Ibid., 63.
16 Ibid., 119–20; Schlereth, *The Chap-Book*, 9.
17 Macleod, *American Little Magazines*, 122.
18 Ibid., 119.
19 Macleod, "The Other Magazine Revolution," 160–4, 97.
20 Hodgson, *Eve, & Other Poems*; *The Chapbook (A Yearly Miscellany)*, edited by Harold Munro, nos. 1–40; Millard, *The Printed Work of Claud Lovat Fraser*.
21 Vancouver Poetry Society, *A Book of Days*, 22; see also Campbell, *Both Hands*, 257 and 257n16.
22 Lloyd Roberts to Lorne Pierce, 6 Nov. 1924, box 1.
23 Parker, "Authors and Publishers," 144.
24 Adams, *Sir Charles God Damn*, 106–30.
25 Ibid., 112.
26 Lloyd Roberts to Lorne Pierce, 14 Feb. and 4 June 1924, box 1.
27 L.C. Page to Ryerson Press, 27 June 1925, box 2.
28 V. Quaglia to Lorne Pierce, 2 Sept. 1925, box 2.
29 Adams, *Sir Charles God Damn*, 131.

30 Lorne Pierce to W.A. Deacon, 23 Jan. 1925, box 2; W.A. Deacon to Lorne Pierce, 16 Jan. 1925, box 2.
31 Lorne Pierce to W.A. Deacon, 20 Jan. 1925, box 2.
32 Adams, *Sir Charles God Damn*, 131–2.
33 Ibid., 133, 138.
34 Emily F. Murphy to Lorne Pierce, 4 Mar. [i.e., Apr.] 1925, box 2.
35 Adams, *Sir Charles God Damn*, 133; Isabel Ecclestone MacKay to Lorne Pierce, 20 Apr. 1925, box 2.
36 Davies Woodrow, "Poets at Home," 145.
37 Adams, *Sir Charles God Damn*, 134–6; Murray, *Come, Bright Improvement!*, 80–1.
38 Adams, *Sir Charles God Damn*, 139–40; Davies Woodrow, "Poets on Holiday," 130; W.H.F. Tenny to Lorne Pierce, 26 May 1924, box 1; "Woodrow, Constance Davies"; Boone, *The Collected Letters of Charles G.D. Roberts*, 321.
39 Quoted in Adams, *Sir Charles God Damn*, 139.
40 Quoted in Campbell, *Both Hands*, 260.
41 Roberts, "The Sweet o' the Year," *To-day* (London), May 1920, 94.
42 Campbell, *Both Hands*, 260.
43 Bliss Carman to Lorne Pierce, 7 Oct. 1925, box 2.
44 *Canadian Recital Tour 1925–1926* (Charles G.D. Roberts), 4. I am grateful to Adrian King-Edwards of Montreal for bringing this ephemeron to my attention.
45 Charles G.D. Roberts to Lorne Pierce, 2 Nov. 1925, box 2.
46 In bibliographical notation, the collation of the book would be summarized in this way: [1]^4. Four leaves. Pages 1–8. (The superscript number refers to the number of leaves in the given gathering. It is followed by the total number of leaves in the book [spelled out]). Copies examined: Queen's University, W.D. Jordan Special Collections, call no. Lorne Pierce PS8273 R99 no. 1, c. 2; Carleton University, Archives and Research Collections, call no. PS8279 R8 no. 1 c. 2 (binding reinforced); Library and Archives Canada, call no. PS8485 O24 S8 c. 4 reserve (three staples hold the leaves together, rather than the usual two); McGill University, Rare Books and Special Collections, uncatalogued (in the original slipcase).
47 Thoreau MacDonald renewed his father's design in 1942 for Mary Elizabeth Colman's *For This Freedom Too* (no. 99) and subsequent numbers. The MacDonald woodcut was dropped with Arthur Bourinot's *The Treasures of the Snow* (no. 140, 1950) but reinstated with William Sherwood Fox's *On Friendship* (no. 152, 1953), which was also the first to have a hardcover binding (still paper, not cloth) and a proper title page. Myrtle Reynolds Adams's *Remember Together* (no. 162, 1955), neatly stating title, author, city,

and publisher, defined the look of the Chap-Books through the flurry of activity that characterized their last years. For more on Ryerson book design, see Speller, "Arthur Steven at the Ryerson Press," 7–44.

48 Roberts, "The Unknown City," in *The Sweet o' the Year and Other Poems*, 2–3.
49 Scott, "The Piper of Arll," in *Labour and the Angel*, 29–35 (ll. 89–90), *Early Canadiana Online*, 1 May 2013.
50 Tennyson, "Gareth and Lynette" (book 2 of *Idylls of the King*) in *The Poems of Tennyson*, 281–323 (ll. 186–7, 272–4).
51 W.H.F. Tenny to Lorne Pierce, 16 Oct. 1925, box 2.
52 Charles G.D. Roberts to Lorne Pierce, 10 Dec. 1925, box 2.
53 Bentley, *The Confederation Group of Canadian Poets*, 17, 111–12, 263.
54 Kathryn Munro (Mrs J.F. Tupper) to Lorne Pierce, 23 Nov. 1925, box 2.
55 Kathryn Munro (Mrs J.F. Tupper) to Blanche Hume, 20 Feb. 1926, box 2.
56 Agreement re: *Forfeit and Other Poems* (section 2), between Kathryn Munro Tupper and the Ryerson Press, [1926], Ryerson Press Collection, Ryerson University Library.
57 Kathryn Munro Tupper to Blanche Hume, 5 Mar. and 26 Apr. 1926, box 2.
58 "Geoffrey Riddehough Fonds."
59 Geoffrey B. Riddehough to Lorne Pierce, 6 Apr. 1926, box 2.
60 Geoffrey B. Riddehough to Lorne Pierce, 21 June 1926, box 2.
61 The poems that Riddehough proposed were "The Prophet's Man," "Weavings," "After Noontide," "Conceit," "Silences," "Abiding," "Acknowledgment," and "Duty" – all of which Pierce accepted – and "A Puritan to a Pagan Friend" and "From Thule" – both of which Pierce rejected.
62 Duncan Campbell Scott to Lorne Pierce, 15 Jan. 1926, box 2.
63 Whalley's letter criticized Pierce's "arbitrary restriction upon religious and patriotic verse." Campbell, *Both Hands*, 262 and 262n39.
64 Riddehough, "Peculium," in *The Prophet's Man*, 8. I am thankful to Lee M. Whitehead, husband of the late Pegeen Brennan, Riddehough's executor, for encouraging me to reprint Riddehough's poems.
65 Riddehough, "Conceit," in *The Prophet's Man*, 10.
66 Donne, "Holy Sonnet 14," 335 (ll. 1, 5–6).
67 Compare the series advertisements from Davies Woodrow, *The Captive Gypsy*, through Leveridge, *A Breath of the Woods*.
68 Bentley, *Confederation Group*, 254–5, 259, 262–4, 267–8; Djwa, "Frederick George Scott," 337–9.
69 Frederick George Scott to Lorne Pierce, 10 Dec. 1925 and 11 Jan. 1926, box 2.
70 Lorne Pierce to Frederick George Scott, 13 Jan. 1926, box 2.

71 Frederick George Scott to Lorne Pierce, 18 Jan. 1926, box 2.
72 Copy examined: Bibliothèque et Archives nationales du Québec, Collection nationale (réserve), call no. C811.52 S4259i 1926. Scott inscribed this copy to the Library of Parliament of Quebec, 25 Aug. 1926.
73 Frederick George Scott to Lorne Pierce, 31 May 1926, box 2.
74 Frederick George Scott to Lorne Pierce, 4 June 1926, box 2.
75 Frederick George Scott to Lorne Pierce, 10 Sept. 1926, box 2.
76 Frederick George Scott to Lorne Pierce, 26 Oct. 1926, box 2.
77 Frederick George Scott to Lorne Pierce, 8 Nov. 1926, box 2.
78 Lorne Pierce to Susan Frances Harrison, 9 Nov. 1928; Susan Frances Harrison to Lorne Pierce, 12 Nov. 1928, box 3.
79 Garvin, *Canadian Poems of the Great War*, 99; "Lilian Leveridge," *Special Collections*, University of Calgary Libraries and Cultural Resources.
80 Lilian Leveridge to Lorne Pierce, 26 Jan. 1926, box 2.
81 Lilian Leveridge, "The Loon," in *A Breath of the Woods*, 4 (ll. 1–8).
82 Johnson, *Collected Poems and Selected Prose*, 81 (ll. 1–9). A lateen is a sail, triangular in shape, fastened to a yard at an angle of forty-five degrees to the mast.
83 Lilian Leveridge to Lorne Pierce, 26 Jan. 1926, box 2.
84 Lilian Leveridge to Lorne Pierce, 16 May 1926, box 2.
85 Gillian Dunks picks up the thread of Leveridge's career, describing the publication of her next two Chap-Books, *The Blossom Trail* (no. 57, 1932) and *Lyrics and Sonnets* (no. 82, 1939). In 1938, Leveridge wrote to Pierce, reluctantly admitting that she would not be able to pay for the 150 unsold copies of the former. Dunks, "Reading the Field of Canadian Poetry in the Era of Modernity, 28–30. Nevertheless, Pierce not only proceeded to print *Lyrics and Sonnets*, but did so in a relatively lavish manner, using a design (bigger size, italic type, new ornaments, unadorned cover) otherwise reserved for Bliss Carman's *Music of Earth*. Clearly, Pierce held Leveridge and her poetry in high esteem.
86 Leveridge, "Sunset in the City," in *A Breath of the Woods*, 10–11.

Chapter Three

1 "The Book of Remembrance," Nathaniel A. Benson Papers, in the possession of his son, Julian Benson, Winnipeg, MB (hereafter Benson Papers). I am grateful to Julian for hosting me in Nov. 2017, for drawing up a chronology of his father's life, and for allowing me to examine his papers.

2   Telegram, John P. Robarts to Emma Benson, 22 July 1966; Kenneth R. Thomson to Julian Benson, 21 July 1966; William G. Davis to Emma Benson, 9 Aug. 1966, Benson Papers.
3   Nathaniel A. Benson, "The Community Must Come First! An Interview with Mackenzie King," *Forbes Magazine*, 1 June 1947. In 1952, Benson also apparently took part in an Indigenous poetry festival outside of Kingston, Ontario, which included "a fire council ceremony" and wampum reading led by Akwesasne Mohawk Chief Ray Fadden (Tehanetorens). See W.A. Deacon, "The Fly Leaf," *Globe and Mail*, 14 June 1952.
4   "Thomas Benson Local Baseball Pioneer, Dies," *Toronto Star*, 28 May 1937; note (dedication torn from book), "To Mother from Kate, Xmas 1899," Benson Papers.
5   Agreement re: *Twenty and After*, between Nathaniel A. Benson and the Ryerson Press, [1927], Ryerson Press Fonds, Ryerson University Library, Toronto.
6   Thomas Benson to Lorne Pierce, 13 Apr. 1927, Ryerson Press Fonds, Ryerson University Library, Toronto.
7   Benson, "Twenty and After," in *Twenty and After*, 1–15 (3, ll. 95–101).
8   Nathaniel A. Benson, "'He Was a Man to Remember!' Sir Charles G.D. Roberts (1860–1943)," ca. 1964–65, Benson Papers.
9   Benson, "The Wanderer," in *The Wanderer*, 1–23 (5, ll. 140–1).
10 Nathaniel A. Benson, "A Minstrel Stolen from Arcadie," Feb. 1966, Benson papers.
11 Nathaniel A. Benson, "The Lampman Cairn at Morpeth," *The Wanderer*, 30.
12 Benson, "He Was a Man to Remember," Benson Papers.
13 Hugh S. Eayrs to Nathaniel A. Benson, 23 Mar. 1937; Nathaniel A. Benson, "Sir Charles G.D. Roberts, the Man and His Work," draft manuscript for *Educational Record*, Benson Papers.
14 Photograph of Charles G.D. Roberts, E.J. Pratt, Pelham Edgar, and Nathaniel A. Benson, Mar. 1939, Benson Papers. Anne Marriott won the second-place prize in the contest.
15 Emma studied math and physics at Victoria College: Julian Benson, in discussion with the author, 4 Nov. 2017. "Poet Married at Hart House: Miss E. Wright, Dundalk, Becomes Bride of Nathaniel Benson, Toronto," unidentified clipping, Benson Papers.
16 Julian Benson, "Nathaniel Anketell (Michael) Benson: Chronology," typescript prepared for the author, Nov. 2017.

17 Hall and Benson, *Improve Your Skiing*.
18 J. Markowitz, "The Bookshelf," review of *The Glowing Years* by Nathaniel A. Benson, Feb. 1938, unidentified clipping, Benson Papers.
19 W.A. Deacon, "The Fly Leaf," *Globe and Mail*, 14 Aug. 1937.
20 Murray, "The Canadian Readers Meet," 149–83 (170); Benson, *None of It Came Easy*, dust jacket.
21 W.A. Deacon, "The Fly Leaf," *Globe and Mail*, 22 Apr. 1944; Benson, *None of It Came Easy*, dust jacket; Julian Benson, "Nathaniel Anketell (Michael) Benson: Chronology."
22 Benson, "The Ballad of the 'Rawalpindi'" (1940), in *One Man's Pilgrimage*, 32–3 (ll. 26–32).
23 "Cincinnati Lounge" (June 1940), ibid., 34–5 (ll. 34–6).
24 "Elegy for Icarus" (Mar. 1942), ibid., 40 (ll. 5–8). For a typical example of end-of-stanza rhythmic silence in Confederation poetry, see Lampman, "Morning on the Lièvres," *Among the Millet and Other Poems*, 21–2. Benson also wrote "A Canadian Elegy of Remembrance" (1945) on the death of President Franklin Delano Roosevelt, *One Man's Pilgrimage*, 51–2; it was broadcast on the NBC Radio Network on the day of Roosevelt's funeral, 14 Apr. 1945.
25 "'Marseillaise' for a Penny Flute," in *One Man's Pilgrimage*, 37.
26 Wordsworth, "Ode: Intimations of Immortality from Recollections of Early Childhood," 478–83.
27 Benson, "The Last Parting," in *One Man's Pilgrimage*, 46–8 (l. 3).
28 Roberts, *Selected Poems of Sir Charles G.D. Roberts*, ix, showing pencilled marks by Nathaniel A. Benson (copy examined: author's copy, gift of Julian Benson).
29 "I knew and loved him as a son from 1926 until I left for NY, 6 weeks before his death on Nov 26, 1943 at almost 84." Nathaniel A. Benson, "An Eastern Journey; or, Travelogue for Ten Thousand Picture Post Cards," letter to Florence Anketell Clarke, 28 July to 6 Aug. 1957, Benson Papers.
30 Julian Benson, in discussion with the author, 4 Nov. 2017.
31 Julian Benson, "Nathaniel Anketell (Michael) Benson: Chronology"; W.L. Mackenzie King to Nathaniel A. Benson, 15 Mar. 1947, Benson Papers.
32 Julian Benson, in discussion with the author, 4 Nov. 2017.
33 Nathaniel A. Benson, "The House That Timothy Eaton Built," Benson Papers.
34 Nathaniel A. Benson, "The Community Must Come First! An Interview with Mackenzie King," *Forbes*, 1 June 1947, 14–15, 28–9 (28).

35 Nathaniel A. Benson, "Arthur Stringer: A Literary Enigma," *University of Toronto Alumni Bulletin*, Apr. 1953, 10–13. "Lately he wrote series of articles for *Marketing*, many other for *U. of T. Alumni Bulletin*, and Canadian Broadcaster." Benson, *None of It Came Easy*, dust jacket.
36 Benson, *None of It Came Easy*, dust jacket.
37 Nathaniel A. Benson, "By-Line Bill (A Full-Hour Musical Play for TV)," Benson Papers.
38 Benson, *None of It Came Easy*, dust jacket.
39 Nathaniel A. Benson, "An Eastern Journey; or, Travelogue for Ten Thousand Picture Post Cards," letter to Florence Anketell Clarke, 28 July to 6 Aug. 1957, Benson Papers.
40 See Moodie, "A Visit to Grosse Isle," in *Roughing It in the Bush*, 12–25.
41 Wally Byam (1896–1962) was an early manufacturer of travel trailers and recreational vehicles. In the 1950s, he organized tours to promote automobile travel and a club was founded in his name.
42 Helen Pierrot to Emma Benson, 4 Nov. 1966, Benson Papers.

Chapter Four

1 For example, Candida Rifkind writes that "the images cut one to another, objects are cut into their parts, and the wind cuts time to blur the distinctions between prophecy and reality. From its opening section, then, *The Wind Our Enemy* adopts the forms and feelings of Anglo-American modernism that the Canadian male poets and editors of the period hoped would take root at home." Candida Rifkind, *Comrades and Critics*, 99.
2 Anne Marriott, "Saskatoon Reading and Talk, 1971," A.1.2, Anne Marriott Fonds, Rare Books and Special Collections, University of British Columbia Library. I am grateful to Laura Cameron and to Jeff Weingarten for their assistance in researching this archive.
3 Ibid.
4 Curriculum vitae [1976], enclosed in Anne Marriott to S.W. Jackman, 3 Jan. 1976, A.1.1; Anne Marriott to Heather Spears, 18 Mar. 1983, A.1.2, Marriott Fonds. "I wrote a lot of short nature verse and sent it to places like the Winnipeg Free Press, and the Portland Oregonian, both of which used poetry on the editorial page (I suppose) and paid a dollar or two for it. And the Regina Leader-Post, though they were more conservative. I had one poem in the Saturday Evening Post. And bombarded the New York Times, and actually sold them one poem! And some magazines in England – Chambers's

Journal was a good market (with rather a 'work from the colonies' tone as far as I remember). Floris [Clark McLaren] and Doris [Ferne] tried the same markets, I am sure." Anne Marriott to Geoff Hancock, 22 Nov. 1984, A.1.2, Marriott Fonds.

5 Irvine, *Editing Modernity*, 93.
6 Anne Marriott to Geoff Hancock, 22 Nov. 1984, A.1.2, Marriott Fonds.
7 "Dilworth, Ira," 297.
8 Anne Marriott to Geoff Hancock, 22 Nov. 1984, A.1.2, Marriott Fonds.
9 Rose, "The Literary Archive and the Telling of Modernist Lives," 231–49; Nelson, "Anne Marriott: Treading Water," 34–49; Rose, "Anne Marriott: Modernist on the Periphery," 147–62; Irvine, *Editing Modernity*, 77–126 (esp. 93–7); Cameron, "'A Strange Gestation,'" 84–6, 92–7.
10 Anne Marriott to Geoff Hancock, 22 Nov. 1984, A.1.2, Marriott Fonds.
11 Ibid.
12 Doris Maude Ferne, Registration of Death, 12 Nov. 1986; Ernest George Ferne, Registration of Death, 14 Mar. 1983; Harry Curtis Ferne and Jessie Dolena Talbot, Registration of Marriage, 27 Oct. 1942, Genealogy, BC Archives, Royal BC Museum, https://royalbcmuseum.bc.ca/. The two sons named in these documents are David M. and Harry Curtis Ferne.
13 Doris Ferne, *Ebb Tide*, Ryerson Poetry Chap-Book no. 93 (Toronto: Ryerson, 1941), biographical note inside front cover. For a list of the six poems that Ferne published in *Contemporary Verse*, see Joan McCullagh, *Alan Crawley and Contemporary Verse*, introd. Dorothy Livesay (Vancouver: University of British Columbia Press, 1976), 69.
14 Doris Ferne, "Memory," in *Victoria Poetry Chapbook*, selected by Alan Crawley (Victoria: Poetry Group, Canadian Authors Association, Victoria and Islands Branch, 1936), 25; in *New Harvesting: Contemporary Canadian Poetry*, ed. Ethel Hume Bennett (Toronto: Macmillan Co of Canada, 1938), 39; in *Muse Anthology of Modern Poetry*, Poe Memorial Edition, comp. Devora Lovell, ed. Dorothy Kissling, Arthur H. Nethercot, et al. (New York: Straub, 1938), 658. Ferne also included "Memory" in *Ebb Tide*, 6.
15 Many Ryerson Poetry Chap-Books continue to circulate as unopened collector's items, and in pursuing this research I have frequently been obliged to slice open folded leaves. In the case of a typical four-leaf (eight-page) Chap-Book, there are two joined edges (in addition to the gutter, where the leaves of a book normally remain attached): the top edge between leaves one and two, and the top edge between leaves three and four. In December

2018, seventy-seven years after its publication, I sliced through these folds in my copy of *Ebb Tide*.

16 Ferne, "Ebb Tide," *Ebb Tide*, 1 (ll. 13–26).

17 Anne Marriott, *The Wind Our Enemy*, Ryerson Poetry Chap-Book no. 80 (Toronto: Ryerson Press, 1939), 2 (part 2).

18 Anne Geddes Bailey, "Re-visioning Documentary Readings of Anne Marriott's *The Wind Our Enemy*," 55–67. Bailey argues that the mode of the poem is ultimately more apocalyptic than documentary.

19 Anne Marriott to Penny Petrone, 20 Mar. 1974, A.1.1, Marriott Fonds, quoted in Cameron, "A Strange Gestation," 94–5. Petrone, working on a conference paper, had written to ask about the conditions under which Marriott wrote *The Wind Our Enemy*: "Had you ever visited Saskatchewan during the Depression for instance?" Penny Petrone to Anne Marriott, 18 Mar. 1974, A.1.1., Marriott Fonds.

20 M. Eugenie Perry to Pelham Edgar, 6 Jan. 1939, file 23, box 5, M. Eugenie Perry Papers, MS-0697, BC Archives, cited in Irvine, *Editing Modernity*, 95.

21 J.F.B. Livesay to Anne Marriott, 26 Nov. 1938, file 10, box 7, A.3.1, Marriott Fonds.

22 Dorothy Livesay, "The Poetry of Anne Marriott," *Educational Record of the Province of Quebec* 65, no. 2 (Apr.-June 1949): 87–90 (87), quoted in Rifkind, *Comrades and Critics*, 103–4.

23 J.F.B. Livesay to Anne Marriott, 7 Dec. 1938 and 17 Jan. 1939, file 10, box 7, A.3.1, Marriott Fonds.

24 J.F.B. Livesay to Anne Marriott, 7 Dec. 1938, file 10, box 7, A.3.1, Marriott Fonds.

25 J.F.B. Livesay to Anne Marriott, 12 Dec. 1938, file 10, box 7, A.3.1, Marriott Fonds.

26 Agreement re: *The Wind Our Enemy* (section 2), between Anne Marriott and the Ryerson Press, undated, Ryerson Press Collection, Ryerson University Library. Marriott signed the contract on 24 Feb. 1939. Anne Marriott to Norma MacRostie, 24 Feb. 1939, file 6, box 7, coll. 2001, Lorne and Edith Pierce Collection, Queen's University Archives.

27 Anne Marriott to Lorne Pierce, 20 Dec. 1938, file 2, box 7, Lorne and Edith Pierce Collection.

28 J.F.B. Livesay to Anne Marriott, 23 Dec. 1938, file 10, box 7, A.3.1, Marriott Fonds.

29 Anne Marriott to Norma MacRostie, 2 Feb. 1939, file 6, box 7, Lorne and Edith Pierce Collection.
30 Ibid.
31 Ibid.
32 "Recvd. the proof looks a nice piece of typographical work." J.F.B. Livesay to Anne Marriott, 16 Feb. 1939, file 10, box 7, A.3.1, Marriott Fonds.
33 Anne Marriott to Norma MacRostie, 24 Feb. 1939, file 6, box 7, Lorne and Edith Pierce Collection.
34 Anne Marriott to Norma MacRostie, 2 Feb. 1939, file 6, box 7, Lorne and Edith Pierce Collection.
35 Anne Marriott to Norma MacRostie, 3 Mar. 1939, file 6, box 7, Lorne and Edith Pierce Collection.
36 Anne Marriott to Norma MacRostie, 3 Apr. 1939, file 6, box 7, Lorne and Edith Pierce Collection.
37 Anne Marriott to Norma MacRostie, 19 Oct. 1939, file 6, box 7, Lorne and Edith Pierce Collection.
38 Production card re: *The Wind Our Enemy*, Ryerson Press Collection, Ryerson University Library. Years later Marriott estimated her royalties to have been slightly higher: "I don't think I even have a copy of 'Calling Adventurers!' and certainly not one, that I know of, of the original 'The Wind Our Enemy' (I heard once Bill Hoffer had a copy for sale for $35.00! My total royalties on the edition were $12.50.)" Anne Marriott to Heather Spears, 8 Nov. 1982, A.1.2, Marriott Fonds. Marriott's calculation overlooks the promotional copies, on which no royalties were paid.
39 Mary Nasmyth Matheson and Goodridge MacDonald had four Chap-Books published each; Theresa E. Thomson had one alone and three coauthored with her husband, Don W. Thomson; and Kathryn Munro, Lilian Leveridge, William P. McKenzie, William Thow, Arthur S. Bourinot, R.E. Rashley, and Elizabeth Brewster each had three.
40 Irvine, *Editing Modernity*, 97.
41 Anne Marriott to Geoff Hancock, 22 Nov. 1984, A.1.2, Marriott Fonds. In a draft of this letter, Marriott wrote, "I always felt I was the outsider in the CV group." This confession supports Marilyn J. Rose's argument that marginality was central to Marriott's creativity: "her poems consistently explore borders and edges, margins and shores, and champion their embrace." Rose, "Anne Marriott," 156–7.

42 Anne Marriott, "Salt Marsh," in *Salt Marsh*, Ryerson Poetry Chap-Books no. 100 (Toronto: Ryerson Press, 1942), 1. Reprinted with the permission of the estate of Anne Marriott.
43 Anne Marriott to Heather Spears, 18 Mar. 1983, A.1.2, Marriott Fonds.
44 Anne Marriott to Geoff Hancock, 22 Nov. 1984, A.1.2, Marriott Fonds.
45 Dorothy Livesay, "Recent Ryerson Chapbooks," *Contemporary Verse* 8 (1943): 13–14 (13), quoted in Irvine, *Editing Modernity*, 100.
46 Margaret Kennedy to Anne Marriott, 14 Dec. 1939, file 11, box 7, A.3.2, Marriott Fonds.
47 Ibid.
48 Anne Marriot to Margaret Kennedy, 21 Dec. 1939, file 11, box 7, A.3.2, Marriott Fonds.
49 Margaret Kennedy to Anne Marriott, 1 Jan. 1940, file 11, box 7, A.3.2, Marriott Fonds.
50 Ibid.
51 Anne Marriott and Margaret Kennedy, "Payload," produced by Rupert Lucas (CBC, 1940), microfilm typescript, Centre for Broadcasting and Journalism Studies Archives, Concordia University (CCBJS), 1. I am grateful to Andrea Hunter for providing access to this and other radio typescripts archived at Concordia University.
52 "Bush Flying," *The Canadian Encyclopedia*, 4 Mar. 2015, www.thecanadian encyclopedia.ca.
53 Strikethrough and italics indicate changes to typescript during production.
54 Anne Marriott to Margaret Kennedy, 15 Dec. 1949, file 11, box 7, A.3.2, Marriott Fonds.
55 Irvine, "The Governor General's Literary Awards," 35–161 (45).
56 Anne Marriott to Heather Spears, 8 Nov. 1982, A.1.2, Marriott Fonds.
57 Fink, with Morrison, "CCBS Bibliography," E-818, E-673, CCBJS.
58 Anne Marriott to Margaret Kennedy, 15 Dec. 1949, file 11, box 7, A.3.2, Marriott Fonds.
59 Anne Marriott, curriculum vitae [1976], Marriott Fonds.
60 Anne Marriott to Geoff Hancock, 22 Nov. 1984, A.1.2, Marriott Fonds.
61 Ibid.
62 Anne Marriott, curriculum vitae [1981], A.1.2, Marriott fonds. Marriott lost precise count of her school broadcasts and estimated a higher total in an earlier CV: "I have had some 100 of these on the air, including five

series on creative writing, the subject I enjoyed most. The majority of the other scripts have been on some aspect of Canadian history, e.g. a series on British Columbia and Confederation, broadcast in 1971." Anne Marriott, curriculum vitae [1976], Marriott Fonds.

63 Anne Marriott to Geoff Hancock, 22 Nov. 1984, A.1.2, Marriott Fonds.
64 Anne Marriott to Margaret Kennedy, 15 Dec. 1949, file 11, box 7, A.3.2, Marriott Fonds.
65 Anne Marriott to Margaret Kennedy, 5 Dec. 1949, file 11, box 7, A.3.2, Marriott Fonds.
66 Ibid.
67 Anne Marriott and Margaret Kennedy, "The Wind Our Enemy," produced by J. Frank Willis (CBC, 1950), microfilm typescript, CCBJS, 19. Marriott also changed the lines "The man who makes bad liquor in his barn / Grows fat on groaning emptiness of souls" (19); the original poem read, "The Finn who."
68 Lorne Pierce to Anne Marriott, 19 Jan. 1950, file 10, box 7, A.3.1, Marriott Fonds. CBC Vancouver was called CBR from 1936 to 1952.
69 Cameron, "A Strange Gestation," 85n14.
70 Anne Marriott to Penny Petrone, 20 Mar. 1974, A.1.1, Marriott Fonds.
71 Anne Marriott, curriculum vitae [1976], Marriott Fonds.
72 Jenefer Curtis, "Lives Lived: Joyce Anne Marriott McLellan (Anne Marriott)," *Globe and Mail*, 7 Nov. 1997, ProQuest Historical Newspapers.
73 Anne Marriott, curriculum vitae [1976], Marriott Fonds.
74 Joyce Moller and Anne Marriott, *A Swarming in My Mind: A Poetry Workbook for Elementary Students*, illus. Janet Chidgey (North Vancouver: Curriculum Services Centre, 1977).
75 Anne Marriott, curriculum vitae [1984], Marriott Fonds.
76 Anne Marriott to Penny Petrone, 20 Mar. 1974, A.1.1, Marriott Fonds.
77 Livesay, "The Poetry of Anne Marriott," 90.
78 Anne Marriott, "After a Meeting of Poets," in *Aqua* (Toronto: Wolsak & Wynn, 1991), 80–1. Reprinted with the permission of the estate of Anne Marriott.

Chapter Five

1 Perry, "Song in the Silence," in *Song in the Silence and Other Poems*, 1–10.
2 M. Eugenie Perry to Lorne Pierce, 23 Oct. 1945, file 6, box 12, Lorne and Edith Pierce Collection, coll. 2001, Queen's University Archives, Kingston. Copies of Perry and Pierce's letters are preserved in both this collection and in the M. Eugenie Perry Papers, British Columbia Archives, Victoria.

Subsequent archival citations in this chapter refer to the Pierce collection, unless otherwise indicated.

3   Jack [? or J.A.C.?] to "my dear Eugenie," Easter Sunday [11 April] 1909, file 1, box 1, M. Eugenie Perry Papers.
4   M. Eugenie Perry to Lorne Pierce, 23 Oct. 1945, file 6, box 12.
5   Another detail in this passage is that the "goldfinch linnet" is not any known species of bird. *Goldfinch* and *linnet* are the common names of different species. The combination of them appears to be another suggestion of ideal beauty through a realistic technique. I am grateful to Mark Abley for pointing out this detail.
6   Keats, "Ode on a Grecian Urn," 984–5 (ll. 11–12).
7   "Perry, M. Eugenie."
8   Ibid.
9   Perry, *Hearing a Far Call*, biographical note inside front cover.
10 "Perry, M. Eugenie."
11 M. Eugenie Perry to Lorne Pierce, 17 Nov. 1946, file 2, box 14.
12 "Victoria Writer Publishes Book," *Colonist* (Victoria), 25 Jan. 1946.
13 Harrington, *Syllables of Recorded Time*, 248.
14 M. Eugenie Perry to Lorne Pierce, 1 Dec. 1945, file 6, box 12.
15 M. Eugenie Perry to Lorne Pierce, 1 Apr. 1945, file 6, box 12.
16 M. Eugenie Perry to Lorne Pierce, 2 Feb. 1946, file 2, box 14.
17 Djwa, *Journey with No Maps*, 104.
18 M. Eugenie Perry to Lorne Pierce, 1 Apr. 1945, file 6, box 12. For the comments on Ebbs-Canavan and Brown, see M. Eugenie Perry to Lorne Pierce, 20 Jan. 1946, file 2, box 14.
19 M. Eugenie Perry to Lorne Pierce, 22 Sept. 1946, file 2, box 14.
20 M. Eugenie Perry to Lorne Pierce, 17 Nov. 1946, file 2, box 14; M. Eugenie Perry, "Nettle-Shy," *Canadian Poetry Magazine* 10, no. 2, Dec. 1946: 23–4; Lorne Pierce to M. Eugenie Perry, 29 Nov. 1946, file 2, box 14.
21 Campbell, *Both Hands*, 412. Chapters 19 and 20 describe Pierce's "hitherto largely unacknowledged" (459) role in fostering a generation of modernist poets and critics. Campbell also indicates the limits of Pierce's cooperation. Irving Layton's blasphemous ego, performed or not, was beyond the pale of what he would support (425).
22 Lorne Pierce to M. Eugenie Perry, 19 Dec. 1944, file 2, box 11.
23 Lorne Pierce to M. Eugenie Perry, 4 Oct. 1946, file 2, box 14.
24 M. Eugenie Perry to Lorne Pierce, 1 Apr. 1946, file 6, box 12.
25 Perry, "Thus Love," in *Hero in Ermine and Other Poems*, 12, lines 32–3.

26 M. Eugenie Perry to Lorne Pierce, 16 Aug. 1945, file 6, box 12.
27 M. Eugenie Perry to Lorne Pierce, undated fragment [Dec. 1943], file 2, box 11.
28 M. Eugenie Perry to Lorne Pierce, 28 May 1944, file 2, box 11.
29 Ibid.
30 M. Eugenie Perry to Lorne Pierce, 3 Dec. 1944, file 2, box 11.
31 M. Eugenie Perry to Lorne Pierce, 28 May 1944, file 2, box 11.
32 M. Eugenie Perry to Lorne Pierce, 1 Apr. 1945, file 6, box 12.
33 Ibid.
34 Perry, *Hearing a Far Call*, 1, ll. 1–2.
35 Lecker, "Canadian Authors and Their Literary Agents," 93–120. Chap-Book poet Doris Hedges of Montreal briefly ran her own literary agency in the 1940s.
36 Agreement re: *Hearing a Far Call* (section 2), between M. Eugenie Perry and the Ryerson Press, 29 Dec. 1942, Ryerson Press Collection, Ryerson University Library.
37 Lorne Pierce to M. Eugenie Perry, 20 Mar., 26 Apr., and 20 June 1944, file 2, box 11.
38 M. Eugenie Perry to Lorne Pierce, undated fragment [Dec. 1943], file 2, box 11.
39 Agreement re: *Hearing a Far Call* (section 8).
40 Advertisement, *Ryerson Poetry 1943* (Toronto: Ryerson Press, [1943]), 2, file 2, box 11.
41 Lorne Pierce to M. Eugenie Perry, 26 Apr. 1944; M. Eugenie Perry to Lorne Pierce, undated fragment [Dec. 1943], file 2, box 11.
42 Memo signed E.H., 1 May 1944, file 2, box 11.
43 Lorne Pierce to M. Eugenie Perry, 3 Oct. 1945, file 6, box 12.
44 Friskney, "Beyond the Shadow of William Briggs Part II," 161–207.
45 M. Eugenie Perry to Lorne Pierce, undated fragment [Dec. 1943], file 2, box 11.
46 M. Eugenie Perry to Lorne Pierce, 2 May 1946, file 2, box 14. Spencer's was one of the stores that agreed to sell copies of Marriott's *The Wind Our Enemy* (see chapter 4).
47 M. Eugenie Perry to Lorne Pierce, 26 Sept. 1945, file 6, box 12.
48 Lorne Pierce to M. Eugenie Perry, 10 Dec. 1945, file 6, box 12.
49 Quoted in advertisement, *Ryerson Poetry 1943* (Toronto: Ryerson Press, [1943]), 3, file 2, box 11.
50 Brown, "Letters in Canada," 305–12 (309, 310).
51 M. Eugenie Perry to Lorne Pierce, 11 Mar. 1944, file 2, box 11.

52 M. Eugenie Perry to Lorne Pierce, 22 Sept. 1946, file 2, box 14.
53 M. Eugenie Perry to Lorne Pierce, undated fragment [Dec. 1943], file 2, box 11.
54 M. Eugenie Perry to Lorne Pierce, 28 May 1944, file 2, box 11.
55 Lorne Pierce to M. Eugenie Perry, 20 June 1944, file 2, box 11.
56 Campbell, *Both Hands*, 388, 389.
57 M. Eugenie Perry to Lorne Pierce, 30 July and 3 Dec. 1944, file 2, box 11.
58 M. Eugenie Perry to Lorne Pierce, 2 May 1946, file 2, box 14.
59 Campbell, *Both Hands*, 306.
60 Ontario, Minister of Education, "Report ... for the Year 1940," Appendix I, "Report of the Superintendent of the Ontario School for the Deaf," 73, *Sessional Papers*, 1941.
61 M. Eugenie Perry to Lorne Pierce, 23 Oct. 1945, file 6, box 12.
62 M. Eugenie Perry to Lorne Pierce, 3 Dec. 1944, file 2, box 11.
63 Lorne Pierce to M. Eugenie Perry, 25 June 1945, file 6, box 12.
64 Lorne Pierce to M. Eugenie Perry, 4 Dec. 1945, file 6, box 12; Lorne Pierce to M. Eugenie Perry, 8 Jan. 1946.
65 M. Eugenie Perry to Lorne Pierce, 28 May 1944, file 2, box 11.
66 M. Eugenie Perry to Lorne Pierce, 3 Dec. 1944, file 2, box 11.
67 M. Eugenie Perry to Lorne Pierce, 30 July 1944, file 2, box 11.
68 M. Eugenie Perry to Lorne Pierce, 1 Apr. 1945, file 6, box 12.
69 M. Eugenie Perry to Lorne Pierce, 11 July 1945, file 6, box 12.
70 M. Eugenie Perry to Lorne Pierce, 29 Mar. 1946, file 2, box 14.
71 M. Eugenie Perry to Lorne Pierce, 23 Oct. 1945, file 6, box 12.
72 Ibid.
73 Ibid.
74 Lorne Pierce to M. Eugenie Perry, 10 Nov. 1945, file 6, box 12.
75 M. Eugenie Perry to Lorne Pierce, 22 Nov. 1945, file 6, box 12.
76 M. Eugenie Perry to Lorne Pierce, 2 May 1946, file 2, box 14.
77 M. Eugenie Perry, "Hummingbird," in *Song in the Silence*, 11.
78 M. Eugenie Perry to Lorne Pierce, 12 Dec. 1945, file 6, box 12.
79 M. Eugenie Perry to Lorne Pierce, 2 Feb. 1946, file 2, box 14.
80 M. Eugenie Perry to Lorne Pierce, 22 Sept. 1946, file 2, box 14.
81 Agreement re: *Song in the Silence* (section 2), between M. Eugenie Perry and the Ryerson Press, 17 Jan. 1947, Ryerson Press Collection, Ryerson University Library.

Chapter Six

1 Adachi, *The Enemy That Never Was*; Nakano, with Nakano, *Within the Barbed Wire Fence*; Kogawa, *Obasan*; Nakayama, *Issei*; Kitagawa, *This Is My Own*; Kogawa, *Itsuka*; Omatsu, *Bittersweet Passage*; Shimizu, *The Exiles*; Miki, *Redress*.
2 Livesay, *Right Hand Left Hand*, 45–6.
3 Lorne Pierce to Dorothy Livesay, 14 Sept. 1928, Dorothy Livesay Fonds, Queen's University Archives, quoted in Thompson, *Dorothy Livesay*, 17. "Explanation" is not the title of a poem in *Green Pitcher*; perhaps Pierce intended "Emergence."
4 Such praise troubles the distinction that might be assumed to have divided his romanticism from her modernism. For a stark classification of Livesay's *Green Pitcher* under the rubric of modernism, see Arnason, "Dorothy Livesay and the Rise of Modernism in Canada," 5–18 (13–15).
5 Benson and Livesay's friendship is attested in Livesay's letter of 5 Nov. 1931 to Jean Morton: "Jinnie, hello, you didn't even tell me ... why the deuce Nat is at O[ntario] C[ollege of] E[ducation]," Livesay, *Right Hand Left Hand*, 40.
6 Macmillan Co of Canada to Dorothy Livesay, 16 Mar. 1928, box 114, Macmillan Company of Canada Fonds, McMaster University Library, scanned copy available online in Cundell, "Dorothy Livesay and 'Call My People Home.'"
7 Publishing agreement for Leo Cox, *Sheep-Fold* (1926), Ryerson Press Archives, Ryerson University Library, Toronto. See also table 4.1.
8 Livesay, *Right Hand Left Hand*, 31.
9 Thompson, *Dorothy Livesay*, 2.
10 For accounts of Livesay's involvement with leftist periodicals in the 1930s, see Mason, *Writing Unemployment*, 69–87; Irvine, *Editing Modernity*, 29–76; Rifkind, *Comrades and Critics*, 35–75.
11 Livesay, *Right Hand Left Hand*, 45.
12 Ibid., 153.
13 Thompson, *Dorothy Livesay*, 3.
14 Aguila-Way, "Griersonian 'Actuality,'" 39–58 (40, 40n5).
15 Quoted in Aguila-Way, "Griersonian 'Actuality,'" 42, 44n6. Aguila-Way offers a comparative analysis of Grierson's propagandistic film about the Japanese Canadian internment, *Of Japanese Descent* (1945), and Livesay's "Call My People Home."
16 Livesay, "The Documentary Poem," 267–81 (267, 269). Livesay regarded Marriott's *The Wind Our Enemy* as a ground-breaking documentary poem.
17 Campbell, *Both Hands*, 22.

18 Ibid., 49.
19 Ibid., 66.
20 Ibid., 68–9.
21 Ibid., 75.
22 Livesay, *Right Hand Left Hand*, 48.
23 Campbell, *Both Hands*, 422–3.
24 Irvine, "The Governor General's Literary Awards," 35–161 (48, 51).
25 Campbell, *Both Hands*, 245.
26 Livesay, introduction to "Call My People Home," *The Documentaries*, 32–3 (32).
27 Ibid., 32.
28 The federal act took effect in 1949. Adachi, *The Enemy That Never Was*, 345; "Case Study 1: Japanese Canadians," Elections Canada, https://electionsanddemocracy.ca/voting-rights-through-time-0/case-study-1-japanese-canadians.
29 Livesay, *Journey with My Selves*, 168.
30 Livesay, introduction to "Call My People Home," *The Documentaries*, 33.
31 Ibid.
32 Dorothy Livesay to Lorne Pierce, 24 Jan. 1949, file 3, box 18, Lorne and Edith Pierce Collection, Queen's University Archives, available online in Cundell, "Dorothy Livesay."
33 Livesay, introduction to "Call My People Home," *The Documentaries*, 33.
34 Earle Birney to Dorothy Livesay, [Mar. 1949], file 4, box 4A, Dorothy Livesay Fonds, Queen's University Archives, available online in Cundell, "Dorothy Livesay."
35 Adachi, *The Enemy That Never Was*, 345.
36 Tiessen and Tiessen, "Dorothy Livesay and the Politics of Radio," 71–86 (77).
37 Fink, with Morrison, "CCBS Bibliography," E-755 (Dorothy Livesay).
38 Raymond Whitehouse to Dorothy Macnair, 19 July 1949, file 4, box 1, Dorothy Livesay Fonds, Queen's University Archives, available online in Cundell, "Dorothy Livesay."
39 Fink, "CCBS Bibliography," E-755.
40 Irvine, *Editing Modernity*, 119–20. Irvine reads the rejection of "Call My People Home" by *Saturday Night* and its publication in *Contemporary Verse* as evidence that Livesay was caught in the "crisis" of trying to write for two different audiences at once – the mass audience of society at large, and the elite audience of modernist poets and critics.
41 Alan Crawley, "About 'Call My People Home,'" *Contemporary Verse* 28 (1949): 23–4.
42 Thompson, *Dorothy Livesay*, 57.

43 Lorne Pierce to Mrs Duncan Macnair, 7 June 1950, file 20, box 2, Dorothy Livesay Fonds, Queen's University Archives, available online in Cundell, "Dorothy Livesay."

44 Agreement re: *Call My People Home*, between Dorothy Livesay Macnair and the Ryerson Press, 25 Oct. 1950, Ryerson Press Collection, Ryerson University Library.

45 Quoted in Thompson, *Dorothy Livesay*, 57.

46 Anne Marriott, "The New Crop of Chapbooks," *Contemporary Verse* 34 (1951): 18–20, quoted in Irvine, *Editing Modernity*, 119–20.

47 Thompson, *Dorothy Livesay*, 57.

48 Mickey Nakashima (Japanese Canadian Citizens Association) to Dorothy Macnair, 5 Mar. 1953, file 1, box 1, Dorothy Livesay Fonds, Queen's University Archives, available online in Cundell, "Dorothy Livesay."

49 Frye, "Poetry," 257–62 (259). This review and several others are discussed in Morrissey, "Portraits of 'Past Actuality,'" 90.

50 Morrissey, "Portraits of 'Past Actuality,'" 108.

51 Livesay, "Call My People Home," in *Call My People Home*, 1–17 (17, ll. 487–8). Subsequent citations are given parenthetically.

52 Thompson, *Dorothy Livesay*, 58.

53 Duberman, *Paul Robeson*, 79–80, 235–6, 280. The title of the poem is "an echo of the Negro spiritual often sung by Robeson, 'Let My People Go'" (Livesay, introduction to "Call My People Home," *The Documentaries*, 33). For other examples of Livesay alluding to African American spirituals, see Rifkind, *Comrades & Critics*, 173–4; Denham, "Lyric and Documentary in the Poetry of Dorothy Livesay," 87–106 (93).

54 Denham, "Lyric and Documentary in the Poetry of Dorothy Livesay," 88.

55 Livesay, "Broadcast from Berlin," in *Archive for Our Times*, 10.

56 Livesay, "Seven Poems: 1," *Day and Night*, 1 (ll. 1–2, 10–11).

57 Livesay, "West Coast," *Day and Night*, 40–8 (40, ll. 4–8).

58 Livesay, "Variations on a Tree," in *Call My People Home*, 18–19 (ll. 16, 18).

59 Birney, "David," *David and Other Poems*, 11.

60 Crawford, *Malcolm's Katie*, 18, part 3, ll. 213–14; Livesay, foreword, *The Documentaries*, v; Livesay, "The Documentary Poem," 269–75.

61 MacLennan, *Two Solitudes*, 143 (ch. 19).

62 Livesay, "Call My People Home," in *The Collected Poems*, 180–94 (181).

63 Aguila-Way, in "Griersonian 'Actuality,'" 51–2, criticizes this section of the poem on the grounds that it misrepresents the couple as establishing a family farm for themselves, like pioneers, when in fact internees were forced to

work for less than minimum wage on land owned by large companies. Does the poem state that the wife and husband own the land that they till? "We lived in a hen coop perched on a farmer's field" (13, l. 385).

64 Livesay, *Journey with My Selves*, 173, quoted in Aguila-Way, "Griersonian 'Actuality,'" 53.

Chapter Seven

1 Harris, *Romantic Moderns*.
2 Djwa, "Al Purdy: Ivory Thots and the Last Romantic," in *The Ivory Thought*, 51–62 (59, 60).
3 Purdy, *Reaching for the Beaufort Sea*, 38.
4 Bentley, "Unremembered and Learning Much," 31–50 (39).
5 Ibid., 38.
6 Bourdieu, "The Field of Cultural Production," 99–120 (109).
7 I.S. MacLaren, "Arctic Al," 119–36 (121).
8 Ibid., 129.
9 Solecki, *Last Canadian Poet*, 53. Further on, Solecki states that "Purdy, in a Nietzschean heave, had to remake himself" (75). In a filmed interview, he elaborates this portrait: "Now, imagine the will here, the will to creative power – that you just keep failing, failing, failing, and then, bang!, a book of poems comes out [*The Cariboo Horses*] ... and you're a somebody." Johnson, *Al Purdy Was Here*, 43:25. Granted, allowances may be made for dramatizing literary biography for the audience of a film.
10 Solecki, *Last Canadian Poet*, 61–2.
11 Ibid., 59.
12 Ibid., 72.
13 Ibid., 56, 58, 68.
14 Ware, "Al Purdy, Sam Solecki, and Canadian Tradition," 227–38 (232).
15 Heath, "'Buried Bones and Ornaments and Stuff,'" 191–211 (193).
16 Davey, "Al Purdy, Sam Solecki, and the Poetics of the 1960s," 39–57 (46, 49).
17 Brewster, "Paper Flowers," in *East Coast*, 2.
18 Brewster, "East Coast – Canada," in *East Coast*, 1.
19 Brewster, *Lillooet*, 3.
20 Brewster, "Poem for Good Friday," in *Roads and Other Poems*, 12.
21 Trehearne, *The Montreal Forties*, 236–307.
22 Ibid., 300–4.
23 Dudek, "The Bee of Words," in *The Searching Image*, 1, ll. 5–12.

24 Dudek, "The Pomegranate," in *The Searching Image*, 5, l. 1.
25 Dudek, "Line and Form," in *The Searching Image*, 11–12, ll. 1–15.
26 Hazelton, biographical note in *Mint and Willow*, inside cover. There is a brief entry on Hazelton in the Database of Canada's Early Women Writers, Simon Fraser University Library, https://dhil.lib.sfu.ca/doceww.
27 Hazelton, "The Night," in *Mint and Willow*, 6–7, ll. 6–8.
28 Hazelton, "To You," in *Mint and Willow*, 11–12, ll. 19–25.
29 Hazelton, "Mint and Willow," in *Mint and Willow*, 1. The metre, trochaic tetrametre, is that of Longfellow's *Song of Haiwatha* (1855).
30 Campbell, *Both Hands*, 409.
31 Ibid., 482.
32 Al Purdy to Lorne Pierce, 5 July 1954, file 10, box 23, Lorne and Edith Pierce Collection, coll. 2001, Queen's University Archives, Kingston. Subsequent archival citations refer to this collection, unless otherwise indicated.
33 Lorne Pierce to Al Purdy, 7 July 1954, file 10, box 23.
34 Al Purdy to Lorne Pierce, 16 July 1954, file 10, box 23.
35 Lorne Pierce to Al Purdy, 20 July 1954, file 10, box 23.
36 Al Purdy to Lorne Pierce, 3–5 Aug. 1954, file 10, box 23.
37 Agreement re: *Running Colours* [*Pressed on Sand*], between Alfred W. Purdy and the Ryerson Press, 25 Aug. 1954, Ryerson Press Collection, Ryerson University Library.
38 Al Purdy to Lorne Pierce, 21 Dec. 1954, file 10, box 23.
39 Purdy, *Reaching for the Beaufort Sea*, 156.
40 "The A-Frame," The Al-Purdy A-Frame Association, www.alpurdy.ca.
41 Purdy, *Yours, Al*, 157.
42 Doyle, "Proteus at Roblin Lake," 7–23 (12).
43 Purdy, "House Guest," in *Poems for All the Annettes*, 27–9, ll. 1–19.
44 Lampman, "The Frogs," (1888) in *The Poems of Archibald Lampman*, 7–10 (ll. 1–2).
45 Purdy, "Bullfrogs," in *The Blur in Between*, 16, ll. 9–13.
46 The original text reads "saves," which appears to be a solecism.
47 Purdy, "House Guest," in *Pressed on Sand*, Ryerson Poetry Chap-Books no. 157 (Toronto: Ryerson Press, 1955), 5. Used with permission of Eurithe Purdy.
48 Yeats, "Sailing to Byzantium" (1927), 1254–5 (ll. 15–16).
49 Roberts, "The Tantramar Revisited" (1886), in *Selected Poetry and Critical Prose*, 51–3 (ll. 47–50).
50 Purdy, "Short History of X County," in *The Crafte So Longe to Lerne*, 3–4, ll. 7–12.

51 Purdy, "The Country North of Belleville," in *The Cariboo Horses*, 74–6, ll. 33–4, 37, 56–7, 65–6, 71–3.
52 Bentley, *The Gay] Grey Moose*, 210, 211.
53 Purdy, *Reaching for the Beaufort Sea*, 31.
54 Thanks to G.D. Currie for bringing to light this correspondence.
55 Alfred M. Purdy [*sic*], "At Roblin Lake," in Milton Wilson, "Recent Canadian Verse: Selected and Edited with General Introduction," *Queen's Quarterly* 66 (1959): 268–311 (292–3).
56 Purdy, "At Roblin Lake," in *The Crafte So Longe to Lerne*, 17–18, ll. 1–10.
57 A further layer of Jewishness might be found in Solecki's argument that Purdy's "At Roblin Lake" responds to (the Jewish Canadian poet) Irving Layton. In Layton's "Cain," the speaker takes an "air rifle" from his son's hand and shoots a frog. If so, it is a layer that Purdy removed when he revised the poem. Solecki, *Last Canadian Poet*, 80–1.
58 Purdy, *Poems for All the Annettes*, 24–5, ll. 29–32.
59 Purdy, "Villanelle [*Plus 1*]," in *The Crafte So Longe to Lerne*, Ryerson Chap-Book no. 186 (Toronto: Ryerson Press, 1959), 4–5. Used with permission of Eurithe Purdy. The square brackets in the title are the poet's.
60 Perkins, *A History of Modern Poetry*, 201.
61 Heath-Stubbs, "The Language of the Age," in *The Triumph of the Muse and Other Poems*, 1 (ll. 1–6).
62 The Space Race began with the Soviet launch of Sputnik 1, the first artificial satellite, in 1957.
63 Solecki, *Last Canadian Poet*, 61–3, 75–6, 251.
64 Kane and French, "Villanelle."
65 McKnight, "Small Press Publishing," 308–18 (311).

Conclusion

1 The two countries did take steps to eliminate piracy before 1962, such as the reciprocal agreement arranged by Thomas Low, Canadian minister of trade and commerce, and President Calvin Coolidge in December 1923. Parker, "Authors and Publishers on the Offensive," 131–85 (155). Aspects of protectionism persisted in US publishing, however, until the United States implemented the Berne Convention in 1989.
2 Purdy, "Trees at the Arctic Circle," in *Rooms for Rent in the Outer Planets*, 38–40.
3 Pierce, *An Editor's Creed*, 3–4.
4 MacSkimming, *The Perilous Trade*, 29–30.

BIBLIOGRAPHY

Archives

Anne Marriott Fonds. University of British Columbia, Vancouver.
Dorothy Livesay Fonds. Queen's University Archives, Kingston, Ontario.
Lorne and Edith Pierce Collection. Queen's University Archives, Kingston, Ontario.
Macmillan Company of Canada Fonds. McMaster University Library, Hamilton.
M. Eugenie Perry Papers. British Columbia Archives, Victoria.
Nathaniel A. Benson Papers. Private collection, Julian Benson, Winnipeg.
Ryerson Press Collection. Ryerson University Library, Toronto.

Books, Articles, and Other Sources

Adachi, Ken. *The Enemy That Never Was*. Toronto: McClelland & Stewart, 1976.
Adams, John Coldwell. *Sir Charles God Damn: The Life of Sir Charles G.D. Roberts*. Toronto: University of Toronto Press, 1986.
"The A-Frame." The Al-Purdy A-Frame Association. www.alpurdy.ca.
Aguila-Way, Tania. "Griersonian 'Actuality' and Social Protest in Dorothy Livesay's Documentary Poems." In *Double-Takes: Intersections between Canadian Literature and Film*, edited by David R. Jarraway, 39–58. Ottawa: University of Ottawa Press, 2013.
Armstrong, Thomas. "Lifting the Lid on Geoffrey Drayton and His Outsider Role in Barbadian Literature." *Arts Etc.* 2013. www.artsetcbarbados.com.
Arnason, David. "Dorothy Livesay and the Rise of Modernism in Canada." In Dorney, Noonan, and Tiessen, eds, *A Public and Private Voice*, 5–18.
Bailey, Anne Geddes. "Re-visiting Documentary Readings of Anne Marriott's *The Wind Our Enemy*." *Canadian Poetry: Studies, Documents, Reviews* 31 (1992): 55–67.

Beattie, Munro. "Poetry: 1920–1935." In *Literary History of Canada*, 2nd ed., vol. 2, edited by Carl F. Klinck et al., 234–53. Toronto: University of Toronto Press, 1976.

"Behind the Diary: A King's Who's Who Biographies: Andrew Haydon (1867–1932)." Library and Archives Canada. http://www.collectionscanada.gc.ca/king/023011-1050.19-e.html.

Benson, Nathaniel A. *The Glowing Years*. Toronto: T. Nelson & Sons, 1937.

– *None of It Came Easy: The Story of James Garfield Gardiner*. Toronto: Burns and MacEachern, 1955.

– *One Man's Pilgrimage*. Toronto: Thomas Nelson and Sons, 1962.

– *Twenty and After*. Ryerson Poetry Chap-Book no. [17]. Toronto: Ryerson Press, 1927.

– *The Wanderer: A Narrative Poem (Sequel to "Twenty and After") and Other Poems*. Ryerson Poetry Chap-Book no. [48]. Toronto: Ryerson Press, 1930.

Bentley, D.M.R. *The Confederation Group of Canadian Poets, 1880–1897*. Toronto: University of Toronto Press, 2004.

– *The Gay] Grey Moose: Essays on the Ecologies and Mythologies of Canadian Poetry, 1690–1990*. Ottawa: University of Ottawa Press, 1992.

– Introduction to *Abram's Plains: A Poem*, by Thomas Cary. London, ON: Canadian Poetry Press, 1986.

– "Unremembered and Learning Much: LAC Alfred W. Purdy." In Lynch, Ganz, and Kealey, *The Ivory Thought*, 31–50.

Birney, Earle. *David and Other Poems*. Toronto: Ryerson, 1942.

Boone, Laurel. *The Collected Letters of Charles G.D. Roberts*. Fredericton: Goose Lane, 1989.

Bourdieu, Pierre. "The Field of Cultural Production." In Finkelstein and McCleery, *Book History Reader*, 99–120.

Bowman, Louise Morey. *Dream Tapestries*. Toronto: Macmillan Company of Canada, 1924.

Brewster, Elizabeth. *East Coast*. Ryerson Poetry Chap-Book no. 145. Toronto: Ryerson Press, 1951.

– *Lillooet*. Ryerson Poetry Chap-Book no. 153. Toronto: Ryerson Press, 1954.

– *Roads and Other Poems*. Ryerson Poetry Chap-Book no. 174. Toronto: Ryerson Press, 1957.

Broadus, Edmund Kemper, and Eleanor Hammond Broadus, eds. *A Book of Canadian Prose and Verse*. Toronto: Macmillan Company of Canada, 1923.

Brown, E.K. "Letters in Canada: 1942. I. Poetry." *University of Toronto Quarterly* 12, no. 3 (1943): 305–12.

Browne, Thaddeus A. *The Belgian Mother, and Ballads of Battle Time*. Toronto: Macmillan Co of Canada, 1917.

Call, Frank Oliver. *Acanthus and Wild Grape*. Toronto: McClelland & Stewart, 1920.
Cameron, Laura, ed. "'So Often I Look up at You and Tell You Things, and You Listen!': The Correspondence of Louise Morey Bowman and Amy Lowell." *Canadian Poetry: Studies, Documents, Reviews* 83 (2018): 56–109.
– "'A Strange Gestation': Periods of Poetic Silence in Modern Canadian Creative Careers." PhD diss., McGill University, 2016.
Campbell, Sandra. *Both Hands: A Life of Lorne Pierce of Ryerson Press*. Montreal: McGill-Queen's University Press, 2013.
– "From Romantic History to Communications Theory: Lorne Pierce as Publisher of C.W. Jefferys and Harold Innis." *Journal of Canadian Studies* 30, no. 3 (1995): 91–116.
Canadian Recital Tour 1925–1926 (Charles G.D. Roberts). Toronto: Ryerson Press, 1925.
Carman, Bliss. *Ballads and Lyrics*. Toronto: McClelland & Stewart, 1923.
– *Far Horizons*. Toronto: McClelland & Stewart, 1925.
– *Later Poems*. Toronto: McClelland & Stewart, 1921.
The Chapbook (A Yearly Miscellany). Edited by Harold Munro. Nos. 1–40. London: Poetry Bookshop, 1919–1925.
Crawford, Isabella Valancy. *Malcolm's Katie: A Love Story*. 1884. Edited by D.M.R. Bentley. London, ON: Canadian Poetry Press, 1987.
Cundell, Cheryl. "Dorothy Livesay and 'Call My People Home' (with Audio Recording)." Historical Perspectives on Canadian Publishing. McMaster University Library. http://hpcanpub.mcmaster.ca/hpcanpub/case-study/dorothy-livesay-and-call-my-people-home-audio-recording.
Dalton, Annie Charlotte. *Flame and Adventure*. Toronto: Macmillan Company of Canada, 1924.
Darnton, Robert. *The Business of Enlightenment: A Publishing History of the Encyclopédie, 1775–1800*. Cambridge, MA: Belknap Press / Harvard University Press, 1979.
Davey, Frank. "Al Purdy, Sam Solecki, and the Poetics of the 1960s." *Canadian Poetry: Studies, Documents, Reviews* 51 (2002): 39–57.
Davies Woodrow, Constance. "Poets at Home." *Canadian Bookman*, Sept. 1925, 145.
– "Poets on Holiday." *Canadian Bookman*, Aug. 1925, 130.
Denham, Paul. "Lyric and Documentary in the Poetry of Dorothy Livesay." In Dorney, Noonan, and Tiessen, *A Public and Private Voice*, 87–106.
"Dilworth, Ira." In *Encyclopedia of Literature in Canada*, edited by William H. New, 297. Toronto: University of Toronto Press, 2002.
Distad, Merrill. "Newspapers and Magazines." In Fleming and Lamonde, *History of the Book in Canada*, 2:294–303.
Djwa, Sandra. "Al Purdy: Ivory Thots and the Last Romantic." In Lynch, Ganz, and Kealey, *The Ivory Thought*, 51–62.

– "Frederick George Scott." In *Dictionary of Literary Biography*. Vol. 92, *Canadian Writers 1890–1920*, edited by W.H. New, 337–9. Detroit: Gale Research, 1990.
– *Journey with No Maps: A Life of P.K. Page*. Montreal: McGill-Queen's University Press, 2012.
Donne, John. "Holy Sonnet 14." In Ferguson, Kendall, and Salter, *The Norton Anthology of Poetry*, 6th ed., 335.
Dorney, Lindsay, Gerald Noonan, and Paul Tiessen, eds. *A Public and Private Voice: Essays on the Life and Work of Dorothy Livesay*. Waterloo: University of Waterloo Press, 1986.
Doyle, Mike. "Proteus at Roblin Lake." *Canadian Literature* 61 (1974): 7–23.
Duberman, Martin. *Paul Robeson*. 1988. New York: New Press, 2005.
Dudek, Louis. "The Role of Little Magazines in Canada." 1958. Reprinted in Dudek and Gnarowski, *The Making of Modern Poetry in Canada*, 205–12.
– *The Searching Image*. Ryerson Poetry Chap-Book no. 147. Toronto: Ryerson Press, 1952.
Dudek, Louis, and Michael Gnarowski, eds. *The Making of Modern Poetry in Canada: Essential Articles on Contemporary Canadian Poetry in English*. Toronto: Ryerson Press, 1967.
Dunks, Gillian. "Reading the Field of Canadian Poetry in the Era of Modernity: The Ryerson Poetry Chap-Book Series, 1925–1962." MA thesis, University of British Columbia, 2013.
Fee, Margery. "Lorne Pierce, Ryerson Press, and the Makers of Canadian Literature Series." *Papers of the Bibliographical Society of Canada / Cahiers de la Société bibliographique du Canada* 24 (1985): 51–71.
Ferguson, Margaret, Mary Jo Salter, and Jon Stallworthy, eds. *The Norton Anthology of Poetry*. Shorter 5th ed. New York: W.W. Norton, 2005.
Ferguson, Margaret, Tim Kendall, and Mary Jo Salter, eds. *The Norton Anthology of Poetry*. 6th ed. New York: W.W. Norton, 2018.
Fink, Howard, with Brian Morrison. "CCBS Bibliography, Volume One: Canadian National Theatre on the Air, 1925–1961." "CBC Radio Dramas." Centre for Broadcasting and Journalism Studies Archives. Concordia University. https://www.concordia.ca/research/broadcasting-journalism/archives/cbc-radio-dramas.html.
Finkelstein, David, and Alistair McCleery, eds. *The Book History Reader*. 2nd ed. London and New York: Routledge, 2006.
Fleming, Patricia Lockhart, and Yvan Lamonde, eds. *History of the Book in Canada*. 3 vols. Toronto: University of Toronto Press, 2004–07.
Foucault, Michel. "What Is an Author?" In Finkelstein and McCleery, *Book History Reader*, 281–91.
French, Donald G. *The Appeal of Poetry*. Toronto: McClelland & Stewart, 1923.

Friskney, Janet B. "Beyond the Shadow of William Briggs, Part I: Setting the Stage and Introducing the Players." *Papers of the Bibliographical Society of Canada / Cahiers de la Société bibliographique du Canada* 33, no. 2 (1995): 121–63.

– "Beyond the Shadow of William Briggs Part II: Canadian-Authored Titles and the Commitment to Canadian Writing," *Papers of the Bibliographical Society of Canada / Cahiers de la Société bibliographique du Canada* 35, no. 2 (1997): 161–207.

– *New Canadian Library: The Ross-McClelland Years 1952–78.* Toronto: University of Toronto Press, 2007.

– "Towards a Canadian 'Cultural Mecca': The Methodist Book and Publishing House's Pursuit of Book Publishing and Commitment to Canadian Writing, 1829–1926." MA thesis, Trent University, 1994.

Frye, Northrop. "Poetry." "Letters in Canada: 1950." *University of Toronto Quarterly* 20, no. 3 (1951): 257–62.

Garvin, John W., ed. *Canadian Poems of the Great War.* Toronto: McClelland & Stewart, 1918.

Gaskell, Philip. *A New Introduction to Bibliography.* Oxford: Clarendon Press, 1972.

"Geoffrey Riddehough Fonds." MemoryBC: The British Columbia Archival Information Network. https://www.memorybc.ca/geoffrey-riddehough-fonds.

Graham, J. Robertson. *Where Canada Begins: A Visitor's Guide to Point Pelee National Park.* Leamington, ON: Friends of Point Pelee, 1991.

Grove, Frederick Philip. *Settlers of the Marsh.* Toronto: Ryerson Press, 1925.

Hall, Frederick Albert, and Nathaniel A. Benson. *Improve Your Skiing: A Comprehensive Handbook on the Day-to-Day Development of Practical Ski Techniques.* New York: Dodge, 1936.

Harrington, Lyn. *Syllables of Recorded Time: The Story of the Canadian Authors Association, 1921–1981.* Toronto: Simon & Pierre, 1981.

Harris, Alexandra. *Romantic Moderns: English Writers, Artists and the Imagination from Virginia Woolf to John Piper.* London: Thams & Hudson, 2010.

Harvey, William. *Scottish Chapbook Literature.* Paisley, Scotland: Alexander Gardner, 1903.

Haydon, Andrew. *Pioneer Sketches in the District of Bathurst.* Toronto: Ryerson Press, 1925.

Hazelton, Ruth Cleaves. *Mint and Willow.* Ryerson Poetry Chap-Book no. 149. Toronto: Ryerson Press, 1952.

"Hazelton, Ruth Cleaves." Database of Canada's Early Women Writers. Simon Fraser University Library. https://dhil.lib.sfu.ca/doceww.

Heath, Tim. "'Buried Bones and Ornaments and Stuff': Purdy's Reliquary Poetics." In Lynch, Ganz, and Kealey, *The Ivory Thought*, 191–211.

Heath-Stubbs, John. *The Triumph of the Muse and Other Poems.* London: Oxford University Press, 1958.

Hodgson, Ralph. *Eve, & Other Poems*. Flying Flame Chapbooks. London: Printed by A.T. Stevens, 1913.
Irvine, Andrew David. "The Governor General's Literary Awards: English-Language Winners, 1936–2013." *Papers of the Bibliographical Society of Canada / Cahiers de la Société bibliographique du Canada* 52, no. 1 (2014): 35–161.
Irvine, Dean. *Editing Modernity: Women and Little-Magazine Cultures in Canada, 1916–1956*. Toronto: University of Toronto Press, 2008.
Judge, May P. *The Way to Fairyland and Other Rhymes*. Ryerson Poetry Chap-Book no. [52]. Toronto: Ryerson Press, 1931.
Johnson, Brian D. *Al Purdy Was Here*. Toronto: Purdy Pictures, Filmswelike, 2016. iTunes.
Johnson, E. Pauline (Tekahionwake). *Collected Poems and Selected Prose*. Edited by Carole Gerson and Veronica Strong-Boag. Toronto: University of Toronto Press, 2002.
Kaestle, Carl F., and Janice A. Radway, eds. *A History of the Book in America*. Vol. 4, *Print in Motion: The Expansion of Publishing and Reading in the United States, 1880–1940*. Chapel Hill: University of North Carolina Press / American Antiquarian Society, 2009.
Kane, J., and A.L. French. "Villanelle." In *The Princeton Encyclopedia of Poetry and Poetics*, 4th ed., edited by Roland Greene. Princeton: Princeton University Press, 2017. Oxford Reference. www.oxfordreference.com.
Keats, John. "Ode on a Grecian Urn." In Ferguson, Kendall, and Salter, *The Norton Anthology of Poetry*, 6th ed., 984–5.
Kitagawa, Muriel. *This Is My Own: Letters to Wes & Other Writings on Japanese Canadians, 1941–1948*. Edited by Roy Miki. Vancouver: Talonbooks, 1985.
Kogawa, Joy. *Itsuka*. Toronto: Viking, 1992.
– *Obasan*. Toronto: Lester & Orpen Dennys, 1981.
Lampman, Archibald. *Among the Millet and Other Poems*. Ottawa: J. Durie, 1888.
– *The Poems of Archibald Lampman*. Introduction by Margaret Coulby Whitridge. Literature of Canada: Poetry and Prose in Reprint. Toronto: University of Toronto Press, 1974.
Laurence, Margaret. *Dance on the Earth: A Memoir*. Toronto: McClelland & Stewart, 1989.
Lecker, Robert. "Canadian Authors and Their Literary Agents, 1890–1977." *Papers of the Bibliographical Society of Canada / Cahiers de la Société bibliographique du Canada* 54, nos. 1–2 (2016): 93–120.
Leveridge, Lilian. *A Breath of the Woods*. Ryerson Poetry Chap-Book no. [13]. Toronto: Ryerson Press, 1926.
Leveridge, Lilian. *Over the Hills of Home and Other Poems*. New York: E.P. Dutton; Toronto: McClelland, Goodchild and Stewart, 1918.

Litster, Thomas Harkness. *Songs in Your Heart and Mine*. Toronto: McClelland, Goodchild and Stewart, 1917.

Livesay, Dorothy. *Archive for Our Times: Previously Uncollected and Unpublished Poems of Dorothy Livesay*. Edited by Dean Irvine. Vancouver: Arsenal Pulp Press, 1998.

– *Call My People Home*. Ryerson Poetry Chap-Book no. 143. Toronto: Ryerson Press, 1950.

– *The Collected Poems: The Two Seasons*. Toronto: McGraw-Hill Ryerson, 1972.

– *Day and Night*. Toronto: Ryerson, 1944.

– *The Documentaries*. Toronto: Ryerson Press, 1968.

– "The Documentary Poem: A Canadian Genre." In *Contexts of Canadian Criticism: A Collection of Critical Essays*, edited by Eli Mandel, 267–81. Chicago: University of Chicago Press, 1971.

– *Green Pitcher*. Toronto: Macmillan Co of Canada, 1928.

– *Journey with My Selves: A Memoir 1909–1963*. Vancouver: Douglas & McIntyre, 1991.

– "The Poetry of Anne Marriott." *Educational Record of the Province of Quebec* 65, no. 2 (1949): 87–90.

– *Right Hand Left Hand*. Erin, ON: Press Porcepic, 1977.

Livesay, Florence Randal. *Shepherd's Purse*. Toronto: Macmillan Company of Canada, 1923.

Lynch, Gerald, Shoshannah Ganz, and Josephine T.M. Kealey, eds. *The Ivory Thought: Essays on Al Purdy*. Ottawa: University of Ottawa Press, 2008.

MacDonald, Wilson. *Miracle Songs of Jesus*. Toronto: Ryerson Press, 1923.

MacInnes Tom. *The Fool of Joy*. Toronto: McClelland, Goodchild and Stewart, 1918.

MacKay, Isabel Ecclestone. *Fires of Driftwood*. Toronto: McClelland & Stewart, 1922.

MacLaren, Eli. *Dominion and Agency: Copyright and the Structuring of the Canadian Book Trade 1867–1918*. Toronto: University of Toronto Press, 2011.

MacLaren, I.S. "Arctic Al: Purdy's Humanist Vision of the North." In Lynch, Ganz, and Kealey, *The Ivory Thought*, 119–36.

MacLennan, Hugh. *Two Solitudes*. Toronto: Collins, 1945.

Macleod, Kirsten. *American Little Magazines of the Fin de Siècle: Art, Protest, and Cultural Transformation*. Toronto: University of Toronto Press, 2018.

– "The Other Magazine Revolution: American Little Magazines and Fin-de-Siècle Print Culture, 1894–1904." MLIS thesis, University of Alberta, 2009.

MacSkimming, Roy. *The Perilous Trade: Book Publishing in Canada 1946–2006*. Toronto: McClelland & Stewart, 2007.

Mason, Jody. *Writing Unemployment: Worklessness, Mobility, and Citizenship in Twentieth-Century Canadian Literatures*. Toronto: University of Toronto Press, 2013.

– *Home Feelings: Liberal Citizenship and the Canadian Reading Camp Movement*. Montreal: McGill-Queen's University Press, 2019.

McIntyre, Tim. "Alan Crawley and *Contemporary Verse*." Historical Perspectives on Canadian Publishing. McMaster University Library. digitalcollections.mcmaster.ca.

McKenzie, D.F. "The Sociology of a Text: Orality, Literacy and Print in Early New Zealand." In Finkelstein and McCleery, *Book History Reader*, 205–31.

McKnight, David. "Small Press Publishing." In Fleming and Lamonde, *History of the Book in Canada*, 3:308–18.

McLaren, Scott. *Pulpit, Press, and Politics: Methodists and the Market for Books in Upper Canada*. Toronto: University of Toronto Press, 2019.

McRaye, Walter. *Town Hall Tonight*. Toronto: Ryerson Press, 1929.

Meriton, John, ed., with Carlo Dumontet. *Small Books for the Common Man*. London: The British Library / New Castle, DE: Oak Knoll, 2010.

Middleton, Jesse Edgar. *Sea Dogs and Men at Arms: A Canadian Book of Songs*. New York: G.P. Putnam's Sons, 1918.

Miki, Roy. *Redress: Inside the Japanese Canadian Call for Justice*. Vancouver: Raincoast Books, 2004.

Milligan, James Lewis. *The Beckoning Skyline and Other Poems*. Toronto: McClelland & Stewart, 1920.

Millard, Christopher. *The Printed Work of Claud Lovat Fraser*. London: Henry Danielson, 1923.

Miner, Jack. *Jack Miner and the Birds and Some Things I Know about Nature*. Toronto: Ryerson Press, 1923.

– *Jack Miner: His Life and Religion* [cover title *Wild Goose Jack: Jack Miner's Autobiography*]. Kingsville, ON: Jack Miner Migratory Bird Foundation, 1969.

Moffat, Gertrude MacGregor. *Book of Verses*. Toronto: Macmillan Company of Canada, 1924.

Montgomery, L.M. *The Watchman and Other Poems*. Toronto: McClelland, Goodchild and Stewart, 1916.

Moodie, Susanna. *Roughing It in the Bush; or, Life in Canada*. 1852. Edited by Carl Ballstadt. Centre for Editing Early Canadian Texts. Ottawa: Carleton University Press, 1988.

Morrissey, Lynda. "Portraits of 'Past Actuality': The Tragedy and Triumph of Japanese Canadians as Portrayed in Historically Based Canadian Literature." PhD diss., University of Ottawa, 2003.

Mount, Nick. *When Canadian Literature Moved to New York*. Toronto: University of Toronto Press, 2005.

Murray, Heather. "The Canadian Readers Meet: The Canadian Literature Club of Toronto, Donald G. French, and the Middlebrow Modernist Reader." *Papers of the Bibliographical Society of Canada / Cahiers de la Société bibliographique du Canada* 46, no. 2 (2008): 149–83.

– *Come, Bright Improvement! The Literary Societies of Nineteenth-Century Ontario.* Toronto: University of Toronto Press, 2002.

Nakano, Takeo Ujo, with Leatrice Nakano. *Within the Barbed Wire Fence: A Japanese Man's Account of His Internment in Canada.* Afterword by W. Peter Ward. Toronto: University of Toronto Press, 1980.

Nakayama, Gordon G. *Issei: Stories of Japanese Canadian Pioneers.* Preface by Joy Kogawa. Toronto: NC Press / Kagami, 1984.

Nelson, Sharon H. "Anne Marriott: Treading Water." In *Re:Generations: Canadian Women Poets in Conversation,* edited by Di Brandt and Barbara Godard, 34–49. Windsor, ON: Black Moss Press, 2005.

Norwood, Robert. *The Piper and the Reed.* New York: George H. Doran / Toronto: McClelland, Goodchild and Stewart, 1917.

Omatsu, Maryka. *Bittersweet Passage: Redress and the Japanese Canadian Experience.* Toronto: Between the Lines, 1992.

Osborne, Marian. *The Song of Israfel and Other Poems.* Toronto: Macmillan Company of Canada, 1923.

Panofsky, Ruth. *The Literary Legacy of the Macmillan Company of Canada: Making Books and Mapping Culture.* Toronto: University of Toronto Press, 2012.

Parker, George L. "Authors and Publishers on the Offensive: The Canadian Copyright Act of 1921 and the Publishing Industry 1920–1930." *Papers of the Bibliographical Society of Canada / Cahiers de la Société bibliographique du Canada* 50, no. 2 (2012): 131–85.

– *The Beginnings of the Book Trade in Canada.* Toronto: University of Toronto Press, 1985.

– "The Evolution of Publishing Canada." In Fleming and Lamonde, *History of the Book in Canada,* 2:17–32.

– "The Sale of the Ryerson Press: The End of the Old Agency System and Conflicts over Domestic and Foreign Ownership in the Canadian Publishing Industry, 1970–1986." *Papers of the Bibliographical Society of Canada / Cahiers de la Société bibliographique du Canada* 40 (2002): 7–56.

Perkins, David. *A History of Modern Poetry.* Vol. 2, *Modernism and After.* Cambridge, MA: Belknap Press of Harvard University Press, 1987.

Perry, M. Eugenie. *Canteen.* Victoria: Clarke Printing Co, 1944.

– *The Girl in the Silk Dress and Other Stories.* Ottawa: Overbrook Press, 1931.

– *Green Timbers and Other Poems.* Toronto: Ryerson Press, 1955.

– *Hearing a Far Call.* Ryerson Poetry Chap-Book no. 102. Toronto: Ryerson Press, 1942.

– *Hero in Ermine and Other Poems.* Victoria: Clarke Printing Co, [1939].

– *Song in the Silence and Other Poems.* Ryerson Chap-Book no. 123. Toronto: Ryerson Press, 1947.

– *Two Hundred and Fifty Thousand Strong: A Survey of the Deaf and Hard of Hearing Organizations in Canada*. [Toronto: Lorne Pierce, 1946].
"Perry, M. Eugenie." Canada's Early Women Writers. SFU Digitized Collections. http://digital.lib.sfu.ca/ceww-767/perry-m-eugenie.
Pickthall, Marjorie. *The Wood Carver's Wife*. Toronto: McClelland & Stewart, 1922.
Pierce, Lorne. *The House of Ryerson 1829–1954*. Foreword by C.H. Dickinson. Toronto: Ryerson Press, 1954.
–, ed. *The Chronicle of a Century 1829–1929: The Record of One Hundred Years of Progress in the Publishing Concerns of the Methodist Presbyterian and Congregational Churches in Canada*. Toronto: United Church Publishing House / Ryerson Press, 1929.
– *An Editor's Creed*. Toronto: Ryerson Press, 1960.
Pratt, E.J. *Newfoundland Verse*. Toronto: Ryerson Press, 1923.
– *The Witches' Brew*. Toronto: Macmillan Company of Canada, 1925.
Purdy, Al. *The Blur in Between*. Toronto: Emblem, 1962.
– *The Cariboo Horses*. Toronto: McClelland & Stewart, 1965.
– *The Crafte So Longe to Lerne*. Ryerson Poetry Chap-Book no. 186. Toronto: Ryerson Press, 1959.
– *Poems for All the Annettes*. 2nd ed. Toronto: House of Anansi Press, 1968.
– *Pressed on Sand*. Ryerson Poetry Chap-Book no. 157. Toronto: Ryerson Press, 1955.
– *Reaching for the Beaufort Sea: An Autobiography*. Edited by Alex Widen. Madeira Park, BC: Harbour Publishing, 1993.
– *Rooms for Rent in the Outer Planets: Selected Poems 1962–1996*. Edited by Sam Solecki. Madeira Park, BC: Harbour Publishing, 1996.
– *Yours, Al: The Collected Letters of Al Purdy*. Edited by Sam Solecki. Madeira Park, BC: Harbour Publishing, 2004.
Radway, Janice A. *A Feeling for Books: The Book-of-the-Month Club, Literary Taste, and Middle-Class Desire*. Chapel Hill: University of North Carolina Press, 1997.
Riddehough, Geoffrey B. *The Prophet's Man*. Ryerson Poetry Chap-Book, no. [11]. Toronto: Ryerson Press, 1926.
Rifkind, Candida. *Comrades and Critics: Women, Literature and the Left in 1930s Canada*. Toronto: University of Toronto Press, 2009.
Roberts, Charles G.D. *Selected Poems of Sir Charles G.D. Roberts*. Toronto: Ryerson, 1936.
– *Selected Poetry and Critical Prose*. Edited by W.J. Keith. Literature of Canada: Poetry and Prose in Reprint. Toronto: University of Toronto Press, 1974.
– *The Sweet o' the Year and Other Poems*. Ryerson Poetry Chap-Book no. [1]. Toronto: Ryerson Press, 1925.
Robertson, Ian Ross. *Andrew Macphail: The Life and Legacy of a Canadian Man of Letters*. Montreal: McGill-Queen's University Press, 2008.

- "Macphail, Sir Andrew." In *Dictionary of Canadian Biography*, vol. 16. Toronto: University of Toronto / Quebec: Université Laval, 2003. http://www.biographi.ca/en/bio/macphail_andrew_16E.html.
Rose, Marilyn. "Anne Marriott: Modernist on the Periphery." In *Wider Boundaries of Daring: The Modernist Impulse in Canadian Women's Writing*, edited by Di Brandt and Barbara Godard, 147–62. Waterloo: Wilfrid Laurier University Press, 2009.
- "The Literary Archive and the Telling of Modernist Lives: Retrieving Anne Marriott." In *The Canadian Modernists Meet*, edited by Dean Irvine, 231–49. Ottawa: University of Ottawa Press, 2005.
Royal, Charles E. *The Trail of a Sourdough: Rhymes and Ballads*. Toronto: McClelland & Stewart, 1919.
Salverson, Laura Goodman. *Wayside Gleams*. Toronto: McClelland & Stewart, 1925.
Schlereth, Wendy Clauson. *The Chap-Book: A Journal of American Intellectual Life in the 1890s*. Ann Arbor, MI: UMI Research, 1982.
Scott, Duncan Campbell. *Beauty and Life*. Toronto: McClelland & Stewart, 1921.
- *Labour and the Angel*. Boston: Copeland and Day, 1898.
- *Lundy's Lane and Other Poems*. New York: George H. Doran; Toronto: McClelland, Goodchild and Stewart, 1916.
Scott, Frederick George. *In Sun and Shade*. Quebec: Printed by Dussault & Proulx, 1926.
Scott, Walter. *The Lay of the Last Minstrel*. Edited by John C. Saul. Toronto: Macmillan Company of Canada, 1925.
Sharman, Lyon. *The Sea-Wall and Other Verse*. Toronto: Macmillan Company of Canada, 1925.
Shimizu, Yon. *The Exiles: An Archival History of the World War II Japanese Road Camps in British Columbia and Ontario*. Wallaceburg, ON: Shimizu Consulting and Publishing, 1993.
Smith, A.J.M., ed., *The Book of Canadian Poetry: A Critical and Historical Anthology*. Chicago: University of Chicago Press, 1943; rev. 1948.
Smythe, Albert E.S. *The Garden of the Sun*. Toronto: Macmillan Company of Canada, 1923.
Spadoni, Carl, and Judy Donnelly. *A Bibliography of McClelland and Stewart Imprints, 1909–1985: A Publisher's Legacy*. Toronto: ECW Press, 1994.
Solecki, Sam. *The Last Canadian Poet: An Essay on Al Purdy*. Toronto: University of Toronto Press, 1999.
Speller, Randall. "Arthur Steven at the Ryerson Press: Designing the Post-War Years (1949–1969)." *Papers of the Bibliographical Society of Canada / Cahiers de la Société bibliographique du Canada* 41, no. 2 (2003): 7–44.
St Clair, William. *The Reading Nation in the Romantic Period*. Cambridge: Cambridge University Press, 2004.

Stephen, A.M. *The Rosary of Pan*. Toronto: McClelland & Stewart, 1923.

Stevenson, Lionel. *The Ordeal of George Meredith: A Biography*. 1953. Reprinted New York: Russell & Russell, 1967.

Tennyson, Alfred. *The Poems of Tennyson*. 2nd ed. Edited by Christopher Ricks. Berkeley: University of California Press, 1987.

Thomas, Hartley Munro. *Songs of an Airman and Other Poems*. Introduction by S.W. Dyde. Toronto: McClelland, Goodchild and Stewart, 1918.

Thompson, Lee Briscoe. *Dorothy Livesay*. Boston: Twayne Publishers, 1987.

Tierney, Frank M. *The Journeys of Charles Sangster: A Biographical and Critical Investigation*. Ottawa: Tecumseh, 2000.

Tiessen, Paul Gerard, and Hildegard Froese Tiessen. "Dorothy Livesay and the Politics of Radio." In Dorney, Noonan, and Tiessen, *A Public and Private Voice*, 71–86.

Trehearne, Brian. *Aestheticism and the Canadian Modernists: Aspects of a Poetic Influence*. Montreal: McGill-Queen's University Press, 1989.

–, ed. *Canadian Poetry: 1920 to 1960*. Toronto: McClelland & Stewart, 2010.

– *The Montreal Forties: Modernist Poetry in Transition*. Toronto: University of Toronto Press, 1999.

Tremaine, Marie. *A Bibliography of Canadian Imprints, 1751–1800*. Toronto: University of Toronto Press, 1952.

Tremblay, Tony, and Ellen Rose. "The Canadian Little Magazine Past and Present: Can Digitizing a Literary Subculture Make a Movement?" *Canadian Literature* 200 (Spring 2009). *Literature Resource Center*, www.canlit.ca.

Trotter, Bernard Freeman. *A Canadian Twilight and Other Poems of War and of Peace*. Introduction by W.S.W. McLay. Toronto: McClelland, Goodchild and Stewart, 1917.

Vancouver Poetry Society. *A Book of Days, 1916–1946*. Toronto: Ryerson Press, 1946.

Vipond, Mary. "Major Trends in Canada's Print Mass Media." In Fleming and Lamonde, *History of the Book in Canada*, 3:242–7.

Wallace, W. Stewart. *The Ryerson Imprint: A Check-List of the Books and Pamphlets Published by the Ryerson Press since the Foundation of the House in 1829*. Toronto: Ryerson Press, 1954.

Ware, Tracy. "Al Purdy, Sam Solecki, and Canadian Tradition." In Lynch, Ganz, and Kealey, *The Ivory Thought*, 227–38.

Whiteman, Bruce, Charlotte Stewart, and Catherine Funnell. *A Bibliography of Macmillan of Canada Imprints, 1906–1980*. Toronto: Dundurn Press, 1985.

Williams, Raymond. *Marxism and Literature*. Oxford: Oxford University Press, 1977.

Wilson, Milton. "Recent Canadian Verse: Selected and Edited with General Introduction." *Queen's Quarterly* 66 (1959): 268–311.

Winship, Michael. "The Rise of a National Book Trade System in the United States." In Kaestle and Radway, *History of the Book in America*, 56–77.

"Woodrow, Constance Davies." Canada's Early Women Writers. SFU Digitized Collections. http://digital.lib.sfu.ca/ceww-527/woodrow-constance-davies.

Wordsworth, William. "Ode: Intimations of Immortality from Recollections of Early Childhood." 1807. In Ferguson, Salter, and Stallworthy, *The Norton Anthology of Poetry*, shorter 5th ed., 478–83.

Yeats, W.B. "Sailing to Byzantium." 1927. In Ferguson, Kendall, and Salter, *The Norton Anthology of Poetry*, 6th ed., 1254–5.

INDEX

Abram's Plains, 44
Acanthus and Wild Grape, 30
Acorn, Milton, 222
Adachi, Ken, 203
agency system, 3, 6n8, 15–17, 23, 27, 32–3, 37, 51, 66
Alfred A. Knopf, 17, 33n66
Allen, Thomas, 15
alliteration, 56, 80, 93, 153, 192, 211, 226–7, 230, 234
allusion, 79–80, 83, 92, 162, 192, 197, 202, 204, 228, 234
anacoluthon, 226
anaphora, 92, 97, 198, 217
Anderson, Annie M., 46
Anderson, Patrick, 158, 213, 218
Anglican Church of Canada, 155, 177
anthimeria, 154
anthologies, 108, 144, 161, 218–19
Appeal of Poetry, The, 31–2
Appleton & Company, 16
Arts and Crafts Movement, 6, 45
assonance, 189, 211, 230
asyndeton, 202
At the Long Sault and Other New Poems, 9, 160
Atwood, Margaret, 175, 203, 222
Auden, W.H., 178

authors: British Columbian, 6, 8, 30, 37, 60–3, 105, 107–11, 155, 178; Jewish, 8, 234n57; Maritime, 6, 36, 38–9, 210; Newfoundland, 6; Ontarian, 6, 13, 18, 21–6, 28–30, 34, 59–60, 67–72, 227; Prairie, 6–7, 20, 36, 112, 150; Quebec, 6, 33–4, 37, 64–6, 177–8; Ukrainian Canadian, 8
authorship: advances, 16, 18; author copies, 19, 60, 79, 115, 117–28, 162–3, 173, 185, 221; authority, 22, 106, 111–15, 142–3, 145, 189; collaborative, 88, 134–5, 139; and community, 107, 156–7; concepts of, 66, 74, 83, 85, 95–9, 103, 106, 134, 160; formation of authors, 67, 69, 107, 111, 148, 161; ghostwriters, 22, 99; gravitation to US, 26; novices, 18, 21, 72, 111, 115; and patronage, 239; payments by authors, 19, 59, 61, 66, 79, 117–28, 163, 166, 173; payments to authors, 36–7, 42–3, 117–26, 138–9, 144, 161, 206; pseudonyms, 155, 170; reading tours, 48–52, 58, 95–6, 145; revision, 185, 192, 200, 202, 221, 231, 234–5; royalties, 17, 48,

60, 65–6, 115, 117–26, 128, 162–3, 173, 177–8; and selling books, 24, 59, 127–8, 161, 163, 177–8; and socialization, 85, 103–4, 106, 111, 134, 139, 142, 146
"Ave! An Ode for the Shelley Centenary," 49

Bailey, A.G., 210, 242
Baird, Irene, 32
ballad, 7, 33, 38, 44, 89, 90
Ballads and Lyrics, 30
Barbados, 7
Bayer, Mary Elizabeth, 236
Beauty and Life, 30
Beckoning Skyline and Other Poems, The, 30
"Bee of Words, The," 214
Belgian Mother, and Ballads of Battle Time, The, 33
Benson, Nathaniel A.: "An Actor's Soliloquy," 103–4; advertising, 89, 94–5; "Ballad of the Rawalpindi," 89; biography, 98–9; "By-Line Bill," 97–8; and Carman, 74, 82, 100; children, 86, 94; "Cincinnati Lounge," 90; death, 102; *Dollard: A Tale in Verse*, 86–8; early life, 75–9; elegy, 74, 79–82, 89–93, 95–7, 100, 103–4; "Elegy for Icarus," 90; *The Glowing Years*, 88; journalist, 74–5, 84–6, 94–5; and King, W.L.M., 75, 94–5, 103; and Lampman, 83–4, 91, 96; "The Lampman Cairn at Morpeth," 83–4, 97; "The Last Parting," 92–3; letters, 74, 99–102; marriage, 85; "'Marseillaise' for a Penny Flute," 91–2; *In Memoriam Principis*, 103; *Modern Canadian Poetry*, 85; *None of It Came Easy*, 98; *One Man's Pilgrimage*, 103–4; and Pierce, 82; *Poems*, 78; and Pratt, 75, 84–8, 102; radio, 103; and Roberts, 75–6, 82–5, 92–3, 96, 100; service, 89; and Stringer, 95–7; teacher, 74–5, 86, 95; television, 74, 97–8; theatre, 86, 94; *Three Plays for Patriots*, 85; tragedy, 98; *Twenty and After*, 78–82; *The Wanderer and Other Poems*, 82–3, 88
Benson, Thomas, 75, 79
best-sellers, 15, 17
Bible, 9, 21, 95, 111, 149, 158, 189, 202, 209, 216, 223, 234
bibliographical descriptions, 52–3, 65, 169, 177
binding, 23, 54, 128, 177
birds, 149, 151–4, 170, 172, 209
Birds before Dawn, 163
Birney, Earle, 9, 156–8, 160, 183, 197, 209, 222, 240
Birney, Esther, 183
blindness, 156
Bobcaygeon Chapbook, A, 46
book collecting, 44, 52, 108n15
book design, 27–8, 34, 53–4, 54n47, 69n85, 221
Book of Canadian Poetry, 180
Book of Canadian Prose and Verse, A, 34
Book of the Rose, The, 48–9
Book of Verses, 35
book reviews, 37–8, 75, 88, 127, 130, 156, 160, 163–6, 173, 175, 185, 187
booksellers and bookselling, 13–14, 24, 128, 164

Bourdieu, Pierre, 2, 206
Bourinot, Arthur, 100, 218, 220
Bowman, Louise Morey, 33, 36
Bradbury, Charles, 46
Brand, Dionne, 175
Brandt, Di, 203
Brébeuf and His Brethren, 88
Brewer, Alice, 236
Brewster, Elizabeth, 210
Brick Books, 1
Briggs, William, 14–15, 17, 26
Broadus, Edmund Kemper, 34
Broadus, Eleanor Hammond, 34
Brooke, Rupert, 88
Brown, Audrey Alexandra, 156, 161
Brown, E.K., 9, 158–9, 165, 218
Browne, Thaddeus A., 33
Browning, Robert, 207
Bulman Brothers, 21
Burr, E.H., 236
By Cobequid Bay, 60
Byron, George Gordon, 207, 211–12
By the Marshes of Minas, 49

Cachalot, The, 38
caesura, 110–11
Call, Frank Oliver, 30, 38
Callaghan, Morley, 32
Canada Council, 106, 144, 146, 239
Canadian Authors Association, 39, 89, 95, 106–7, 134, 138, 156–9, 170–1, 216. *See also* Victoria Poetry Group
"Canadian Authors Meet, The," 6
Canadian Bookman, 39, 50–1, 155
Canadian Forum, 4, 38–9, 108, 144, 158, 236
Canadian literature, 203, 227, 240, 241–2

Canadian Literature Club, 89
Canadian Magazine, 36–7, 59
Canadian Mercury, 39
Canadian Pacific Railway, 86
Canadian Poetry in English, 219
Canadian Poetry Magazine, 89, 108, 113, 155–8, 165, 178, 210, 216, 220
Canadian Publicity Company, 21
Canadian Twilight and Other Poems of War and Peace, 28–30
Canadian Writers' War Board, 89
Caple, Kenneth, 142, 183
Cappon, James, 48
Carillon Chap-Books, 242
Carman, Bliss, 30–1, 34, 38, 47–8, 50–1, 67–9, 158, 240. *See also* Benson, Nathaniel A.; Purdy, Al
Carr, Emily, 107
Carsley, Sara, 6
Cary, Thomas, 44
Catley, Elaine M., 6, 236
Catullus, 238
CBC, 107, 135, 138–42, 146, 165, 182–3, 190
Challenge to Time and Death, 160
Chapbook, A, 46
chapbook: concepts of, 44–7, 66; 166
Chap-Book, The, 45–7
character, 62, 109–10, 136, 150–1, 165, 189, 197–8, 211, 230, 227, 230
chiasmus, 234
children, 7, 244
"Chimney Tops," 59
Chop-Book, The, 46
chorus, 98, 136–8, 153, 187, 190, 192, 198, 200, 202
Christian Guardian, 13, 67, 69
Christian Science, 108

circumlocution, 133
"City of the End of Things, The," 71
Clarke, George Elliott, 203
Clarke Printing Company, 166
class, 7, 44–5, 57, 203, 207–8
Coates, Carol, 210
Cogswell, Fred, 116, 211, 242
Coleman, Bromley, 47
Coleridge, Samuel Taylor, 216
Collected Poems of Raymond Knister, The, 180
Colman, Mary Elizabeth, 203
Combustion, 236
coming-of-age narrative, 149
Companionship and the Crowd, 57
conceit. *See* metaphor
Confederation Poets, 9, 30, 38, 47–8, 57, 64, 67, 160, 206–7, 224. *See also* Carman, Bliss; Lampman, Archibald; Roberts, Charles G.D.; Scott, Duncan Campbell; Scott, Frederick George
conferences, 160, 165
confessional poem, 79, 160
consecration, 82, 106, 111
Contact, 4, 242
Contemporary Verse, 4, 107–8, 130, 159, 170, 179, 184–5, 210
Continuations I and *II*, 214
contracts. *See* publishing: agreements
Copeland & Day, 17
copyright, 12, 17, 19, 23, 26, 43, 48–9, 51, 60, 66, 79, 135, 162–3, 185, 241
Cox, Leo, 6, 177–8
Crawford, Isabella Valancy, 152, 197
Crawley, Alan, 107–8, 130, 134, 156, 170, 179, 184
Cumming, R.D., 8, 116

Dafoe, John Wesley, 86
Dalhousie University, 37
Dalton, Annie Charlotte, 7, 35, 50
Dance on the Earth, 6n11
D. Appleton. *See* Appleton & Company
Darnton, Robert, 2
David and Other Poems, 9, 160, 165, 197
Davies Woodrow, Constance, 50, 57–9, 67
Davis, Bill, 74
Deacon, W.A., 49, 89
deafness, 7, 14, 149, 167–73
decadence (1890s), 45–6, 88
deixis, 83
de la Roche, Mazo, 32
Delta, 236
design. *See* book design
diacope, 150
dialectic, 189, 192
Dickinson, Clarence Heber, 6n8
diction, 30, 37, 204, 206, 216, 226, 233
disability, 7, 153, 156, 172–3. *See also* deafness
documentary poem. *See* Livesay, Dorothy; Marriott, Anne
Dollard des Ormeaux, Adam, 86, 100
Doran, George H., 23, 27
Dostoevsky, Fyodor, 9
dramatic lyric, 33–4
dramatic monologue, 103, 109, 161
Drawn Shutters, 37
Drayton, Geoffrey, 7, 8n15
dream, 34, 55–6, 62, 71, 75, 80, 82, 96, 98, 104, 150, 204, 208–9, 217, 220–4
Dream Tapestries, 33
Drummond, William Henry, 20

Dudek, Louis, 4, 9–10, 204–5, 213–16, 218, 235, 242
Duncan, Sara Jeannette, 37, 162
Dussault & Proulx, 65
Dust Bowl, 109, 112–14, 142

Ear Trumpet, The, 7, 50
Earth's Enigmas, 49
East Coast, 210–11
East of the City, 214
Eaton, Evelyn, 163
Ebbs-Canavan, Frances, 108, 127, 156
Ebb Tide, 108–11
Edelstein, Hyman, 8
Edgar, Pelham, 84–5, 171
editing, 15, 22–3, 29–30, 31–2, 41–2, 57–9, 61–2, 116, 127, 148–9, 158–9, 173, 176, 181, 184, 206, 219
"Edmonton, the Gateway," 36
Educational Record, 85
Eggleston, Wilfrid, 36
elegy, 196. *See also* Benson, Nathaniel A.
Elegy Written in a Country Churchyard, 71
Eliot, T.S., 4–5, 39, 63, 105–7, 160, 178, 207, 210, 212
Elmslie, Susan, 203
epic. *See* long poem
Enemy That Never Was, The, 203
enjambment, 111, 152, 227
E.P. Dutton (publisher), 67
Europe, 214
"Eve of St Agnes, The," 139
Execution Poems, 203

Faerie Queene, The, 214
Fahrni, Mildred, 181

faith, 62, 67, 109, 203, 212–13
Fallis, Samuel Wesley, 14–15, 41–3, 49–50
Fancy Free, 210
fantasy, 7, 79, 111
Far Horizons, 30
Ferne, Doris. *See under* Marriott, Anne
Fewster, Ernest, 6, 47, 50
Fiamengo, Marya, 145
Fiddlehead, The, 210–11, 218–19, 242
Fiddlehead Poetry Books, 1, 242
Finch, Robert, 38, 77
fin de siècle. *See* decadence
Fires of Driftwood, 30
First Nations, 8, 217
First Statement, 4, 213
First World War, 11–12, 14, 20, 27, 33–4, 36, 38, 40, 46, 48, 64, 67, 95
Flame and Adventure, 35
Fletcher, John Gould, 160
Fool of Joy, The, 27
Forbes, 75, 94–5
"Forest of Mine," 34
Forfeit and Other Poems, 59–60, 210
Foucault, Michel, 2
Fountain, The, 116
Fraser, Alexander Louis, 6, 38, 60
Fraser, Claud Lovat, 46
Fraser, Hermia Harris, 108, 156–7
French, Donald G., 31–2, 40
free verse, 57–8, 155, 157–8, 170, 208, 211, 215–16, 224, 240
Frye, Northrop, 175, 187
F.W. Robertson (printer), 78

Garden of the Sun, 34
Gardiner, James G., 75, 98

gender, 6, 105, 143, 173, 175, 203
genres (other than poetry):
fiction, 18, 32, 48, 96, 144–5;
encyclopedias, 20; history, 20;
natural history, 21–6. *See also under*
Benson, Nathaniel A.; Marriott,
Anne; Perry, M. Eugenie
geographical poem, 48, 67, 71–2, 128,
130–5, 191, 211–12
Gogol, Nikolai, 9
Goldsmith, Oliver, 211
grace, 201–2
Graphic Press, 180, 242
Gray, Thomas, 71, 91
Great Depression, 3, 86, 158, 212.
See also Dust Bowl
Green Pitcher, 35
"Grey Seas Are Sobbing," 58
Grove, Frederick Philip, 18, 32
Gundy, S.B., 15
Gustafson, Ralph, 165
Gypsy Heart, The, 58–9

Haas, Maara, 8
Hamlet, 86
Hanlon, John. *See* Mitchell, John
Hanlon
Hardy, Thomas, 46, 77
Harrison, Susan Frances, 6, 66, 115, 236, 239
Haydon, Andrew, 18–20
Hazelton, Ruth Cleaves, 216–18
Heath-Stubbs, John, 236–8
Heighton, Steven, 222
Hémon, Louis, 32
Henryson, Robert, 116
Herbert, George, 213
heroic couplets, 211

Hicks, J.P., 155
history of the book, 10
home, concepts of, 187, 191–2, 199, 203
Hopkins, Gerard Manley, 170
Houghton Mifflin Company, 16
House in the Water, The, 48
Housman, A.E., 77
Hubbard, Elbert, 45
Huxtable, H.L., 116

"Iceberg, The," 93
idealism, 9, 11, 15, 31–2, 41, 47–8, 55–7, 67–72, 74–5, 82, 94, 149–50, 158, 179, 203, 205, 229, 231, 236, 242
Idylls of the King, 56
illustration, 17, 19, 21, 23, 38, 44, 46, 87
imagery, 7, 56, 68, 71, 133, 177, 198, 204, 208–9, 227–8
imagism, 31, 130–1, 160, 187, 214, 230
imperialism, 6
inclusivity, 6–8
Industry and Humanity, 94
Innis, Harold, 16
"In November," 38
In Sun and Shade, 65–6
Internet Archive, 11
In the Battle Silences, 64
Invisibility Project, 203
Ireland, 6
irony, 187, 229–31, 233
"Ishtar," 216

Jackes, Lyman B., 36
Jack Miner and the Birds, 21–6
Jackson, A.Y., 206

James, Henry, 46
Japanese Canadians, internment of, 175–6, 181–3, 185–203
Japanese Canadian Citizens' Association, 185
Jeffrys, C.W., 17, 38
Jesuit Relations, the, 86, 100
John Lane, 37
Johnson, Pauline, 20, 33, 68
Jordan, W.D., 9
Joynes, Agnes, 36, 203
Judge, May P., 7

Keats, John, 139, 154, 205, 216
Kennedy, Margaret, 134–9, 142
Kindred of the Wild, The, 49
King, William Lyon Mackenzie, 43
Klee Wyck, 107
Klein, A.M., 218
Knight Errant, The, 5, 46
Knister, Raymond, 31–2, 180
Knopf. *See* Alfred A. Knopf
Knowles, Elizabeth, 34

Lakeside Press, 46
Lally, E.B., 168
Lampman, Archibald, 9, 38, 42, 71, 158–60, 170, 224. *See also under* Benson, Nathaniel A.
Lampman, Archibald Otto, 61
Lane, Patrick, 222
Later Poems, 30
Later Poems and New Villanelles, 66
Laurence, Elsie Fry, 6
Laurence, Margaret, 6
"Laurentian Shield," 135
Lawrence, D.H., 208–9
Lay of the Last Minstrel, 35

Layton, Irving, 209
L.C. Page and Company, 27, 48–9
Leacock, Stephen, 32, 211
Lee, Dennis, 7
"Let My People Go," 188–9
Leveridge, Lilian, 30, 67–72, 115, 155
Lewis, Cecil Day, 178
libraries, 11, 48, 145, 161, 164, 169, 180, 243
Lillooet, 211–12
"Line and Form," 215
lines, layout of, 200–1, 228
"Lines Composed a Few Miles above Tintern Abbey," 71–2
Litany before the Dawn of Fire, 50
literary agents, 106, 111, 113–16, 162
literary prizes, 77, 84–5, 85n14, 107, 138, 158, 160, 164, 170, 177, 180–1, 206, 220, 231
Litster, Thomas Harkness, 27–8
little magazines, 4–5, 39, 45–6, 106, 130, 236, 239–40, 242
Livesay, Dorothy: 35, 77–8; and Benson, 177; "Broadcast from Berlin," 191; *Call My People Home*, 175–6, 181–203; children, 178; *Day and Night*, 113, 161, 178–9; *The Documentaries*, 181, 192; documentary poem, 175, 179, 182, 189, 192, 196–7; *Green Pitcher*, 177–8; and Grierson, 179; and Knister, 180; marriage, 178; and Marriott, 107, 113–14, 116, 130, 134, 146, 185; and Pierce, 175–7, 179–84, 202–3; *Poems for People*, 180–1; radio, 179, 182–4, 190; "Seven Poems, " 191; *Signpost*, 178; and socialism, 175–6, 178,

187; "Variations on a Tree," 192; "West Coast," 191
Livesay, Florence Randal, 34
Livesay, J.F.B., 111–16, 127
Lochhead, Douglas, 75
Log of a Halifax Privateer, The, 39
long poem, 79, 86–8, 105, 113, 116, 138–9, 149, 152, 166, 175, 187, 211
"Loon, The," 68
Lost Shipmate, The, 58
Lowell, Amy, 36
Lowry, Malcolm, 182
Lundy's Lane and Other Poems, 27
lupus, 7, 14
lyric, 58, 71, 88, 96, 103, 111, 113, 130, 159–60, 185–9, 211–14, 224, 227, 230
Lyrics Unromantic, 165

MacDonald, Erskine, 34
MacDonald, J.E.H., 15, 27, 30, 52–3
MacDonald, Thoreau, 15, 30, 54, 221
MacDonald, Wilson, 18, 36, 50–1
MacInnes, Tom, 27
Mackay, Isabel Ecclestone, 30
MacLennan, Hugh, 198
MacMechan, Archibald, 38–9, 46
Macmillan Company of Canada 17, 32–5, 84, 108, 113–14, 177–8
Macnair, Duncan, 178, 181, 185
MacNeice, Louis, 160, 178
Macphail, Andrew, 34, 37
Macrae Smith Company, 60
magazines, 13, 16, 35–9, 49, 57, 59, 67, 69, 96, 107–8, 144, 148, 155–7, 170, 184, 210, 213, 216, 236. *See also* little magazines
Makers of Canadian Literature, 42–3, 47–9

Malcolm's Katie, 197
marketing, 19, 51–2, 60, 127–8, 163–4
Marlatt, Daphne, 203
Marquis, Thomas Guthrie, 43
Marriott, Anne: "After a Meeting of Poets," 146; *Aqua*, 111, 146–7; and Brewster, 211; *Calling Adventurers!*, 134–9; children, 145; "City," 131; comedy, 139–40; and Dilworth, 107; documentary, 136, 141; drama, 136, 140, 143; early life, 106–7; educational scripts, 139–41, 145; and Ferne, 107–11, 112–13, 127; film, 106, 141–2, 146; history, 141; "Holiday Journal," 130; and Kennedy, 134–9, 142; and Livesays, 111–16, 127–8, 130–4; *A Long Way to Oregon*, 144; marriage, 141; "Night Traveller," 130; novel, 144–5; "Payload," 135–9; and Perry, 108, 134; and Pierce, 106, 112, 115–16, 128–34, 138, 142, 145; "Prairie Graveyard," 131; "Prayer of the Disillusioned," 130; radio, 106, 127, 134–44, 146; "The Rose and Dagger," 111; *Salt Marsh*, 116, 128–34, 165; *Sandstone*, 128; short stories, 140–1, 144–5; "Still I Cheat Myself," 130; "Storm over a Garden," 131; *The Wind Our Enemy*, 10, 105, 107–16, 127–9, 134–5, 142–4; "Woodyards in the Rain," 130–1
Martin, Fred, 164
Masefield, John, 85
Masses, 178
Matheson, Mary, 6, 236
McClelland & Stewart, 1, 15, 27–32, 69, 227

McCrae, John, 37–8
McGill Fortnightly, 4, 39
McGill University, 37
McKenzie, D.F., 2
McKenzie, William P., 203
McLaren, Floris Clark, 107, 130, 165
McLellan, Gerald, 141
McLeod, G.J., 15
McRaye, Walter, 20–1
"Memory," 108
Meredith, George, 44
metaphor, 63, 88, 109, 152–4, 191, 214, 224, 228, 233–4
metaphysics, 233, 235
Methodism, 8–9, 13, 177, 179, 202
Methodist Book and Publishing House. *See* Ryerson Press
metre. *See* prosody
Middleton, Jesse Edgar, 28
Milligan, James Lewis, 30
Milton, John, 152
Miner, Jack, 21–6
Mint and Willow, 216
Miracle Songs of Jesus, 18
Mitchell, John Hanlon, 6, 36
modernism, 4–5, 8–10, 38–9, 58, 74, 98, 105, 109, 148, 157–9, 161, 173, 180, 204–18, 221, 226, 231, 236, 238–40, 242
Moffat, Gertrude MacGregor, 35
Monro, Harold, 46
Monroe, Harriet, 4
Montgomery, L.M., 27, 100
Moodie, Susanna, 100
Moonlight and Common Day, 33
Moore, E.J., 25
Morris, William, 6, 45
"Mountain that Watched, The," 33–4

Multiculturalism Act, 8
Munro, Alice, 150
Munro, Kathryn, 6, 59–60, 203, 210
Murakami, Sachiko, 203
Murphy, Emily, 50
Muse Anthology of Modern Poetry, 108
Museum of Kindness, 203
Musgrave, Susan, 222
music, 50, 56, 70, 75, 89–90, 97, 101, 142, 177, 183–4, 188–9, 206, 210, 215, 234
Muskoka Assembly, 50, 76
Musson Book Company, 64
My Star Predominant, 180

Nakashima, Mickey, 185
National Film Board, 141, 146, 179
nationalism, 6, 9, 11–12, 17, 47, 53–4, 62, 64, 67, 79, 94, 131–9, 142, 149, 164, 174–6, 180, 188, 201–3, 208, 210, 222, 227, 242. *See also* home, concepts of
National Society of the Deaf and Hard of Hearing, 167–8
Natural History Society (Victoria), 170
nature poem, 34, 38, 48, 67–72, 81, 83, 131–4, 162, 170, 205, 210, 214, 216, 231–6, 240, 243–4
Newfoundland Verse, 17
New Frontier, 178
New Harvesting, 108
New Outlook, 57, 67, 69, 88, 155
New Poems, 49, 51
New Republic, 113
News of the Phoenix, 9, 180
Newson, W.V., 7
newspapers, 36, 39, 45, 59, 61, 67, 74, 85–6, 88, 97, 107–8, 127, 145–6,

148, 155–6, 161, 165–6, 182, 185, 197, 206, 216, 220, 240
New York Nocturnes, 97
Nietzsche, Friedrich, 207, 223
noble savage, 217
northern development, 135–8, 141–2
Northern Review, 4, 210
Norwood, Robert, 27
Nova Scotia Chap-Books, 39, 46
Now You Care, 203

occasional verse, 33, 83, 103
ode, 235
"Ode: Intimations of Immortality," 92
Odyssey, The, 187, 196
On Canadian Poetry, 159
Ondaatje, Michael, 222
Ontario Publishing Company, 36
"Open Letter," 38
Orchards of Ultima Thule, The, 39
Osborne, Marian, 34
Osler, William, 34
Ostenso, Martha, 36
Over the Hills of Home, 30
Overture, 9
Ovid, 79–80

Pacific Northwest Writers' Conference, 160, 165
Page, P.K., 9, 156, 158, 213, 218
paper, 23, 25, 46, 53
paradox, 56, 95, 137, 154, 192, 196, 204, 220–1, 227–31, 238–9
parallelism, 189, 197–8
Parker, Gilbert, 37
paronomasia, 80
parsimony, 43–6
Paschal Lamb, 108

pastoral, 71, 162, 228–9
Paul Pero, 8, 116
"Peculium," 62
Pen and Pencil Club, 37
Pentland, Barbara, 136, 138
Percival, W.P., 84
peripety, 150
Perry, M. Eugenie: book publication, importance of, 161, 166; *Canteen*, 166; Chap-Books, promotion of, 164–5; children's column, 155; early life, 155; "Fall of the Mighty, 170–1; garden, 170; *The Girl in the Silk Dress*, 155; *Hearing a Far Call*, 116, 156, 161–6, 173; *Hero in Ermine and Other Poems*, 155–6, 161; history/survey, 167–9; "Hummingbird," 172; literary circle, 156–7, 170; and Livesay, 156, 161; and Marriott, 148, 156, 164; "Nettle-Shy," 158; and Pierce, 149–50, 158–9, 161–74; radio, 165–6; as reader, 160–1; sister, 167; *Song in the Silence and Other Poems*, 149–54, 169–74; tragedy, 161–2; *Two Hundred and Fifty Thousand Strong*, 167–9, 172
Phelps, Arthur Leonard, 46
Philistine, The, 5, 45
Pickthall, Marjorie, 30, 37–8, 69, 158
Picture Gallery of Canadian History, 17
Pierce, Clifford, 14
Pierce, Edith (née Chown), 14–15
Pierce, Lorne: education and early career, 8–9, 14–15; missionary on Prairies, 179–80; and modernism, 9–10, 158–9; parliamentary inclusivity, 6–8, 58, 175, 218,

242; role as publisher, 1–7, 15–27, 184–5, 241–3; and Ryerson Poetry Chap-Books, creation of, 36, 39–41, 44, 47–55, 57–60. *See also under* Benson, Nathaniel A.; Livesay, Dorothy; Marriott, Anne; Perry, M. Eugenie; Purdy, Al

Pioneers and Prominent People of Manitoba, 20–1

Pioneer Sketches in the District of Bathurst, 18–20

Piper and the Reed, The, 27

"Piper of Arll, The," 56

Poems, 64

Poems and Lyrics of the Joy of Earth, 44

Poetry (Chicago), 4, 36, 107, 184, 210

poetry, concepts of, 31–2, 37, 58, 69, 202–3, 207–8, 210, 215, 226

point of view, 151

polyptoton, 80, 187, 226

"Pomegranate, The," 214

Pomeroy, Elsie, 160

Pool of Stars, A, 210

Pound, Ezra, 5, 207, 213–14

Pratt, Claire, 102

Pratt, E.J., 17, 35, 38, 102, 113, 157, 160, 178, 205, 209. *See also under* Benson, Nathaniel A.

Pratt, Lenore, 6

Preview, 4, 213

price, 46, 59, 79, 163, 177

print runs, 5, 11, 23, 26, 44, 46, 51–2, 79, 163, 166, 173

printing, 13, 19–20, 23, 25, 27–8, 34, 45–6, 65, 78, 116, 128, 164, 166, 177

proofreading, 116

propaganda, 113–14, 141

Prophet's Man, The, 60–3

prosody, 32, 33, 34, 48, 68, 71, 80, 91–3, 110–11, 130, 137, 152–3, 161, 206, 208–9, 211–17, 224, 226, 230, 239, 244

publishing: agreements, 60–1, 65, 79, 115–26, 162–3, 166, 173, 177–8, 184–5, 221; concepts of, 66, 149; educational (*see* school books); general conditions of, 1–4, 12, 15–17, 241; original, and challenges to, 17–18, 26–7, 32, 42–3; reprinting, 51; risk avoidance, 14, 20–1, 43, 60, 79, 114–15; subscription, 163–4; and US market, 24–6, 60, 241. *See also* self-publishing

Purdy, Al: "At the Quinte Hotel," 238; and Buckley, 206; "Bullfrogs," 224; *The Cariboo Horses*, 227, 231; and Carman 206, 208–10, 224; combined poetics, 204–5, 209, 226, 231, 239, 240; "The Country North of Belleville," 227–31; *The Crafte So Longe to Lerne* 205, 221, 227–39; *The Enchanted Echo*, 206, 208, 219; "Far Traveller," 220; and history, 227, 230; "House Guest," 221–6; "Inside the Mill," 208–9; "Lament for the Dorsets," 205; "Landscape," 218–19; "Meander," 220; *North of Summer*, 206–7; "On the Flood Plain," 229; and Pierce, 210, 218–21, 240; *Piling Blood*, 208; *Poems for All the Annettes*, 221, 224, 231, 238; *Pressed on Sand*, 205, 219–21, 224–6; and Roberts, 226, 228, 242; "At Roblin Lake,"

231–6; *Rooms for Rent in the Outer Planets*, 222; "Short History of X County," 227–31; "Spring Song," 229; "Still Life in a Tent," 207; *The Stone Bird*, 207; *Sundance at Dusk*, 208; "Villanelle [*Plus 1*]," 236–9; "Wilderness Gothic," 231
Purdy, Eurithe, 222
Pushkin, Alexander, 9
Putnam, 27

Queen Mab, 44
Queen's Quarterly, 144, 231, 236
Queen's University, 9, 14, 30, 47, 179

race, 8, 133, 138, 142, 175–6, 188–9, 196, 198–203, 217, 233–4
Radway, Janice, 2
Rashley, R.E., 75
readers and reading, 69, 93, 100, 111, 114, 134, 160–1, 165, 183–5, 204, 222, 235, 243
realism, 18, 31, 105, 109–11, 149–51, 158–9, 204–5, 211–12, 240
Redpath, Beatrice, 37
Redpath Roddick, Amy, 164
refrains, 162, 227
regionalism, 160. *See also* geographical poem
Reid, Robert, 164
Reilly and Lee, 25
repetition, 80, 93, 137, 153, 189–90, 197, 234
representation (political). *See* responsibility
responsibility, 6–8, 174, 176, 179, 182, 202–3

"Return, O Shulamite," 36
review copies. *See* marketing
rhyme, 32, 55–6, 68, 92, 110–11, 137, 152, 154, 161, 192, 198, 208, 211, 214, 226, 230, 244
rhythm. *See* prosody
Riddehough, Geoffrey, 60–3
Rising Village, The, 211
Roads and Other Poems, 212–13
Robarts, John, 74
Roberts, Charles G.D., 9–10, 41, 47– 59, 67, 71, 115, 138, 160, 226, 228. *See also under* Benson, Nathaniel A.
Roberts, Dorothy (Gostwick), 7, 57–8, 75
Roberts, Lloyd, 48–9
Roberts, Theodore Goodridge, 57–8, 100
Robeson, Paul, 189
Robinson, Edwin Arlington, 211
romanticism, 8–10, 33, 37, 47, 56–7, 67–72, 74–5, 79–80, 82–3, 86, 96, 98, 103, 148, 150, 157, 173, 204–18, 221–4, 226, 228, 235–6, 240, 242
Ronald P. Frye & Company, 11
Rosary of Pan, The, 30
Royal, Charles E., 30
Royal Society of Canada, 181
Russia, 9, 15
Ryerson, Egerton, 13, 15
Ryerson Poetry Chap-Books: advantages of, 103, 145–9; 157; as creative mould, 171; limits of, 103, 127, 134; midpoint of series, 161. *See also under* Pierce, Lorne
Ryerson Press: origins of, 13–14

sales, 3, 13, 15, 17, 24–6, 44, 49, 59–60, 65, 127–8, 163, 166, 178, 185, 206
Sandiford, Peter, 16
Sandwell, B.K., 39
Sangster, Charles, 44
Sapir, Edward, 38
satire, 155, 211–12
Saturday Evening Post, 96
Saturday Night, 86, 94, 108, 165, 184
school books, 3, 6n8, 16, 17, 32, 139, 145, 158
Schroeder, Andreas, 144
Scotland, 8
Scott, Duncan Campbell, 9, 27, 30, 38, 42, 56, 61, 159–60, 209
Scott, F.R., 6, 9, 135, 158
Scott, Frederick George, 64–6
Scott, Walter, 35
Sea Dogs and Men at Arms, 28
Searching Image, The, 213–16
Sea-Wall and Other Verses, The, 35
Second World War, 74, 89, 90–2, 108–9, 115, 130–1, 142, 151, 154–8, 162–3, 166–7, 175, 179, 181–2, 187, 189, 206
Selected Poems, 64
Selected Poems of Bliss Carman, The, 158
self-publishing, 3, 19, 23, 25, 35, 44–5, 59, 61, 65–7, 78–9, 148, 155, 161, 163, 166–9, 206
self-reflexive poem, 56, 63, 71, 83, 133, 154, 214, 223, 226, 228, 230–1
service, 9, 15, 27, 149–50, 173
Service, Robert, 30, 207
Settlers of the Marsh, 18
Shakespeare, William, 162, 86

Sharman, Lyon, 35
Sheaf of Verse, A, 242
Sheehan, Katherine, 75
Sheepfold, 177–8
Shelley, Percy Bysshe, 44, 47, 68, 80
Shepherd's Purse, 34
simile, 153, 201
Sir Charles G.D. Roberts, 160
Skelton, O.D., 16
small press, 4–6, 106, 146, 149, 169, 173
Smith, A.J.M., 9, 38–9, 63, 158, 170, 180, 207, 211, 218
Smythe, Albert E.S., 34
Social Gospel, 9, 176
socialism, 214. *See also under* Livesay, Dorothy
social justice, 114, 148, 173, 175, 187, 202–3
Some Animal Stories, 48
"Song My Paddle Sings, The," 68
Song of Israfel and Other Poems, The, 34
Songs for Swift Feet, 58
Songs in Your Heart and Mine, 28
Songs of an Airman and Other Poems, 30
Songs of the Common Day, 49
Songs of the North, 57
sonnet, 57, 62–3, 83, 88, 108, 153–5, 172, 214, 216, 224
Souster, Raymond, 6, 242
Spender, Stephen, 178
Spenser, Edmund, 214
spirituality, 15, 22, 31, 37, 48, 57, 67, 174, 176, 180, 205, 207, 209–10, 213, 218, 224, 233, 235, 240, 242, 244
Stanhope Press, 34

stanza, 33, 68, 71, 91–3, 112, 127, 133,
    187, 189, 202, 204, 208, 213–16,
    226, 229–31, 239
Stephen, A.M., 30, 47, 50
Stevens, A.T., 46
Stevens, Wallace, 39
Stevenson, Lionel, 63, 210
Steveston, 203
St Lawrence and the Saguenay, The, 44
Stone & Kimball, 17, 45–7
Straub, Carlyle, 108
Stringer, Arthur, 7, 95–7
sublimity, 30, 80, 197, 204, 207, 210,
    216, 226, 228, 233
"Sunset in the City," 69
Sunshine Sketches of a Little Town, 211
Swayze, Fred, 102
*Sweet o' the Year and Other Poems,
    The*, 47, 51–7
symbolism, 91, 189
synaesthesia, 153–4
syntax, 133, 152

Tabata, Amy, 181
Tabata, Susumu, 181–2
"Tantramar Revisited, The," 71
Tâo, 210
tapinosis, 208
temperance, 9
Tenny, W.H.F., 50, 57–8
Tennyson, Alfred, 56, 68, 207
Testament of Cresseid, The, 116
textbooks. *See* school books
"This Is a Photograph of Me," 203
Thomas, Dylan, 238
Thomas, Hartley Munro, 30
Thomas Nelson & Sons, 86
Thomson, Ken, 74

Thomson, Roy, 74, 99
Thomson, Theresa, E., 236
Three Meridians, 7
Three Poems, 46–7
Three Sea Songs, 39
Time, 4
"To Life," 68–9
Tolstoy, Leo, 9
topographical poem. *See*
    geographical poem
Toronto Daily Star, 85
"To the Students of Liège," 28–9
Trail of a Sourdough, The, 30
Trotter, Bernard Freeman, 28–30
Twelve Profitable Sonnets, 39
Two Solitudes, 198
type and typography, 2, 19, 23, 25,
    27–8, 45–6

Union Theological Seminary (New
    York), 14
United Church of Canada, 14, 67,
    155
United Theological College
    (Montreal), 15
Unit of Five, 9, 161
University Magazine, 37–8
University of Alberta, 61
University of British Columbia,
    60–1, 107, 139, 157, 183
University of Toronto, 9, 14, 37–8,
    77, 85, 177
"Unknown City, The," 55–7, 228
"Unsleeping, The," 47

Vagrant of Time, The, 51
Vale of Luxor, The, 7
Vancouver Poetry Society, 46–7, 50

Vancouver Sun, 206
Véhicule Press, 1, 214
Verlaine, Paul, 46
Victoria Daily Times, 127
Victoria Literary Society, 160, 164
Victoria Poetry Chapbook, 108, 128
Victoria Poetry Group, 107–12, 156
villanelle, 66, 236–9

Walker, E.W., 6n8
Warwick Brothers and Rutter, 27
Waste Land, The, 107, 212
Watchman and Other Poems, The, 27
Watson, John, 9
Watt, Frederick B., 36
Way to Fairyland and Other Rhymes, 7
Weaver, Robert, 144
Week, The, 96
Wesley Building, 14–15
Western Recorder, 155, 160
Whalley, George, 61
Whitehouse, Raymond, 183–4
White Lilac, 37
White Narcissus, 32

Wiebe, Rudy, 144
Wilde, Oscar, 88
wilderness, 227
Willey, Christina, 36
Williams, Raymond, 2
Wilson, Ethel, 130
Wind Our Enemy, The, 3, 10
Witches' Brew, The, 35
Woman at Dusk and Other Poems, 96
Women's Arts Association of Canada, 116
Wood Carver's Wife, The, 30
Woolf, Virginia, 205
word play, 56, 63, 154, 215, 229, 233
Wordsworth, William, 33, 71, 92, 209, 213
Wright, Emma, 85
Writers' Craft Club, 242

XII Poems, 6n11

Yeats, W.B., 46, 160, 226
Yeigh, Frank, 36
Yes, 236